Skills for Success

Skills for Success

A Career Education Handbook for Children and Adolescents with Visual Impairments

KAREN E. WOLFFE, EDITOR

Foreword by DEAN W. TUTTLE

PRESS
New York

Printed in the United States of America

Library of Congress Cataloging-in-Publication Data
Skills for success : a career education handbook for children and
    adolescents with visual impairments / Karen E. Wolffe, editor.
        p.   cm.
    Includes bibliographical references.
    ISBN 0-89128-943-7
    1. Children, Blind—Education.   2. Visually handicapped children-
-Education.   3. Career education.   4. Vocational education.   5. Life
skills—Study and teaching.   I. Wolffe, Karen E.
HV1638.S55 1999   98-8121
371.91'1—dc21   CIP

The publication of *Skills for Success* was funded in part by the following foundations in Dallas, Texas:
The A. L. Chilton Foundation; Carl B. and Florence E. King Foundation; Delta Gamma Foundation of Dallas; The Gurvetch Foundation; Roberta Coke Camp Fund of Communities Foundation of Texas, Inc.; Roy and Christine Sturgis Charitable and Educational Trust Foundation; Southwestern Bell; Van London Memorial Fund of Communities Foundation of Texas, Inc.; and the WHO Foundation.

W.H.O.
FOUNDATION
Women Helping Others

*To my mother, June Wolffe, whose nurturing
and high expectations motivated her children to set
career goals for themselves and then achieve them.
With heartfelt thanks and love.*

Contents

CHAPTER 4 Encouraging Socialization   77

Deborah Chen

CHAPTER 5 Developing Compensatory Skills   97

Jamie Dote-Kwan

CHAPTER 6 Promoting Opportunities to Work   125

Deborah Chen and Jamie Dote-Kwan

CHAPTER 7 Providing Realistic Feedback   139

Jamie Dote-Kwan and Deborah Chen

Part Three The Elementary School Years   160
Sandra Lewis

CHAPTER 8 Conveying High Expectations   163

CHAPTER 9 Encouraging Socialization   187

CHAPTER 10 Developing Compensatory Skills   213

CHAPTER 11 Promoting Opportunities to Work   235

Foreword

It has long been my conviction that, in order to be well-rounded, children need to learn three things: how to love—that is, how to have enough of self to be able to share it with another; how to work—how to be able to contribute to the welfare of another; and how to play—how to be able to enjoy life and to engage in activities that renew the spirit. In my own work I have observed that even though many visually impaired students receive a strong academic education, graduate after graduate struggles with finding employment. With the failure to find work often come the loss of confidence and the erosion of self-esteem.

As long ago as the early 1970s I first began reading in general education literature about the need for career education early in a child's schooling. I heard many of my colleagues observe from time to time that, if career education is important early in a sighted child's life, how much more important it is in the life of a student with a visual impairment. I waited expectantly during the seventies and eighties for someone to produce a practical guide that applied the principles of career education to the specific needs of visually impaired students in the lower and middle grades. During this time, it was refreshing to find the occasional creative teacher who had taken the initiative to adapt a career education program for a specific child. However, most teachers did not have the time or background to do much more than superficial forays into this little-known area of the curriculum.

Thanks to Dr. Karen Wolffe, you and I now have that long-needed guide. In *Skills for Success: A Career Education Handbook for Children and Adolescents with Visual Impairments* she has effectively integrated practical suggestions for the development of daily living skills, personal-social skills, and occupational skills into a systematic handbook on career education for preschool, elementary school, and middle school grades that specifically addresses the special and unique needs of students who are visually impaired. The life skills being taught address both the child's needs for making successive transitions into higher school grades and needs for lifelong functional skills that are essential for leading a full and satisfying life. The practical, realistic, and optimistic outlook offered on career education also includes insights from contributors who discuss the needs of students from a family, rural, urban, or multicultural perspective, as well as other needs of students with multiple disabilities. A career exploration program for visually impaired students in middle school and beyond is included as well to encourage students to go into their communities to learn about the myriad career possibilities available to them.

Many visually impaired students reach their late teen years naive about the world of work. Through no fault of their own, numerous youngsters who are academically trained have little or no work experience and thus little practical understanding of the labor market, jobs, and how one progresses through jobs to capture one's career goals. With structured systematic intervention and strong healthy expectations, students are better able to achieve a more successful pattern of career development. *Skills for Success* can help teachers, orientation and mobility instructors, school counselors, case managers, and rehabilitation teachers become the partners of families in guiding the career development of students with visual impairments throughout the entire school spectrum from preschool through high school. The rest of us, too, are able to profit from Dr. Wolffe's experiences and positive outlook by learning how to motivate and assist visually impaired students to reach for their best. Thank you, Karen, for this insightful and sensitive book.

Dean W. Tuttle, Ph.D.
Professor Emeritus of Special Education
University of Northern Colorado

Acknowledgments

There are many people who have contributed to *Skills for Success: A Career Education Handbook for Children and Adolescents with Visual Impairments* and I would like to acknowledge as many of them as possible. First, I would like to thank the American Foundation for the Blind (AFB) staff, and, in particular, Mary Ann Siller, National Program Associate in Education at AFB's Southwest office in Dallas, Texas, who wanted to provide assistance to families and teachers and who recognized that there was a critical need for a book on career education solely devoted to children with visual impairments. Through the fundraising efforts of Mary Ann, the production of *Skills for Success* was generously supported by the following foundations in Dallas: The A. L. Chilton Foundation; Carl B. and Florence E. King Foundation; Delta Gamma Foundation of Dallas; The Gurvetch Foundation; Roberta Coke Camp Fund of Communities Foundation of Texas, Inc.; Roy and Christine Sturgis Charitable and Educational Trust Foundation; Southwestern Bell; and Van London Memorial Fund of Communities Foundation of Texas, Inc. In addition, the Women Helping Others (WHO) Foundation provided a generous grant for the printing of *Skills for Success*. I, AFB, and AFB Press would like to express our sincere appreciation to these organizations for their contributions.

Additional support from AFB was widespread—Carl R. Augusto, President; Judy Scott, Director, AFB Southwest; and Susan Jay Spungin, Vice President, National Programs, all encouraged and endorsed the development of this book. However, the lion's share of the work was done by Natalie Hilzen, Editor-in-Chief, and Kathy Campbell, Editor, of AFB Press. They helped organize and edit the book, and I am forever indebted to them for their efforts.

I would also like to thank my partner in life, my husband, Terry Hirsh, for his support and patience throughout the development and publication of *Skills for Success*. His willingness to read and edit what I wrote and his resulting insights are gratefully acknowledged as one of the most important contributions to this book. His background as a special educator, children's caseworker, and transition counselor made his insights all the more relevant to this project and I thank him for his willingness to share his expertise. Most important, I appreciate his being patient with me as I spent hours, days, weeks, and months at the computer with the manuscript.

In addition, I owe a huge debt of gratitude to the contributing authors Anna Lee Braunstein, Lila Cabbil, Deborah Chen, Jamie Dote-Kwan, Jane Erin, Julie Lee Kay, Sandra Lewis, Kevin O'Connor, Elaine Sveen, and Victoria Tripodi. These individuals have shared their knowledge and experience in a practical and stimulating way that encourages the implementation of career education activities with youngsters at different ages and in a variety of settings. Furthermore, we were fortunate to have received input from some of the most capable peer reviewers in the blindness and visual impairment fields, namely, Jana Almquist, Tanni Anthony, Diane Fazzi, Theresa Postello, and Sharon Sacks. I was also fortunate to have the assistance of Karen Thomas, who helped me track down resources and other information to share with readers.

Finally, I would like to thank all the children and young adults who have taught me and the others who contributed to this handbook how best to instruct them in what they need to know to be successful in life.

About the Contributors

Karen E. Wolffe, Ph.D., is a career counselor and consultant in private practice in Austin, Texas, and Co-project Director of the Full Option Curriculum for the Utilization of Social Skills (FOCUS) project funded by the Office of Special Education Programs, U.S. Department of Education, to create materials for teaching social skills to students with visual impairments. In addition to being a writer and instructor in the Transition to the American University Program and career development courses at the Hadley School for the Blind in Winnetka, Illinois, Dr. Wolffe is the author of *Career Counseling for People with Disabilities: A Practical Guide to Finding Employment,* a guide for rehabilitation counselors and educators, and the co-author of *The Transition Tote System: Navigating the Rapids of Life,* a comprehensive set of organizational and career education materials developed for high school students with visual impairments.

Formerly a faculty member in the Department of Special Education at the University of Texas, Austin, Dr. Wolffe also served as director of the Job Readiness Clinic. She is a nationally known lecturer, presenter, and researcher on the importance of career education in the lives of children and adolescents with visual impairments, transition issues, employment concerns, social skills development, and literacy in the workplace.

Anna Lee Braunstein, M.Ed., is an itinerant teacher in the San Juan Unified School District in Sacramento, California. She has more than 30 years of experience in the education of students with visual impairments. In 1994, Ms. Braunstein received the Education Award from the Northern California Chapter of the Association for Education and Rehabilitation (AER) of the Blind and Visually Impaired for her development of the Career Caravan, which has been used in career curriculum programs in California and in teacher training courses in that state and in Canada.

Lila Cabbil, M.S., is Supervisor of Occupational Information and Children's Services at Upshaw Institute for the Blind in Detroit, Michigan. She is an adjunct faculty member for the Multicultural Experience in Leadership Development Program in the College of Urban Labor and Metropolitan Affairs at Wayne State University and also teaches in the Occupational Therapy Assistant Program at Wayne County Community College. Mrs. Cabbil provides rehabilitation teaching services to children, youths, and adults, and has conducted leadership training in multicultural competency to numerous corporations, schools, religious institutions, and government and nonprofit agencies.

Deborah Chen, Ph.D., is Professor in the Department of Special Education at California State University, Northridge, where she teaches in the areas of severe disabilities and early childhood special education. She has had diverse experiences in working with young children with multiple disabilities and sensory impairments and their families as a respite care provider, early interventionist, program administrator, teacher trainer, and researcher. Dr. Chen has given numerous presentations and published extensively on the topic of early intervention for infants and preschoolers who are visually impaired, deaf-blind, and have multiple disabilities and sensory impairments.

Jamie Dote-Kwan, Ph.D., is Professor of Special Education and Coordinator of the Teacher Training Program in Visual Impairments and Blindness at California State University in Los Angeles. Dr. Dote-Kwan's research and publications focus on caregiver-child interactions and early home environments of young blind children and specific intervention strategies for working with young children whose multiple disabilities include visual impairment.

Jane Erin, Ph.D., is Associate Professor in the Department of Special Education, Rehabilitation, and School Psychology at the University of Arizona in Tucson, where she coordinates the program to prepare teachers of students with visual impairments. She is also editor-in-chief of the *Journal of Visual Impairment & Blindness*. Her writing and research interests are in the education of students with visual and multiple disabilities, in braille reading, and in parent and family issues related to visual impairment.

Julie Lee Kay, M.A., is Associate Dean of Parent/Family Education at the Hadley School for the Blind in Winnetka, Illinois. Previously she worked as Transition Program Supervisor with the Texas Commission for the Blind and as Lead Teacher in Career Education at the Texas School for the Blind and Visually Impaired.

Sandra Lewis, Ed.D., is Associate Professor at Florida State University in Tallahassee, where she coordinates the Program in Visual Impairment. She is Executive Editor of *RE:view*. Previously she was the Coordinator of Educational Assessments at the California School for the Blind. Dr. Lewis has worked as an educator of visually impaired individuals of all ages and in a variety of settings, including a private agency and a residential school.

Kevin O'Connor, M.A., C.S.P., is a faculty member of Loyola University in Chicago, Illinois. He is a professional speaker, management consultant, and marriage and family counselor. The parent of a child who is visually impaired, Mr. O'Connor is the author of three books. He is the immediate past president of the National Association for Parents of the Visually Impaired (NAPVI) and has frequently presented programs related to visual impairment throughout the United States and Canada.

Elaine Sveen, Ed.D., is Superintendent at the Minnesota State Academy for the Blind. She has been a teacher of blind and visually impaired individuals, as well as a consultant to public schools. Her writing and research interests are on topics related to parents and transition issues and model programs for family training. She is past president of the National Association for Parents of the Visually Impaired (NAPVI) and is a parent of a visually impaired child.

Victoria Tripodi, Ed.D., is Principal of the New York Institute for Special Education in the Bronx. She is also an adjunct professor at Teachers College, Columbia University, in New York City and at Dominican College in Orangeburg, New York. Her 22 years of experience as an educator in the field of visual impairment includes classroom teaching and consultant work throughout the United States.

Introduction

Karen E. Wolffe

The purpose of *Skills for Success: A Career Education Handbook for Children and Adolescents with Visual Impairments* is to provide teachers, parents, and others who are interested in helping or working with youngsters with visual impairments with activities to stimulate and encourage these children to grow up to be what they want to be, to become the best that they can be, to identify and refine their natural talents and interests, and, to become productive citizens. *Skills for Success* is a book about career education and lifelong learning. Written to establish a foundation that will enable visually impaired children to compete and cooperate with sighted children, it provides practical learning experiences in the environments that children frequent: school, home, and community.

THE SIGNIFICANCE OF CAREER EDUCATION

The basic premise of career education is that individuals learn best when they understand the relationship between what they do at home or school and what they want to do in the future. If children understand that by picking up their toys, they will find what they want to play with more readily, avoid stumbling over and possibly breaking their things, and please their parents, they are far more likely to learn to pick up after themselves than if they are constantly cajoled or badgered or the toys are taken care of by others. If students want to participate in an overnight excursion in which campers must set up their own campsites and fend for themselves, they are more likely to learn how to clear an area of rocks and sticks, drive a stake, tie down tent lines, and cook a

1

meal on a campfire than if they learn these activities merely as lessons in a classroom. And if teenagers want to attend a rock concert, they are more likely to learn how to budget money and save toward the cost of admission than if parents assign them the same fiscal responsibility without the same concrete goal. Learning to take care of possessions, participating in campsite preparation, cooking outdoors, and budgeting money are all examples of career education activities with transferability into adult responsibilities, including work. Employers expect workers to take care of tools and equipment they have issued to them to perform their jobs. They expect workers to be able to prepare for and implement their work-related tasks in much the same way that a Scout leader expects campers to fend for themselves. And all workers are expected by their employers to demonstrate responsibility with company resources, particularly with fiscal resources.

In the examples just discussed, the children are aware of the advantage or the reason for learning. Career education is about helping young people understand how what they learn is connected to their future goals. The learning process becomes more pertinent because they can relate what they are doing in the classroom to what they want to do in the future.

Career education, then, is not solely about preparing for and getting jobs. It is mainly about preparing for all the roles one plays over the course of a lifetime, such as child, student, worker, friend, life partner, parent, and mentor. Career education usually is infused throughout the curriculum by the efforts of teachers and parents to make learning meaningful. For example, when parents establish savings accounts for their children, they help their children learn mathematics through money management. When teachers ask students to work together on class projects, they help the students learn to cooperate and communicate effectively with their peers and further their understanding of the academic concepts under scrutiny. However, for children and adolescents with visual impairments, career education cannot be incorporated merely into traditional classroom and community settings; it needs to be a part of an expanded core curriculum in which they receive additional instruction (Hatlen, 1996; Wolffe, 1996; Wolffe, Roessler, & Schriner, 1992). (For more about the expanded core curriculum, see Chapter 1.) *Skills for Success* therefore provides teachers and parents with a means to make career education activities a part of the educational experience of children with visual impairments.

STRUCTURE OF THE HANDBOOK

Part One of this book contains two chapters. Chapter 1 introduces the reader to career education content as it is presently integrated into the everyday lives of young people with or without disabilities. The history of the career education movement is reviewed and its current status is considered. The major components of the career education model are highlighted, and examples are provided for implementation. In addition, the unique needs of children with visual impairments are discussed, and the impact of vision loss on learning and instructional strategies is explained. Specifics related to the difficulties that visually impaired children encounter concerning incidental learning are also presented. And the importance of the expanded core curriculum and career education, in particular, is related in detail. In Chapter 2, the reader is introduced to the rationale for the proposed emphasis on career education for children and adolescents with visual impairments—as a direct response to the high rates of unemployment among adults who are visually impaired and to the prevailing concern about quality of life for people who are unable to support themselves in a society that values employability above almost all other matters. These issues need to be addressed in a meaningful way for today's children to lead successful, productive lives. Research related to people with visual impairments and prospective employers is also discussed. Suggestions for changing current patterns of underemployment and unemployment, as well as for improving the overall quality of visually impaired people's lives, are offered as well.

To make the material in this book readily accessible to as broad an audience as possible, the learning activities presented are divided by relevance to specific age groups. Parts Two, Three, and Four detail, respectively, career education activities for preschoolers, elementary school students, and middle school students with visual impairments. For each age level, the activities are intended to facilitate the acquisition of skills and competencies that are necessary to enable children to enter the next prevailing environment and to provide the foundation skills for daily activities and success in life. For example, the activities in Part Two, written by Deborah Chen and Jamie Dote-Kwan, are designed to prepare preschool children to enter the school system; those in Part Three, written by Sandra Lewis, are designed to help elementary school students to move into middle school; and those in Part

Four, written by Julie Lee Kay, are intended to prepare middle school students for high school. All activities are designed to help build a foundation for life by teaching children functional skills needed to develop and maintain relationships, acquire high levels of self-esteem, and participate in vocational and avocational endeavors. A program developed for high school students, *The Transition Tote System: Navigating the Rapids of Life* (Wolffe & Johnson, 1997), complements *Skills for Success* for older students.

In each of these parts of the book, activities are presented that address the unique career education needs of visually impaired children. In addition to the career education content that all children need, children who are visually impaired also benefit from structured activities to promote high expectations of themselves, refine their social skills, develop compensatory skills, provide opportunities to work, and afford opportunities for the receipt of realistic feedback (Wolffe, 1996). These skills and behaviors, along with the rationale for their inclusion in *Skills for Success,* are briefly described as follows:

- Children and adolescents with visual impairments need to have adults and peers in their lives who will convey to these young people their high expectations of them. Society, in general, has reduced expectations for people with disabilities, and children with visual impairments are often not expected to participate or compete actively in traditional age-appropriate activities. Therefore, structured activities that promote inclusion and participation in a wide variety of home-, school-, and community-based endeavors enable visually impaired youngsters to develop and demonstrate their competencies. When people without disabilities see that young people with disabilities can do things for themselves and others, their expectations for those young people rise. Enhanced performance often follows enhanced expectations.
- Socialization does not always occur in a casual or unstructured manner for young people with visual impairments, partly because many social nuances are typically learned through observation. By watching how other children interact, with whom, and with what result, sighted children learn to socialize and develop relationships. Without reliable or functional sight, visually impaired children often need to participate in structured learning activities that help them develop social skills.

They need to learn not only how and when to exhibit facial expressions and other nonverbal social cues to convey social messages to others, but how to interpret others' social expressions and behaviors.

- A visual impairment frequently necessitates the acquisition of alternative techniques or compensatory skills to read, write, travel, and manage one's daily life. For youngsters with visual impairments, compensatory skills may include reading and writing with braille or optical devices; traveling with a long cane or such low vision devices as telescopes; and performing activities of daily living using adaptive tools and equipment with speech output, large print, or tactile markings (see Chapter 1 for more information on low vision).

- Opportunities for young visually impaired people to work have often been severely restricted because of the public's lack of awareness of the capabilities of people with visual impairments and because of the lack of accessible work environments. Many young people with visual impairments graduate from high school and college without ever having held jobs. Not having the opportunities to work as children or young adults diminishes their chances of obtaining well-paid jobs as adults.

- It is often difficult for children with visual impairments to receive realistic feedback because people tend to overrate or underrate their abilities on the basis of mythical notions of inferiority or superiority. Early writers who wrote about people who were blind tended to portray them as either helpless or superhuman. Consequently, some people may believe it is amazing that visually impaired individuals can dress and feed themselves, travel independently, and make change when paying money for purchases. Other people may believe that all visually impaired people are gifted singers, lawyers, orators, or visionary clerics. Depending on their perspectives, then, people may either laud children with faint praise or pay little or no attention to their achievements. What children really need is honest, realistic feedback about their behaviors, performance, and physical appearance.

All the chapters of *Skills for Success* deliberately follow the same pattern. The learning-activity content area (high expectations, socialization, compensatory skills, opportunities to work, or realistic feedback) in each age-related part is discussed, along with the relevance of learning activities. A list of activities is then introduced, along with ways in which teachers or families can engage visually impaired children in developing the particular skills. Next, critical points to cover in the instruction are highlighted, and helpful hints for making the activities meaningful or varying them to promote generalization of the targeted skills are presented. For example, an activity performed in school, such as learning to read a city map or bus schedule, may also be encouraged in the community to see if the students can apply the skills learned at school elsewhere. Strategies for assessing the students' acquisition of the skills are included in the section on evaluation tips. In addition, related learning activities, written by Jane Erin, are presented that focus on modifications for students with multiple disabilities.

To reflect the importance of the roles of parents and family members and the diversity of issues that need to be considered in relation to career education for visually impaired children, information from a family, multicultural, rural, and urban perspective has been included in the handbook. Kevin O'Connor writes about concerns that relate to families, Lila Cabbil discusses multicultural considerations, Elaine Sveen provides a rural perspective, and Victoria Tripodi offers an urban perspective.

Part Five of this book presents the Career Caravan and is followed by the Resources section. The Career Caravan is Anna Lee Braunstein's overview of a career education program, which includes sample lesson plans. Braunstein, a teacher in California who has taught students with visual impairments in middle school and high school, shares many of her ideas for applying the information contained in *Skills for Success* in a practical, easy-to-understand format. In addition to describing the program and presenting lesson plans, the Career Caravan includes examples of form letters and student worksheets. In the Resources section, annotated related readings from books and journals, as well as videotapes, are listed. Information about Internet listservers is also presented. Furthermore, organizations that may be of interest to readers are included with contact information (postal addresses, telephone numbers, and E-mail or Web-site addresses).

Skills for Success provides a variety of activities and resources for teaching career education skills to children and young people with visual impairments. Teachers, parents, rehabilitation specialists, and other service providers will benefit from the materials while they endeavor to improve the likelihood that the young people with whom they work will find and retain jobs after their academic training. These materials are designed to supplement the regular classroom curriculum and to enable visually impaired students to develop the work skills and habits they will need to be successful in their careers.

References

Hatlen, P. (1996). The core curriculum for blind and visually impaired students, including those with additional disabilities. *RE:view, 28,* 25–32.

Wolffe, K. (1996). Career education for students with visual impairments. *RE:view, 28,* 89–93.

Wolffe, K., & Johnson, D. (1997). *The transition tote system: Navigating the rapids of life.* Louisville, KY: American Printing House for the Blind.

Wolffe, K. E., Roessler, R. T., & Schriner, K. F. (1992). Employment concerns of people with blindness or visual impairment. *Journal of Visual Impairment & Blindness, 86*(4), 185–187.

PART ONE

Career Education for Youngsters with Visual Impairments: Paths to Successful Employment

Karen E. Wolffe

Preparation for the world of work begins as early as the preschool years for most children. To be fully integrated in the community and to lead satisfying lives, individuals need to be competent, confident, and independent and to have the chance to work. Part One of *Skills for Success* introduces readers to career education and explains the critical importance of the skills, behaviors, and competencies that youngsters with visual impairments need to develop and later build on as they grow up and engage in occupations. Chapter 1 presents the basic principles of career education, a brief history of the career education movement within the context of general education, and the specific career education needs of young people with visual impairments. The career development stages—awareness, exploration, preparation, and placement—are described to enable parents, family members, teachers, and other service providers to encourage the young people with whom they live or work toward life success. Chapter 2 focuses on employers' perceptions—what employers expect of young people graduating from school and entering the workforce. It highlights the academic skills, thinking skills, and personal qualities employers seek in prospective employees and discusses how young people with visual impairments can demonstrate their competence and employability. The chapter also includes a review of the important studies related to the integration and employment of adults with disabilities and the conclusions drawn by the studies' authors from their findings.

CHAPTER

The Importance of Career Education

In 1971, Sidney Marland, commissioner of the U.S. Department of Education, introduced career education as a major innovation in the curricula at all levels of education. Before then, educators had been concerned that what was being taught in the typical classroom was not relevant to the demands of adult life. Career education offered a system for blending career-relevant content—daily living skills, personal and social skills, and occupational skills—that researchers (Brolin, 1995, 1997; Brolin & Kokaska, 1979; Kokaska & Brolin, 1985) had identified as being important for students of all ages to learn. Brolin and Kokaska had also defined the competencies in each of these content areas that they believed were essential for young people to acquire to move successfully from school to work environments and to assume the responsibilities of adulthood. The competencies that they identified within each content area were as follows:

- daily living skills, including the ability to manage money and a household; care for one's personal needs; rear children; buy, prepare, and consume food; buy and care for clothing; demonstrate responsible citizenship; use recreational facilities; and get around in the community;
- personal and social skills, such as the ability to attain self-awareness, acquire self-confidence, achieve socially responsible behav-

ior, maintain effective interpersonal skills, become independent, make adequate decisions, and communicate with others; and

- occupational preparation skills, for example, the ability to explore and become knowledgeable about occupational possibilities; choose and plan for an occupation; exhibit appropriate work habits and behaviors; seek, obtain, and maintain employment; exhibit sufficient physical and manual skills; and learn specific occupational skills (Brolin, 1997).

BASIC ASPECTS OF CAREER EDUCATION

The career education model encouraged process learning—that is, learning by doing. According to this model, the presentation of learning activities in environments where they would naturally occur, such as performing mathematical calculations in a store to make a purchase, rather than in a classroom setting, makes the content more meaningful to students. The use of a process-learning approach in natural environments, rather than traditional methods of learning content, such as reading, writing, or listening in a classroom or clinical environment, enables students with visual impairments to perform experiential activities at home, on the job, or in the community.

Proponents of career education support a lifelong approach to learning and encourage that children be exposed to career education content from the time they are born to the time they complete high school. This content is incorporated into the regular education curriculum and presented in the following distinct yet interrelated learning stages: career awareness, exploration, preparation, and placement. Career awareness activities are introduced as early as possible in children's lives, preferably in preschool but certainly no later than kindergarten, and are emphasized in the elementary grades. Career exploration activities are presented in the late elementary grades or in middle school or junior high school (grades 6, 7, and 8 or 7, 8, and 9, respectively). Career preparation activities are integrated into the high school curriculum and extend into postsecondary educational environments. During the placement stage, career education activities are presented through community-based continuing education, in-service training, or on-the-job skills training while students are in high school or after they have graduated.

NEEDS OF VISUALLY IMPAIRED CHILDREN

The stages of career education—awareness, exploration, preparation, and placement—are the same for children with visual impairments as for those who are sighted. However, the absence of visual information or, in the case of children with low vision, the absence of reliable visual information, inhibits incidental learning, a way of learning that is prevalent with sighted children: learning by chance, from the environment, usually through observation. In this book, the term *visual impairment* is used to encompass any degree of vision loss, including total blindness. The term *low vision* is used to describe a vision loss that is severe enough to interfere with the ability to perform everyday tasks and cannot be corrected to normal by conventional eyeglasses, contact lenses, medication, or surgery but permits people to use vision as a primary channel for learning.

A sighted child may see other children outside playing a game of hide-and-seek. The child can observe where the other children are hiding and how "good" their hiding places are. An observant child will see which children are hiding together, whether some children are being excluded or ostracized, and whether the "seeker" is cheating—peeking or not waiting the full count. The child will also see what the other children are wearing and may notice what colors blend into the landscape and what colors stand out and "give away" the hiding children. Through this observation and incidental learning, the child determines what role he or she would want to play in the game and how to execute his or her duties. The same kinds of observations occur day after day in the lives of sighted children and provide them with a wealth of information about how people manage their lives, socialize with one another, and work.

INCIDENTAL LEARNING AND WORK

Without vision or with impaired vision, it is difficult to learn incidentally about work roles, the types of jobs available, what tasks are inherent in different jobs, and what work behaviors are expected of employees. Therefore, visually impaired children and adolescents need to participate in structured learning activities, such as those detailed in this book, rather than to rely on happenstance. When career education content is presented using structured activities such as these, young people with visual impairments are far more likely to move successfully from home and school into adult roles. The activities included in *Skills for Success* may be guided by parents, extended family members, teachers, or other service providers, such as school counselors, rehabilitation personnel, or orientation and mobility (O&M) instructors. In addition, children and adolescents can perform many activities independently.

Essential Competencies

Young people with visual impairments need to acquire a wide range of competencies during each stage of career education.

Career Awareness Competencies
- learning what work is without being able to observe workers visually
- learning what kinds of jobs are being performed by immediate and extended family members, neighbors, family friends, and others in the community
- developing work habits, such as following instructions, assuming responsibility for oneself and one's possessions, getting to places on time, knowing whom to go to for assistance, attending to tasks, completing tasks in a timely fashion, and participating in cooperative play
- developing work skills, including sorting like objects, putting things together, cutting, matching to size or shape or texture, building, taking apart, coordinating oneself and one's tools, using assistive devices and adapted tools, learning organizational skills, and acquiring basic academic skills (including speaking and listening, counting, and recognizing letters)
- learning incidentally about secular and religious holidays; seasons and representative activities; temporal concepts (for example, morning versus evening, the number of hours in a day, days in a week, weeks in a month, and months in a year); social rules and mores; clothing worn by different workers; and jobs performed behind the scenes
- becoming aware of different tasks within everyday jobs, such as kitchen and household chores like washing and drying dishes, setting the table, refilling condiment containers, sweeping or mopping

the floor, vacuuming, and dusting; working in the yard and garden; washing and vacuuming family vehicles; and caring for pets
- learning the roles that chores play in promoting responsibility, reciprocity, self-esteem, self-worth, and the development of skills

Career Exploration Competencies
- learning to organize time as a result of increasing demands (that is, understanding how to keep family and community activities, religious activities, and extracurricular and school activities in balance) and to manage money and resources
- learning to adjust to increasing responsibilities at home and in the community (including volunteering, paid work for family members and neighbors, and work for school and extracurricular activities)
- learning to handle additional demands for developing skills (such as academic skills, computer skills, and communication skills, both spoken and written; physical prowess; and alternative techniques related to the extent of the visual impairment)
- understanding fully the work performed by family members, family friends, teachers, and other significant adults in their lives, and key community workers
- exploring the identified areas of vocational interest (relying on such activities as reading, informational interviews, field trips, guest speakers, and job shadowing, a technique in which a job seeker follows an employee during the performance of the employee's work duties)
- developing additional positive work habits (knowing the value of attendance, punctuality, and cooperation; being able to follow complex instructions, both written and oral; and managing time and space)
- being able to articulate interests, abilities, and challenges (self-awareness)

Career Preparation Competencies
- having well-developed academic skills (such as listening, speaking, reading, writing, arithmetic, science, and history)
- participating in values clarification (that is, being able to recognize what is truly important in one's life, such as health, financial security, family living, independence, integrity, and freedom)

- being able to set personal and vocational goals
- understanding resources (how to allocate time, money, materials, space, and energy)
- developing refined interpersonal skills (such as sociability and the ability to work on teams, teach and lead others, and negotiate and work with different kinds of people)
- learning to acquire, evaluate, and use information; organize and maintain data files; and use computers efficiently to communicate
- being able to select, use, and maintain equipment and tools (including high, medium, and low technology)
- having well-honed thinking skills, namely, having the ability to think creatively and to solve problems
- being flexible and self-reliant
- having a high level of self-esteem
- being able to correlate interests, abilities, and values with career options
- having job-seeking and job search skills
- obtaining work experience (either volunteer or paid work)

Career Placement Competencies
- getting work experiences (paid, if possible) during and after school
- refining of work-related skills and habits
- gaining access to information from adults in chosen fields (through internships, apprenticeships, or job shadowing)
- focusing and refining of interests and experiences in line with career goals
- preparing for postsecondary education and training
- participating in meaningful, career-related postsecondary training
- networking for support after graduation
- planning for life and career

Transition Planning

Throughout the 1970s and into the 1980s, career education flourished in regular and special education as educators sought a means to make the learning environment more pertinent to the world of work. Special educators, including teachers of visually impaired students, often identified career education objectives in students' Individualized Education Programs (IEPs), along with academic goals and objectives. Since the passage of Public Law 94-142, the Education for All Handicapped Children

Act, in 1975, IEPs have provided a means for identifying the needs of special education students in order to stipulate what services are required to meet their needs. P.L. 94-142 was amended and renamed the Individuals with Disabilities Education Act (IDEA) (P.L. 101-476) in 1990.

In 1977, Congress passed the Career Education Implementation Incentive Act (P.L. 95-207), which introduced career education activities into school curricula throughout the United States. When the act expired in the early 1980s, Madeleine Will, assistant secretary of the U.S. Office of Special Education and Rehabilitative Services, introduced the term *transition,* which essentially replaced the term *career education* within the educational bureaucracy. Transition was defined as the period, usually between ages 16 and 22, when students prepare for independent living and work after high school graduation. One beneficial outcome of the new federal emphasis was that transition planning was mandated in 1986 through an amendment to P.L. 94-142. The 1986 amendments to P.L. 94-142 and, subsequently, IDEA (P.L. 101-476) required that transition services be addressed in special education students' IEPs by their 16th birthdays or as early as the 14th birthday, if deemed necessary to ensure the attainment of identified goals and objectives. This focus on transition-related services and goals underscored the need for career education activities. However, the shortcoming of this new emphasis was that transition services were required only for 16 year olds (or, in some instances, 14 year olds). In the original career education model, transition planning and career education content were to be applied throughout a child's life, and formalized instruction was intended from the time a child entered the educational system.

CAREER EDUCATION FOR YOUNG PEOPLE WITH VISUAL IMPAIRMENTS

Skills for Success underscores the need for early and continued intervention for children and young adults with visual impairments in regard to career education. Working as a team, parents and teachers can assist children in learning career-related concepts that may help them find and retain satisfying jobs later in life (see How Parents and Teachers Can Facilitate Teamwork in this chapter). Although career education is important for all young people, it is essential for students with visual impairments. Because many young visually impaired children are unable to receive visual information in a consistent and reliable fashion and thus cannot learn incidentally, they need to be taught many of the skills that sighted children pick up through observation. Therefore, the aim of the contributors to this book is to focus on the unique career education needs of students with visual impairments, including the following:

- the need for others to have high expectations of them
- the need for them to be engaged in structured activities to promote socialization
- the need for them to develop compensatory skills, such as the ability to read and write in braille or use optical devices, travel safely with mobility tools, and use and maintain adaptive technology
- the need for them to be included in activities in which they receive realistic feedback
- the need for them to have opportunities to work—both in volunteer and paid work experiences

The discussion that follows provides fuller descriptions of the specific needs of visually impaired children and young adults. These needs vary widely and relate both to the development of personality and organized patterns of behavior and to the development of specific employment-related skills, all of which form the basis of successful social and work life. So critical are these needs that subsequent chapters of *Skills for Success* contain activities designed to address them and to promote the development of related skills.

Expectations

It is only when others expect certain outcomes for children that they come to expect the same for themselves. Many adults and other children with whom youngsters who are visually impaired have contact, however, will have diminished or absent expectations for them. Therefore, a crucial factor in the lives of young children with visual impairments is that others need to have expectations that they can and will grow up to establish families of their own, live interdependently in their communities, and work to support themselves and their families. Early in their lives, visually impaired children need to be asked the following kinds of questions that sighted children are asked:

- What do you want to be when you grow up?

- What are you best at doing?
- What do you like best about school?
- What do you do for fun?

Others at home, in the community, and at school should expect children with visual impairments to participate actively in a full range of endeavors. The key for visually impaired children is active participation—not passive inclusion. Within their families, children with visual impairments need to be expected to do as their siblings and parents do—to contribute to family decision making and to engage in activities together, as well as to help each other. Parents should expect their visually impaired children to perform their responsibilities with the same standards as their sighted children. Furthermore, significant others (grandparents, family friends, other relatives) need to be asked or reminded to treat children with visual impairments as they would treat all children and not do things for visually impaired children that the children can do for themselves.

Teachers and other service providers should expect students with visual impairments to perform to standards comparable to those set for their sighted classmates, when their needs for adapted materials, equipment, and other individual learning requirements have been provided. Likewise, assignments should be of the same quantity and quality as those given to other students in the class. Although some visually impaired students may need more time than their sighted counterparts to complete assignments initially, or may need modified assignments of various kinds, the goal should be to move as quickly as possible to the same standards expected of other students in the class. Grades received by visually impaired students need to be earned and meaningful when compared to the norm. In addition, students with visual impairments need to participate in class projects and other group efforts within the educational purview and be expected to contribute in meaningful ways.

In the area of community and social life, community leaders and group members need to expect active participation and contributions from young people with visual impairments. They should expect appropriate social behaviors and model these behaviors for those visually impaired youngsters who become involved in community activities. People who are not familiar with visual impairments need to be made aware of the strengths and real, not imagined, challenges of the children with whom they will have contact. Scout leaders, recreation

HOW PARENTS AND TEACHERS CAN FACILITATE TEAMWORK

To support young people in pursuing their interests and developing their abilities, it is essential for parents, teachers, and other concerned adults to work together. The following are some strategies that parents and teachers can follow to foster teamwork in the career education process.

Parents

- Schedule and attend informal meetings that include the key participants in children's lives to discuss their expectations and goals for the children. (Key participants may include family members, a vision teacher, regular classroom teachers, O&M instructors, therapists, rehabilitation counselors, and other service providers.)

- Volunteer for class and community-based activities.

- Volunteer on the playground and at school-sponsored events.

- Accompany students on field trips.

- Sponsor or support extracurricular activities.

- Invite teachers and other service providers to work with children at home and in the neighborhood.

- Communicate regularly with school and rehabilitation personnel about children's strengths and weaknesses, interests and values, achievements and challenges.

- Attend and actively participate in formal meetings, such as IEP meetings.

Teachers

- Use a daily or weekly notebook to inform parents of what is being done with their children and encourage them to inform teachers of what they are doing at home.

- Schedule and attend meetings about students that include all the key participants in their lives.

- Sponsor or support extracurricular activities.

- Videotape students performing activities that their parents and other interested adults may not realize they can do and share the videotape with these adults.

- Encourage parents and other concerned adults to come to class to teach the students about their career and life activities.

- Attend community-based meetings of consumer and parent groups where students, parents, and other interested persons can be met.

- Telephone or visit parents to express concern or enthusiasm for what their children are doing in school.

supervisors, coaches, religious leaders, and others need to understand how young people with visual impairments can be fully included in the community activities in which they want to participate.

Socialization

Vision mediates learning, and nowhere is this more apparent than in the realm of social skills. So many of the social nuances that gain people entry into groups and help them establish and maintain relationships are based on nonverbal cues. For example, people generally make eye contact with others before speaking to them and, depending on their facial expression, will either engage others in conversation or choose not to do so. Often, sighted children will visually scan a playground or recreation area to see who is with whom and what interesting activities other children are doing in which they would like to participate. Without vision or with severely impaired vision, these visual cues are meaningless or can be easily misinterpreted.

With vision, children observe what body postures and facial expressions are pleasing to others and which are displeasing. They learn subtle cues, such as a wave, a nod, a wink, and a shrug of the shoulders, for conveying information; how and when to use these nonverbal forms of communication; and how others react to them when they use such cues. Children with impaired vision need to be systematically taught how to produce nonverbal cues like gestures and postures, as well as the kinds of reactions those cues are likely to elicit from others.

Basic socialization involves communication with others. Communication involves at least two people and depends on reciprocity: The parties engaged in a communication exchange give a little bit of information and then expect to receive a little bit of information in return. Sometimes, without realizing the impact of their behaviors on others, children with visual impairments monopolize conversations or do not participate in them. They do not see expressions of boredom or notice when people turn to them for input. They therefore need to be taught how to listen and speak in near-equal measure to engage successfully in the social interactions that form the fabric of everyday life.

Compensatory Skills

Compensatory skills, or alternative techniques, are the means or systems that enable people with visual impairments to perform activities that most people do using vision: walking, reading, writing, calculating, taking care of themselves and their belongings, taking care of others, and gaining access to and using equipment and tools, among other actions. To promote the effective achievement of educational and developmental goals among visually impaired students, educators and parents developed and disseminated *The National Agenda for the Education of Children and Youths with Visual Impairments, Including Those with Multiple Disabilities* (Corn, Hatlen, Huebner, Ryan, & Siller, 1995). Goal 8 of *The National Agenda* recommends that instruction for students with visual impairments "reflect the assessed needs of each student in all areas of academic and disability-specific core curricula." This notion of a disability-specific core curriculum was detailed by Hatlen (1996) in his proposed expanded core curriculum for students with visual impairments. In addition to the core curriculum, or general educational curriculum, covering such areas as language arts, mathematics, health, fine arts, economics, vocational education, science, physical education, social studies, business education, and history, the expanded core curriculum is intended to focus on compensatory and functional academic skills that students with visual impairments need to develop: communication modes, such as reading and writing with braille; the use of low vision devices and adapted computer hardware and software; O&M; social interaction skills; independent living skills; recreation and leisure skills; career education; technology; and visual efficiency skills (that is, being able to maximize the use of whatever vision that is retained and to use low vision devices like magnifiers and other aids that are intended to help maximize vision and enable the student to read at rates commensurate with fully sighted peers).

Compensatory and functional academic skills are explained in Chapter 2, in the discussion of employers' concerns related to literacy demands in the workplace, and technology skills are interwoven in Chapter 2 and throughout the book. Social interaction skills, what the contributors to *Skills for Success* call socialization, were discussed earlier in this section and are reviewed in light of employers' expectations in Chapter 2. Each of the other expanded core curriculum areas— O&M, independent living skills, recreation and leisure skills, and visual efficiency skills—are briefly reviewed in the following discussion. All areas of the expanded core curriculum are incorporated into *Skills for Success*'s recommended activities. The expanded core curriculum, together with the regular education curriculum, is essentially a part of this book because career education includes all these areas.

O&M

Basic O&M skills, which enable children to know where they are and how to get from where they are to where they want to be in space, are learned with the assistance of O&M instructors. These instructors work with individuals who have visual impairments in the environments where they live and work, namely, the home, the school, and the community. O&M for young children involves learning such basic concepts as top, bottom, left, right, up, and down. Gradually, depending on their needs, children learn how to use such techniques as trailing and sighted guide technique and equipment such as modified or long canes to get around in their environments. In cases in which youngsters meet the criteria of dog guide schools and become experienced travelers, they may choose to learn to work with dog guides.

Independent Living Skills

Independent living skills, often referred to as activities of daily living, include home and personal management tasks (taking care of one's living quarters, grooming and hygiene, shopping and cooking, and managing time and money, among other activities) that make living independently possible. In general, what is taught in traditional home economics classes is not sufficient to meet the specific needs of youngsters with visual impairments. The enhanced core curriculum teaches students about adapted devices and tools, as well as alternative techniques for performing these activities.

Recreation and Leisure Skills

Although physical education classes are valuable and appropriate for many visually impaired students, they frequently do not provide students with a full range of options for leisure-time activities. A structured recreation and leisure skills component within the expanded core curriculum supports the development of recreation and leisure skills by visually impaired children. Students are encouraged to participate in a wide range of activities, including team sports with adaptations (using equipment with auditory signals, for example) and individual athletic endeavors. Students also learn about the range of recreational opportunities in their communities without having to rely on sight to find out what is available to them.

Visual Efficiency Skills

Many students with low vision can benefit from instruction in using what vision they have more efficiently. Teachers of students with visual impairments are responsible for performing functional vision assessments and for teaching students how to use effectively the vision they still retain (Hatlen, 1996). Students with low vision frequently acquire low vision devices and must be taught how to use them in the environments in which they live, work, and play.

Realistic Feedback

Throughout their lives, children and young adults with visual impairments probably will be compared against a sighted norm. Therefore, they need to receive realistic feedback from their families, teachers, and other service providers to know how their performances stack up against those of their sighted counterparts. This is not to say that they should be held to unrealistic expectations to perform in areas in which visual acuity is a determining factor in a person's ability to do something—for example, driving a car or accurately describing a complex graphic. However, when the tasks in which they are involved are "doable" by someone with a severe visual impairment, it is important that young people receive input from those who care about them that describes accurately how their performances compare to those of their peers.

If children receive messages from significant persons in their lives that are based on untruths or exaggerations, they cannot develop an accurate knowledge of their own abilities or talents. Although some people may believe that because a blind child can find the notes on a piano, he or she has a remarkable talent or gift in music, it is important for that child to understand his or her own musical abilities, experiences, and preferences. Some teachers working with children with low vision for the first time may think they are doing the children a favor by giving them less work or less challenging work than sighted children. However, this attempt to "be kind" actually sends a message signaling that the teachers do not think the children can perform as well as or do as much as their sighted classmates or that they are not as capable. From examples such as these, the interrelationship between realistic expectations and realistic feedback becomes clear.

If teachers give high grades to children with disabilities for work that is not up to standard and on which they would have scored lower than children without disabilities in the belief that these children performed as best they could, the children will not learn how their work compares to other children's work while they are in school. They will then be hardpressed to understand their employers' expectations for their performance when they graduate from school. By understanding how they are performing in comparison to others their age, young people with visual impairments can compete realistically and more successfully for openings in postsecondary training and academic programs and, ultimately, for jobs.

Opportunities to Work

Beginning with responsibilities at home, children with visual disabilities need to have opportunities to work. Chores done at home, in school, and during community activities help young people realize their self-worth and ability to contribute. Throughout their lives, youngsters need to be encouraged to work—to do things for themselves, for their families, and for others, whether it is picking up their clothes and toys, making their beds, taking out the trash, washing or drying the dishes, or feeding the family pet. Receiving an allowance for the performance of such chores is one way in which children can understand the relationship between work and paid compensation. At school, children with visual impairments need to be assigned duties similar to those of their classmates, including handing out supplies, tidying up the classroom, taking care of class pets or gardens, running errands, and helping the teacher in any way possible. The opportunities to work during community activities are as diverse as the activities in which children participate, for instance, helping to take care of younger children, collecting money at bake sales, sorting collected goods during a food drive, and helping with equipment at athletic events.

In general, it is less critical that children be paid than that they actively participate and contribute. By helping and giving of themselves, children gain self-respect and develop a high level of self-esteem. Opportunities to work are crucial to the life success of individuals with disabilities. Many people over the course of their lives will expect youngsters with disabilities to be unable to work, to do for themselves, or to contribute to society. These misconceptions can be dispelled by showing that such youngsters are capable. To work is to demonstrate competence and ability.

NATIONAL LONGITUDINAL TRANSITION STUDY

One effective way to understand how children with visual impairments compare with their peers with other disabilities and those without disabilities is to follow their progress over time. In the mid-1980s, the U.S. Congress mandated the National Longitudinal Transition Study of Special Education Students (NLTS) to analyze the transition of young people with disabilities from secondary school to early adulthood. The researchers involved with the survey were asked to compare the performances of children with and without disabilities over a five-year period.

In the first comprehensive NLTS report, *Youth with Disabilities: How Are They Doing?* (Wagner et al., 1991), youngsters with visual impairments were noted as performing well in school with little likelihood of dropping out. However, in spite of their good performances in school, the employment rate for those who were not college bound was only 23 percent, half the rate of young adults with disabilities as a whole. Only half the young people who had been out of high school up to two years had held paid jobs the preceding year, compared to 70 percent of all young people with disabilities. Among the young people who were employed, those with visual impairments were significantly more likely to be paid at or below minimum wage. Although the NLTS study did not attempt to explain the reasons for these discrepancies, an earlier investigation of the employment concerns of visually impaired adults provided insights. At the top of their list of concerns was the adults' belief that they had received inadequate help in getting information about career opportunities and in developing their job-seeking skills while in school (Wolffe, Roessler, & Schriner, 1992).

What Happens Next? Trends in Postschool Outcomes of Youth with Disabilities (Wagner, D'Amico, Marder, Newman, & Blackorby, 1992), the 1992 NLTS report, drew attention to the results that were published in the 1991 study. It reported that students with visual impairments continued to be successful in school but were not employed after graduation. Only 17 percent of students with visual impairments who were out of school three to five years were working full time, and 12 percent were working part time. The majority—71 percent—were unemployed. Only three other groups of young people with disabilities had unemployment rates as high or higher: those with orthopedic impairments (78 percent), those with multiple disabilities (83 percent), and those who were deaf-blind (84 percent). By comparison, in the general population, nearly 70 percent of young people who were out of school three to five years were employed. The report of the 1992 NLTS study did not specify why the disparities exist. However, two important points can be inferred from the study: First, visually impaired young people seem to be staying in school longer and focusing on the development of academic skills, whereas those with other disabilities and many of those without disabilities are gaining work experience and networking in the community with prospective employers. Second, although research has indicated that paid work experience of any kind during high school is associated with higher levels of employment in early adulthood, few young people with visual impairments work while they are enrolled in secondary school programs (Wehman, 1992).

In most of the other areas that were investigated in the 1992 NLTS study—participation in postsecondary education, living independently, and social involvement—students with visual impairments were performing as well or better than students with other disabilities. That is, 48 percent of the students with visual impairments were attending postsecondary school either full or part time, 46 percent of the young adults who had been out of school three to five years were living independently, and 81 percent of those who were out of school reported that they were socially involved.

The conclusions drawn from the NLTS findings reinforce the need for career education for young people with visual impairments. These reports demonstrate empirically the need for early intervention to develop the outcomes that parents, teachers, and other concerned individuals want for children and adolescents with visual impairments—productive and satisfying lives in the mainstream of society. By exposing children as young as preschoolers to concepts related to the satisfaction of accomplishments and working as a team, adults can help ensure these children's later successes.

References

Brolin, D. E. (1995). *Career education: A functional life skills approach* (3rd ed.). Englewood, NJ: Merrill.

Brolin, D. E. (1997). *Life-centered career education: A competency-based approach* (5th ed.). Reston, VA: Council for Exceptional Children.

Brolin, D. E. & Kokaska, C. J. (1979). *Career education for handicapped children and youth.* Columbus, OH: Merrill.

Corn, A. L., Hatlen, P., Huebner, K. M., Ryan, F., & Siller, M. A. (1995). *The national agenda for the education of children and youths with visual impairments, including those with multiple disabilities.* New York: American Foundation for the Blind.

Hatlen, P. (1996). The core curriculum for blind and visually impaired students, including those with additional disabilities. *RE:view, 28*(1), 25–32.

Kokaska, C. J., & Brolin, D. E. (1985). *Career education for handicapped individuals* (2nd ed.). Columbus, OH: Merrill.

Wagner, M., D'Amico, R., Marder, C., Newman, L., & Blackorby, J. (1992). *What happens next? Trends in postschool outcomes of youth with disabilities.* Menlo Park, CA: SRI International.

Wagner, M., Newman, L., D'Amico, R., Jay, E. D., Butler-Nalin, P., Marder, C., & Cox, R. (1991). *Young people with disabilities: How are they doing?* Menlo Park, CA: SRI International.

Wehman, P. (1992). *Life beyond the classroom: Transition strategies for young people with disabilities.* Baltimore: Paul H. Brookes.

Wolffe, K. E., Roessler, R. T., & Schriner, K. F. (1992). Employment concerns of people with blindness or visual impairments. *Journal of Visual Impairment & Blindness, 86,* 185–187.

2

Employers: What Do They Want?

Getting a job is a complex process. It involves a broad range of varied activities. But ultimately a successful job candidate is someone who understands what a prospective employer needs and how to help meet those needs. Like everyone else, people who are visually impaired who want to be employed need to match their abilities and skills to what an employer wants to accomplish. It is therefore important for young visually impaired people and their parents, teachers, and other service providers to know the concerns employers may have in hiring people in general and in hiring people with disabilities in particular. This chapter presents an overview of some of the more significant research of the late 1980s and 1990s pertaining to the employment of individuals with disabilities. It also examines employers' general perceptions of public school graduates and their impact on hiring practices.

OUTCOME STUDIES ON THE LIVES OF DISABLED ADULTS

In the mid- to late 1980s, the International Center for the Disabled (ICD) commissioned Louis Harris and Associates to survey Americans with disabilities, special educators, and employers to try to get an accurate picture of how individuals with disabilities were faring in the United States. The Harris surveys—*The ICD Survey of Disabled Americans: Bringing Disabled Americans into the Mainstream* (Harris, 1986), *The ICD Survey II: Employing Disabled Americans* (Harris, 1987), and *The*

ICD Survey III: A Report Card on Special Education (Harris, 1989)—provide some interesting insights into the socioeconomic status, labor market participation, and access to education of people with disabilities. Highlights from these reports are described next.

First ICD Survey

The initial ICD survey (Harris, 1986) looked broadly at the lives of disabled Americans and their status in society following the legislative mandates of the 1970s for inclusion in neighborhood schools and communities. More than 70 percent of the 1,000 disabled Americans who were surveyed believed their lives had improved in the decade before this report, and two-thirds believed that federal legislation had helped improve the quality of their lives. However, the findings on what it meant to be a disabled American in the mid-1980s were disturbing:

- Americans with disabilities had less education than did those without disabilities.
- Americans with disabilities, particularly elderly disabled people, were much poorer than were those without disabilities.
- Americans with disabilities were far less likely to have active social lives than were those without disabilities.
- Americans with disabilities were far more likely to be unemployed than were those without disabilities.
- Disabled Americans were less involved in community life than were Americans without disabilities.
- Almost 60 percent of disabled Americans believed that their disabilities had prevented them from reaching their full potential.

More than any other indicator, however, the lack of employment defined what it meant to be a disabled person in the mid-1980s in the United States. Two-thirds of the Americans with disabilities aged 16–64 who were surveyed were unemployed. Only 1 person in 4 worked full time. Although two-thirds of those who were unemployed said they wanted to work, at the time of the survey 96 percent were out of the labor market—meaning that they were not actively seeking work.

Second ICD Survey

The second ICD survey (Harris, 1987) was based on 921 interviews with top managers, equal employment opportunity managers, department heads, and line managers. Overall, these managers had positive feelings about their disabled employees' job performances. The majority believed the costs of accommodations were not prohibitive (the survey was conducted before the passage of the Americans with Disabilities Act, ADA, of 1990), and 48 percent said that they had made accommodations for disabled employees. Additional highlights from the study were as follows:

- Large companies were more likely to hire people with disabilities than were small companies.
- Companies that had not hired people with disabilities said that the lack of qualified applicants was their greatest deterrent.
- Only 37 percent of the companies reported having an established policy or program for hiring employees with disabilities.
- Three-fourths of those surveyed considered job discrimination to be a barrier to employing disabled persons.
- The managers rated minority groups and elderly people as better potential sources of employees than people with disabilities.

Third ICD Survey

The third ICD survey (Harris, 1989) specifically investigated how special education systems had served the needs of students with disabilities. Surveys were conducted with 702 public school teachers, 198 students with disabilities, and 1,000 parents of disabled students. Significant points from the study were these:

- The teachers believed that the education of students with disabilities had improved since the passage of P.L. 94-142 in 1975.
- Nearly 80 percent of the parents reported that they were satisfied with the special education system. However, only 43 percent thought that the transition from school to work was effective, that is, that graduates had acquired the skills to live independently, work, maintain their jobs, and develop social relationships.
- Most of the parents rated their children's schools positively on the attitudes of teachers toward parents of disabled children (76 percent), physical access to school facilities (73 percent), and efforts to integrate disabled children and children without disabilities in school activities (70 percent).
- Preparing students for work received the lowest ratings from both parents and educators. Only 11 percent of the parents and

15 percent of the teachers believed that the schools did an excellent job preparing students for work after graduation from high school.
- Less than half the students over the age of 17 had received job counseling or job placement services.

The findings of this study give some insight into why most students with visual impairments did not do well on the employment ratings in the National Longitudinal Transition Study described in the previous chapter. Students often receive academic instruction but little else during their public school years. What is missing from the curriculum is the development of the skills that have been identified as essential for success in careers—social skills, compensatory skills, and work-related skills—together with activities that promote high expectations and realistic feedback.

Follow-Up Survey

In 1995, the National Organization on Disability contracted with the Harris organization to do a follow-up survey of the employment status of disabled people on the fifth anniversary of the ADA. The study, *The N.O.D./Harris Survey on Employment of People with Disabilities* (Harris, 1995), addressed two major factors—the attitudes of corporate employers toward workers with disabilities and the impact of the ADA on the integration of disabled employees in the workplace (for example, the removal of physical barriers and increased employment). The findings included the following:

- Seventy percent of the employers believed the ADA should not be changed, and 82 percent believed that the opportunities provided by the ADA are worth the cost of implementation.
- Although the proportion of companies that made accommodations in the workplace increased from 51 percent in 1986 to 81 percent in 1995, the percentage of companies who hired people with disabilities in that period increased only from 62 percent to 64 percent.
- Corporate managers viewed their disabled employees' work performance positively (17 percent rated it "excellent," and 59 percent rated it "very good").

Conclusions for People with Visual Impairments

The studies of adults with disabilities and employers highlight the critical need for career education activities in school, at home, and in the community for youngsters with visual impairments. Career education activities, including those aimed at promoting daily living skills, personal social skills, and occupational skills, need to be implemented as early as possible in the lives of all children. Children with visual impairments also need activities to convey high expectations of them and realistic feedback because both self-esteem and evaluative information are in short supply as a result of the general public's lack of awareness about the abilities of children and young adults with disabilities. In addition, children with visual impairments need to develop compensatory skills, such as reading and writing in braille; using low vision devices, adaptive technology, and other adapted tools; and traveling with alternative techniques.

Two other areas are fundamental to the success of visually impaired people: socialization and opportunities to work. As was discussed in Chapter 1, without the ability to see, children are at great risk of failing to learn the nuances of appropriate social behavior because most children learn social skills incidentally, not in structured lessons at home or in school. Moreover, children with visual impairments need to have opportunities to work while they are in school. It is through work and work-related experiences that children discover what they like and do not like about various occupations and learn vocational skills on the job or experientially. But perhaps most important, it is through their work experiences that youngsters learn the requisite work behaviors to maintain employment and advance in their chosen occupations.

EMPLOYERS' CONCERNS

For many years numerous employers have expressed their concerns about the inadequate preparation of students for the world of work. (For information on what family members can do to help students develop skills that may meet employers' expectations, see How Adults Can Help Visually Impaired Students Meet Employers' Expectations in this chapter.) Their anxieties are not specific to young adults with visual impairments, but are relevant to these young adults as they enter into

HOW ADULTS CAN HELP VISUALLY IMPAIRED STUDENTS MEET EMPLOYERS' EXPECTATIONS

Employers have identified four types of skill areas that are essential for success in the world of work: academic skills (reading, writing, calculating, listening, and speaking), thinking skills (the ability to learn, reason, think creatively, and make decisions), personal qualities (a sense of responsibility, self-esteem, and sociability), and workplace competencies (the ability to use resources, demonstrate interpersonal skills, apply information, learn about systems, and work with technology). Parents and family members, teachers, and other concerned adults can take a variety of steps to help children with visual impairments develop the skills that meet these expectations.

Families

- Encourage children to read by reading with them, taking them to neighborhood libraries and regional libraries for people who are visually impaired, and providing accessible books.

- Encourage children to write thank-you and other notes, party invitations, diaries, letters to grandparents and other relatives, and to-do lists in both print and braille; write notes to children in their preferred medium.

- Take children shopping and help them participate in money exchanges, such as figuring out sales taxes, savings discounts, and the correct change when paying for purchases.

- Encourage children to help prepare food, measure quantities, follow recipes, and then experiment with recipes (like doubling or halving them). Teach them how to use kitchen appliances and tools, first with supervision and then without it.

- Help children practice saying their names, addresses, telephone numbers, and ages, as well as both parents' full names and telephone numbers at work, and the telephone numbers of other relatives.

- Help children learn effective listening skills by modeling the skills (paying attention to them when they are speaking, responding to their questions honestly and thoughtfully, paraphrasing what they have said, and asking questions to review what was said).

the same work environment as their sighted counterparts. Employers' concerns are well articulated in a series of reports produced in the early 1990s by the U.S. Department of Labor (DOL) Secretary's Committee on Achieving Necessary Skills (SCANS), including, *What Work Requires of Schools* (DOL, 1991), *Learning a Living* (DOL, 1992a), and *Skills and*

Teachers

- Instead of doing things for students, help them think about and resolve problems and perform activities.
- Have students order books and supplies from vendors.
- Provide opportunities for students to participate in school-sponsored work activities, such as fundraising carnivals, ticket sales for athletic events, and community volunteer efforts like car washes and picking up litter in parks.
- Reinforce the performance of naturally occurring activities of daily living (for example, washing dishes after snacks and hanging up costumes used in a play).
- Have students help with class projects, such as taking care of plants or animals in the classroom, passing out supplies, and collecting classroom assignments or tests from other students.
- Expect students to take care of their own books, supplies, assignments, notebooks, and clothing.
- Institute cooperative learning projects and group planning of field trips and other special events.
- Encourage students to help younger students with their schoolwork and extracurricular activities.
- Ask students to read and share what they have read with others through book clubs or book reports presented orally and in writing.
- Discuss current events with students and assign reports on various topics.
- Encourage students to submit written work to the school newspaper.

Other Concerned Adults

- Encourage children to participate in community-based activities like Scouting; sports; recreational activities; and volunteer activities at nursing homes, hospitals, humane societies, and other organizations.
- Provide supports (such as reading, observations, and orientation to new environments) to foster children's active participation in community activities.
- Ask children what they want to be when they grow up.
- Hire children to help with everyday chores: babysitting, pet care, yard work, garden work, and car washing and maintenance.

Tasks for Jobs (DOL, 1992b). Some of these issues are examined in the discussion that follows.

In general, people in hiring positions are concerned about high school graduates' having acquired basic educational skills: academic skills (such as reading, writing, calculating, listening, and speaking), thinking skills (for example, the ability to learn, reason, think creatively, and make decisions), and personal qualities (such as self-esteem, sociability, and being individually responsible). Furthermore, they have identified five additional competencies that young adults need to demonstrate in the workplace: the ability to use resources (allocate time, money, materials, space, and staff), demonstrate interpersonal skills (work on teams, teach others, and work with different types of people), apply information (obtain and evaluate data, organize and communicate information, and use computer equipment), understand systems (social, organizational, and technological), and work with technology (select and maintain equipment and tools and apply technology).

To be successfully integrated into the workplace, young people with visual impairments need to acquire the skills and competencies that employers look for in new employees. In the following discussion, these skills and competencies are examined with regard to the alternative techniques and unique skills that students with visual impairments need to develop and demonstrate to be considered as employable. Although personal qualities are referred to as basic skills in the SCANS literature, for the purpose of this discussion they are treated separately.

BASIC SKILLS

Basic skills are the foundation on which all other skills are built. They are the core skills—academic skills and thinking skills—that are essential to the ability to perform a job.

Academic Skills

Academic skills for students with visual impairments include the same basic skills—reading, writing, calculating, listening, and speaking—that all young people strive to acquire to become literate.

Reading

Reading is performed primarily for oneself—to acquire information, instruct, or entertain. For most students with visual impairments, the preferred media for reading are large print and braille, but those with additional physical or cognitive impairments sometimes need to use audiotapes for reading. In addition, some students with low vision read print with the help of optical devices, reading machines, optical character recognition systems, or human readers. Reading aloud is usually done either to demonstrate competence or to entertain others.

Writing

Depending on one's ability to see, writing for oneself involves making notations by hand or in braille, typing, word processing, or audiotaping. Braille or print are the preferred means for writing down information for future reference, unless a physical or cognitive impairment necessitates an alternative, such as audiotaping. Electronic note-taking devices (with braille or typewriter keyboards) and microcassette recorders make taking notes without pencil and paper easier for many visually impaired students. However, the retrieval of information using such systems may not be as quick as writing notes on paper because such systems rely on batteries or electricity, which makes them less dependable than paper and pencil or slate and stylus.

Writing for others usually requires print output, either handwritten or computer generated. For students who do not have legible handwriting, computers have made this task much less difficult. With computer technology and speech or braille output, students can proofread their work before producing it in print for sighted coworkers or acquaintances. In addition, students need to be able to sign their own names; being able to add one's signature to documents, forms, and applications is an essential skill.

Calculating

Students with visual impairments frequently perform mathematical calculations with a talking calculator, computer, paper and pencil, or abacus, and those with functional vision may use a calculator with a large-print display or a light-emitting diode readout. To be successful on the job and to lead a responsible adult life, prospective employees need to be able to perform basic mathematical functions, such as addition, subtraction, multiplication, and division. The functional arithmetic skills that are indispensable in adult life include balancing a checkbook; computing gross versus net wages, sales taxes, and percentage discounts; analyzing tax liabilities; and figuring out the rate of return on investments.

Speaking

Speaking involves using words orally or employing sign language to convey messages to others. What people say may create a powerful impression on others. If an individual speaks well and uses proper grammar and vocabulary, he or she will probably be highly regarded by others, but if the person speaks improperly and uses incorrect grammar and misunderstood words and concepts, he or she will not. For people with visual impairments, one concern is concept integrity. Sometimes children who are blind hear a word used and believe they understand what it means; however, they may be confused by the word because they have never seen or experienced the object or concept about which they are talking. Thus, children with visual impairments need to be taught the meanings of words they are using, and the concepts that are embedded need to be verified for their accuracy.

Listening

The ability to listen effectively is important for everyone, but it is a critical skill for people who are visually impaired. For many visually impaired individuals, listening is the primary means of obtaining information. Listening enables them to form impressions of others without seeing them, as well as to stay informed about current events, follow conversations or lectures, and discern what is going on in the environment. By listening carefully and asking for clarification when comments or concepts do not make sense, visually impaired students can gather quantities of information in a timely fashion.

Thinking Skills

The abilities to learn, reason, think creatively, and make decisions are essential thinking skills for integration into the workplace. One way in which to promote thinking skills is by having youngsters solve their own problems. Wording questions for children by asking, "How *could* you do this?"; "What ideas do *you* have for solving this problem?"; "How have you heard of other people fixing such a problem?" rather than by saying, "The way you ought to do this is . . ." teaches them to solve their own problems.

In general, people learn to think by being asked to think, rather than by having others think for them. They learn to think creatively by having problems presented to them and by being asked for their ideas—all kinds of ideas—to help solve the problems. Children who are blind may need to hear others' accounts of how they have solved problems in great detail, so they can add new perspectives to their problem-solving repertoires.

PERSONAL QUALITIES

Individual responsibility, self-esteem, and sociability are essential qualities for entering and maintaining relationships with others. When children are given chores to do and expected to participate in activities as equals, they learn to accept individual responsibility. When they are encouraged to help those who are less fortunate or in need, they grow confident and develop high levels of self-esteem. Young people who are nurtured but not catered to, are encouraged to take risks and are comforted and reassured when they fail or rewarded and praised when they succeed, and are allowed to express themselves honestly but learn not to impose their ideas on other people develop and implement strong social relationship skills.

These three areas—academic skills, thinking skills, and personal qualities—are the basic attributes that employers look for in new employees. Therefore, young people who are entering the labor market need to be able to demonstrate competence in these areas. In addition, those with visual impairments need to be able to demonstrate the alternative techniques they use in applying the foundation skills in their daily lives to employers who are probably unfamiliar with these techniques.

WORK-RELATED COMPETENCIES

Ability to Use Resources

The ability to use resources (to allocate time, money, materials, space, and staff) is crucial in the modern workplace. Young people need to understand that their time on the job is the boss's time and that all the resources available at work, such as time, money, materials, space, people, and equipment, are valued and valuable to the overall well-being of the company and, ultimately, to the well-being of the employees. To retain a job, they need to be able to manage the resources to which they have access. Employers expect employees to be prepared to use the resources available to them, and this requirement typically demands effective organizational skills.

Interpersonal Skills

Employees need to be able to demonstrate strong interpersonal skills. Most employers look specifically for employees who can and will work on teams, teach others how to perform and improve on the job, and work with different kinds of people (for example, people from different ethnic and cultural backgrounds and religions, older and younger people, and people of both sexes). Social skills enable employees to get along and work well with each other. People are social by nature, and in a modern society this phenomenon is most reflected in the workplace—that is, people obtain, advance in, and maintain employment largely because of their social skills. They need to be able to understand the overt and covert social rules that guide the society and to prescribe to themselves acceptable behavior on the basis of their understanding of these rules.

Information Management Skills

The modern workplace requires employees to be able to use information—lots of information—competently. Using information involves obtaining and evaluating data, organizing information, communicating information effectively to coworkers, and being able to use computer equipment to manage and retrieve stored information. In other words, employees must be able to cull relevant data from their work, synthesize information, and convey important facts to others.

Knowledge of Systems

Employees need to be aware of the systems—social, organizational, and technological—in the workplace. They are expected to understand how the social hierarchy at work functions and how they fit into it. They need to know the organizational structure of the companies they work for and how it interfaces with the social structure. In today's computer-driven workplace, employees should also have a basic understanding of how networks operate and how companies use local and global networks to generate and monitor business. They are expected to be able to use their knowledge of the social, organizational, and technological systems to help solve any problem that may arise in the work environment.

Ability to Use Technology

Employees need to be able to select, use, and maintain appropriate equipment and tools to perform their job duties and to describe the computer hardware and software with which they are familiar. Furthermore, employees need to be able to demonstrate their competence with technology. This is an especially important point for young people with visual impairments because the equipment they use may differ from the equipment used by other employees. Hence, young visually impaired adults must be prepared to demonstrate that they can perform the required work with their adaptive technology (talking computers, braille output devices, screen enlargers, and reading machines, among other devices).

AGENDA FOR FUTURE SKILLS DEVELOPMENT

Given that employment requires people to be aware of the needs of employers, how can visually impaired youngsters become more attuned to these needs? Parents, siblings, extended family members, neighbors, and family friends, as well as service providers, can help by infusing career education activities into as many of young people's environments as possible. The following chapters in *Skills for Success* provide readers with activities that are specifically focused on the needs of young people with visual impairments and are intended to help them build skills from the preschool years through the middle school years and beyond. By using these activities to form the basis of thoughtful efforts to promote the abilities of individual youngsters, parents, teachers, and other concerned adults can do much to help students with visual impairments grow up to work and contribute fully to their own well-being and to the well-being of others in their communities. They can also speak with each other to form a productive dialogue in support of career education for children with visual impairments. The chapters in the next section demonstrate some ways to begin.

References

Harris, L. (1986). *The ICD survey of disabled Americans: Bringing disabled Americans into the mainstream.* New York: International Center for the Disabled.

Harris, L. (1987). *The ICD survey II: Employing disabled Americans.* New York: International Center for the Disabled.

Harris, L. (1989). *The ICD survey III: A report card on special education.* New York: International Center for the Disabled.

Harris, L. (1995). *The N.O.D./Harris survey on employment of people with disabilities.* New York: National Organization on Disability.

U.S. Department of Labor, Secretary's Committee on Achieving Necessary Skills. (1991). *What work requires of schools.* Washington, DC: Author.

U.S. Department of Labor, Secretary's Committee on Achieving Necessary Skills. (1992a). *Learning a living.* Washington, DC: Author.

U.S. Department of Labor, Secretary's Committee on Achieving Necessary Skills. (1992b). *Skills and tasks for jobs.* Washington, DC: Author.

PART TWO

The Preschool Years

Deborah Chen

Jamie Dote-Kwan

Jane Erin

*Activities for Children Who Need
Additional Modifications*

Experiences in the family are the most influential in the early years of children's lives. It is from them that children learn crucial information about themselves and the world around them. They learn what others expect of them and develop a sense of what to expect of themselves. It is during early childhood that youngsters acquire their basic social and communication skills. Early intervention programs and preschool settings introduce children with visual impairments to the compensatory skills they will use throughout their lives, including the ability to read and write in braille, orientation and mobility techniques, and adapted strategies for home and personal management. In addition, both preschool programs and home-based instruction give young children opportunities to learn about work and to establish work habits. Through all these learning experiences, children also receive feedback from others about their performance. It is important for all children to be given feedback that is honest, reinforces desirable skills and traits, and promotes positive change in their lives.

The following chapters on preschool activities draw from what is known about instructional practices that provide effective preschool experiences for young sighted children who are not disabled, for preschoolers with severe disabilities, and for preschoolers who have visual impairments. Developmentally appropriate practice (DAP), a hallmark of early childhood education (Bredekamp & Copple, 1997), stresses the need for diverse experiences that support learning in a variety of social and cultural contexts on the basis of children's interests and strengths. These experiences involve children as active learners and focus on play to promote social, emotional, and cognitive development. DAP emphasizes the importance of teachers' working in partnership with families, respecting family and cultural differences, and providing flexible structure.

According to this philosophy, children are taught through planned activities in organized physical environments that meet instructional objectives. Preschool teachers organize and monitor the physical setting—arrange the placement of furniture, select the materials that are needed, group the children, plan the amount of time required, guide the roles of involved adults, and identify the children's expectations—to enhance each child's learning experience. At the same time, they stimulate the children's curiosity, interests, and participation in planned activities so they can take advantage of "teachable moments" and opportunities for incidental learning.

Part Two of this book focuses on activities for preschoolers that provide the foundation skills and behaviors children need to assimilate successfully and easily into their next prevailing environment: elementary school. These activities may be considered early career education in that they foster the abilities that children need for successful social and work lives and can be performed at home, at school, or in the community. They are presented as examples that teachers, parents, and others can use to generate additional ideas for structured activities that will ultimately increase visually impaired children's expectations of themselves, help them refine their social skills, develop compensatory skills and an awareness of work, and give them opportunities to receive realistic feedback.

CHAPTER

3

Conveying High Expectations

Deborah Chen and Jamie Dote-Kwan

Many of the activities through which expectations can be communicated to young children who are visually impaired are routine tasks of daily living such as taking care of oneself and one's possessions. Although adults often perform significant portions of these activities for children, especially for infants and toddlers, they convey important subtle information related to self-esteem and self-confidence by allowing youngsters to participate to the utmost extent. When well-meaning adults perform routine daily living tasks for visually impaired children that they would expect sighted children to perform by themselves or with the assistance of others, they are conveying a message that they do not have the same expectations for children with visual impairments. Adults also convey their expectations of children through activities in which they allow them to participate, for example, going with their classmates to visit unusual places or to meet community workers. Children pick up on these messages from adults and raise or lower their own expectations for themselves to match those of the adults.

Career education hinges on the premise that all children can achieve according to their innate abilities. To recognize their abilities, children need to be challenged to do for themselves and encouraged to participate fully in home, school, and community activities. If they are expected to do well or to excel, they often will. Likewise, if they are expected to do poorly or do little, they usually will. Furthermore, the sense of accomplishment they gain from participating tends to be self-reinforcing. This chapter presents activities that enable children with visual impairments to demonstrate their competencies, feel confident, and prepare for new environments.

TAKING CARE OF ONESELF AND ONE'S POSSESSIONS

Children who learn how to take care of themselves and their belongings are on the road to becoming independent, well-organized adults. Preschoolers with visual impairments need specific opportunities to acquire simple self-care skills and to participate in other related tasks at home and at school. The adults in their lives—family members and teachers—can play a key role in this regard.

There are numerous activities in which adults can involve children. However, this chapter focuses on teacher-directed, structured activities that family members or other caregivers can also perform at home.

It is important for teachers of children with visual impairments to begin by asking families about their child-rearing philosophy and practices. Families vary in their expectations about the self-care responsibilities of their young children and have different expectations for children at various ages. An emphasis on early autonomy and independence is not a universal family value or priority (Lynch & Hanson, 1992). For example, in some families, preschoolers are expected to feed and dress themselves, whereas in others, adult family members dress, feed, and bathe the children throughout the preschool years.

Certain activities convey high expectations, and it is often helpful for teachers to point out that although sighted children will observe other family members engaging in self-care tasks such as brushing teeth, sorting laundry, or making sandwiches and are motivated to imitate and then perform these tasks, children with severe visual impairments may not. But teachers also need to be aware that if family members value interdependence, rather than independence, they may not be comfortable with the typical preschool emphasis on self-help skills. Therefore, teachers need to balance respect for a family's values and priorities with their own professional judgments and the philosophy of their educational programs.

In preschool classrooms, daily routine presents natural opportunities for young children with visual impairments to learn basic self-care skills and to assume responsibility for their belongings. Teachers can effectively take advantage of these opportunities by using ecological inventories and working with the instructional team. An ecological inventory, or list of the daily activities in the child's environment, can be developed by noting a child's environments, identifying his or her usual activities, and observing his or her classmates in daily activities to determine the skills needed for participation and self-care (Dote-Kwan, 1995a, 1995b; Downing, 1996). (A sample ecological inventory appears in the appendix to this chapter.) Implementing a predictable routine for children to store belongings on their arrival at school, to put "work" in backpacks or bags to take home, and to gather their belongings at the end of the school day can do much to promote organizational skills. Similarly, self-care skills can be enhanced through predictable sequences for washing and drying hands and for other personal hygiene activities at appropriate times, such as cleaning hands after an art period or a messy play period and before a snack or lunchtime, and going to the bathroom on arrival at school and again before returning home.

The instructional team identifies the learning priorities for each child. For example, the goal for one child may be to complete an entire task independently, whereas the goal for another child may be to complete the last step of the task at the same time as classmates do to make the transition to the next activity in the group. In addition, team members from various disciplines (an orientation and mobility [O&M] instructor, a speech and language therapist, a physical or occupational therapist, and a behavior specialist [a psychologist, social worker, teacher, or other professional who has specific training in positive behavior support strategies]) identify how opportunities to work on their discipline-specific objectives can be integrated into the natural preschool routine (Chen, 1995c; Demcheck & Downing, 1996). This approach helps young children with visual impairments to generalize their skills across different situations. For example, O&M skills can be practiced in the hall and on the playground, speech and language skills can be worked on during circle time and on the playground, occupational therapy objectives may be focused on at play and snack times, and compensatory skills or functional vision can be addressed during snack and circle times. When opportunities to work on specific skills are taught throughout the day, the children are more likely to learn them. Using an instructional team approach is essential for developing a meaningful and coordinated program for children with disabilities.

Activities

- Have the children place their possessions in cubbies or similar designated places at the same times every day and after appropriate activities.
- Establish a routine with the children to wash and dry their hands at specific times.
- Have the children go to the toilet at appropriate times.
- Encourage the children to clean up after play activities, using the same routine (put toys away, straighten out play mats, and make sure desks or play areas are clean).
- Develop a routine with the children to get ready to go home (for example, help them learn to place their belongings in their backpacks and then put on their jackets, backpacks, and gloves).

Critical Points to Cover

- Reinforce the names of classmates by identifying their cubbies with appropriate media (for example, using braille or print labels, pictures, or tactile markers that represent each child—a bell for Tom, a ring for Maria, a pet for Monroe, and a doll's shoe for Marnee).
- Introduce the sequence of activities at the beginning of the day and reinforce the sequence (for instance, when the children arrive, ask them what they do first—hang up their coats—then ask what activity comes next).
- Encourage the children to use language to indicate their choices, for example, by asking, "What do you want to do now: play with blocks in the block center or play in the house area?"
- Engage the children in conversation throughout the day by asking about their preferences for certain activities, for example, "Who likes to read books?"; "What do you want to do when we go outside?"; "What are you going to do when you get home?"; "What did you learn in school today?"
- Use descriptive language, such as "Marcia is washing her hands, and it's your turn next," to let children with visual impairments know what is happening.

- Use language to build concepts, for example, "When do we wash our hands?"; "You have sticky fingers"; "Timmy's hands are dirty"; "You played in the water, and your shirt is wet"; and "Where do these toys belong?"

Helpful Hints

- If family members identify self-care skills as a priority for their children, help them conduct an ecological inventory of their home routines to identify specific learning opportunities and adaptations to support the children's active participation. For example, show them how to organize their bathrooms so the children can locate their toothbrushes and toothpaste. Discuss other opportunities for the children to take care of their belongings (such as combs, hairbrushes, or washcloths) at home or to put dirty clothes in the laundry basket or toys in a toy chest after play.
- Conduct an ecological inventory (see the appendix in this chapter) of the preschool routine to identify opportunities to work on self-care skills and take care of possessions.
- Conduct a discrepancy analysis of individual children's performance of each skill involved in an activity (a systematic notation of the difference between expected and actual behaviors) to identify instructional cues, adaptations, or supports that are needed by each child to participate actively (Dote-Kwan, 1995a). (See the appendix to this chapter for a sample discrepancy analysis.)
- Consult the O&M instructor to determine how the preschool environment may be organized to promote independent access to materials and where they are located.
- Consult the O&M instructor to identify the appropriate times and settings when children with visual impairments may use different techniques, that is, trailing and the sighted guide technique or cane travel. (For information on these techniques, see *The Art and Science of Teaching Orientation and Mobility to Persons with Visual Impairments* [Jacobson, 1993].)
- Ask yourself, how do the children perceive the environment? Close your eyes. What do you hear? Does environmental clutter make it difficult for visually impaired children to discriminate relevant stimuli? What is the auditory environment like? Does

background noise (such as that made by a heater, an air conditioner, traffic, or music) interfere with what is being said?

- Evaluate the sensory characteristics of the classroom environment by asking questions such as these:
  1. Can the visually impaired children locate essential areas through visual cues? For example, do activity centers need to be defined clearly by using floor coverings in different colors and bookshelves to create partitions or by marking activities with related equipment or materials, such as by using the water table to indicate the messy play area or water play area and Play Doh or other art supplies to identify the arts and crafts table?
  2. Is there confusing visual clutter in the learning environment?
  3. Does the visual environment need to be simplified to focus the children's attention?
  4. Is there ambient noise, such as from the ventilation system, that interferes with the children's auditory attention?
- Build opportunities in the day for preschoolers to be able to complete a task independently. This requires allowing sufficient time whenever possible, for instance, having children put on their socks and shoes by themselves or having them put toys in the toy box after play. Identify times during the day when the schedule can be flexible so it does not matter if children take more time than expected. For example, there may not be enough time in the morning for a child to dress independently before having to leave for school; however, later in the day, after returning home from school, the child may have sufficient time to dress into play clothes independently.
- Set up a buddy system so the children with visual impairments can observe sighted children participating in self-care activities. For example, a child with low vision can sit close to his or her buddy, and they can put toys away together, or a blind child can touch his or her buddy's hand while the buddy tells the child what he or she is doing.
- Provide immediate, consistent, and positive verbal reinforcement for children's efforts, for example, by saying, "I like the way you are brushing your teeth"; "Thank you for hanging up your coat."
- Provide immediate and constructive feedback to assist the children in completing tasks when they are having difficulty.

- Implement a regular system of feedback for individual children, that is, select a specific time at the end of the day to review their performance of a targeted behavior or skill. This time provides the opportunity for the children not only to receive positive and constructive feedback about what they do well, but to talk about what areas need additional work or assistance. For example, a parent or family member may want to devote ten or fifteen minutes each afternoon or evening to a discussion about what has transpired that day in school or in an after-school program. By following the children's progress, concerned adults can help reinforce the importance of these activities.

- Orient the children to the classroom environment and encourage them to explore it tactilely when appropriate.

- Provide tactile or high-contrast name and other labels for cubbies and other areas.

- Set up a tangible schedule or calendar box by placing a series of containers together and use object and picture cues, such as a picture of a carton of milk or the actual carton, to symbolize a snack, or a washcloth to represent cleaning hands before and after the snack, to help visually impaired children form a mental sequence of specific activities. By working with objects that symbolize specific activities in the order of their occurrence to represent a schedule, or "calendar," children learn to anticipate activities and mentally form a sequence of the day. At the beginning of each day, ask the children to feel each box and object until they have gone through all the containers in succession. Then have them remove the first object, perform the activity, and, when finished, place the object in a "finished" box, which is separate from the rest of the calendar box. After the children have used the calendar box a few times, observe whether they have searched for and identified the objects in sequence (Chen, 1995c; Huebner, Prickett, Welch, & Joffee, 1995; Rowland, Schweigert, & Prickett, 1995).

Evaluation Tips

- When an activity is about to begin, ask the children what they will do, for example, "What do you do before a snack?" or "It's time to go home. What do you do?"

- If self-care skills are priorities for the family, find out the children's level of participation in self-care activities at home. Once the children have worked on these skills at school, ask the family whether there has been any change in the level of the children's independence in self-care skills at home.
- Observe whether the children anticipate the daily schedule and initiate any of the self-care tasks, such as putting their backpacks in their cubbies at the beginning of the school day, hanging up their coats or canes, and going to the play area.
- Observe and take notes on whether the children require verbal or physical prompts to complete a task or how well they can complete the requirements independently (for example, are their hands clean and dry after the children wash them?).

For Children Who Need Additional Modifications

- For children with multiple disabilities whose self-care routines need to be carried out by others, encourage the use of signals for "start" and "stop." These signals may be as simple as shaking an arm or tapping a hand, but they need to be consistently reinforced so the children have some control over the events in a routine. Encourage all family members and other caregivers to respond to children's signals to continue or discontinue an activity; for example, during eating, the children may open their mouths to indicate they want another bite and turn their heads and close their mouths to refuse a bite.
- At home with the family caregivers, work in play routines at the end of self-care routines to build motivation, for instance, playing in the bath after washing is over, singing a favorite song after dressing, or bouncing on a beach ball after toileting.

ENCOURAGING COMMUNITY INVOLVEMENT: VISITS TO FAMILIAR PLACES

It is important for adults to expect young children with visual impairments to participate in the same activities that sighted children of the same age typically undertake. By encouraging visually impaired preschoolers to have these experiences, adults demonstrate that their

FROM A RURAL PERSPECTIVE

Young children with visual impairments are rare in any community, large or small. In many rural communities, a visually impaired child may be the first child born in the area with such an impairment, and hence the child and his or her family may feel isolated. Setting expectations for a visually impaired child can become an issue for the family, neighbors, and local service providers when there is no other visually impaired child in the community to observe or use as a comparison to help determine what may be typical.

In the early years of children's development, parents and other family members in rural communities begin to face the challenge of learning how to give most effectively the support visually impaired children need to lead independent and satisfying lives. This may prove to be a difficult undertaking because few resources are available. With appropriate information, parents can begin to refine their parenting styles to suit the needs of their visually impaired children. They can obtain this information by going to the local school district's special education library, local library, or bookmobile or consulting parent advocacy organizations. They can also take correspondence courses and order materials on the development of visually impaired children from the Hadley School for the Blind (see Resources) and obtain information from other organizations. Through these correspondence courses, parents can learn step-by-step teaching techniques, methods to address and expand their child's strengths, and ways to encourage and reinforce their child's learning and development, as well as straightforward methods for teaching visually impaired children.

Despite the sense of isolation and limited resources parents may encounter, rural environments offer some distinct advantages for visually impaired preschoolers. In farming communities, children have the opportunity to pet, feed, and touch animals and, in doing so, can develop basic concepts and learn the value of chores by helping to feed the animals. At a farmers' market or in a garden, they can learn object concepts by exploring visually or tactilely the shapes and textures of various vegetables and fruits. These hands-on experiences help visually impaired preschoolers learn about the world around them.

Elaine Sveen

expectations for them are equal to the expectations for their sighted classmates. When children with visual impairments are not allowed to go on field trips or participate in extracurricular activities with their classmates because of adults' anticipation of difficulties with mobility, anxiety about imagined dangers, or misconception of the relevance of the activity to visually impaired children, they learn that adults expect less of them than of other preschoolers. Sometimes adults may impose restrictions on children's activities precisely because they believe that youngsters without vision will be unable to benefit from inclusion, and this belief is then passed on to the children. Involvement in community activities, such as shopping at a supermarket or a department store, often occurs naturally with parents or other family members. Other activities, such as field trips and planned outings, are often the responsibility of school and community organizations. However, specific activities for individual children will vary according to their families' priorities, the philosophies of the program, and community resources. In supporting home-school collaboration, teachers need to identify family values, concerns, and resources in developing instructional goals and learning experiences that children need. This collaboration is facilitated by the MAPS process—Making Action Plans (Forest & Pearpoint, 1992)—formerly known as the McGill Action Planning System (Forest & Lusthaus, 1990; Vandercook, York, & Forest, 1989). MAPS identifies families' dreams and goals for children and their perspective of an ideal day. For example, a family may not want their child to engage in messy activities such as finger painting with pudding because they believe that food should not be wasted and that children should be kept clean.(For additional information on MAPS, see Chapter 4.)

Since young children usually learn about the surrounding community through activities with their families and preschool or similar programs, field trips to new places (such as a pumpkin patch), as well as family outings to familiar places (such as a neighborhood park), play a key role in learning. During these outings, families and teachers can help young children with visual impairments learn the purpose of the trips, what happens in each place, appropriate behaviors for various community settings, and strategies for active participation. In addition, field trips give children greater understanding of the world and can support their development of concepts. For example, a trip to a supermarket may be part of a cooking activity to build the children's understanding of where food is obtained and how it is prepared. It is necessary to differentiate between outings that involve the entire class and those that may involve one or two children. For instance, the entire group may walk to a park to play or may go to a pumpkin patch, but it may be more appropriate to have two children walk to a grocery store with an adult.

To build an understanding of their communities, it is important for young children with visual impairments to participate in experiences that can become familiar and predictable. In this regard, it is helpful to ask family members about the types of community activities that are part of their routines so they can identify the places the children frequently go to and those that they may not have experienced. In addition, given the variety of possibilities, it is useful to know at which grocery stores the families shop, so the stores that will be the most meaningful to the children can be identified. For example, shopping at a large supermarket is significantly different from shopping at a small mom-and-pop store. And, some families may buy bread from a bakery rather than from a supermarket. Similarly, if a family goes to a Laundromat to wash clothes, visiting a Laundromat may be included in the community activities for the class.

Activities

- Discuss with the children places they visit with their families.
- Ask the children to list and discuss community outings they have gone on in preschool.
- Identify lesson topics that need the concrete experience of a community trip, for example, learning about farm animals versus zoo animals and learning about dentists, eye doctors, and other health care professionals.
- Plan community outings, such as going on a picnic, to a farm, or to the post office, depending on the children's learning objectives.

Critical Points to Cover

- Provide information about the purpose of the trip ("We're going to the grocery store to buy apples and sugar to make applesauce" or "We're going to have our snack at the park").
- Ask the children questions about their other experiences with outings, for example, "Who has been to the store with their parents?" or "What did you do when you went to the park on Sunday?"
- Discuss the steps in the trip (for example, "We'll walk to the supermarket. Jusef can find the apples. Jessica can find the sugar. I'll bring the money to pay for the groceries." Or, "Everyone needs to hold hands and walk with a buddy to the park. We'll play on the swings and slide and then have a snack").
- Use appropriate language, such as "We're passing the bakery. Can you smell the freshly baked bread?" to orient children while en route and at the destination.

Helpful Hints

- Consult with the O&M instructor to identify the most appropriate route for a walking trip. Discuss how and when the children with visual impairments may use different techniques (trailing, sighted guide technique, or cane travel) when traveling to and from the community site, as well as at it.
- Encourage adult family members to participate in outings to provide extra adult supervision and opportunities for home-school collaboration on children's learning activities.
- Use a checklist to make certain that all important aspects of an outing, such as its purpose, expectations for the children's behaviors, O&M techniques, safety rules, and the responsibilities of adults, are covered.
- On the basis of each child's Individualized Education Program (IEP), identify with the instructional team the learning objectives for each child that can be incorporated into the field trips. The application of O&M techniques, language and communication skills, functional vision skills, and social skills are some examples of objectives that can be integrated into trips to relate to the IEP, the written plan of instruction by the team for any child who receives special education services, which includes the child's present levels of educational performance, annual goals, short-term objectives, specific services needed, duration of services, evaluation, and related information.

Evaluation Tips

- When the activity is about to begin, ask the children specific questions to ascertain their understanding of the trip, for example, to identify toys they want to take to the park or what they need to buy at the grocery store for a particular recipe.
- When children enter the program, ask their families about the types of outings that are part of their routines. Find out how the children participate in these outings and whether family members have any concerns about their participation. After the children have participated in these outings during the school day, ask families whether there has been any change in the level of the children's participation during family outings. Encourage the family to maintain diaries that document the children's participation.

- Observe and take notes on the children's participation in the outings. For example, did the children find the apples? What O&M techniques did they use?

For Children Who Need Additional Modifications

- Bring an object home after each trip that will remind the children of the events of the trip. A shell from a trip to the beach or a paper bag from the grocery store will remind children of the activity. Soon after the trip, and again several days later, bring out the object and encourage the children to act out the events of the trip. For children who use gestures or sign language, associate actions with the events of the trip: the motion of pulling on a fishing line or reeling in a fish may become the symbol for fishing as well as a reminder of a visit to the pier.
- Encourage children with a classmate who uses a wheelchair to share information by helping the classmate find the best ways to enter and exit a building. For example, if the class visits the grocery store, point out that there are doors that need to be opened and doors that open by themselves. Ask the child who uses a wheelchair which type he or she likes best and ask the others which they like to use when they are pushing their classmate's wheelchair.

ENCOURAGING COMMUNITY INVOLVEMENT: VISITS TO COMMUNITY WORKERS

Children learn what others expect of them and thus develop their own expectations through daily experiences with their families, participation in their communities, and observation of others. Because visually impaired preschoolers may not have the benefit of constant visual input and resultant incidental learning, they need enhanced, planned opportunities to learn about their communities through firsthand experiences. It is useful for teachers of young visually impaired children to review the information about the community and world that is covered in the standard preschool curricula and developmentally appropriate stories that are expected for children who are entering kindergarten. By doing so, a sys-

FROM A FAMILY PERSPECTIVE

Visiting People and Places in the Community

Whenever family members are about to say "no," "can't," or "better not" about visiting places in the community, they need to think twice before saying it. There are many places in the community visually impaired children may wish to visit. As long as family members ensure the children's safety, there is no harm in the children's trying to learn about these places. Indeed, there can be considerable benefits, not only in learning new things but in building self-esteem on the basis of reasonable risk taking. "Ordinary" trips can be extraordinary for any preschooler, but they can be especially exciting for children who are visually impaired. Before the family's next trip to the grocery store, hardware store, or bank, think about how you can make the trip interesting and also educational. Examples include letting the child speak to a local police officer who is on street patrol or at the shopping center, feel the keys of a cash register, help bag the groceries at the grocery store, or count out loud as items are placed in a shopping cart.

Other places that are fun and interesting to visit include a police station, firehouse, bakery, post office, restaurant, construction site, veterinarian's office, and physician's office, as well as unusual places (like an artist's studio, a furniture upholsterer's shop, a local factory, a garbage dump, and a local airport). During visits to these places, ask the workers if they have time to explain what they are doing. If they find it difficult to describe their activities, narrate for them as you watch them work.

In approaching community workers, explain your child's visual impairment, since they may have never met a child with a vision loss. For example, you can say, "May we ask you a few questions about your police car? Jane can't see it with her eyes, but she can touch it, and she has a few questions to ask you." This kind

tematic approach to appropriate field trips can be developed that may help impart this information, with opportunities for repeated experiences and for learning activities that build on previous experiences. The focus of field trips for three year olds should be simpler than those for four- or five year olds. For example, children of different ages may visit a fire station, but the younger children may be expected to examine the wheels of the fire truck tactilely, while the older children may explore the entire exterior of the vehicle. Three year olds may be interested only in trying on the firefighters' hats and boots, whereas older children may also have questions about their clothing and tools.

Typical preschool trips in the community to learn about community workers and what they do include visits to fire stations, physicians' offices, bakeries, post offices, or fast-food restaurants. Hands–on learning

of explanation will both ease any discomfort others may have and model an appropriate explanation for a child who will need to learn to do so later on. Remember that they may never have had an opportunity to interact with a person with a visual impairment before. You are teaching them while they are teaching your child, and this can ultimately create a more receptive environment for your child.

Since visually impaired children frequently cannot see or see well, it is important to let a child know where you are and what your are doing in running commentaries, for example, "We just passed the bank, and boy is it crowded!" "I'm going to turn on Route 22 and go about three miles to the post office. Then, we'll go inside and talk to Mr. Roberts when we get some stamps." These and other descriptions of location, time, and distance can help preschoolers who are visually impaired gain a sense of where they are in their surroundings.

Ask your child's orientation and mobility (O&M) instructors for tips on how to walk and travel with him or her in various circumstances, such as when you are in a hurry, when you are taking a leisurely pace, and when there is a lot of time and your child can practice some independent travel. (Of course, in the latter case, a family member will remain close by for safety.) Checking with the instructors will help ensure that O&M skills are reinforced at home as well as in school.

Not every outing will be joyous, so you need to be ready for times when a child misbehaves. One strategy that many parents use when children under age 12 misbehave in a car is to pull over, stop the car, and tell them that the trip cannot continue until they calm down. *Children: The Challenge* (Dreikurs & Soltz, 1987) describes additional techniques to use with children.

Make a journal or a storybook of these adventures and then read them to your child at the end of each week. This is an important way to review the learning and share the excitement.

Kevin O'Connor

opportunities and real experiences are essential for children with visual impairments to develop an accurate understanding of the world. For example, children who are blind cannot see how a fire hose is stored on a fire truck; however, tactile exploration will allow them to examine a rolled-up fire hose. Similarly, tactile exploration of a stationary fire truck will enable the children to compare the size of the truck with that of their families' vehicle. Children with visual impairments will not be able to handle and explore every piece of equipment. Some items (such as a hot oven or the blade of an axe) may be too dangerous or too far away (like the upright ladder of a fire truck), and other items may be too big or too long (for example, the entire fire hose) for the children to gain a complete perspective from tactile exploration. Therefore, it is helpful to identify specific items for systematic tactile exploration—those that the children will have an opportunity to touch but not to explore completely and those that require additional experiences (such as verbal descriptions, comparisons, and models) to enhance their understanding of the community site. More than one trip to the same place gives children with visual impairments opportunities to confirm previous tactile impressions, to integrate fragmented bits of information, and to build on existing knowledge about the place. Opportunities to talk with people like firefighters, post office workers, and physicians about what their work is like help reinforce children's understanding, are enjoyable, and make vivid impressions.

Activities

- Ask the children which community workers are familiar to them, for example, "Who delivers the mail?" and "What does the mailman wear?"
- Ask the children which community workers are unfamiliar to them, based on their answers to the question about which community workers may be familiar to them. For example, if a plumber is unfamiliar to them, then explain what this worker does in his or her job.
- Develop a coordinated curricular plan involving trips to community work sites, that is, a plan based on the state preschool curriculum guides, community resources, family input, and the program's curriculum philosophy.

Critical Points to Cover

- Ask the children whether they know anyone with the particular job being discussed.
- Discuss the roles and responsibilities of each worker with the children.
- Identify what each worker wears for his or her job.
- Ask the children whether they would like that kind of job. If they would, ask why; if they would not, ask why not.

Helpful Hints

- Let the contact person at the community site know that children with visual impairments need to touch equipment and explore the environment to learn about the place. Make arrangements for the children to be able to handle and explore specific pieces of equipment and selected items at the site. If possible, borrow some items for in-depth exploration in the classroom before the visit and for discussion after the trip.

- Consult the O&M instructor to determine the most appropriate route for a walking trip. Discuss how and when the children with visual impairments may use different techniques when traveling to and at the community site, such as trailing and sighted guide techniques, or cane travel.

- Prepare the children for the trip by discussing where they will be going. Ask "What do you think will be there?"; "Who will be there?"; and "What will we see?"

- Point out key components of the trip—particular people or community workers children will meet, related items or equipment these workers may use, certain smells and sounds children will encounter, or other landmarks. The number and complexity of these details should fit the children's ages and abilities.

- Give visually impaired children an opportunity to explore the environment systematically.

- Encourage tactile exploration, when feasible.

- Foster children's understanding of part-to-whole relationships by providing verbal labels and descriptions as the children examine selected items. For example, ask them to identify the wheels of a fire truck and explain where the wheels are located in relation to the hose and other equipment on the truck.

- Provide verbal labels and descriptions of the objects as the children examine them, for instance, "The fire truck is a big red truck" and "The firefighter wears a hard hat and black rubber boots."

- Prompt children to ask and answer questions by saying, for example, "What's this?"; "How does it feel?"; "Do you have any questions?"

- Build on field-trip experiences through stories, games, art activities, and creative play, especially right after the children have been on a trip.

- Use field-trip experiences to help children integrate concepts that are being introduced through other activities. For example, a trip to a petting zoo to learn about zookeepers or to the humane society to learn about veterinarians is a natural component of a unit on pets and the classification of animals.

- Provide a broad range of experiential learning opportunities that are developmentally appropriate, from unusual places, such as a potter's studio or a humane society, to traditional community sites, such as a fire station, a bakery, a physician's office, a post office, or a farm.

Evaluation Tips

- Ask children what various community workers do during the day.
- Ask children to share what they learned on or liked about the trip.
- Ask the children with low vision to draw pictures related to the trip; ask blind children to talk about what they did on the trip or ask them to identify souvenirs or objects related to the trip.
- Provide a model of the real equipment (such as a fire truck) that the children explored and ask them to identify the components of the model.
- Develop experience stories that are based on the children's narratives about the trip to highlight the children's experiences and what they remember. For example, "We went to a farm. The cows had calves and ate grass. We ate apples. The pigs smelled stinky and played in mud." Write these stories in braille or large print, as appropriate.
- Send the experience stories home for the children to tell their families. Ask families about the children's storytelling abilities.
- Arrange for a repeat trip to a particular place. Compare the children's discussion of the trip after the second visit to that of the first visit.

For Children Who Need Additional Modifications

- Provide opportunities for children to meet adults with similar disabilities to theirs and to notice these people doing work or carrying out activities. Emphasize skills that the children may learn to do as adults, as well as the similarities between their and the adults' adaptive tools, for example, "Mr. Gomez uses a wheelchair like yours, but it is much bigger" or "Ms. Daugherty's hearing aid is the same as yours."

MAKING REALISTIC COMPARISONS WITH SIGHTED PEERS

Although it is important for young children with visual impairments to be expected to participate in activities that are typical for their ages, the severe vision loss and additional disabilities that some may have may require adaptations to activities and realistic adjustments to certain expectations. Thus, it is important for teachers to have expectations that are developmentally appropriate for preschoolers—that is, expectations that preschoolers with visual impairments can participate in activities done by sighted preschoolers of a similar age—but to understand the importance of the use of appropriate modifications for vision loss. For example, if students in a class are coloring pictures, those without functional vision may benefit from having a wire screen under their papers, so they will have tactile feedback as they color. Similarly, if children are playing at the water table, those with low vision may benefit from the addition of food coloring to the water to make the water easier to see. In addition, in having high expectations for preschoolers with visual impairments, teachers need to consider several factors, including the children's experience (at home and in the community), abilities, motivation, personality, type and severity of the visual impairments, and other learning needs, as well as the families' and community's expectations. Since the complex combination of these factors will contribute to each child's performance and developmental outcome, it is necessary to adopt a holistic perspective.

It is natural for family members, teachers, and other adults to compare children with visual impairments to sighted children, especially when the children are in inclusive environments. Similarly, it is highly likely that young children with visual impairments will compare themselves to their sighted classmates and will need support to develop high but realistic expectations for themselves. Both sighted and visually impaired children benefit from opportunities to learn, play, and grow together in their homes, schools, and communities. Teachers and family members need to develop specific strategies for encouraging and supporting their social interactions, cooperative play, and friendships (Chen, 1995a). For example, if a sighted classmate is invited to the park to play with a blind child, he or she needs to be shown how to get the blind child's attention, and the blind child needs to be shown how to share a toy or how to play a game with the sighted classmate. It is important to note at this point that teachers' observations of how young sighted children perform may be helpful for developing instructional programs for young children with visual impairments when they are used as a basis for conducting ecological inventories and task analyses (Chen, 1995c; Demcheck & Downing, 1996), rather than as benchmarks for rating the development of the visually impaired children.

Activities

- With the preschoolers in mind, list the usual sequence of steps in specific activities by saying them aloud, for example, "wash and dry your hands," "get a carton of milk," and "sit at the snack table."
- Identify the natural cues (for instance, do the visually impaired children see other children or the tray with milk cartons, and do they hear the teacher's directions?) and instructional cues (such verbal prompts as, "Do you want some milk?" or such physical prompts as showing the children the tray with the milk cartons) involved in the sequence to determine whether the natural cues are sufficient for eliciting the children's participation or whether the children need additional input.
- Select needed adaptations, such as high-contrast picture or braille cards for bingo, to support the visually impaired children's active participation.
- Determine what the expected behaviors are for particular children. For example, do the children take turns on the swing or clean up after playing with toys?
- Ask children to identify similarities and differences between themselves and their classmates on the basis of physical features, family characteristics, and personal preferences, for instance, whether they have blonde, brown, or black hair; are boys or girls; have brothers or sisters; or like pizza. ("We look with our eyes, and Jimmy uses his fingers to 'see' things.")
- Ask children to identify their own strengths (for example, how well they ride a tricycle, dance, run, or sing).
- Ask children what activities they think they need help in performing (such as tying shoes, going to the bathroom, or getting a toy from a high shelf).

Critical Points to Cover

- Everyone is different, but everyone shares certain similarities.
- Each person can do something well.
- Everyone needs some assistance in different areas.

Helpful Hints

- Preschoolers with visual impairments benefit from planned, repeated, and systematic active learning experiences. In this way, children learn to anticipate activities, develop concepts and skills related to specific activities, and generalize this learning to other activities. Thus, it is necessary to introduce and implement activities in an organized way, give the children opportunities to experience the activities at regular intervals, and provide adaptations to support the children's active participation.
- Conduct ecological inventories to identify typical preschool activities and how to support visually impaired children's participation. An example of an ecological inventory of a visually impaired child playing in a sandbox that involves cooperative play includes the following skills: locating available space in the sandbox, finding toys that are not being used, responding to another child's request for a sand toy, asking other children for a desired sand toy, digging a hole with another child, taking turns filling a bucket with sand, and building sand mounds with another child. The discrepancy analysis included in the appendix to this chapter demonstrates how these activities can be supported.
- Children benefit from being with each other. Preschoolers with visual impairments benefit from inclusive experiences with sighted children because these opportunities support social interactions, play, and language development, and sighted children benefit from learning about differences and similarities in how children learn.
- Support the sighted children's understanding of children's visual impairments by creating an environment in which children feel comfortable asking and answering questions. For example, if a sighted preschooler asks, "What's wrong with his eyes?," a child with a visual impairment should be encouraged to explain in his or her own words—"They don't work. I use my hands to look at things."

- After consulting the family members, members of the instructional team need to identify learning priorities for each child with a visual impairment: for example, should the present focus be on social skills or early literacy skills for this child?
- Some parents or caregivers may have questions about the development of their children with visual impairments and may compare the children with sighted children. They may ask, "How does my child compare with children who can see?" or "How is my child doing compared to other blind children?" It is important to explain that these are complicated questions and, if possible, to provide appropriate information about the wide range of developmental milestones that are typical for children, sighted or visually impaired.

It is also important to communicate that all children develop in their own unique ways. Some sighted children are verbal at 15 months, whereas others are quiet at age 2. Some children walk independently at 9 months, and others do not walk until 15 months. Although infants who are blind usually take more time to walk independently, this is not always the case. For example, a totally blind girl, who was born 3 months prematurely, was ambulatory at 12 months—earlier than some sighted children. Research (Skellenger, Hill, & Hill, 1992; Priesler & Palmer, 1989) indicates that most children who are blind or who have low vision take longer to learn how to play with toys and other children than do most fully sighted children. Nonetheless, by using intervention strategies, teachers and families can build on children's strengths to enable the children to develop and achieve appropriately.

Evaluation Tips

- Observe and record the visually impaired children's initiations, responses, and interactions with their classmates.
- Collect data on the children's performance on selected IEP objectives.

For Children Who Need Additional Modifications

- Find concrete ways to represent words that are used to compare people, for example, touching the heads of boys who are tall and short; comparing the pitches of voices with signs for high or low; or the color of hair with signs for brown, black, yellow, red, and white.

- For students who do not use spoken words, teach a sign for "same" to use when calling their attention to similarities with other children, for example, hair of the same color or shoes of the same style.

- Encourage the children without disabilities to notice how children with disabilities do the same things that they do: "Billy goes to gym class by pushing his own wheelchair" or "Maria tells when she's mad by banging on the table, and I tell when I'm mad with words."

- Use a signal for "I need help" (such as a red flag, a raised hand, or a light to be turned on) that all children in a class can use. Explain to the children that everyone asks for help sometime and that is important to know when they need help from others.

References

Bredekamp, S., & Copple, C. (Eds.). (1997). *Developmentally appropriate practice in early childhood programs* (rev. ed.). Washington, DC: National Association for the Education of Young Children.

Chen, D. (1995a). The beginnings of communication: Early childhood. In K. M. Huebner, J. G. Prickett, R. R. Welch, & E. Joffee (Eds.), *Hand in hand: Essentials of communication and orientation and mobility for your students who are deaf-blind.* (Vol. 1, pp. 185–218). New York: AFB Press.

Chen, D. (1995b). Guiding principles for instruction and program development. In D. Chen & J. Dote-Kwan (Eds.), *Starting points: Instructional practices for young children whose multiple disabilities include visual impairment* (pp. 15–28). Los Angeles: Blind Childrens Center.

Chen, D. (1995c). Understanding and developing communication. In D. Chen & J. Dote-Kwan (Eds.), *Starting points: Instructional practices for young children whose multiple disabilities include visual impairment* (pp. 57–72). Los Angeles: Blind Childrens Center.

Demcheck, M.A., & Downing, J. E. (1996). The preschool child. In J. E. Downing, *Including students with severe and multiple disabilities in typical classrooms: Practical strategies for teachers* (pp. 63–82). Baltimore, MD: Paul H. Brookes.

Dote-Kwan, J. (1995a). Essential steps for getting started. In D. Chen & J. Dote-Kwan (Eds.), *Starting points: Instructional practices for young children whose multiple disabilities include visual impairment* (pp. 29–41). Los Angeles: Blind Childrens Center.

Dote-Kwan, J. (1995b). Teaching daily living skills. In D. Chen & J. Dote-Kwan (Eds.), *Starting points: Instructional practices for young children whose multiple disabilities include visual impairment* (pp. 73–78). Los Angeles: Blind Childrens Center.

Downing, J. E. (1996). *Including students with severe and multiple disabilities in typical classrooms: Practical strategies for teachers.* Baltimore: Paul H. Brookes.

Dreikurs, R., & Soltz, V. (1987). *Children: The challenge.* New York: Sheed and Ward.

Forest, M., & Lusthaus, E. (1990). Everyone belongs with the MAPS Action Planning System. *Teaching Exceptional Children, 22*(2), 32–35.

Forest, M., & Pearpoint, J. C. (1992). Putting kids on the map. *Educational Leadership, 50*(2) 26–31.

Huebner, K. M., Prickett, J. G., Welch, T. R., & Joffee, E. (Eds.). (1995). *Hand in hand: Essentials of communication and orientation and mobility for your students who are deaf-blind.* New York: AFB Press.

Jacobson, W. H. (1993). *The art and science of teaching orientation and mobility to persons with visual impairments.* New York: AFB Press.

Lynch, E. W., & Hanson, M. J. (1992). *Developing cross-cultural competence: A guide for working with young children and their families* (2nd ed.). Baltimore: Paul H. Brookes.

Priesler, G., & Palmer, C. (1989). Thoughts from Sweden: The blind child goes to nursery school with sighted children. *Child: Care, Health, and Development,* 45–52.

Rowland, C., Schweigert, P. D., & Prickett, J. G. (1995). Communication system, devices, and modes. In K. M. Huebner, J. G. Prickett, R. R. Welch, & E. Joffee (Eds.), *Hand in hand: Essentials of communication and orientation and mobility for your students who are deaf-blind* (Vol. 1, pp. 219–260). New York: AFB Press.

Skellenger, A. C., Hill, M., & Hill, E. (1992). The social functioning of children with visual impairments. In S. L. Odom, S. R. McConnell, and M. A. McEvoy (Eds.), *Social competence of young children with disabilities: Issues and strategies for intervention* (pp. 165–188). Baltimore: Paul H. Brookes.

Vandercook, T., York, J., & Forest, M. (1989). The McGill Action Planning System (MAPS): A strategy for building the vision. *Journal of the Association for Persons with Severe Handicaps, 14,* 205–215.

APPENDIX
Evaluating a Preschooler's Skills, Performance, and Learning Needs in Daily Activities

The procedures for conducting an ecological inventory, discrepancy analysis, and routine analysis and for completing Making Actions Plans, formerly known as the McGill Action Planning System (MAPS) (Forest & Lusthaus, 1990), are derived from research on the instruction of students with severe disabilities in inclusive settings (Downing, 1996). These are tools that can help teachers and families evaluate the skills that children need to participate fully in an activity, how they perform these skills, and whether additional sensory information is needed for them to perform the activity. An ecological inventory involves observing the preschool environments in which the activities are performed, identifying usual activities, and observing typical classmates in daily activities to determine the skills needed for participation (Dote-Kwan, 1995a; Downing, 1996). An example of an ecological inventory of playing in the sandbox is presented in Table 3.1.

The use of ecological inventories helps ensure that a child's experience in school is functional and age appropriate and involves naturally occurring and motivating activities for children who are visually impaired (Dote-Kwan, 1995a). A discrepancy analysis uses an ecological inventory of the skills involved in an activity and identifies the visually impaired child's performance on each skill. As is shown in Table 3.2, a plus sign used in the analysis indicates that the child demonstrates the expected skills, and a minus sign indicates that the child does not have the required skills. In the latter case, the teacher determines whether to teach the skill or make adaptations.

Table 3.1

Ecological Inventory of Playing in the Sandbox

Environment: Playground at the preschool

Activity: Playing in the sandbox

Skill area: Cooperative play

Skills:

1. Locates available space in the sandbox

2. Finds toys not being used

3. Responds to another child's request for a sand toy

4. Asks other children for a desired sand toy

5. Digs a hole with another child

6. Takes turns filling a bucket with sand

7. Builds sand mounds with another child

Preschoolers who are visually impaired have specific learning needs that are related to their vision loss. Thus, families and teachers have to promote their sensory development and ability to gain access to information and allow them more time to receive information, to respond, and to complete tasks (Chen, 1995b). For example, it takes more time to identify an object through touch than through vision. An analysis of daily routines is helpful in identifying the areas in which a child needs additional sensory information and when the child will need additional time to complete the activity.

A routine analysis identifies steps in a routine, natural cues, expected child behaviors, and adult input (Chen, 1995c). It assists the teacher in identifying whether natural cues are sufficient for eliciting a child's participation or whether the child will need additional input. Table 3.3 illustrates a routine analysis of a blind preschooler's arrival at school.

Note that the blind child in Table 3.3 will need more time than a sighted child to locate the classroom, put his or her things away, and to find the play area. Examples of adult input encourage the child to use sensory information. Table 3.4 shows the preschool schedule and examples of daily activities in which teachers can work on key career education components of promoting high expectations and socialization skills, developing compensatory skills, and providing opportunities for realistic feedback. It also demonstrates how objectives related to

Table 3.2

A Discrepancy Analysis of a 4–Year–Old Blind Boy Who Is Engaging in Sandbox Play with His Sighted Peers

Items in Ecological Inventory	Cues	Child's Performance Rating	Behavior Discrepancy	Teaching Tip or Adaptation
1. Locates available space in sandbox	Space for the child to sit	–	Sits on other children	A peer lets the child know where there's room
2. Finds toys not being used	Toy on sand	–	Feels area directly in front of him	An adult prompts the child to search in a left-to-right semicircular pattern
3. Responds to another child's request for a sand toy	"Gimme the shovel"	+		
4. Asks other children for a desired sand toy	Hears another child pounding on the bucket to get the sand out	+		
5. Digs a hole along with another child	Has shovel. The other child says, "Wanna dig?"	–	Does not know where the other child is digging	The other child guides the blind child's hand to the sand area for digging
			Cannot scoop with a shovel	An adult says, "Push down into the sand" and uses a hand-over-hand prompt to angle the shovel so the child can scoop independently
6. Takes turns filling a bucket with sand	Empty bucket	–	Can fill the bucket but does not know how to take turns	An adult prompts the peer to say, "Your turn."
7. Builds sand mounds with another child	Mound of sand The other child says, "Let's make this"	–	Does not know what the other child is making	An adult prompts the child to ask the peer, "What is it?" and then prompts the peer to respond

Table 3.3

Routine Analysis of a 4–Year–Old Blind Girl's Arrival at School

Steps in the Routine	Natural Cues	Expected Child Behaviors	Adult Input
Prepares for an activity; marks beginning, middle, end; and makes a transition to another activity	Characteristics of the environment, or what others do to engage the child's attention and participation	Participates actively and follows instructions	Different means of communication (such as directions, comments, gestures, and physical prompts)
Locates the room	Walkway, open door, familiar voices	Locates landmarks, walks to the classroom using appropriate O&M skills	"Find the walkway"; "Listen for Mrs. Sanchez's voice"; "Look for the open door"
Greets the adults and classmates	Seeing or hearing others; greeting by the teacher "Good morning, Maria"; greeting by class-mates, "Hi, Maria"	Acknowledges and responds to greetings, initiates greetings	"Look everybody, Maria's here"; respond to Maria's greeting
Locates her cubbie	Marked cubbie	Finds her cubbie and name card	"Put your things away"
Puts things away	Cubbie, other children's belongings	Hangs up her jacket, stores the backpack	"Hang up your jacket"; "Where does your backpack go?"
Goes to the play area	Children in the play area	Walks to the play area and chooses toys	"You can go play now"

different areas, such as those determined by an O&M instructor, speech and language therapist, and teacher of visually impaired students can be integrated throughout the day. These specialists work with the preschool teacher as an instructional team to share goals and information. Although the specialists may introduce the initial strategies for identified objectives and provide direct instruction to the child, the classroom teacher and other staff use them as well, so the objectives are being addressed in all activities and throughout the day. In this way, the visually impaired child will have a preschool learning experience that is meaningful and meets his or her learning needs.

MAPS can be used as a process for gathering together the significant people in a preschooler's life—parents, child, other family mem-

Table 3.4

Infusing Career Education Components and Discipline-Specific Objectives into the Daily Preschool Schedule

Schedule Item	Behavior Reflecting High Expectations	Behavior Reflecting Socialization Skills	Behavior Reflecting Compensatory Skills	Behavior Reflecting Realistic Feedback
Arrival	Puts away backpack; hangs up jacket (O&M)	Greets the adults and classmates (S&L)	Locates her cubbie and identifies her name card (VI)	
Free play	Puts toys away	Makes requests, shares materials (S&L)	Locates the play area and toys; finds a classmate to play with (VI)	Follows rules
Circle time		Sings songs, identifies who is present	Locates the circle area; counts the days of the week; identifies the weather	Discusses activities for the day, moves to the next activity
Centers	Cleans up the work area; role-plays community workers	Dresses up–role-plays; makes requests; shares materials (S&L)	Makes a book, "All about Me"; does a classification activity; sorts real objects (VI)	Moves to the next activity; follows directions; completes tasks
Outside		Takes turns, makes requests, plays with classmates, makes choices (S&L)	Walks to the play-ground and locates the preferred play equipment (O&M)	Follows rules
Rest room	Goes to the toilet; washes hands (VI)	Requests help	Walks to the rest room; locates the toilet, sink, soap, towel, and trash can (O&M)	Follows the routine
Snack	Pours juice; uses a napkin; serves self; cleans up (VI)	Makes choices; says "please" and "thank you" (S&L)	Locates the table; passes out napkins; counts out cups (VI)	Follows the routine
Story time	Reads "The Firemen Saved the School"	Waits her turn; asks questions; answers questions (S&L)	Listens; follows the story by identifying related objects (VI)	Follows the routine
Goes home	Puts on her jacket and gets her backpack	Says good-bye	Locates her cubbie	

Note: Abbreviations indicate behavioral goal related to skill development and determined by a member of the instructional team, as follows: O&M = O&M instructor, S&L = speech and language therapist, VI = teacher of visually impaired students.

bers, teachers, related service providers, and classmates—to develop an action plan for experiences in the typical preschool setting. During the meeting, a facilitator and a recorder are needed to address the following questions (Vandercook, York, & Forest, 1989), which have been adapted for a preschooler:

1. Who is the child?
2. What have been his or her school and other experiences?
3. What is your dream for the child?
4. What is your fear about what will happen to the child?
5. What are the child's strengths, gifts, and abilities?
6. What are this child's needs?
7. What would the child's ideal day at school be like, and what must be done to make it a reality?

After the participants share their perspectives about the preschooler, they develop a plan of action and take responsibility for implementing it. The MAPS process is particularly useful for facilitating a team approach, promoting family-school collaboration; identifying long-term and meaningful goals; and creating a sense of community.

In a preschool curriculum for children who are visually impaired, the key career education components of promoting high expectations, encouraging socialization, developing compensatory skills, providing realistic feedback, and promoting opportunities to work are all interrelated. Children learn compensatory skills in their "work" at the preschool and at home with other people and by others having high expectations for them and providing realistic feedback. Through the use of the techniques described here, preschoolers who are visually impaired can have a greater enhanced opportunity to develop skills for success.

4

Encouraging Socialization

Deborah Chen

Children who are visually impaired, like all children, learn about the world beyond them through socialization. Therefore, they need to learn to socialize appropriately and to engage in social interactions effectively. This chapter presents activities that facilitate the acquisition of all-important social skills. To be integrated into the school environment, it is essential that children learn to play and study cooperatively. Social skills help them connect with one another and work well together.

Social skills are vital for building lasting relationships and working effectively with supervisors and coworkers in adulthood. Many of the social amenities are learned in childhood through play and group activities in school and the community. This chapter presents techniques to develop social skills in preschoolers who are visually impaired through the use of creative play, storytelling, cooperative play, and similar activities.

DEVELOPING THE CONCEPTS OF SELF AND IDENTITY

The ability to interact socially in an effective way is built on many elements, among them an awareness of, respect for, and sensitivity toward others. Young children develop an awareness of other people and their feelings and needs through family and other early interactions. As they establish an understanding of their own emotions, wants, and likes and dislikes, they can begin to understand those of other people through the give-and-take of daily life. For some children who are visually impaired, the development of such concepts as self, others, and the various emotions and characteristics of each may be difficult and may need to be supported. Activities that enhance the development of concepts need to be planned and provided so children can begin to establish the building blocks for interacting with others and for understanding the effect of their behavior on others without visual cues. Such experiences will help visually impaired preschoolers develop a strong, accurate sense of self-awareness.

Young children learn about who they are through observing, interacting, listening, and communicating with their parents, siblings, other relatives, teachers, and people in the community. Sighted children can see the physical features, types of clothing, and gender characteristics of the people in their environment and begin to notice whom they resemble and whom they do not. However, children who are visually impaired will not learn about these differences and similarities through observation. Since children need to learn early about their own identities and those of others, very early, creative and pretend play experiences can assist those with visual impairments to develop an understanding of these characteristics. Games at home and in preschool are effective ways in which children can explore the concept of roles and identity. For example, children may play "dress up" and take turns being "Mommy" or "Daddy" or "baby." (Teachers should be sensitive to a family's values regarding traditional roles that the family may expect for their sons and daughters. For example, not all families will approve of their 3-year-old son dressing up as "Mommy.")

Preschoolers are naturally curious about their bodies and gender differences (Chen, 1993). In preschool, they readily identify themselves by gender, age, and other characteristics. They usually have opportunities to discuss their families during sharing time, art activities, and other "all about me and my family" activities. Young children learn they belong to different groups: They have a family, they are children, they are boys or girls, and they are members of a preschool group.

Activities

- Have children list personal-identity information, such as their names, ages, addresses, and telephone numbers.

- Ask children about their physical features and personal characteristics, for example, the color and length of their hair or their skin color.
- Have children list the members of their families.

Critical Points to Cover

- When appropriate, celebrate the children's birthdays and involve the birthday children in counting the correct number of candles for the cake.
- Everyone has an identity. By answering such questions as how old they are and when their birthdays are, the children can heighten their sense of their individuality. As they discuss such topics as their place in the family order, this sense can be further enhanced.
- Everyone is different. Ask the children to identify the characteristics of their classmates. They may specify gender, age, hair or skin color, visual status, height, or other physical features. Some questions to ask children include "How are boys different from girls?"; "What different games do you play?"; and "Who likes to play dress up?"
- Everyone belongs to a group; some group members' characteristics are similar, and some are different. Having the children distinguish how many people are in their families and who their family members are helps them understand their identities and the characteristics of their family members and others in the community.

Helpful Hints

- Divide the group into subgroups to enable the children to discuss their individual physical characteristics.
- The concept of gender is important for preschoolers to understand because they need to know that they belong to a particular sex and that the sexes have different characteristics. (Ask the children if they are boys or girls or if they can name other boys or girls in the preschool.) However, issues related to sexual differences and other topics bordering on the area of sex education are sensitive ones for families; teachers need to be particularly careful about how they approach these topics.

- The use of terms to label private body parts for children may be appropriate during toileting, bath time, and dressing activities. However, some families may not be comfortable with the use of the words *penis* and *vagina* to identify gender differences or may be concerned about their children's self-exploration in general.
- Although the discussion of gender differences is sensitive, it may be even more complicated if teachers have emphasized the concept of tactile exploration for children with visual impairments. Therefore, the way in which gender is explored needs to be well thought out, based on program philosophy and discussions with families. In addition, traditional differences between boys and girls (such as their clothing, length of hair, type of play, and toys) may not be helpful in many contemporary preschools, given that formerly traditional differences have been blurred in these areas. Some parents or other family members may want to talk about gender differences in relation to family members. Teachers will need to discuss the philosophy of their program and understanding of developmentally appropriate behaviors related to gender issues with families.
- Involve the family in the child's self-identity activities, for example, by asking for photographs of the family and about favorite activities, the roles of family members, and related information for the child to construct an "all about me and my family" book.

Evaluation Tips

- Observe visually impaired children's responses to directions, such as "All the boys line up to wash their hands" and "All the girls go out to play."
- Observe and take notes on the children's responses to questions about their identity, for example, questions about their ages, members of their families, and their birthday months.
- Observe and record the children's ability to name their classmates and to identify whether the classmates are boys or girls.

For Children Who Need Additional Modifications

- Use consistent storage places for the children's personal materials and make sure that the children with disabilities can distin-

FROM A FAMILY PERSPECTIVE

Helping Children Learn About Themselves and the World

As obvious as this might sound, remember that your children cannot see what you see or cannot see it as well. Phil Hatlen, Superintendent of the Texas School for the Blind and Visually Impaired, once remarked that the world for a child with a visual impairment reaches to the length of the child's arm. Parents and other family members need to constantly remind themselves that even if their children have some vision, touching and talking are key ways they will learn to "see."

Help your children know all the "who, what, when, and where" details about themselves. Do not assume they will just know this information or will find it out on their own. Their access to this information will be through you.

Developing the Concept of Self-Identity

One way your family can help your visually impaired child develop confidence in his or her own abilities is to encourage the child to ask questions, take risks, and learn from successes and mistakes by giving him or her informative feedback. This feedback may include discovering ways in which to help the child become comfortable in speaking to classmates and others about his or her visual impairment.

Your preschooler will occasionally talk to you about vision, and it is good to be as frank and truthful as possible with your child. These discussions will take place many times over the following years, and it is best to be open and honest early on. Your child may also need your help in finding the appropriate words to explain his or her visual impairment. Again, draw out the child first. When your child asks, "How do I tell my new friends that I'm blind?" you might ask right back, "That's a great question. How would you do that?" This dialogue will promote more self-reliance for your child and also will tell you what is on his or her mind.

When my son was first diagnosed as having a visual impairment, I was consumed with the question, "What does he see?" A friend of mine who is an optometrist gave me the following advice: "He sees what he sees. Don't compare it. Accept it. That will help him accept it. What he sees is normal for him. And, he may never know what perfect sight really is, but he will know what his sight is, and that will be okay." For me, this advice has stood the test of time.

Kevin O'Connor

guish the storage spaces for other children's materials. For example, for children who learn tactilely, make sure that each child's basket has a tactile symbol that represents its owner.

- Make sure that the children who do not use or understand words have signs to represent themselves and that they are greeted with these signs. These "name signs" can vary according to each child's level of language. They can refer to a special feature of the child, such as a long braid or curly hair; they can incorporate the first letter or two of the child's name; or they can be arbitrary signs that the child will learn to associate with himself or herself. Also, create signs for familiar people. If the children do not understand signs, the name symbols can involve touching a feature (such as braided hair or a beard) that represents a person.

DEVELOPING THE CONCEPTS OF SELF-IDENTITY AND SELF-ESTEEM

Self-esteem—feeling good about oneself and feeling confident in one's abilities and accomplishments—plays a significant role in the development of self-identity, which relates to how a person describes himself or herself. Among the ways in which people answer the question, Who are you? are usually descriptions of family or group connections and occupational information. Among the ways in which children develop positive self-esteem are by growing up in a responsive, caregiving environment; having a sense of who they are; realizing their strengths and abilities; and receiving positive support and feedback about their actions from their families and teachers. All young children need opportunities to take risks, to try out their abilities, to experience success, and to learn from their mistakes through supportive instruction. Preschool is an environment in which these opportunities can be presented to children with visual impairments to increase their self-esteem and confidence in their own abilities.

It is important to note that children's understanding of their visual impairments often is related to their self-identity and self-esteem. Teachers and family members need to give the children information about the children's visual impairments in words that the children can understand. The children should be encouraged to ask questions and to develop comfortable responses to other people's questions.

A sense of community among children in the preschool can be built by using an adapted format of Making Action Plans (MAPS), formerly known as the McGill Action Planning System (Forest & Lusthaus, 1990), to help the children identify their interests, preferences, abilities, and learning needs. The MAPS process is essential for planning meaningful educational goals for young children with multiple disabilities, particularly in inclusive environments. (For a sample MAPS, see the appendix to this chapter.) It provides a forum for families, for members of the interdisciplinary instructional team, and for classmates to come together to determine the children's strengths, gifts, talents, and learning needs; for parents to explain their hopes, dreams, and anxieties for the children's future; and for the group to describe an ideal day for the children and to build needed supports and adaptations to enable the children to belong to the school group and to participate in school activities.

Activities

- Have the children talk about their talents and strengths.
- Establish the children's specific learning needs and essential supports and ask the children what they are learning in school, what they do well, and who they can ask for help. These needs and supports can be determined through the Individualized Education Program (IEP) and the MAPS process. For example, orientation and mobility (O&M) may be a priority for a blind child who requires O&M instruction and will need to learn how to ask for help in exploring unfamiliar or new areas like playgrounds.
- Determine how the preschool community—both children and adults—can interact to create a sense of identity through belonging to the preschool, for example, by creating school teams for clean-up activities or by assigning jobs for children to do with adults.

Critical Points to Cover

To give the children a sense of identity, of belonging to a family or classroom, and of having friends, ask them the following questions:

- What are your favorite playthings?
- What games do you like to play?
- What things do you dislike?
- Who are your friends?
- What activities are you good at doing?
- What are you learning to do?
- What kind of help do you need?
- Who do you help?
- Who helps you?

Helpful Hints

- Divide the classroom into small groups according to existing friendships or preference to encourage the children with visual impairments to discuss their strengths and talents, as well as learning needs.
- On the basis of an ecological inventory (see Chapter 3) of the preschool schedule, identify opportunities for the children with visual impairments to demonstrate their abilities and to experience success. For example, if children excel in singing or playing ball, provide them with regular musical activities or opportunities to play on the ball team.
- Offer choices and encourage decision making, for example, "Do you want juice or milk at snack?" or "Do you want to play on the swing or in the sandbox?" Nonverbal children will need to touch, smell, or taste (using edibles) object cues (see Chapter 3) to indicate their preference.
- Provide realistic feedback on the children's performances and support their understanding of alternative strategies. For example, if Antonio did not put all his blocks back in the container, he can be told, "You did a pretty good job, but you missed a couple of blocks. Look by the chair." Antonio can then be shown how to scan his play area tactilely to find all the blocks.

Evaluation Tips

- Use the questions listed under Critical Points to Cover to discover changes in the children's or classmates' responses.
- Observe and take notes on the children's ability to make choices.
- Observe and record the children's independence and accuracy in doing a good job, for example, putting their blocks away.
- Ask family members about the children's comments about their preferences, strengths, and interests.

For Children Who Need Additional Modifications

- Reinforce the choices that children make, even if they are not what adults would prefer. For example, when a child spits out food and makes a face, he or she is making a choice. Offer another type of food or, if that is not an option, wait a short time before offering another bite.

- Find opportunities for children to use their best skills when working with other classmates. For example, if children enjoy playing rhythm instruments or washing dishes, find opportunities for them to do so and to recognize these skills as part of the classroom activities.

- Recognize and reinforce appropriate behaviors and responses. This recognition can include praise; however, some children need more concrete rewards, such as the opportunity to hear a favorite audiotape or the chance to rub some scented oil or lotion on their hands. Often children with behavioral difficulties get more attention when they behave inappropriately. To feel positive about themselves, they need to have the opportunity to feel good about the things they are doing well.

- Allow children to perceive the results of their own actions. For example, when milk spills, show them how it flows to the other side of the table and drips to the floor; when they choose to go without a jacket on a cool day, allow them to do so, but only for short periods.

ENCOURAGING COOPERATIVE PLAY

When children play with one another and enjoy playing together, they learn many important social lessons. Discovering such important information as how to take turns, listen to each other, and share toys is essential for the building of early friendships and is the foundation for later social and work interactions.

Preschoolers require consistent opportunities to play with others to develop social skills. There are many places in which they can interact with other children, including in their homes, day care centers, parks, community recreation programs, and preschool programs. A primary goal of preschool programs is to promote the socialization of young children by giving them opportunities to play, interact, and communicate with each other.

FROM A MULTICULTURAL PERSPECTIVE

Learning about their cultural heritage—values, beliefs, language, religious practices, modes of dress, food, music, traditions, and ways of doing things—is an integral component of children's social development. The social norms or rules of families in large part flow from their cultural identity and are learned casually and incidentally through family stories, household traditions and celebrations, and the work that family members do. For example, children imitate their family members' customs, ways of speaking, gestures, and facial expressions, and the reactions of these family members reinforce or modify the children's behavior. This process of social modeling shapes each child's concepts of self, identity, and self-esteem.

The different rules of specific cultures may dictate behavioral expectations that do not match the norms of the classroom. For example, in some Eastern cultures, children show respect for their elders and people in authority by looking down, whereas, in Western cultures, the norm is to look directly at the person with whom one is speaking as a sign of respect and integrity. Therefore, families and teachers need to be alert to cultural differences and to support and help children develop skills for operating in a multicultural world. Children's social confidence emerges from their acceptance by others and leads to a stronger self-concept. This sense of self evolves from children's discovery and explorations of themselves. Infants engage in tactile and visual exploration of their own and others' bodies. As they recognize the faces and other attributes (such as vocal qualities, body aroma, or facial hair) of people around them, they begin to distinguish "what is me" from "what is not me." At the age of 2, sighted children can see differences in physical characteristics, but children with visual impairments often cannot. By giving information to visually impaired children and responding to their questions about differences among people in an unbiased manner, adults can model antibiased behaviors and help build the children's cultural self-esteem.

At ages 3 and 4, children become adept at noticing differences among people and matching people according to their differences. They are constantly asking "Why?" When seeing someone wearing a turban, for instance, a child may ask, "Why is that man wearing a funny hat?" Moreover, they are greatly influenced by the distortions and stereotypes that are perpetuated through books, cartoons, toys, television, and folklore.

An awareness of gender, race, ethnicity, and disability—four key aspects of identity—occurs sometime before age 5. During this period, children classify

Children who are visually impaired need specific opportunities to learn how to socialize with other children. Regular contact with peers establishes a foundation for developing friendships that are essential for social and emotional health.

Preschools are natural environments for learning to play with others. Cooperative play may involve sharing toys, such as Legos, Tinker-

people by these characteristics and ask questions about others' similarities to or differences from them. Learning about similarities and differences gives them the opportunity to affirm their belief that they are unique and important. A strong sense of self and an appreciation of their cultural identities, self-acceptance, self-worth, and self-respect set the stage for how they will interpret beliefs, attitudes, actions, and behavior as they grow older.

Furthermore, children need to learn about and be prepared to deal with the many societal ambiguities and prejudices regarding race, disability, gender, religion, and socioeconomic class. For example, they may be told that all people are equal but meet people at school, at home, or in the community who say disparaging things about or actively avoid people of different racial-ethnic or religious groups.

Since visually impaired children frequently rely on the interpretations of sighted persons, an awareness of the specific meaning of disability in various cultures is essential for supporting a positive self-concept and building self-esteem in children from different cultures. Views related to the cause of the disability range from those that emphasize fate to those that place responsibility on the person or his or her family. For example, in some cultures a disability is considered punishment for sins; others consider it a blessing from God; while still others have the opinion that it is the result of some action of the mother or father taken during the pregnancy. Children with disabilities may be treated differently from their siblings depending on the cultural perspective of the family. In some cultures, children with disabilities are thought to be totally dependent on their parents, who are expected to do everything for the children—to feed, clothe, bathe, and support the children throughout their lives.

Teachers and others who learn about and take into consideration the views, feelings, and practices of families from different cultural groups can foster the learning of everyone who is involved with the visually impaired children. In addition, classroom environments need to include curricular materials; toys; books; games; videos; music; language; and pictures, decorations, and other artifacts that represent the diversity of the cultures of the children in them. And family members need to be encouraged to participate in classrooms to expose preschoolers to their language, games, religious holidays, ethnic customs, and traditions, as well as to tell stories about their cultural heritage.

Lila Cabbil

toys, or blocks, or imaginative role-playing. Although 3 year olds will have less complex role-playing than 5 year olds, they will imitate real-life experiences, such as talking on the telephone, cooking, shopping, or going to the doctor. Older preschoolers can create scenarios from less realistic props, for example, by using Fisher-Price toys to play "house" or using blocks to build a fort. Some preschools separate children according to age, whereas others mix children of different ages. If the group is a mixed-age group, the older children may become role models and helpers to the younger ones.

Activities

- Have the children relate familiar real-life experiences that can form the basis of imaginative play, such as visiting the doctor, shopping for groceries, going on a picnic, and making dinner.
- Provide props, such as pots and pans, empty food packages, and grocery bags, to help the children engage in role-playing.
- Organize an area with a table, shelves, and playhouse furniture and have the children interact in imaginative play.
- Identify and provide toys, such as those that make sounds, that will encourage the sighted and visually impaired children to play together.
- Select and implement strategies to encourage peer interactions and cooperative play, such as asking two children to share materials (like a glue bottle) or to play with something that requires the efforts of two children (for example, a seesaw).
- Have each child invite another child to play a game (for instance, a computer game) or to play with such toys as large building blocks or tricycles.

Critical Points to Cover

- Provide the language to label and identify selected toys, objects, and activities.
- Show the sighted children how to invite the visually impaired children to play, how to share toys, and how to respond so the visually impaired children understand.
- Show the visually impaired children how to invite the sighted children to play, how to share toys, and how to respond so the sighted children understand.

Helpful Hints

- Identify opportunities for cooperative play, for example, by selecting toys that will promote interactions between children who are visually impaired and sighted children (such as large building blocks, toy cars, dress-up clothes, pots and pans, a sandbox, a water table, and a seesaw).

- Develop turn-taking games, such as duck, duck, goose; Simon says; or red light, green light, that support interactions.
- Provide verbal descriptions of what is happening for the child with visual impairments to support parallel and interactive play with others. For example, "John is making a tower with blocks and you are making a long line" or "Nikki has put a block on John's and now it's your turn to stack one."
- Identify and use toys and play activities that are preferred by both a visually impaired and a sighted child to encourage interaction between the children.
- Observe, support, and do not interfere with the children's activity once they are playing together.
- Share strategies with families for providing structured activities to support their children's interaction with peers and for providing regular contact with other children, for instance, making play dates and encouraging children to get together at the playground.

Evaluation Tips

- Ask children with visual impairments who their friends are at school.
- Ask sighted children what games they like to play and activities they like to do with their friends who are visually impaired.
- Observe and record the types and length of cooperative play activities between visually impaired children and sighted children. In addition, note how the children initiate and maintain cooperative play activities and their responses to each other.
- Discern whether families comment about their children's remarks about their sighted or visually impaired classmates.

For Children Who Need Additional Modifications

- For students with physical disabilities, find and use toys and materials that respond to relatively little movement and can be used by two children playing together. Examples include balloons on strings or mobile toys, towels or sheets that can be used for hiding, or toy drums and pianos.

- Teach the children without disabilities how to wait long enough for children with disabilities to take their turns. Talk with them about how their classmates with disabilities let others know that they are having fun, are finished, or want a toy or other play material.

- For children with physical disabilities, identify and use easy-to-operate toys and activities, such as remote-control cars, switch-activated computer games, mobiles, and rolling toys, with which they can be actively engaged along with their classmates without disabilities.

FOSTERING COMMUNICATION SKILLS

Communication is the basis of social interaction, and communication skills are important for all children. Whether to make their needs and preferences known or to play games that lead to more significant social relationships, children need to be helped to learn how to communicate effectively.

Young children learn the art of conversation by observing others and by talking with adults and other children. Many children who are visually impaired do not always find it easy to identify whose turn it is to speak, how to stay on the topic, and when to pause and wait for a response. Some children with visual impairments may have limited opportunities to observe or engage in conversations. Others may overhear conversations but cannot make sense of them because the language is abstract and the referents are unknown. Some adults tend to talk to children only to make requests or provide directions. These experiences do not encourage the children to develop the give-and-take of conversation.

Some children with visual impairments may repeat what was said by the previous speaker or ask off-topic questions to initiate or take their turns in conversations. (In the former situation, for example, an adult may ask, "Do you want a cookie?" and the child may reply, "Want a cookie?" In the latter instance, in reply to the adult's question, "Do you want a cookie?" the child may ask, "Where's Daddy?"). Visually impaired children frequently may also have difficulty engaging in socially appropriate nonverbal behavior, such as facing or looking at a person who is speaking to them, and may sometimes engage in stereo-typical behaviors or mannerisms (hand flapping, body rocking, and eye pressing) that are distracting to other people; some develop such stereotypical behaviors early for self-stimulation. Furthermore, visually impaired children may miss the nonverbal cues of other children that invite or terminate interaction. Thus, it is necessary to support the communication skills of preschoolers with visual impairments by providing specific activities, such as offering a snack to other children or asking another child if he or she wants a turn on the swing, that support the art of communication among children.

Young children should learn how to communicate their ideas and feelings to each other in acceptable ways. Teachers can use both planned activities (for example, show-and-tell time) and unplanned situations (for instance, resolving an argument) as opportunities for facilitating children's communication skills.

Activities

- Have the children interact with each other by planning activities that involve play centers, music, or a playground.
- Establish ways to facilitate peer interactions, for example, by sharing materials or by prompting the children to ask each other questions.
- Develop strategies for encouraging children to solve problems and to negotiate differences, such as by asking them how to decide who will take a turn on a swing first and who will be second or what should happen if a child knocks over another's tower of blocks by accident.
- Develop role-play situations for older preschoolers, for example, by acting out what children should do if they get lost or separated from their parents at a shopping mall.
- Help the children participate in group discussions by calling on them.

Critical Points to Cover

- Ask children questions about the topic they are sharing and encourage others to ask questions by saying, for example, "Does anyone want to ask Jennifer a question about her baby brother?"

- Ask the children questions about a misunderstanding by saying, for example, "What happened? Why is Bobby crying?"
- Help the children to identify solutions to their problems, such as by asking, "How can we help Maria feel better?" or "We only have one bike and you both want to ride it. What can we do?"
- Provide words to help describe a child's feelings, for example, "You're crying. Do you think you may feel sad because you miss your mother?"

Helpful Hints

- Conduct an ecological inventory (see Chapter 3) of the preschool routine to identify planned opportunities to engage children in conversation, such as during "show and tell" or in a group discussion after a field trip.
- Develop and implement a program philosophy of seizing "teachable moments" to discuss children's feelings and to engage the children in problem solving. For example, in the case of one child hitting another, the two children can talk about what happened, how they feel, and what they could do to resolve the situation.
- Give children with visual impairments frequent opportunities to engage in conversations with other children and to overhear others in the give-and-take of conversations.
- Assist children with visual impairments in developing appropriate nonverbal communication skills, such as facing the person with whom they are talking, limiting stereotypical body movements, and keeping their hands off the person. Support the children's role-playing with friends to practice these skills.
- Help sighted children learn how to engage the children with visual impairments and how to respond to the visually impaired children's unconventional behaviors, for example, by saying the children's names and touching them on the arms or asking them to stop rocking or to turn around.
- When it is developmentally appropriate to do so, have the children practice acceptable communication skills through role-playing.
- Collaborate with family members to encourage the visually impaired children's communication with children at home and in other settings.

Evaluation Tips

- Observe and take notes on the visually impaired children's initiation of and participation in conversations with other children.
- Record the topics of conversation and the number of turns that the children take in conversations.
- Observe and take notes on changes in the children's nonverbal communication behavior.
- Note the sighted children's use of identified strategies for engaging the children with visual impairments and how visually impaired children respond.
- Ask family members about the children's communicative behaviors at home and in other situations.

For Children Who Need Additional Modifications

- Use pictures, photographs, or objects to let the visually impaired children know what event will happen next. Use a special symbol to stand for unexpected events so the children will learn to expect the unexpected. This symbol can be a blank card, an empty box, a card with a question mark, or just an arbitrary texture that the child will learn to associate with something unexpected.
- When the children cannot indicate their wants or needs with words or signs, let them know with a touch on the hand before they are lifted or moved. Use the signal consistently so they know what to expect when touched.
- Position children with disabilities so they can hear and observe conversations among others. For example, if the class is grouped around the teacher, make sure the children with physical disabilities are in the middle of the group, not at the side, so they can hear the conversation and others will make eye contact with them as they talk with one another.
- Provide concrete responses to the behaviors that the children initiate. For example, when children smile, respond with a smile or touch; when they vocalize, move close to them to let them know they have communicated that they want attention.
- Teach a gesture or routine for greeting and saying good-bye to others and prompt children to greet and say good-bye to others appropriately. The most appropriate routines include standard

gestures such as waving, shaking hands, or hugging familiar people. A touch on the back of the hand for leaving may be appropriate for a blind child who cannot understand verbal greeting or leave-taking.

- For children who do not use language, find ways to help them recall and review events that have occurred. Sequencing pictures or using objects to represent activities in their order of occurrence will remind them about the relationship between one step in a sequence and the next step. Presenting a garden trowel and empty flower pot may remind children of the time when they planted a flower, and may prompt a trip to check on the garden.
- For nonverbal children with physical disabilities, use switch-activated audiotape recorders or programmed augmentative devices to allow them to "talk" to other children. Begin with a few simple phrases, such as "Do you want to play?," "I want a drink," or "Let's sing a song." Encourage the other children to respond as if the disabled children were using their voices to say these things.

References

Chen, D. (1993). Early childhood development. In *First steps: A handbook for teaching young children who are visually impaired* (pp. 3–16). Los Angeles: Blind Childrens Center.

Forest, M., & Lusthaus, E. (1990). Everyone belongs with the MAPS Action Planning System. *Teaching Exceptional Children, 22*(2), 32–35.

APPENDIX
Making Action Plans

The Making Action Plans (MAPS) process is used to determine the educational goals for young children with multiple disabilities and is based on the information gathered from family members or caregivers, an interdisciplinary instructional team, and the individual child's classmates. Provided here is the sample MAPS for Amy, a 3-year-old blind girl, in which participants consider seven pivotal questions, and then, based on their answers, prioritize the actions that need to be introduced.

1. **Who is Amy?**

   Amy is a very active 3 year old. She is an only child who lives with her parents and grandparents.

2. **What have been her school and other experiences?**

   Amy was in an early intervention home-based program in another city. She began this preschool program last month when her family relocated to this area. She had eye surgery to reattach both retinas when she was a baby and may now have some light perception.

3. **What is your dream for Amy?**

   That she will be like other children and attend the neighborhood school.

4. **What is your fear about what will happen to Amy?**

   That she will continue to have difficulty being with other children. She cries and moves away when other children try to interact with her. We are afraid she will never have any friends with whom to play.

5. **What are Amy's strengths, gifts, and abilities?**

   She is very active and fearless. She likes to play on the swings and slides on the playgrounds, and she loves to swim. She also likes music.

Table 4.1

Making Action Plans (MAPS) Process for Amy

Steps in Action Plan	Initiator of Action	Schedule
1. Find out how to help Amy sleep at night	Mother will talk to doctor Teacher will talk to behavior specialist	By next week
2. Organize program schedule to include opportunities for physical activities	Teacher	By next week
3. Identify Amy's preferences for classmates and who likes to play with her	Teacher	By next week
4. Develop games for Amy and classmates	Adaptive physical education instructor and teacher	In 2 weeks
5. Infuse O&M instruction during day	O&M instructor and classroom staff	In 2 weeks
6. Infuse speech and language therapy objectives into the daily routine	Speech and language therapist and classroom staff	In 2 weeks

6. **What are Amy's needs?**

   She needs to develop her speech and play skills. She does not sleep at night and is sleepy and grumpy in the morning.

7. **What would an ideal day be like and what must be done to make it a reality?**

   Amy has had a good night's sleep. She gets up and helps with her bath and dressing and eats breakfast. Her mother drops her off at school. There are physical activities that encourage Amy to play with other children, that increase her orientation and mobility skills, and that tire her out so she will sleep at night. She does not need a nap during the day because of her sleeping problems. (For a step-by-step plan on how to make this scenario a reality, see Table 4.1.)

CHAPTER

5

Developing Compensatory Skills

Jamie Dote-Kwan

Preschoolers with visual impairments need to learn basic compensatory skills to prepare for subsequent life challenges. It is at the preschool level that they develop the skills that form the foundation on which their school and work efforts will rest. They learn basic concepts, build their language and computational skills, and acquire orientation and mobility (O&M) techniques. They also need to learn and refine alternative techniques for performing many tasks that sighted children perform visually.

The compensatory skills that visually impaired children acquire as preschoolers will be expanded and refined during their academic careers in the areas of reading and writing by using braille or low vision devices; by applying advanced O&M skills; and by performing mathematical calculations using the Nemeth code, an abacus, or a talking calculator. The early development of knowledge and skills in these areas is important for preschoolers with visual impairments to engage in meaningful activities related to career awareness and exploration. The development of early work skills, such as learning to sort or put things together, is enhanced by the preschoolers' ability to solve problems, exhibit one-to-one correspondence, and understand the concepts of same and different.

In this chapter, a series of activities is presented that helps build the basic compensatory skills that preschoolers need to make the transition from preschool to elementary school and to perform and compete with other children during and after school.

CONCEPT DEVELOPMENT

Concepts are the representational mental schemes that children acquire through their multiple experiences with objects and events (Barraga, 1976). Concepts underlie every area of the curriculum—and life. The development of concepts begins with the recognition that objects exist (object permanence), followed by the identification and naming of objects. In addition to object concepts (such as dog, cat, and ball), the characteristics of objects (like big, little, short, tall, smooth, and rough), and spatial awareness (such as top, bottom, on, off, in, and out), there are action concepts (like jumping, running, and hugging) and abstract concepts (such as space, time, and number). Sighted children see objects in their entirety. With young children who are visually impaired, it is imperative to examine their knowledge of specific concepts and elaborate on their understanding via activity-based experiences, rather than merely through verbalization.

Preschool teachers of children with visual impairments need to review state-adopted curricula and skills inventories, such as the Oregon Project for Visually Impaired and Blind Preschool Children (Anderson, Boigon, & Davis, 1991) (see the Resources section of this book), to identify the specific concepts and curricular content that are appropriate for each age level and necessary for understanding stories and other content areas. For example, 3 year olds first develop concepts related to themselves (such as the concept of a nose, a mouth, eyes, and ears) and their personal belongings (like backpacks, shoes, bowls, and cups). Four- and 5 year olds develop concepts related to more distal objects, such as clouds, horses, dogs, the sun, and trees. When possible, this information needs to be shared with the children's families, who can help to support the children's development in these areas.

Instruction in concepts has to be sequenced and systematically taught to children with visual impairments. The development of object concepts begins with children having concrete experiences with a specific object. For example, a young girl may encounter her first dog when she visits her grandmother, who has a golden retriever. For this initial experience to be truly meaningful, she should be given the opportunity to explore the dog tactilely. This tactile exploration should be mediated by a family member or teacher to ensure that the child examines all the critical features of the dog (for example, the dog's ears, nose, paws, tail, fur, and body) carefully and safely. These critical features are referred to as defining features; that is, they distinguish a dog from other four-legged animals (such as a cat, cow, or horse). The adult's mediation of this experience can involve placing the child's hands on the various defining features and verbally describing what the child is actually feeling. To develop and refine the child's concept of dog further, the adult needs to expose the child to a variety of dogs (a poodle, German shepherd, and terrier, for example) over time. These multiple exposures help the child recognize that dog is a class of objects with a number of types within it. At each initial exposure to a different type or example of a dog, the adult can facilitate the child's development of the concept, dog, by showing or talking to the child about the similarities between the particular dog and her grandmother's golden retriever.

Activities

- Have the children identify familiar and common objects in their environment, including body parts and personal belongings.
- Have the children select multiple examples of the same class of objects (such as a poodle, collie, or terrier, in the case of dogs).
- Have the children identify common and novel examples of the same class of object (like a dining room, kitchen, or coffee table).
- Ask the children to define tactile, visual, and other characteristics of objects and their classes (for example, that a cat can be soft, fluffy, and white and that it is an animal).

Critical Points to Cover

- Assist the children in exploring the critical features of an object systematically.
- Mediate the exploration by guiding the children's hands and verbally describing the major features.

- Provide multiple opportunities to interact with the original exemplar of the object and a variety of objects of the same class.

Helpful Hints

- Give the children ample time to feel comfortable before approaching the object, especially when dealing with animals.
- Place the individual child's hand on top of your hand, allowing only his or her fingertips to touch the object, if the child is resistant to exploring the object tactilely.
- At a later point, expand this activity to include examples that may be exceptions to the class of objects in terms of the critical or defining features, such as a dog without a tail or a dog with long or short ears.

Evaluation Tips

- Ask the children to describe the critical features of the object.
- Give the children a novel example of a class of object and ask, "What is it?"
- Ask the children to compare two different examples of an object concept (such as a poodle and a dalmatian) and describe how they are the same and how they are different.
- Provide the children with a field of three objects (two objects of the same concept and one object that is different) and ask them to identify the one that does not belong.
- Have the children point out their body parts that correspond to those of a dog (like the nose, ears, and eyes), particularly if dogs have been the class of objects explored.

For Children Who Need Additional Modifications

- For children with severe physical disabilities, make sure they have the opportunity to touch and explore toys and objects while in different positions, so they use their muscles in various ways and understand that objects do not look the same from different positions and angles.
- For children with physical disabilities, use mobiles or standing frames of polyvinyl chloride pipe to suspend objects where the

children can make contact with them and initiate movement with little pressure. Position the objects so the children can use their own movements to activate the objects.

- Teach a sign or provide a picture symbol for "same" and use it when the children are presented with similar objects (for example, two apples, two shoes, or two combs). Symbols for "same" may include standard signs, such as two index fingers tapped together, or adaptations of signs, such as rubbing palms together. A picture symbol for "same" may show two familiar objects that are exactly alike. When the children have mastered the concept of same, begin to introduce the concept of different, along with pairs of contrasting objects.

- Use the same materials during routines when the children are learning the function of an object (for instance, the use of a cup, a brush, or tape). When the children recognize the function of the object, begin to vary the characteristics of the object (for example, substitute a larger cup or a coarser brush). Encourage the children to choose a preferred object from several items.

- Teach concepts during activities and incorporate the use of several senses. After an activity, use the children's most effective learning medium (vision, touch, or hearing) to review the steps of the activity in a sequence. To review a cooking activity, for instance, use several pictures of the class making pudding; a sequence of object symbols like a pudding box, a milk carton, and a spoon; or an audiotape recording that describes the steps in making pudding.

- Provide tangible experiences of the concepts of more and less, and heavier and lighter. Make sure that these experiences allow the children to touch, grasp, hold, and manipulate materials to compare their characteristics. For children with physical disabilities who cannot hold objects in their hands, use small fabric or plastic bags with loops or handles so they can hold different amounts and weights of objects with either hand.

- For children who can follow basic routines, occasionally include an inappropriate object in a routine. Wait for them to reject the object or request a different object before restoring the needed material. For example, in a toothbrushing routine, put out toothbrushes and cups along with hairbrushes. Wait to see if the children ask for toothpaste.

CONCEPTUAL UNDERSTANDING OF SPATIAL AWARENESS

Because some visually impaired children frequently do not have the benefit of incidental learning that is facilitated by sight, concepts need to be introduced to them in a planned and sequenced way and systematically taught. In general, they need to experience a concept first through motor activity, then through object manipulation, and finally through representational or symbolic experiences. Keeping this instructional sequence in mind, teachers can identify activities that allow children to experience a concept physically through motor activity. For instance, to gain an understanding of the concept, top, children can walk to the top of a staircase, climb to the top of a ladder, and climb to the top of a jungle gym. They may initially need to have the activity demonstrated to them and to be moved through it. Although the children's experience may be verbally mediated by saying, for example, "You're going to the top of the stairs," it is not important for the children to verbalize what they are doing at this level of experience. After the children have had physical experiences with the concept, the next level in the sequence of instruction is object manipulation. Using the same concept, top, the children can then place objects on top of a box, on top of a chair, on top of a bookcase, and so forth. Initially, the children will respond to the verbal directions and perform the activity demonstrating their understanding of the concept. Eventually, a book or other object can be placed on top of the bookcase and they can be asked, "Where's the book?" If they respond correctly, they have demonstrated an understanding of the concept.

The final level is the representational, or symbolic, understanding of a concept in two-dimensional form (such as enlarged or raised-lined drawings). (A raised-line drawing board can be used to make a raised-line drawing. The board consists of a thin sheet of rubber attached to a firm backing of such material as cardboard or wood, over which a disposable sheet of plastic is fastened. Writing on the plastic with a pen, pencil, or stylus produces raised lines that can be perceived tactilely rather than the indentations that would be formed by writing with firm pressure on paper.) Teachers can begin with simple worksheets with basic shapes. For example, they can give children a simple raised-line drawing of a ladder. Then the children can use stickers or pushpins, rather than pencils or crayons, to indicate the top of the ladder, so they can correct their mistakes more easily and get feedback about where they have marked their responses. Once the children have mastered simple worksheets, teachers may use more complex worksheets or materials directly from the general education classroom.

Activities

- For the physical-experience level of learning concepts, have the children perform a concept with their entire bodies or specific body parts (like placing their bodies behind a box. Encourage them to verbalize what they are doing (such as by saying, "I'm behind," or "I'm behind the box").
- For the object-manipulation level, have the children act out or demonstrate the concept of using concrete familiar objects (for example, by placing their shoes behind a bookcase). Encourage them to verbalize what they are doing (such as by saying, "put behind," "shoes behind," or "I put my shoes behind the bookcase").
- For the representational or symbolic level, have the children demonstrate the concept by using simple enlarged or raised-line drawings of pictures of a cat sitting behind a box and of a cat sitting next to a box, for instance. The children can select the picture that illustrates the concept. Encourage the children to verbalize their selection (such as by saying, "Here it is, the cat behind").

Critical Points to Cover

- Identify a concept to teach in the classroom or on the playground.
- Identify activities at each level in the instructional sequence just described. For example, for the concept, in, have the children go into a sandbox or place toys in the sandbox.
- Vary the materials used and plan a sufficient number of activities so the children can generalize the concept across different situations.

Helpful Hints

- Use the same terminology consistently, such as "top," not "over" or "on," and refer to the children when possible, as in "the top of your head."
- Use materials that are readily available in the children's environment and are familiar to the children.

FROM A FAMILY PERSPECTIVE

Conceptual and Literacy Skills

Remind yourself often that teaching conceptual and literacy skills to preschoolers is no easy task—even when they are fully sighted. Be patient with your child and with yourself. Also remember that learning will stop when the enjoyment stops! Like most of the activities in this handbook, the activities for teaching conceptual and literacy skills can provide many possibilities for family involvement. Teach actively, but for short periods of time, and make sure to stop before everyone is frustrated and tired. Try to end play on a high note so children will want to perform the activity again.

When teaching your visually impaired child about the concept of colors, use lots of descriptive words. Although children who are totally blind cannot see colors, it is important for them to hear color words and to gain a sense of the concept of colors, since colors are an integral part of the sighted world. Therefore, parents need to say these words often and try to describe them. For example, you could describe the color blue as being cold like ice, the color pink as being soft like the petal of a flower, and the color red as being hot like fire.

Whenever you are helping your child understand the concept of spatial awareness, try to have your child touch whatever you are acquainting him or her with because his or her experiences need to be tactile as well as auditory. Helping children recognize important landmarks, such as fast-food restaurants, ice

- In developing the lesson, experience the activity before asking the children to perform it. Close your eyes and get a sense of how it may feel for the children to perform the activity.
- Provide a variety of experiences using the same motor pattern, but different equipment or materials, such as climbing up some stairs and then climbing a ladder of the slide.
- Use tactile books that represent concepts with textured symbols or small objects, such as those made by Oakmont (see the Resources section) to illustrate and reinforce basic concepts in the two–dimensional format.

Evaluation Tips

- Use objects other than those initially presented to teach a concept and ask the children to demonstrate the concept.
- Use two-dimensional worksheets (enlarged or raised-line drawings) and ask the children to describe them. For example, on a

cream parlors, and stationery stores, as you pass them not only lets them in on what everyone else is seeing, but gives them some awareness of place. When you are at McDonald's, for example, let them feel the arches and the Ronald McDonald statue.

When your child is older, to minimize public attention and his or her potential embarrassment and to help him or her become oriented in space, try to explain location, texture, distance, and time quietly if there are other people around. Many blind adults orient themselves this way. During a workshop, for example, they will quietly ask a sighted associate, "Who is across from me?" and "Which way is the presenter facing?"

To help your child learn literacy skills, learn braille yourself and encourage other family members to do so. Although many sighted parents find it difficult, if not impossible, to learn to read braille with their fingertips, you can learn to read braille visually. Vision teachers can suggest resources for learning braille, such as the free correspondence course for parents that is offered by the Hadley School for the Blind (see Resources).

Once you have learned to read and write in braille, label objects in the house with braille strips, so your child can get accustomed to the idea of braille. For optimal learning, introduce just a few labeled objects at a time, and review them often. Also encourage your child to dictate stories to you and write them out in braille. Then read the stories aloud to your child while he or she "reads" the braille.

Kevin O'Connor

raised-line worksheet with a circle on top of a box, ask, "Where's the circle?"

- Place objects in various positions and ask the children to describe the location of the objects.
- Administer the Boehm Test of Basic Concepts (Boehm, 1971) (available from the Psychological Corporation in San Antonio, Texas), for children with low vision. This test assesses young children's understanding of basic concepts, such as in and out, top and bottom, and few and many, by using two-dimensional drawings.

For Children Who Need Additional Modifications

- Use a consistent sign or gesture to indicate movement in a particular direction, for example, a touch on the shoulder to mean "up" and a touch on the knee to mean "down." Use this sign before a child is assisted in moving.

- For children with physical disabilities, find concrete ways to reinforce concepts of space and distance. Blind children who do not move by themselves due to cerebral palsy or other conditions may be confused about distance and may use time only to monitor how far they have gone. Maintaining physical contact with the floor or wall (for example, pushing a broom ahead of them while riding in their wheelchairs) may provide more feedback about the physical space and landmarks they are passing. A "curb feeler" for automobiles can be attached to the wheel of a wheelchair to give a child auditory feedback about contact with wall surfaces.

READING AND WRITING SKILLS: PERSONALIZED STORIES

To obtain access to the information they will need to become part of the world and to be successful and competitive individuals when they grow up, visually impaired children, like all children, need to be literate. To reach their full potential, then, they need to develop early literacy skills. "Literacy begins to develop at birth; it does not wait until a child reads his first words or even until he opens his first book. Literacy is a basic process, set in motion long before actual reading and writing take place, and it involves all of the child's development" (Stratton & Wright, 1991, p. xi–xii). Early literacy involves the development of four areas: early sensory-motor abilities, used in such activities as the discovery of objects, object manipulation, cooperative use of both hands, and scribbling; sensory acuity and efficiency in all remaining sensory channels, reflected in listening skills and tactile-kinesthetic skills for children who are functionally blind; the formation of basic concepts; and literacy awareness, represented in exploring, using, and enjoying books and stories.

Emergent literacy is the process by which young children begin to develop concepts related to written language or reading or writing. In general it is developed through early interactions with the symbolic representations of language (for example, recognizing the "Golden Arches" as McDonalds, scribbling, and telling stories from pictures). However, many of these common everyday experiences of sighted children are not readily available for children with visual impairments. The limited exposure many visually impaired children have to numerous forms of symbolic examples of language (such as books, signs, labels, and advertisements) is further exacerbated by the children's inability to observe and experience the communicative aspects of these forms in such guises as grocery lists, greeting cards, and notes (Lamb, 1996). Research has shown that as a group, potential braille readers are particularly at risk of entering school having learned fewer literacy concepts than have potential print readers (Craig, 1996). This difference is attributed to a lack of exposure to print and symbolic examples of language and to a lack of understanding of the importance of reading and writing in society.

Through the creation of stories based on children's experiences, families and teachers can promote early literacy skills. After special events, such as going for a haircut, visiting a beach, or attending a birthday party, family members and teachers can ask the children to dictate a few short sentences that can be written in the appropriate medium (braille or print) for them. The children can identify and attach concrete objects such as a lock of hair, a sand dollar, or a party hat, to illustrate their stories. Children with low vision can use markers or crayons to create simple illustrations for their stories. Blind children can use crayons on a textured surface, such as a piece of screen attached to a board, to create drawings in relief. Initially, families and teachers can read the children's stories aloud while the children follow along with their eyes or hands, depending on the reading medium (a process called coactive reading). The children's stories can be placed together to create theme books, such as "Things I Like To Do," "Places I Have Been," or "Special Days."

Activities

- Set up activities like having monthly classroom birthday parties, learning a new game, or having a guest visit the class and record the children's verbal descriptions in a written format to include in daily or weekly journals, thank-you notes, or letters.
- Have the children dictate letters or stories that can then be written and read by teachers or parents.
- Provide a writing center in the classroom where children can write or draw freely. This center should include a variety of adaptive devices to create tactile text or drawings, such as a Sewell Raised-Line Drawing Kit, a braillewriter, a slate and sty-

lus, or a tracing wheel with a rubber pad, as well as simple magnification devices, markers, crayons, and a variety of textured paper for children with low vision. (Using a Sewell Raised-Line Drawing Kit, available from the American Printing House for the Blind [see Resources], children can create a raised-line drawing by writing on a rubberized board with a ballpoint pen and cellophane sheets.)

- Have the children dictate a few short stories about special events, such as going to the beach, attending a wedding, or going on a vacation trip.
- Have the children illustrate their stories with real objects or simple drawings.

Critical Points to Cover

- Encourage the children to follow along with their fingers or eyes while reading the story with an adult.
- Encourage the child to turn the pages of the books.

Helpful Hints

- Do not attempt to correct the children's grammar or choice of words.
- Use double or triple spaces between lines of braille or enlarged text to enable children to follow the text without difficulty.
- Make the covers of the books tactilely interesting, make the pages in different shapes, or use various types of paper so the pages arouse the children's interest.
- Provide natural examples of enlarged or brailled text throughout the classroom by using labels to designate specific areas, such as the block area or rug area, or to indicate information about the class, such as the day of the week, the cafeteria menu, the names of the class helpers, or the list of student names and birth dates.

Evaluation Tips

- Ask the children open-ended questions related to their stories or drawings, such as "What was the best part of your day?" or "What did you do there?"

- Collect representative samples of the children's written work (for example, stories, letters, and notes) as indicators of increased competence.
- Gather representative examples of the children's drawings as indicators of increased competence.
- Ask the parents to participate in an early literacy curriculum by sending home one book per week with each child, along with a form requesting feedback on the child's questions and comments about the book.

For Children Who Need Additional Modifications

- Create books about the children's experiences, using real objects or parts of objects to represent entire objects. For children with fine motor difficulties, use heavy cardboard for pages and cut the pages so a small section on each page sticks out and can be easily grasped for turning.
- Use adapted keys on the braillewriter, such as extended keys, which allow a child to press keys without exerting as much strength; enlarged keys, which enable a child to press keys without using finger discrimination; or one-handed braillewriters, which allow the user to press keys on either side of the space bar before the cell is imprinted. For those who cannot exert pressure, use an electronic braillewriter or an adapted braillewriter, such as the Mountbatten. (All these items are available from distributors of braillewriters, including Howe Press and the American Printing House for the Blind. See the Resources section.) Encourage the children to experiment with pretending to write stories and experiences even before they are ready to learn the letter symbols. They may do this by pressing random keys on the braillewriter, just as a sighted child scribbles before writing.
- For children who do not use conventional literacy media, teach them to use audiocassettes as a way of preserving information. Young children may use audiocassettes to tell about their experiences, make lists of things needed for a task or activity, or record "letters" to send to friends. For children who cannot operate standard audiocassette players, consider the use of switches to allow them to activate the devices without assistance.

- For children who cannot use print or braille, consider other ways of preserving ideas, including picture sequences and arrays; tactile symbols; and iconic systems, such as Bliss symbols. These systems can organize ideas so that a child can express experiences by drawing pictures, recognizing those of others, or sequencing tactile symbols or objects to describe or recall an experience.

READING AND WRITING SKILLS: INTERACTIVE READING WITH CHILDREN

Reading stories that are meaningful to young children will extend and reinforce their own experiences. It facilitates language development by extending the children's experiences and knowledge of language patterns and structures and by increasing their vocabulary, word knowledge, and interest in words (Stratton & Wright, 1991). It also introduces children to the conventions of print and braille, such as punctuation, left-to-right progression, sequential concepts of a story (that is, there is a beginning, a middle, and an end), and the language of literature (for example, "Once upon a time . . ."). Interactive reading incorporates strategies like asking open-ended questions or acknowledging, repeating, and expanding children's utterances that encourage the children's active participation during reading sessions. Involving young children in the experience of fluent reading exposes them to the benefits of reading in everyday life, such as the acquisition of information, the communication of messages and thoughts, and entertainment.

Because the visual presentation (pictures) of a book and the facial expressions and gestures of the reader are often inaccessible to children with visual impairments, the written text used in interactive reading needs to convey the meaning of the story. To ensure that the meaning of stories to be used in the preschool classroom can be conveyed and the children's interest can be engaged without visual cues, teachers need to preview the books to be read to the children with their families. Also, teachers need to choose stories that convey activities that the children have experienced. For example, a story about a trip to a farm may have less meaning to children who live in the city or who have never been to a working farm than it will to children in rural areas. However, city children may be able to relate better to a story about going to the grocery store or spending the day with a grandparent, since they may have experienced these activities.

Teachers and families need to select a consistent time of day and place to read to children, such as the rug area of the classroom after lunchtime or a rocking chair at home before bedtime. Readers need to rely on their voices to convey aspects of the story, and to read with expression to describe an event or the moods or actions of characters. They can use animated intonation to create anticipation and excitement about what is about to happen. Teachers and families can encourage active participation during the reading by asking open-ended questions, such as "What do you think will happen next?," and by acknowledging and expanding on the children's utterances. For example, when reading the story "Goldilocks and the Three Bears," the reader can respond to the questions, "What is porridge?" by saying to the children, "Porridge is hot cereal. Have you ever had hot cereal?"

Activities

- Have the children answer open-ended questions; for example, in the story, "Goldilocks and the Three Bears," ask, "What do you think will happen?," "Why did Goldilocks run away?," or "Who is most like Goldilocks?"
- Have the children answer questions about facts in the story, for example, "What did Goldilocks find in Mama Bear's bowl?"
- Have the children follow the braille text with their fingers by using books from Twin Vision, Seedlings (see the Resources section), or the On the Way to Literacy series, which are books that combine print and braille on facing pages so that blind and sighted people can read together.
- Have the children hold the books and turn the pages to help them understand the way books are held and read.

Critical Points to Cover

- Point out the front of the book and top of the page.
- Identify the title of the story.
- Ask the children what they think the story is about.
- Ask what the children liked about the story.

Helpful Hints

- Select developmentally appropriate books.
- Schedule a consistent story time.
- Preview stories and gather necessary props.
- Develop a list of questions to engage the children's attention.
- Ask the children questions to maintain their interest in the story, for example, "What do you think will happen next?" "How do you think she feels?" or "What could she do to find her dog?"
- Help the children understand the story line by substituting real objects, when possible, for the pictures used in printed books.
- Provide materials that the children have memorized, such as nursery rhymes, short poems, and songs, in the appropriate medium (large print or braille).
- Provide simple picture books with reduced visual clutter for children with low vision.
- Use repetitive and predictable stories, such as *Brown Bear, Brown Bear, What Do You See?* (Martin, 1992) and *The Very Hungry Caterpillar* (Carle, 1986), to build the children's familiarity with and participation in providing responses.

Evaluation Tips

- Ask the children to retell the story, nursery rhyme, or poem.
- Have the children act out a story or nursery rhyme, using simple props.
- Have the children describe a specific character or event in a story or nursery rhyme.
- Have the children draw a picture or create a tactile illustration for a story.
- Check periodically to determine if the children are on the correct page and line of text when they are reading.

For Children Who Need Additional Modifications

- For children who do not use spoken language, a loop-tape (repeating tape) system can allow them to participate in stories read by others. Before reading, the person who will read a story records a phrase that is repeated throughout the story. Each time that phrase is about to be said during reading, the reader prompts the child, who activates the tape using a switch and thereby participates in the story.

- Arrange object stories—stories that include a number of familiar objects in a sequence. Encourage the children to select and display the appropriate object to their classmates when it is named in the story. For children with physical disabilities and those with a limited understanding of words, classmates can present two objects as choices when an object is named and allow the children to identify the one that was named.

COMPUTATIONAL SKILLS: ONE-TO-ONE CORRESPONDENCE

The development of computational and problem-solving skills in preschool children with visual impairments can be facilitated through everyday experiences at home and in the preschool classroom. Early computational skills include knowledge of a one-to-one correspondence and number concepts.

One-to-one correspondence is the pairing of one class of objects with another class of objects. Sighted preschoolers have numerous opportunities in their daily lives to observe examples of this concept. Each place setting at the table with its plate, glass, napkin, and various utensils for each person seated at the table is an example of one-to-one correspondence at home. Similarly, a piece of paper and a pencil that are passed out to each child during an art activity is an example of one-to-one correspondence that can be observed in the preschool classroom. It is important for teachers to explain to families that merely telling blind preschoolers that Mommy, Daddy, and their siblings have a place setting before them or that each child in the class has a piece of paper and a pencil is not meaningful enough to build the concept of one-to-one correspondence. Rather, active participation in setting the table or passing out art supplies is necessary. A visually impaired preschooler can help set the table by placing a plate on the table in front of Daddy's chair, one in front of Mommy's chair, one in front of a sibling's chair, and then in front of his or her chair, thereby experiencing this concept. The process can then be repeated with the glasses, napkins, and eating utensils to build an understanding of the concept. In the classroom, having a preschooler with a visual impairment pass out papers and pencils to the entire class may not be practical, but the child can assist the teacher or a sighted classmate in passing out papers and pencils to a smaller group.

Activities

- Have the children pass out school supplies (paper, glue bottles, or scissors) to small groups of children.
- Have the children pass out candy or treats at parties.
- Have the children give everyone sitting at the table a cracker or a cookie.

Critical Points to Cover

- Have the children engage actively in the entire process, beginning with getting the items from a cupboard or closet.
- Monitor the children carefully, so everyone gets only one of each item (for example, one sheet of paper, one pencil, one napkin, or one plate) and individuals are not skipped or missed.

Helpful Hints

- Identify whether helping to set the table is a priority in the family routine. If it is, share strategies with the parents. If it is not, identify other appropriate opportunities for the children to experience one-to-one correspondence, for example, giving a cookie to each person or having a glove for each hand and a shoe for each foot.
- Make sure all items in one category are identical in size, shape, and texture; for instance, that all the plates are white with flower borders, round, ceramic, and of salad size.
- Provide a point of reference for the children when they pass out the items, such as by using a chair as a point of reference for each person's place setting or handing the item directly to the person.
- Provide a point of reference for where the children should begin and end the process each time, such as by placing a plate in front of Daddy's chair first and moving around the table clockwise until they are back at Daddy's chair.

- Extend this activity to introduce beginning number concepts by having the children stand at the cupboard with an adult and count out the appropriate number of items needed for setting the table (for example, "one plate, two plates, three plates, four plates").
- Encourage the children's development of problem-solving skills by asking the following questions:
    1. "Why do we need four plates?"
    2. "If we need four plates, how many napkins do we need?"
    3. "What kind of foods do we eat with a fork?"

Evaluation Tips

- Ask the children to give everyone at the dinner table a napkin.
- Observe the children's follow-through.
- Ask the family members about the children's participation in setting the table at home.
- Observe and take notes on the children's level of independence and accuracy in passing out materials.

For Children Who Need Additional Modifications

- For children who cannot grasp objects to place in one-to-one correspondence, use a wand with a magnet on the end to enable them to pick up objects and place them on pictures or forms on a metal sheet.

COMPUTATIONAL SKILLS: NUMBER CONCEPTS

The development of number concepts begins with understanding one-to-one correspondence and the ability to rote count from the number 1 to, at least, 20. To promote the development of such concepts, teachers and families can give children with visual impairments numerous opportunities throughout the day to count things. They can have them count the number of days in a week, the number of children present in the class, the number of blocks they have put away in the cupboard, and the number of eating utensils required for mealtime. Initially, teachers and family members can count aloud and encourage children to count along. The children need to practice counting alone and together using real objects. If objects for the concept are not available (for example, in counting the number of days that have already passed in the month), teachers or family members can provide an auditory signal, such as clapping, to signify each day.

Activity

- Once the children are able to count using a one-to-one correspondence, have them count aloud a specific number of objects, such as four plates, six bottles of glue, or two chairs. After they have counted the objects, ask them, "How many do you have?"
- Have the children give an adult a specific number of items (such as four books, six blocks, or three sheets of paper).

Critical Points to Cover

- Identify whether the children will use objects, other tangibles, and auditory or tactile cues in the counting activity. (An auditory cue may be clapping to signify a day of the week; a tactile cue may be touching a child's hand once for each day or for each object being counted.)
- When counting objects, have the children count using a systematic pattern, such as a left-to-right or from top to bottom progressions.
- When counting objects, make sure the children are tactilely manipulating a different object as they count and not the same object over and over again.
- Ask the children how many of the objects they have.

Helpful Hints

- In the beginning of teaching the concept of numbers, make sure that the objects chosen are the same size, shape, and texture.
- Monitor the children carefully, so they do not double or triple count the same object or miss or skip objects.
- Provide a starting and stopping place for counting (for example, move the glue bottles from the shelf to the table or count large objects, like chairs, using a left-to-right progression).
- Extend this activity to introduce comparisons, such as more, less, fewer, and greater, by counting out a smaller or larger number of objects and asking the children, "Who has more?" or "Who has less?"

Evaluation Tips

- Create tactile or enlarged worksheets that require the children to mark a specific number of items with crayons, pushpins, or stickers.
- Ask the children to get a sufficient number of supplies (such as scissors, paper, and glue bottles) for a small group of children.
- Record notes on the children's accuracy in counting aloud a specific number of objects.

For Children Who Need Additional Modifications

- For children who use wheelchairs or walkers, provide collections of small objects to carry in a hanging bag or waist pack, so they can examine and compare sets of objects when they are not busy. For children who throw or drop small objects frequently, enclose the objects in a mesh or net bag, so they can manipulate them and perceive numbers of objects without losing the materials.

INDEPENDENT PROBLEM SOLVING

Like other children, young children with visual impairments need to make observations about their environment to make discoveries and draw conclusions. Problem solving involves divergent thinking (that is, moving or extending a thought in different directions) and developing more than one possible solution to emerging problems. For example, if children cannot get glue to come out of a bottle, they can get another glue bottle, ask for help, borrow a classmate's bottle, or use adhesive tape or a stapler. Restricted sensory input resulting from impaired vision may limit the children's ability to learn about available options and may encourage them to rely on one solution or on another person. Although it is natural to want to protect children from making mistakes or from encountering difficulties, children learn from trying solutions to problems and from having opportunities to try again when their solutions do not work. Family members and teachers need to encourage young visually impaired children to take appropriate risks and to support their learning from making mistakes.

It is important for families and teachers to encourage children to develop their own solutions to minor dilemmas in activities that they have already mastered and within clearly established routines. The familiarity of the activities and routines will give the children the supporting framework and self-confidence to take risks and try different solutions. For example, during mealtime, families can provide an insufficient number of utensils for the people who are eating, so children will have to determine whether to substitute a spoon for a fork or a plate for a bowl or whether to wash the dirty forks and bowls. Initially, the children may be unaware of the options available to them and will require assistance from an adult in the form either of an indirect prompt, such as "I wonder what else we could use to eat with?," or a direct prompt, such as "Can we use a fork?"

Another way teachers or families can facilitate the development of problem-solving skills is to create obstacles within established routines. For example, when the children are returning to the classroom from recess or lunch, teachers can lock or block the door that is normally used to enter the room. They can then observe the children and note their reactions. After making several attempts to turn the doorknob, do the children move toward another door? Teachers may need to make the children aware of this option. Teachers can create a sound, such as turning the doorknob of the unlocked door, or have another child or adult enter or exit the open door. If these auditory prompts are unsuccessful, then teachers can provide an indirect or direct verbal prompt, such as "Is there another way to get into the room?" or "Have you tried the other door?"

Activities

- Have the children develop their own solutions to minor problems by providing an insufficient amount of material for a group of children (for example, having only five pencils for six children).
- Have the children overcome obstacles within established routines, for example, by having an empty tube of toothpaste or by not having a bar of soap available when it is time to brush their teeth or wash their hands.
- Have the children verbalize all the options or choices that they think are available for solving a problem.

Critical Points to Cover

- Select activities that the children have already mastered, such as opening a door or walking to the attendance office.

- Change only one aspect of the activity, for example, do not take away soap and provide an empty tube of toothpaste at the same time.
- Reinforce the children's problem-solving efforts, regardless of the outcomes.

Helpful Hints

- Identify specific places in familiar routines to introduce opportunities for solving problems. For instance, if children routinely enter the classroom through a specific door or walk down a particular passageway, then these would be ideal places in which to set up problem-solving scenarios. Placing a trash can in the passageway to block it would provide an obstacle that children would have to overcome. Another example may be removing toothpaste and soap from a routine, if the teacher ordinarily provides them for the children, to see how the children respond.
- Consider the children's abilities and temperaments in "creating" problems; do not make the problems too difficult and frustrating for the children.
- Begin with "easy" problems, so the children will experience success and be motivated to try solving future problems.
- Give the children ample time to be creative and develop alternatives.
- At first, make the choices for solutions obvious either by placing them in close proximity to the children (for example, moving spoons within the children's immediate reach) or by providing indirect or direct verbal prompts.

Evaluation Tips

- Repeat a problem if the children required assistance initially, noting whether they were able to generalize the solution to other situations.
- Ask the children to describe what they did and the outcome of their actions.
- Ask the children, after the problem has been resolved, "What else could you have done?"

FROM AN URBAN PERSPECTIVE

Although more children with visual impairments live in urban than in rural areas, their number is still small in comparison to their sighted classmates and those with other disabilities. The greatest advantage for visually impaired preschoolers of living in urban areas is likely to be the availability of professional and interdisciplinary services and community-based supports, such as parent groups. However, a great disadvantage may be the absence of close-knit communities or extended family members.

Because of the frequent accessibility of services in urban areas, families can enroll their children with visual impairments in early childhood intervention programs that are center based and can participate in outreach programs in which teachers and therapists come to their homes to provide specific services to the children. In addition, people, resources (organizations and agency services), and materials (such as books, videotapes, adapted toys, and educational materials) are more likely to be readily accessible in urban areas, where public transportation is frequent and widespread. Through these resources, families can learn appropriate ways to help their young children with visual impairments develop and can observe other children with similar impairments and discuss the children's developmental milestones and alternative techniques for teaching the children with teachers and caregivers.

Children in urban areas may not have some of the concrete, direct learning experiences that are more readily available in rural environments, such as visiting farms to explore animals and crops growing in their natural environments. Thus, they may need to be taken on field trips to rural areas to gain these experiences. Visits to zoos, community gardens, and farmers' markets are viable alternatives for visually impaired children who are unable to travel to rural areas but would like to learn firsthand about animals, fruits, and vegetables. Since a major task in career education during the preschool years is to encourage visually impaired children to explore and learn about the environment, these kinds of hands-on learning experiences are essential to their early development.

Victoria Tripodi

For Children Who Need Additional Modifications

- When the children's adaptive equipment needs to be fixed, make them aware of what is not working properly and, when appropriate, arrange for them to be present while the equipment is being repaired. For example, if a screw has fallen out of eyeglasses or the seatbelt on a wheelchair needs to be replaced, show the children how the equipment is repaired. When possible, provide choices about replacement parts or aesthetic features of the equipment.

O&M: EXPLORATION OF THE ENVIRONMENT

O&M for young visually impaired children is designed to increase the children's orientation to their surroundings, both at home and in school, and the children's ability to move freely and safely in and explore the environment. These skills should be infused within the children's daily routines and throughout various settings. Teachers and families need to collaborate with the children's O&M instructors to identify when, where, and how specific O&M techniques should be used by particular children.

When working with an individual child, it is helpful for a family member or a teacher to support the child's exploration of the indoor environment. In a familiar environment that is stable (that is, free of moving objects and people) and free of clutter, a teacher or family member may place a favorite sound-producing toy or object (such as a ticking clock, a radio, or a squeaky monkey) near the child to observe his or her reactions: Does the child move toward the toy or attempt to retrieve it? When playing a game of hide-and-seek with a toy, the teacher or family member can ask the child to find it. Initially, the teacher or family member can place the object out in the open, close to the child. As the child locates and retrieves the toy, the teacher or family member can strategically move it farther away and can partially or completely hide it behind furniture, such as a bookcase or sofa. If the child has difficulty locating the toy, the teacher or family member can provide additional cues. For example, he or she may ask, "Is the sound getting louder or softer as you walk toward the sofa?" or "Have you looked over by the sofa?" While motivating the child to move in and explore the environment, the family member or teacher can also help the child understand his or her surroundings. As the child explores the environment tactilely, the teacher or family member can verbally mediate his or her experience by describing the objects he or she encounters, for example, by saying, "That's the rocking chair. It's made of brown corduroy. It's old but comfortable." If the child provides communicative utterances, the teacher or family member needs to be sure to acknowledge, repeat, and expand them. For example, when the child locates the big chair and says, "chair," the adult should reply, "Yes, that's the rocking chair. Isn't it soft and comfortable?"

Activities

- Have the children engage in a game of hide-and-seek in which they need to locate objects in an enclosed area.
- Have the children answer questions to encourage exploration by saying, for instance, "Have you looked behind you? To your right?"
- Have the children pair up with sighted children who can play the game of finding objects.

Critical Points to Cover

- Select an environment that is familiar to the children and that is static.
- Ensure initial success by placing toys or objects out in the open near the children.
- Facilitate exploration of the environment by verbally mediating the children's movement through space and support the children's behaviors and communicative utterances.
- Reinforce the children for their efforts, regardless of the outcome.

Helpful Hints

- Consult with the O&M instructor about specific techniques that the children should be encouraged to use, for example, searching techniques, trailing, body protection, and cane use. (For more information on these techniques, see *The Art and Science of Teaching Orientation and Mobility to Persons with Visual Impairments* [Jacobson, 1993].) Analyze the preschool environment for realistic travel routes (such as from the bus stop to the classroom, from the classroom to the bathroom, and from the classroom to the cafeteria).
- Use toys or objects in the hide-and-seek game that are interesting and motivating to the children.
- Support (with tactile and verbal prompts) the children at the level necessary to keep them interested and engaged in the activity.
- Provide stability and structure in the environment by storing toys in the same place and keeping the furniture in expected

locations. When changes to the environment are made naturally (for example, during new learning activities), have the children participate in making changes.

- Designate a specific place in the home or in the classroom as a
safe area to move or play in by using an area rug or a piece of
linoleum.

- When the children use O&M techniques, give them positive reinforcement about how well they are performing the techniques.

Evaluation Tips

- Ask the children to describe where they found the toy and what
objects they encountered while searching for it.

- Ask the children to describe the physical layout of the area
selected for exploration.

- Ask the O&M instructor about the children's progress in acquiring
orientation skills, such as sound localization or the use of landmarks.

- Ask family members about the children's ability to get around
at home and in other settings.

For Children Who Need Additional Modifications

- For children with physical disabilities, provide opportunities to
move to and from objects. Encourage them to talk about how
an object sounds or looks as they move farther away from it.
For example, place objects at an appropriate height for children
to reach by rolling, crawling, wheeling a wheelchair, or requesting to be moved by another person. Children can be encouraged to comment by brief statements by others regarding the
object approached: "Look how big the ball is! We're getting
close to it now."

- Give children with physical disabilities ways to control how they
are moved; for example, make it their job to say "now" or to tap
the family member's arm when they are ready to be lifted and
let them decide when they want to be moved faster or slower
in the wheelchair.

- Use object and picture cues (see Chapter 3) to remind children
who do not have language of their destination when they are
traveling over a long route. For example, if the children are

going to the playground, give or show them a picture of the swings or a swatch of rough cloth that is similar to the seat on the swings.

- Identify a landmark that can be shown to the children when they enter a new room of their homes or a new area of the school that will help them understand where they are going. If necessary, affix an object to the wall or doorway, such as a piece of a fluffy blanket to a bedroom door, that will serve as a reminder.

- For children who need to be moved from place to place, find ways to offer them choices, for example, by asking, "Who do you want to go with you? Do you want to carry your tape recorder or your fuzzy blanket with you?"

References

Anderson, S., Boigon, S., & Davis, K. (1991). *The Oregon Project for Visually Impaired and Blind Preschool Children* (5th ed., rev.). Medford, OR: Jackson Educational Service District.

Barraga, N. C. (1976). *Visual handicaps and learning: A developmental approach.* Belmont, CA: Wadsworth.

Boehm, A. E. (1971). *Boehm Test of Basic Concepts: Test manual.* New York: Psychological Corp.

Carle, E. (1986). *The very hungry caterpillar.* New York: Putnam.

Craig, C. J. (1996). Family support of the emergent literacy of children with visual impairments. *Journal of Visual Impairment & Blindness, 90,* 194–200.

Jacobson, W. H. (1993). *The art and science of teaching orientation and mobility to persons with visual impairments.* New York: AFB Press.

Lamb, G. (1996). Beginning braille: A whole language-based strategy. *Journal of Visual Impairment & Blindness, 90*(3), 184–189.

Martin, B. (1992). *Brown bear, brown bear, what do you see?* New York: Henry Holt.

Stratton, J. M., & Wright, S. (1991). On the way to literacy: Early experiences for visually impaired children. *RE:view, 23*(2), 55–61.

6

Promoting Opportunities to Work

Deborah Chen and Jamie Dote-Kwan

To become aware of the nature of work and the kinds of work people do, children need to learn what work is. They can learn about work and work responsibilities by doing household and school-centered chores. A variety of activities to promote the awareness of work and opportunities to work and suggestions for implementing them are discussed in this chapter. These activities introduce children with visual impairments to the breadth of jobs available in the community. Children learn about many of these real jobs through make-believe or role-playing.

One goal of a career education curriculum is to prepare children and youths for work as adults. This chapter demonstrates clearly how early these activities can and need to be introduced. By establishing early in children's lives the notion that they can work and are expected to work, teachers and family members can enhance the likelihood that children will become self-supporting adults as these expectations become their own.

LEARNING ABOUT WORK

Young children are introduced to the concept of work and the roles that people play through observation and participation in their families, schools, and communities. Preschool teachers usually introduce children to the concept of work-related responsibilities by assigning them classroom jobs, discussing the various jobs of family members, and teaching them about community workers. Some classroom responsibilities, such as putting toys away after playing with them, should involve all the children. Others (such as taking attendance sheets to an administrative office or passing out snacks) may be assigned to individual children on a rotation basis. Creative and pretend-play experiences will help visually impaired children develop an understanding of the roles and responsibilities of family members and community workers. Different roles and responsibilities can be learned through such games as playing with dolls and playing at household chores. However, teachers need to be sensitive to the family's attitudes toward the traditional work-related roles for men and women. For example, family members who view cooking and feeding babies as female responsibilities will not approve of their young sons pretending to do these chores. Thus, it is important to discuss the family's values, traditions, and customs with the family members (Lynch & Hanson, 1992) and explain the purpose of the imaginative-play and dress-up activities, discuss any concerns the family members may have, and seek solutions that will support family members' promotion of their children's development.

Preschoolers can develop an understanding of work (both paid and unpaid jobs) as it relates to the various jobs of family members. They can begin to understand that each person has a responsibility to contribute to the welfare of his or her family and community. In addition, they can develop an awareness of the roles of workers in the community, the various duties of adults in the preschool, and the contributions that children can make to their families and preschool.

Activities

- Ask children to list the jobs of family members, both children and adults.
- Have children describe the jobs performed by people at the preschool, both children and adults.
- Ask children to identify jobs that are carried out by community workers they know about.
- Ask children what jobs they would like to have when they grow up.

FROM A FAMILY PERSPECTIVE

Learning About Work

Whether they are helping someone else or managing an independent task, children learn what work truly consists of in the family, as well as outside the home. Doing their own chores helps them to become participating family members and discover what they are capable of doing. All children, regardless of their disabilities, need to learn about and expand their abilities. When their siblings see that visually impaired children can and need to contribute to the family, then any rivalry, jealousy, and feelings about special status frequently decrease, and self-esteem increases.

When possible, allow children who are visually impaired to explore the products of their work with questions or through direct tactile experience. Since the children's experience of the world reaches just to the end of their arms, parents have to find ways to get the world closer to them.

Kevin O'Connor

Critical Points to Cover

- Introduce the concept that everyone in a family has a job and ask the children, "What jobs does your mother have? What jobs does your father have?"
- Ask children what kinds of jobs they have.
- Discuss the preschool program and the work of all participants with the children, by asking them, "What are the teachers' jobs? What are the children's jobs?"
- Explain the various tools that different people use in their jobs.
- Encourage the children to brainstorm all job possibilities on the basis of their experiences in their families and at school.
- Discuss field trips to community sites and the jobs of community workers. (See Chapter 3 for a discussion on visits to community sites and workers.)
- Identify reasons for all people to work and contribute to their families and communities.
- Ask children to discuss what would happen if people did not do their jobs.
- Have the children talk about the jobs they like and dislike.
- Ask the children what they want to do when they grow up.

Helpful Hints

- Develop a plan for learning about work that is developmentally appropriate for the age group. The plan needs to be based on the program's philosophy, state guidelines, family priorities, and the ages and experiences of the children. Questions and discussions about jobs with 3 year olds will be simpler than those with 4- and 5 year olds. For example, "What do you do after you finish riding the tricycles?" is a simpler question than "What do you do at home for your allowance?"
- Develop a tangible job chart for different children to have designated jobs each day; for instance, wiping the table after a snack can be represented by a sponge. Jobs can be rotated and the children's name cards can be written in large print and braille, so all children have an opportunity to identify their own names and to recognize others'.
- Develop lists with pictures and tangible objects on the basis of the children's brainstorming about the various jobs of different people. For example, pictures and objects used to discuss the work of a nurse or a custodian may include various equipment, such as a thermometer, bandages, a hammer, or a ladder.

Evaluation Tips

- Record children's responses to questions and discussions related to the topic of jobs.
- Ask family members whether the children ask questions or comment about work and jobs.
- Assist the children in developing stories about preferred jobs or what they would like to do as adults.

For Children Who Need Additional Modifications

- Reinforce the idea that some parts of activities are not always fun but need to be done regardless of appeal; these are called work. Other activities are meant to be fun and are chosen as activities for leisure or recreation; these are called play. Schedule activities in which something fun usually follows something unpleasant or difficult. Find ways to let the children know that adults enjoy some tasks and do not enjoy others. When daily activities or schedules are reviewed, talk about which times are work times and which are play times.

LEARNING FROM ROLE MODELS

Young children should be exposed to a variety of role models to develop their dreams and aspirations about careers, jobs, and adult life. Their parents and other family members serve as primary role models. Young children with visual impairments also need to meet and learn about others with visual impairments—workers in the community and elementary and high school students who are leading productive and satisfying lives to develop high expectations for themselves. Similarly, it is important for families of young children with visual impairments to interact with these role models not only to learn about what they do, but to help develop their children's expectations.

Articulate visually impaired elementary and high school students who are willing to talk about their preferences, abilities, interests, jobs, and responsibilities can share their hobbies, knowledge of technology, and related areas of interest; talk about their visual impairments and helpful strategies for overcoming difficulties; and answer questions. Young visually impaired children also need to meet visually impaired adults who work in a variety of community jobs, particularly those whom the children are likely to encounter, such as teachers and office workers. Teachers and family members need to integrate visits with these community workers into community-involvement activities.

Activities

- Have the preschoolers name older children with visual impairments who may be considered role models.
- Have the selected role models discuss with the preschoolers the types of information and activities that are developmentally appropriate for preschoolers. The activities need to engage children in hands-on experiences using objects. Information about a selected job needs to appeal to the preschoolers' curiosity. For example, a high school student may talk about his or her dog guide and how he or she gets to a job rather than what he or she does at the community library.

- Obtain props, objects, or equipment and have the children explore them to build an understanding of a person's responsibilities and interests in a particular job. For example, if a mail carrier visits the class, he or she can bring a mail bag or a box used to store mail; a visiting custodian can bring a tool box with various tools that the children could handle.
- Coordinate specific lesson topics and learning objectives with opportunities for the children to interact with role models. For instance, during a meeting of preschoolers and older students, have the older students describe learning braille or using a long cane.

Critical Points to Cover

- Explain what various workers in the community or at school do in their jobs.
- Discuss how the workers travel to their jobs.
- Explain whether the workers read regular print using low vision devices, read large print, or use braille.
- Describe the tools that various workers use in their jobs.
- Review the types of special equipment that can be used in different jobs; for example, a visually impaired office worker may use a computer that talks.
- Discuss the use of a long cane or a dog guide by workers.
- Encourage the children to ask questions about the workers who are discussed in class.

Helpful Hints

- Identify active and articulate elementary and high school students who are interested in interacting with the preschoolers and discuss how they can assist the children in developing aspirations for the future. Itinerant teachers who serve visually impaired students are an important source for identifying role models.
- Involve family members in these opportunities to interact with their children's role models to increase not only their expectations of the children but their children's expectations of themselves.
- Invite the role models to class to talk to all the students. These opportunities will also build high expectations and positive atti-

tudes among sighted children toward their visually impaired classmates.

Evaluation Tips

- Compare the visually impaired children's discussions of their ideas about the future and jobs as adults before and after their interactions with the role models who are visually impaired.
- Compare the families' discussions of their expectations about their children's future before and after interactions with role models who are visually impaired.
- Discuss the sighted children's expectations about future jobs for their classmates with visual impairments.

For Children Who Need Additional Modifications

- Find workers in the school environment who will allow students to try their jobs briefly. For example, will the janitor allow the children to help push a mop for a few minutes? Will the gardener allow the children to help plant a flower? Try to arrange more than one visit with each person, so the children can observe work routines. For instance, the janitor has to mop the hallway every Monday, not just once; the gardener has to water the flowers frequently after they have been planted.
- After visits to workers, help children recall each job and associate it with the correct person. For children who hear, audiotape the voices of workers saying "hello" and then match the voices with the objects or tools that the workers use.
- Find adults who have disabilities that are similar to the children's and arrange for the children to visit them. Talk about whether these adults do their jobs differently from others. For example, is an adult's desk at a different height because of a wheelchair? Does the adult use a sign language interpreter when he or she goes to meetings?

HELPING AT HOME

Participating in chores or having a job at home and in the preschool are important responsibilities for young children to learn. These experiences help preschoolers develop an awareness of the various roles and responsibilities of each individual in their families and in the preschool. Two- and 3 year olds should be able to perform simple home tasks (such as putting toys, clothing, and personal belongings away; feeding pets; or putting dirty clothes in a hamper) with minimal assistance from adults (Loumiet & Levack, 1993). Four- and 5 year olds can help empty small wastebaskets into larger receptacles; wipe off tabletops, counters, or other small areas; and tidy up their beds. Teachers can discuss with family members their family's values, the priorities for their children, and the primary roles and responsibilities of family members.

Since families of diverse cultural backgrounds may have different expectations and roles for family members, the recommendations of a preschool program may conflict with some families' values and beliefs. Therefore, it is important to acknowledge the different cultural expectations that families may have regarding the particular roles and jobs of family members and the families' child-rearing practices. For example, in some families, it may not be acceptable for a girl to wear pants or to engage in rough and tumble play. Furthermore, some families may believe that children with visual impairments should not be expected to assume the roles and responsibilities that they demand of their sighted children.

It may be necessary for teachers to work with families who hold different values and beliefs to identify alternative ways of providing essential learning experiences for young children who are visually impaired. Teachers need to remember that the critical characteristics or underlying process of any learning experience are not tied to a single activity. Children can learn about roles and responsibilities in many different ways. What is important is to balance the family's perspectives with professional judgment about individual children's learning needs. To do so effectively, teachers need to gather information about each family's values, concerns, priorities, and practices; convey their professional suggestions sensitively; and collaborate with the family members to support the development of their visually impaired children.

By brainstorming with families, teachers can identify possible jobs in the home (including helping with laundry, picking up leaves, and emptying trash cans) that children can perform with minimal assistance. Family members can begin by selecting one or two jobs that they would expect their children to perform, such as picking up toys and putting dirty clothes in the hamper, and introduce these responsibilities to the children by discussing the importance of having everyone in the family help out. Initially, the children may require verbal and physical prompts to complete these tasks. Once the child's responsibilities for selected jobs are firmly established, family members may need to provide social and tangible reinforcements for completing the tasks, as well as specific consequences for not doing so. For example, if the children do not pick up their toys, families would not allow them to get other toys until they do so.

Activities

- Identify with families the possible household chores that their preschoolers can perform and ask the children what their jobs are at home.
- Ask the children to list their jobs at school.
- Have the children describe the jobs at home and at school that they like or dislike.
- Have families develop a system of consequences for the children that are related to the completion or noncompletion of assigned chores; for example, after the children help clean up after lunch, they can play outdoors.
- Ask the children to explain what happens if they do not perform assigned jobs.

Critical Points to Cover

- Discuss with the children the importance of everyone pitching in and helping around the home.
- Provide specific consequences for the children when they do not do their chores at school, for instance, they will not be able to go outside to play.
- Consistently reinforce children with praise when they complete their jobs or chores.

Helpful Hints

- Interview family members about their expectations for the children's responsibilities in the home.
- Conduct ecological inventories (discussed in Chapter 3) to identify possible jobs and chores in the home and in the

preschool classroom. After these chores have been determined, give each child a job board that lists his or her jobs in an accessible and understandable format, such as pictures of some aspect of the task or labels in braille or large print.

- In the preschool classroom, young children can perform a variety of jobs with minimal assistance from the teacher. These jobs include erasing the chalkboard, watering the plants, emptying the trash, putting up and taking down chairs, or being flag or attendance monitors.
- Develop a tangible job chart for different children to have specific jobs each day; for example, the job of getting the snack can be represented by a cup. Jobs can be rotated and the children's name cards can be written in large print and braille, so all the children have an opportunity to identify their own names and to recognize others'.

Evaluation Tips

- Observe whether the children initiate their chores without needing verbal reminders.
- Note whether the children attempt to examine their job boards without prompting.
- Observe and record whether the children complete their chores independently or require verbal reminders or physical assistance to complete them.

For Children Who Need Additional Modifications

- Find ways to break tasks down into small steps and to identify the steps that children with severe disabilities can perform. These tasks may simply involve carrying or holding objects (for example, on a wheelchair tray) or dropping objects (for instance, into a wastebasket, hamper, or "finished" box), or they may be more complex; in either case, emphasize the children's role in participating in the job.
- For children with physical disabilities, consider jobs that they can do in different positions; for example, washing dishes on a prone stander, which supports them while leaning against a specially designed inclined board; using a crumb catcher to clean

the rug while lying on the side; or wiping a table while kneel-ing or being propped up against the back of a chair.

- Use objects and pictures to help the children understand jobs that need to be done; for example, a picture of socks or pants or a piece of fabric similar to the clothing item attached to a draw-er can help remind the children where these things are stored when they are getting dressed.
- At the start of a job that involves materials or objects, place all the materials in a row from left to right or in a slotted box, so the children understand the order in which the steps of the task should be done.

EARNING AN ALLOWANCE

In the world of work, people are paid for performing assigned jobs. Earning an allowance is a natural way for young children to experi-ence the relationship between performing as expected and receiving compensation for particular chores. Families may have different expec-tations and requirements for giving their children allowances. Some may not be able to afford to give their young children allowances. Oth-ers may not believe that children should be given a certain amount of money at regular intervals. Still others may believe that children should receive a regular allowance without having any particular chore-relat-ed responsibilities. Some families may want children to earn their allowances by completing all the designated tasks. Some may require their children to save a portion of the allowance, whereas others may believe that the total amount is the children's to spend. If a family has an allowance system for the visually impaired child or is willing to establish one, teachers need to obtain information about the family members' expectations of the child's responsibilities. It is helpful for a teacher to explain to the family the benefits of having the child active-ly experience the relationship between completing assigned jobs and getting paid for them. These experiences will foster the child's devel-opment of high expectations of himself or herself, a positive self-iden-tity, and a sense of responsibility.

Four- and 5 year olds can learn the value of working or perform-ing an assigned job for monetary compensation. This experience allows them to develop a sense of pride in accomplishments and may help eliminate the need for them to be nagged about their assigned jobs and responsibilities. One way in which children can receive special compensation is by receiving a modest sum of money for the jobs they perform at home when these jobs are in addition to those involving their own personal belongings. For example, they would not get paid for picking up their toys, making their beds, or putting their dirty clothes in the hamper, but they would be paid for jobs that contribute to their entire families' welfare, such as feeding a pet, setting the table, emptying small trash cans from bathrooms and bedrooms, and picking up the leaves in the yard. Families can discuss the concept of earning an allowance with their visually impaired children and identify jobs that the children would be willing to do to earn an allowance. The amount of money they pay to the children will vary according to the families' economic level. One possible arrangement is to have a 4 year old receive a modest allowance of from 50 cents to one dollar per week for performing two or three jobs regularly.

Activities

- If families are willing and comfortable with the concept, ask them to list specific responsibilities that their preschoolers have for self-care.
- Ask families to select jobs that will allow their preschoolers to earn an allowance.
- Collaborate with the family members to develop a plan for how and when the allowance will be paid to the children and how the allowance may be spent.
- Ask children to list the jobs for which they receive an allowance.
- Have the children explain the rules related to earning their allowance.
- Ask children how much money they receive as an allowance and how they spend it.

Critical Points to Cover

- Observe the children in their preschool classrooms and have the family members observe the children performing home routines to identify jobs that the children can accomplish with minimal assistance.

- Discuss with the families and children the concept of getting paid for doing a job or chores.
- Ask families to involve the children in family discussions to identify the jobs the children would like to do to earn their allowance.
- Ask families to involve the children in family discussions regarding how and when the children may spend their allowance.
- Help the children and family members decide on the consequences (earning no allowance) of not performing the jobs.
- Assist family members and children in establishing a clear agreement about the expectations and rules of earning the allowance.

Helpful Hints

- Assist the family in developing tangible job charts for the children's assigned jobs for each day of the week. Use an object to identify the job for the day, for instance, a sponge to indicate wiping off the table or a piece of rabbit food to represent feeding the pet rabbit.
- Suggest that families establish a consistent pay day, for example, every Saturday or Sunday, for giving the children their allowance.
- Discuss the need to help the children to put their allowance in an appropriate place, such as a wallet, coin purse, or piggy bank.
- Discuss with the children the need to help them identify how and when they may want to use the money. For example, discuss the benefits of saving to buy a desired toy versus buying a candy bar immediately.

Evaluation Tips

- Ask family members about the children's expected behaviors for earning an allowance and help them develop the following strategies:
  1. Observe whether the children anticipate the jobs for that day.
  2. Observe whether the children check their job charts on a daily or regular basis.
  3. Observe and make notes on whether the children complete their jobs for the week without needing verbal reminders.

For Children Who Need Additional Modifications

- For children who do not yet understand or value money, give basic rewards right after they complete their tasks. These rewards may include experiences like taking a walk or playing with a favorite toy, or tangibles, such as a snack or a drink. As soon as the children perform the tasks regularly for these rewards, substitute abstract representations and delay presenting the rewards. For example, place a picture of a favorite toy on the calendar at the end of the day and tell the child that he or she will get to play with it then.

- For children who respond well to a token system, which uses small symbols such as pennies or chips to be saved for a reward, pennies can be used as tokens as long as they will not put them into their mouths. Even though they may not understand the value of money, the children can learn to understand how money is used by receiving pennies for some tasks or responsibilities.

- For children with physical disabilities, devise banks in which to store money that they can use themselves. Transparent plastic containers work well as banks because the openings in the lids can be cut as large as the children need them to be, and a child with vision can see the money after it has fallen into the containers.

References

Loumiet, R., & Levack, N. (1993). *Independent living: A curriculum with adaptations for students with visual impairments: Vol. 1. Social competence* (2nd ed.). Austin: Texas School for the Blind and Visually Impaired.

Lynch, E. W., & Hanson, M. J. (1992). *Developing cross-cultural competence: A guide for working with young children and their families* (2nd ed.). Baltimore: Paul H. Brookes.

CHAPTER

Providing Realistic Feedback

Jamie Dote-Kwan and Deborah Chen

Career education for young children involves the development of work habits (such as learning to follow instructions, daily schedules, and classroom routines and learning to assume responsibilities for oneself and one's belongings) and the development of work skills (such as sorting, matching, and putting things together). Activities in these areas give preschoolers with visual impairments opportunities to acquire knowledge of appropriate job-related behaviors and skills. In addition, these activities offer opportunities for them to receive realistic feedback concerning their performance within meaningful contexts.

The activities in this chapter are designed to encourage realistic feedback about preschoolers' performance. Feedback of this kind can teach children important lessons and ultimately help them become more responsible and independent. It is important for visually impaired children to know and follow the same class rules as their sighted classmates, so they and others develop a sense that they can perform as well as anyone else. The children need to know the consequences of misbehaving in school or during community activities and how their work compares to their classmates' work and to their own previous efforts. They can benefit from learning strategies to monitor their own progress in school, at home, and in the community. To promote the communication of realistic feedback, the activities in this chapter encourage the use of alternative techniques and auditory or tactile cues for monitoring progress. These techniques help the children control changes in their behavior and be aware of the acquisition of skills. By introducing children to normative standards, teachers, parents, and other family members establish a framework for children to work within and to develop at rates commensurate with their sighted classmates.

DEVELOPMENT OF WORK HABITS: FOLLOWING CLASSROOM AND SCHOOL RULES

Showing pride in accomplishing tasks, demonstrating a willingness to try new things, and requesting assistance with a problem are work-related behaviors that 2- and 3 year olds can begin to demonstrate. Four- and 5 year olds can follow simple classroom and school rules and routines, keep materials organized in assigned areas, seek assistance appropriately when faced with a problem, and initiate and complete school assignments with minimal help (Loumiet & Levack, 1993). These skills lay an important foundation for the development of job-related skills.

Some people—with or without disabilities—cannot obtain or keep jobs because they lack appropriate job-related social skills (Kokaska & Brolin, 1985), such as punctuality or working cooperatively with others. The development of positive attitudes toward work in general and toward goal-oriented work habits in particular is difficult to influence by direct instruction, but can be promoted through the establishment of a classroom that is oriented toward achievement.

Preschool teachers can establish classroom rules by discussing with the children the need for certain rules to ensure the safety of all children and promote opportunities for everyone to learn, for example, by saying to the children, "Listening to others prevents people from interrupting one another and lets us hear things that are important, like today we'll have a visitor." They can also allow the children to participate in creating the classroom rules, so the children establish a sense of ownership of and commitment to them. Rules should be simply stated in positive terms and should tell the children what to do, for example, "Keep your hands to yourself" and "Listen to others," rather than "No hitting" or "No talking." In addition, it is necessary to create situations in which the children can model the appropriate behaviors to one another.

It is important to reinforce the rules consistently, praising the children for complying with the rules and reminding them firmly when they fail to comply. Once the rules are firmly established, it is necessary not only to continue to encourage children for complying with the rules, but to provide consistent and specific consequences for the children who fail to comply. For example, if a child runs in the room and the rule is to walk, have the child go back outside and walk into the classroom; if a child hits another child, ask the child to apologize and sit quietly for a few minutes. Teachers also need to seek the support of parents by making them fully aware of the school rules and disciplinary procedures.

Activities

- Have the children participate in establishing a short list of three to seven rules that are developmentally appropriate. For example, saying, "listen to others" is more appropriate for younger children to understand than saying "be polite." Similarly, saying "keep hands to yourselves" is easier for preschoolers to comprehend than saying "be respectful of others' property."
- Have children review and discuss the purpose of the rules.
- Ask children to remind one another about the rules, when necessary.
- Have children discuss a problem and identify possible solutions, for example, "What could we do if two children want to ride the same tricycle?"
- Have children role-play situations to practice expected classroom behaviors.

Critical Points to Cover

- Discuss with the children the need for rules. Ask them, "What would happen if everyone spoke at the same time?" and "What could happen if we all ran into the classroom instead of walking?"
- Discuss with the children the rewards and consequences for either following or failing to follow the rules.
- Provide consistent and positive verbal reinforcement when children comply with the rules.

- Provide specific consequences, such as quiet time or apologizing, for children who fail to comply with the rules.

Helpful Hints

- Provide class rules for the children in accessible and understandable formats, such as photographs, pictures, braille, or large print.
- Inform all adults (such as paraprofessionals and parent volunteers) who are working in the classroom of the rules as well as rewards and consequences of following the rules.
- Inform the children's families of the rules and rewards and consequences of following the rules.

Evaluation Tips

- Note whether the children are following the rules and are reminding one another of them.
- Observe and take notes on whether children follow the rules independently or require verbal or tactile reminders.

For Children Who Need Additional Modifications

- If there are exceptions to the rules because of a child's disability, talk with the rest of the class about the reasons for the exception. For example, in a class of nondisabled children, a child with severe disabilities may make sounds during work time when the other children are expected to be quiet. The other children need to understand that the child with disabilities is learning to communicate with his or her voice, but that they already know this skill and are learning when *not* to use their voices.
- If nonverbal children break a rule or behave inappropriately, they should be helped to behave in the proper manner, according to the rule, and then praised for it. This approach makes it more likely that the children will follow the rules in the future and minimize the risk that they will remember only a reprimand or the experience of being told no. Children with communication difficulties may behave inappropriately because they do not understand the rules or what behavior is expected of them.

DEVELOPMENT OF WORK HABITS: FOLLOWING DAILY SCHEDULES AND ROUTINES

For all young children, following a classroom schedule or routine requires that they remember to do a task, to perform the task efficiently and correctly, to complete the task independently, and to move from one activity to the next. The daily routine of the preschool classroom provides numerous opportunities for children with visual impairments to practice making the transition from one activity to another and completing tasks independently. It is essential for teachers to establish a schedule of activities in the classroom.

After teachers have established a schedule of activities, they need to develop predictable routines for completing those activities. These routines should include a clear beginning or introductory step or steps, a series of sequenced steps, and an ending or culminating step or steps. It is important for teachers to use consistent language and gestures to prepare the children for the beginning and end of an activity and to involve them in preparing or gathering materials and cleaning up (Chen, 1995). Teachers can conduct a routine analysis to make it easier for them to establish the steps in the routine, as well as the expected teacher and child behaviors. (For a sample routine analysis, see the appendix in Chapter 3.) For example, the steps in the routine for snack time may include the following:

1. The teacher announces it is snack time (introduction).
2. The children wash their hands.
3. The children sit down at the table.
4. The teacher announces the choices for the snack.
5. A child passes out a napkin to everyone.
6. Another child passes out a cup to everyone.
7. The children say or point to the items they want.
8. The teacher acknowledges and assists the children, when necessary.
9. The children eat their snacks.
10. The teacher announces that snack time is over.
11. The children clean up their snack area.
12. The children get up from the table and throw their trash away (conclusion).

Activities

- Provide a consistent, predictable class schedule for the children to follow.
- Have the children help prepare or gather materials for activities and clean up after the activities.

Critical Points to Cover

- Introduce the sequence of activities at the beginning of each day.
- Introduce the sequence of tasks at the beginning of each activity if the tasks vary from day to day; for example, art periods may include coloring, painting, or playing with Play Doh.
- Give the children ample time to complete the activity.
- Give the children ample warning before moving to the next activity, by saying, for example, "You have five more minutes before we need to clean up and go to lunch." Such warnings help the children make the transition from one activity to another. Use a bell or timer to signal the amount of time left to complete the activity.

Helpful Hints

- Provide a class schedule for the children in accessible and understandable formats, such as photographs, pictures, tangible objects, or tactile symbols.
- Develop predictable routines for storing belongings when the children arrive at school and for gathering their belongings and putting them and their "work" in backpacks or bags to take home.
- Expand this activity to weekly schedules. The Classroom Calendar Kit and Individual Calendar Kit, which are available from the American Printing House for the Blind (see the Resource section at the end of this book), are large visual and tactile calendars that depict one month at a time.

Evaluation Tips

- When making the transition from one activity to another, the children need to know where they should be and what they should be doing. For example, after recess, ask the child, "What do we do after recess?" or "Where do we go?"

- Observe whether the children anticipate the daily schedule and initiate any behaviors that indicate that they know the next activity, for example, if the children wash their hands after recess in anticipation of having snacks.
- Observe and record whether the children require verbal, gestural, or physical prompts to move to the next activity.

For Children Who Need Additional Modifications

- Maintain a consistent routine and find ways to help the children anticipate what will happen during the day, such as by giving them a picture calendar or an object calendar box (see Chapter 3). For children with short memory spans, begin by helping them associate a tangible object with an activity and keeping that object with them during the activity to reinforce the association of the object with the event. For example, if a child always wears a cap to go outdoors, the cap can be given to him or her when preparation begins, so the child understands that he or she will be going out. Later the button from the cap can be placed in a sequence of objects that stands for the order of the day's activities to represent the time of day when the child will go outdoors.
- Use a consistent signal to let the children know when they will be moving to a new activity. Consider each child's abilities and disabilities in creating this signal; for a hearing-impaired child with low vision, showing a picture of the next activity may be appropriate, whereas for a blind child, a bell on a timer may communicate that a change will take place.
- Emphasize the concepts of past and future in communication activities. When reviewing the daily schedule, refer to events in the past, as well as to those that will occur.
- When the schedule includes an event that is outside the normal routine, prepare the children for the unfamiliar event. The type of preparation will vary, depending on the child; pictures of the event to come may work for some, whereas a brief description or a related object symbol will help others understand. If the event is likely to be frightening or unpleasant (for example, a visit to the dentist), the children may be more responsive if they

have an opportunity to visit the dentist's office, greet the receptionist, and sit in the dental chair before a later visit in which dental work will be performed. Identify a few routines that can be consistently performed both at home and in school and try to ensure that they are carried out each day at the same time (for example, at mealtimes or during a song routine).

- Provide times during daily routines when the children can choose preferred activities. Use objects or pictures to let them know the choices that are available.

DEVELOPMENT OF WORK HABITS: FOLLOWING DIRECTIONS

Preschool provides many opportunities for young children to learn how to follow directions—an ability that is basic to all aspects of living and working in a community. Whether the directions are in verbal or written form, the abilities to attend, comprehend, and implement directions are essential in both academic and work-related endeavors, as well as in activities of daily living. Following written directions on a worksheet, verbal instructions about how and when to play at certain activity centers, and directions to complete an art activity or to operate a Nintendo game are all examples of following instructions. Young children with visual impairments need to be particularly attentive to directions, especially verbal ones, because they may not have sufficient vision to see what their sighted classmates are doing and then follow along themselves. For example, when the teacher tells the children to get their crayons from their desks, the sighted classmates may miss this verbal command, but they can see that the other children are getting out their crayons.

Children should be asked to follow directions for tasks that are clearly within their current repertoire to perform. Teachers and families need to select activities or tasks that are plainly within the daily routine and that the children have consistently performed with minimal or no assistance to ensure success. Children learn to follow directions after they have had experience following simple, one-step commands, such as "James, put the spoon on the table" or "Erin, pick up your doll." Families and teachers need to monitor these one-step commands to ensure

FROM A FAMILY PERSPECTIVE

Development of Work Habits: Following Rules

Doing chores and earning allowances are important to children's feelings of inclusion at home, and so, too, is learning to follow rules and procedures. Try to state the rules in positive terms, so that following them will help children build skills, rather than cause them to rebel and misbehave. For example, instead of "Don't talk!" say "Remember how important it is to listen so we can all watch the movie together." "Don't run in the parking lot" can be rephrased as "Let's walk through the parking lot and see what adventure awaits us."

Experiment with the words and phrases you use. Some psychologists and many parents believe that children do not even hear the word *don't*.

Development of Work Habits: Following Routines and Directions

Sequential routines help give visually impaired children security and predictability. Getting dressed, making a meal, and even resolving conflicts in the family are all worthy patterns to notice and talk about repeatedly. Brainstorming with children and making lists of "How we get dressed" and "How we shop for groceries," for example, eventually make these activities automatic and teach the children basic organizational principles. For instance, by talking as a family about the morning routine in which Mom gets everyone up, makes and serves breakfast, then rushes everyone to get dressed and leave the house; breaking the routine down into its components; and asking such questions as "Why is Mom responsible for waking us all up?" the family can establish more manageable and less stressful routines.

Similarly, make the skill of following directions as natural and enjoyable as you can. Instead of ordering, cajoling, and nagging children to follow directions, make positive statements and involve the children in every step. Cooking, for example, is an activity in which you can subtly teach that following directions is essential for an edible outcome. Try not to fuss over any mess—you and your children can clean it up later! It can be fun to make two or three recipes simultaneously—one that follows the directions exactly, another in which you are more creative, and a third in which you leave out a critical ingredient (such as eggs, butter, or baking soda). Then let the family decide which recipe is which. Keep your sense of humor, enjoy your children for these few teaching moments, and stop when the fun stops. There is always tomorrow. If a power struggle develops, it is best to drop the activity. You will have other opportunities to teach conflict resolution; on this occasion, try to teach your child to follow directions—as long as doing so remains exciting.

Kevin O'Connor

that the children comply with them and are given positive reinforce-ment for their efforts. This consistency will help the children under-stand the importance and rewards associated with following commands. Activities, such as the game Simon Says and the song "Hokey Pokey," can also be used by families and teachers to encourage the following of simple commands. Once the children have mastered the skill of hear-ing a direction and then performing a specific behavior immediately, they can be given directions that expand the time between receiving the direction and performing the task. For example, when teachers or families remind the children at the beginning of an activity to put away their toys or school materials when they are finished, they will require the children to remember the direction until the activity is completed. When a teacher asks the children to go to the office after recess, he or she is requesting a delay in the children's performing a direction.

Activities

- Have the children complete tasks that are easy and motivate them (for example, by telling them, "Sit down for a snack" or "Get your toys").
- Ask the children to comply with frequently used directions that are task related (for example, the directive "Wash your hands").
- Have the children complete common directions that occur in songs and games, such as in "Hokey Pokey" when they are directed to put their right foot in the circle.
- Give the children a direction that involves a time delay in the performance of a task, for example, telling them to wash their hands after recess.

Critical Points to Cover

- Observe the children in their preschool classroom and home routines to identify activities that they can accomplish with minimal assistance.
- Monitor the children's performance and reinforce them with feedback, so there is consistency and follow-through.
- Start by giving the children simple one-step commands (such as "stand up" or "sit down") and then follow them by giving one-

step directions (such as "fold your paper in half") that can be acted upon immediately.

- Reinforce the children's genuine efforts with positive words and actions, regardless of the outcome.

Helpful Hints

- Ask the children to repeat the direction or directions to help them remember the directions and to ensure that they heard the directions correctly.
- Provide the children with pictures or tactile cues, such as a photograph of the school office or the key to the office on a keychain, to remind them of what they are to do.
- Analyze the tasks in an activity and put them in sequential steps when giving the children directions that require multiple responses. (For example, for passing out art supplies, ask the child to go to the cupboard, get the paper, give one sheet to everyone, go back to the cupboard, get the scissors, and give a pair of scissors to everyone.)
- Give the children ample time to complete the requested task.

Evaluation Tips

- Observe whether the children show any hesitation or reluctance to complete a task.
- Observe and make notes on the level of assistance (verbal or physical prompting) the children need to complete a requested task.
- Observe and record the types of directives given (such as one-step or two-step) and length of the directions the children are able to complete.

For Children Who Need Additional Modifications

- After directions or prompts are given for an activity, make sure the children have plenty of time to respond before giving them assistance. Many children with physical and mental disabilities require a longer-than-average time to understand and process directions. If the children still do not respond after the delay, repeat the directions once and then try to provide the instructions in other ways; for example, by demonstration instead of words. Make sure the children are noticed and receive attention when they do follow directions. This approach makes it more likely that they will carry out directions the next time they are given them.

- Find ways for children with physical disabilities to participate in giving directions to their classmates. For example, if the other children are doing acrobatics and a child with disabilities cannot participate, let him or her tell the others what stunts to do. For children who do not use language, try having them choose a card with the name of a stunt or make another choice that will allow their classmates to follow the directions.

DEVELOPMENT OF WORK HABITS: PUTTING AWAY BELONGINGS

The development of organizational skills begins at a young age. Children learn from adults, who model and demonstrate their own organizational skills. For example, children observe people putting away an item in the same place each time immediately after it has been used. Organizing the preschool classroom and locating furniture in consistent places also promote independent access to materials and supplies, such as crayons and papers. Two- and 3 year olds can be expected to pick up toys and return them to a shelf or toy chest independently (Loumiet & Levack, 1993). Four- and 5 year olds should be able to put away toys with multiple pieces (for example, Duplos or blocks) and their personal belongings (such as jackets, lunch boxes, or backpacks), returning them to where they are stored.

To assist children in putting away their toys and belongings teachers and families can give them small baskets or containers for storage. Handles on the baskets enable the children to carry the baskets to a specific play area, pick up Duplos (large Legos), place them in the baskets, and return the baskets to a closet or toy shelf independently. Initially, the children may need assistance in putting away toys or materials in the form of hand–over–hand guidance or turn-taking (alternating between putting one Duplo away and then having another child or adult put the next one away). Teachers and family members can try to make a game of who can put the toys away the fastest. This approach will make the task more enjoyable. The children need to be given positive reinforcement for completing tasks and verbal reminders, if necessary.

Activities

- Have the children pick up toys and return them to the shelf.
- Have the children hang up their jackets.
- Have the children use small baskets or containers for storing toys with multiple pieces.
- Ask the children to put away their lunch boxes when they arrive at school and after lunchtime.

Critical Points to Cover

- Have a consistent routine for putting toys or materials away. For example, when the children enter the classroom, they need to hang up their jackets in the closet, and before they get another toy with which to play, they have to put away the toy they are no longer playing with.
- Provide ample time for the children to clean up or put away their materials or toys. Do not be in a hurry to get to the next activity.
- Initially, reinforce the children for their efforts, regardless of the outcome. For example, if the children put away most of the pieces of a puzzle and miss one or two pieces, say "You did a good job of putting most of the puzzle away. Let me help you with the rest."

Helpful Hints

- Mark shelves and containers with large print, pictures or photographs, braille, or tangible symbols of the toys or objects.
- Provide small metal containers with lids to store crayons, markers, scissors, and tape.
- Within the workspace, present materials in an organized manner. Use trays, boxes, and dividers to define space and to help the children organize their drawers or cupboards.
- Leave materials and belongings (such as clothing, toys, crayons, toothpaste, and toothbrushes) in consistent and easily accessible locations so the children can find and return them independently.
- Emphasize to family members how important organizational skills are for children with visual impairments. Encourage them to involve their children in preparation and cleanup activities at home, when possible.

Evaluation Tips

- Observe whether the children attempt to put away toys and materials independently.
- Observe and record whether the children require verbal or physical prompts to complete tasks or how well they can complete the tasks independently (for instance, whether they put away all the Duplo pieces in their containers and return the containers to the shelf in the closet).
- Ask family members about the children's participation in these types of cleanup activities at home.

For Children Who Need Additional Modifications

- Use a "finished" box or basket to indicate where materials should go when a task is completed. For children who understand gestures or signs, model the "finished" sign each time things are stored to reinforce that this is the end of the task.
- Make sure that storage places are accessible to children who have physical disabilities. For example, a clothes hamper may be a good place to store toys for a mobile child in a wheelchair because it is taller than a toy box and can be easily reached from the wheelchair.

DEVELOPMENT OF WORK SKILLS: SORTING

Basic mechanical skills, such as sorting, putting things together, and taking things apart, which are important for later vocational endeavors, are also essential for many academic activities and daily functional living. For example, finger dexterity and wrist flexibility are essential for braille reading, and the skill of coordinating two hands so they work together (promoted by sorting, stringing beads, and sewing cards) is necessary not only for braille reading but for performing simple everyday activities, such as fastening clothing, removing lids from jars or containers, and using a key to open a door. Teachers and families need to take care in selecting activities to ensure that the children understand the tasks, develop skills, and generalize concepts. For example, the use of pegs or shapes for a sorting activity may not be meaningful or motivating for some children who may benefit from functional activities using actual objects, but others may more easily generalize the concept of shapes to enhance their academic skills.

To develop sorting skills with young children, teachers and families can begin with only one characteristic of an object, such as size, and two elements, such as big and little. Initially, teachers and families need to provide objects that are grossly different, and as the children develop sorting skills, they can be given objects that are similar. For example, for sorting big and little circles, teachers and families can begin by providing 3-inch and 1-inch diameter circles, not 1-inch and 1½-inch diameter circles. They can start the activity by verbally describing the task to the children, by saying, for example, "Today you're going to sort by size. I want you to place all the little circles in that container and all the big circles in this container." Then they can model the behavior and help the children perform the task a few times, perhaps with hand–over–hand guidance, if necessary. If the children seem to understand the task, then teachers and families can have them finish it independently.

After the children can sort big and little circles of various sizes, they can sort different shapes, such as big and little squares, then big and little triangles, and so forth. Because they have focused on the same characteristic of objects (such as size) and then on a variety of types of objects, they can generalize this concept beyond circles. After the children can sort by two elements (for example, big and little), they can then be introduced to three elements (such as big, medium, and little) and eventually to four or five elements. The next major progression in sorting is to sort by two object characteristics. For example, teachers and families can have them sort by size and color (such as big blue, big yellow, little blue, and little yellow circles) or by size and texture (such as big rough, big smooth, little rough, or little smooth circles).

Activities

- Have the children initially sort objects with only one specific characteristic, such as size, shape, color, or texture.
- Ask the children to sort simple concrete objects.
- Have the children sort objects and increase the number of differentiating characteristics of the objects, for example, a big red circle versus a little blue square.

Critical Points to Cover

- Describe and model the task for the children.
- Check to make sure the children understand the task before having them work independently.

Helpful Hints

- Be sure all the objects used for sorting are identical in all characteristics but one, such as size, shape, color, or texture.
- Use a cookie sheet or tray to provide a defined work space. The curved edge around the tray prevents items from falling off the table or moving out of the children's reach.
- Use the Work-Play Trays available from the American Printing House for the Blind (see the Resources section of this book).
- Use consistent terminology, such as "little," not "small" or "tiny," until the children understand the concept.
- Provide a sample in each container that will represent what is to be placed in it; for example, tape a little circle on the outside of one container and a big circle on the outside of another.
- Have the containers match the objects to be placed in them; for instance, a container for little circles can be smaller than a container for big circles, or a yellow bowl and a red bowl can be used for sorting yellow and red blocks.
- Use the Colored Shape Cards or Plexiglas Blocks with the Light Box available from the American Printing House (see the Resources section) for children who have low vision.

Evaluation Tips

- Have the children verbally describe what they are doing and check their own work. For instance, a child can say, "I'm putting all the big ones in this bowl and all the little ones in this bowl."
- Have the children sort objects not used during the instructional period to ensure that they have generalized the skill beyond the instructional activity.
- Observe and make notes on whether the children require verbal or physical prompts to complete the task or how well they can complete the task independently.

- Document the children's progress on a checklist that follows a developmental progression, such as the following:
    1. sorts by size—2 elements (big and little)
    2. sorts by size—3 elements (big, little, and medium)
    3. sorts by shape—2 elements (circle and square)
    4. sorts by shape—3 elements (circle, square, and triangle)
    5. sorts by color—2 elements (red and blue)
    6. sorts by color—3 elements (red, blue, and yellow)
    7. sorts by color—4 elements (red, blue, yellow, and green)
    8. sorts by size and shape—4 elements (big, little, circle, and square)
    9. sorts by size and color—4 elements (big, little, red, and blue)
    10. sorts by shape and color—4 elements (circle, square, red, and blue)

For Children Who Need Additional Modifications

- If the children are not ready to match or sort, encourage them to find only objects that match a sample object. For example, help them to find only the spoons in a set of silverware and to put the spoons in a tray. Emphasize only the concept of spoon until they can successfully find these items. Later, a second, contrasting object, such as a fork, can be introduced.
- Find ways to call the children's attention to features that make two objects the same during daily activities. For children who are blind and have physical disabilities, make sure their experience includes awareness of the features of larger objects, such as chairs, doors, and trees, as well. Frequently, children are exposed only to certain aspects of these objects and do not recognize similarities that make the objects part of the same class.

DEVELOPMENT OF WORK SKILLS: PUTTING THINGS TOGETHER

When children learn to put things together or take them apart, they are learning basic functional skills that will serve them throughout their lives and in their future work. They are learning to manipulate objects, follow directions to make a product, problem solve the relationships between objects, and so forth. As in the activity for sorting, these early efforts to help young visually impaired children develop work skills provide teachers and families with opportunities to give them realistic feedback about their performance, including how well and how quickly they completed the task.

At the beginning of a project that involves putting things together, teachers and families can have the children gather all the necessary pieces or parts. For example, if children are putting together a puzzle, building a house with blocks, or making a car with Duplos, they can be assisted in selecting all the required pieces or parts. Depending on the specific learning objectives and the children's development needs, teachers and families need to present a model of the finished project and provide ample opportunities for children who are blind to explore it tactilely. They need to give clear, simple verbal directions to children for completing the project and, if necessary, to demonstrate each step and then to encourage the children to show each step, too. When the children complete the project, teachers and family members need to have the children check their creations against the model. Once the children have mastered a particular activity or task (for example, making a car with Duplos), teachers and families can have them choose the pieces themselves and make an object without a model. After the children have mastered the basic idea, they should be allowed to create their own variations, such as cars with two, three, or four wheels.

Activities

- Have the children use manipulative and constructive toys that are motivating to them.
- Have the children complete models by copying or imitating each step that has been demonstrated.
- Ask the children to create things without using a model to encourage exploration and creative expression.
- Encourage the children to repeat a task even after they have completed it successfully, to help them increase their speed and sense of accomplishment.

Critical Points to Cover

- Gather all necessary pieces or parts to complete an object or toy before asking the children to begin the project.

- Provide a model of the completed object or toy for the children to copy.
- Give the children ample time to complete the construction of the object or toy.
- Encourage the children's creative endeavors.

Helpful Hints

- Conduct an ecological inventory (see Chapter 3) to identify tasks that focus on the skill of putting things together and that are age appropriate and meaningful for children with visual impairments. For example, visually impaired children may find Duplos easier to manipulate than Legos because they are larger. Likewise, young children may need to work at putting together 5- to 7-piece puzzles whereas those who are older may be able to complete 20- to 25-piece puzzles.
- Interview family members to identify tasks that will reinforce this skill at home.
- Use a cookie sheet or tray to provide a defined work space. The curved edge around the tray prevents items from falling off the table or from moving out of the child's reach.
- Use the Work–Play Trays available from the American Printing House (see the Resources section).
- If a task is particularly difficult or elaborate, break it into sequential steps. For example, when making a paper cutout, such as a turkey, have the children start with the head, then do the body, and then attach the head to the body.
- Give the children step-by-step directions using pictures or concrete models at different levels of completion.

Evaluation Tips

- Ask the children how they put together the toy or object.
- Observe whether the children use any problem-solving skills, such as trial and error, in trying to put things together.
- Observe whether the children follow the step-by-step directions when they are provided.
- Observe and take notes on the types of things the children are able to put together independently and on the amount of time they take to put things together.

For Children Who Need Additional Modifications

- Teachers and families need to consider ways to help children with physical disabilities stabilize materials when they are putting things together. The use of rubber mats, lipped trays and pans, clamps, or two-sided adhesive tape can free children from using one hand to stabilize materials, so they can use both hands to manipulate materials.

- Emphasize the satisfaction of working with materials and create routines to make the use of these materials even more satisfying, such as a sound effect associated with a particular movement or a turn-taking game in which each child adds something new to a clay figure. Refrain from comparing one child's production to another's, but point out its unique characteristics.

References

Chen, D. (1995). Understanding and developing communication. In D. Chen & J. Dote-Kwan (Eds.), *Starting points: Instructional strategies for young children whose multiple disabilities include visual impairment* (pp. 57–72). Los Angeles: Blind Childrens Center.

Kokaska, C. J., & Brolin, D. E. (1985). *Career education for handicapped individuals* (2nd ed.). Columbus, OH: Charles E. Merrill.

Loumiet, R., & Levack, N. (1993). *Independent living: A curriculum with adaptations for students with visual impairments: Vol. 1. Social competence* (2nd ed.). Austin: Texas School for the Blind and Visually Impaired.

PART THREE

The Elementary School Years

Sandra Lewis

Jane Erin
*Activities for Students Who Need
Additional Modifications*

When children enter elementary school, they are making a significant transition from home and part-time early childhood programs to full-time school and more structured, challenging academic programs. They are expected to participate in group and individual activities that test their ability to follow instructions, respond appropriately to adults and classmates, organize their materials, and be responsible for their actions. As they did in preschool, children with visual impairments need to encounter high expectations for their performance in elementary school. They need to learn that they will be expected to participate actively in school and after-school activities. They need to understand that people constantly evaluate each other and thus that their teachers and peers will constantly evaluate their school performance. And they need to refine their social skills by learning how to communicate with others and to express information about themselves comfortably.

During their elementary school years, students with visual impairments will not only spend considerable time honing their compensatory skills and applying these skills to their academic and avocational pursuits, but will benefit from assuming additional work responsibilities at home and in school. They need to receive feedback on all their efforts. Evaluating oneself is critical to improving skills that need to be mastered. But once children have met their own standards of performance, they need to be challenged to meet the standards being set by their peers—with and without disabilities. Realistic feedback helps children understand how they are performing in comparison with others.

Part Three of this book focuses on activities that elementary school students with visual impairments can perform at home, in school, and in the community that facilitate career education. Like the activities in the preceding preschool section, these activities are not meant to be all-inclusive; they are designed as a springboard for the development of additional activities by teachers, parents and other family members, and other service providers.

CHAPTER

8

Conveying High Expectations

As was pointed out earlier in this book, all children tend to internalize the expectations that others have for them. Therefore, to have high expectations of themselves, children with visual impairments need to perceive that others have high expectations of them. To believe that they will grow up to be contributing members of society, visually impaired children first need to know that they can be active participants in their families, in school, and in their communities. This chapter underscores the need for this critical component in the career education of children with visual impairments and introduces readers to activities that will help children demonstrate competence in school and after-school activities.

In many ways, expectations and competence are parts of a circle. When children are expected to perform well, their chances of doing so increase. And, when they display competence, people come to see them as competent and expect them to be so. Ultimately, children then become competent and know themselves to be such. Some of the activities presented in this chapter are intended to enhance youngsters' organizational and self-help skills; some are geared toward encouraging children to help other people, including their families. All the activities are designed to give youngsters responsibilities and to develop skills that reflect high expectations.

TAKING CARE OF ONESELF AND ONE'S POSSESSIONS: ORGANIZATIONAL SKILLS

Caring for and keeping their belongings organized are skills that most youngsters take many years to learn, yet these skills are important and relate to their future success. The ability to locate needed items quickly reduces the amount of time required to accomplish even simple tasks, thereby increasing efficiency. The acquisition of this skill is particularly important for adults who are visually impaired because they may not be able to easily and quickly scan an entire environment to identify where a needed paper or tool is located. In addition, individuals who are organized are generally perceived by others as having capabilities, competence, and productiveness—qualities that sighted people do not always expect visually impaired people to have.

Sighted children learn organizational skills primarily by watching others at home, at school, and in the community. They see how similar items are arranged in stores, how related materials are stored in school closets and on shelves, and how their clothes are placed in their drawers. Sighted youngsters also observe the wide variety of organizing tools that are available, including notebooks, pencil cases, stacking trays, file folders, containers, and special shelving.

In addition to being expected to learn by observation, sighted children also are expected to practice organizational skills. It is not unusual for school notebooks and desks to be checked for neatness. Families may ask their children to place their folded underwear into drawers, put groceries in the pantry, empty the dishwasher, or help clean the garage on Saturday. Each activity gives the youngsters an understanding of and appreciation for the need to keep order in their world, as well as the techniques to maintain that order.

It is important that adults have high expectations for children with visual impairments, especially in regard to organizational skills. In addition to helping with activities that require their use of organized work spaces, the children need to become aware of tools, strategies, and techniques for maintaining order and for organizing their possessions.

Activities

- Encourage visually impaired children to return used materials and belongings to specific places. For example, they can place

FROM A FAMILY PERSPECTIVE

Conveying High Expectations: Organizational Skills

Organizational skills are important for your visually impaired child to learn because he or she will need them at home to locate items essential for daily living, at school to help find the necessary tools for his or her education, and at work in the future to help perform the tasks of a specific job.

Look around your home to find the spots that are naturally organized and those that may need some additional organization. The more predictable your environment is, the better that environment is for your visually impaired child. It is important to help your child organize the home environment with you. The less vision your child has, the more he or she will benefit from living in an organized home. Because the organization of the home environment will become predictable for your child, and, consequently will enable him or her to function independently within it, your child will come to understand how important organizational skills are in other areas of his or her life, such as in school and in socializing.

Kevin O'Connor

their shoes under their beds or by the front door when they take them off, rehang their used towels on towel bars after their baths, and return their braillewriters to appropriate storage spots after they finish their homework.

- Ask the children to help put away groceries or other items after a shopping trip. While they are doing so, the adults who are present can explain the organizational systems they use and their rationales for placing items in specific places. (For example, "I keep all the canned vegetables on the right and the canned fruits on the left of this shelf. Dried foods like macaroni and rice go in this drawer.")

- Involve the children in other activities that require the use of organized spaces, such as setting the table ("You can always find the salad plates here"), emptying the dishwasher ("Spoons go in the tray on the right"), putting away laundry ("Put your pajamas in the top drawer"), or replacing used garden tools ("The shovel hangs on the wall next to the hoe").

- Describe the various organizational systems that are used. For example, teachers or family members can tell youngsters that they are looking for papers in a file folder that are arranged alphabetically and can then ask the children to help locate the papers. Or family members can explain that all the unpaid bills are kept in a box on the desk and that they need help finding a particular bill.

- Ask children to help set up their own organized environments. For example, family members can involve children in determining in which drawers clothing items or toys are to be stored, and teachers can ask them to decide where their braille paper, magnifiers, and other school supplies are to be kept.
- Take regular trips with the children to office supply and variety stores to become familiar with the hundreds of gadgets, containers, and materials that one can use to organize one's space, things, and papers.

Critical Points to Cover

- People organize their spaces and materials in ways that seem logical to them.
- There is no single correct way to organize one's things.
- Organized spaces and materials make everyone's lives easier because people do not have to spend much time looking for what they need or want.
- Organization is important at home, at school, and on the job.

Helpful Hints

- Youngsters with visual impairments may not be aware of all the ways that people organize their papers, materials, and work and living space; when possible, they need to be shown others' systems and tools and be allowed to explore the systems tactilely or up close.
- Allow for a gradual improvement in the children's skills and reward the children's approximations of the desired result. Organizing without the benefit of good vision demands more of children than adults may realize.
- Provide for the natural consequences of disorganization as much as possible. That is, the natural consequence of not keeping school papers organized may be missed assignments and poor grades; the natural consequence of not putting open soda cans beyond one's papers may be spills.

- Supply the students with defined spaces, such as storage boxes, lipped trays, drawers, cabinets, card files, and shelves.

Evaluation Tips

- Have other teachers and family members observe students using systems spontaneously to organize their materials.
- Present the students with scenarios or stories that describe individuals who are not well organized. Ask them what advice they would give to these people.
- Ask the students to describe the benefits of keeping one's belongings organized. Ask them to suggest the possible consequences of being disorganized.

For Students Who Need Additional Modifications

- To help students with physical disabilities to be more independent, provide storage spaces in their classrooms that they can reach without assistance, such as a cubbyhole at elbow height, a desk with an open front, and a coat hook that can be easily reached.
- Provide enough time at the beginning and end of activities for students to store materials, and give them positive reinforcement for putting things away.
- When students need assistance in completing tasks, encourage them to choose individual helpers to take responsibility for the success of the tasks. Explain to the students that it is not enough for them to say to the helpers, "I need my social studies book." Rather, they should provide specific instructions: "Could you please get my social studies book? It is in my red book bag in the yellow basket with my name on it."
- Create identifying symbols or features, such as printed name tags, happy face stickers, or Velcro stickers, that can help the students identify their belongings.
- Present students who are learning to make choices with two items (for example, cups or brushes) before beginning a routine. Encourage them to practice selecting the item that belongs to them. At first, offer two distinctively different items and later, present two similar ones.

FROM A RURAL PERSPECTIVE

In rural communities, visually impaired children may be the only children with this impairment in the entire school system. Because rural school systems are often unfamiliar with the educational needs of visually impaired children, it may be difficult for a child with a visual impairment to receive an appropriate educational experience.

School districts in rural areas often need to design unique programs for visually impaired students without the ongoing support of local experts. Frequently, teachers of visually impaired students and other related service personnel must provide services on an itinerant basis because the local schools cannot support full-time teachers or other service providers for such few children.

Information about the expectations and unique methods and educational needs of the children is vital in designing programs. Teachers and organizations serving children who are visually impaired may be unavailable or located far from the area and thus may be unable to respond immediately. Therefore, school districts are often forced to search for high-quality specialized services and the information they need to design programs. Sometimes they form cooperatives with other school districts or send children to residential schools for blind children because they are unable to provide daily, disability-specific services.

Once these obstacles are addressed, rural school districts, in general, are capable of responding to the individual needs of students. Because they tend to be small, they often do not have rigid systems that are apt to respond with prescriptive programs for students instead of those that take into account the needs of individual children. Furthermore, because of their small number, people in rural communities often tend to be more connected to each other, have a greater awareness of the needs of their communities, and have a stronger sense of themselves as members of their communities than people living in larger, more densely populated areas. Therefore, when a specific need arises, such as for transportation or equipment, they may be able to get together in a cooperative way to solve the problem creatively.

In the area of career education, teachers and families need to expose visually impaired students to job-related experiences as early as possible in their development. Work-related activities for elementary school students occur at home, in relatives' or neighbors' homes, and at school. Such activities may include taking care of pets or farm animals, helping tend a garden, assisting at a garage sale, and helping in the school's recycling program.

Elaine Sveen

- Involve the students in taking materials out at the beginning of tasks and in putting them away at the end. Even if they are unable to carry or manipulate the materials, allowing them to hold the materials, open or close the closet door, or touch the container in which the materials are stored can reinforce the idea that the materials will remain in a specific place until they are needed again.

COMMUNITY INVOLVEMENT: HELPING OTHERS

All children, including those with visual impairments, may need help from others to complete difficult tasks. However, many visually impaired children have a variety of needs that sometimes require additional assistance. These students often are not provided with natural opportunities to help others in turn. Because many acts of kindness among people occur spontaneously and nonverbally, such as when one person sees another struggling to carry too many items and holds a door open for that person, youngsters with visual impairments may not be aware of the mutual dependence of people. It might be easy for these students to have the impression that they are the only people who ever need or desire assistance. Students who are visually impaired benefit from teachers' and families' creating situations in which the students' assistance is genuinely necessary. In these situations, unlike those involving assigned chores, teachers and families need to emphasize the help that the youngsters are offering at a particular moment, not the tasks.

Activities

- Ask a visually impaired child to bring snacks to family members who may exclaim, "I'm so tired tonight, I can hardly move!"
- Encourage children to carry objects for adults whose "arms are full."
- Have children read stories to younger students at school or to younger siblings while other family members cook dinner.
- Ask children to help during trips to a supermarket, for instance, by saying, "If you can get bread for me, I can get in line to pay and we'll be out of here faster."
- Ask children for assistance by saying, for example, "This bag (or jar) is hard for me to open. Would you see if you can do it for me?"
- Ask a student to show other students where items at school are stored.
- Ask students to help struggling classmates or younger students with tasks they themselves have already mastered, such as by say-

ing, "You know how to turn the computer on, will you show Andy how it's done?"

- Encourage the children to participate in school, church, Scouting, or community service group activities.

Critical Points to Cover

- Everyone needs assistance sometimes.
- Everyone gives and receives assistance at times.
- Sometimes people say when they need help, but at other times, they need to be asked how they can be helped.
- When a person has been helpful, it is polite to thank him or her and to offer to return the favor in some way.

Helpful Hints

- Because these activities are intended to build the children's sense of self-worth, offers to help others should involve previously mastered activities that children can perform with relative ease.
- Students may need positive verbal feedback on how their assistance was helpful. For example, allow the children to overhear positive descriptions of the results of their helping others, such as, "I wouldn't have been able to get all the groceries inside in one trip if I hadn't had help."
- Model for the youngsters the various ways to say "thank-you" to those who offer assistance.
- Help the students recognize situations in which their assistance may be useful.
- Family members can help children to determine their ability to contribute by saying, for example, "I have to get ready for dinner, which involves setting the table, putting the bread on a plate, and washing the lettuce. Which of these steps can you help me with?"
- Older children can be taught to understand that when they receive assistance, it is their responsibility to find a way to reciprocate.

Evaluation Tips

- Ask the students to describe how they feel when they help someone who needs assistance.

- Role-play with the students to discover the techniques they can use to offer and refuse assistance.
- Ask parents or other family members whether they have observed their children spontaneously offering assistance to others in various situations at home and in the community.

For Students Who Need Additional Modifications

- Students with disabilities can take responsibility for assisting in grocery store routines. Students who use wheelchairs can carry grocery items on a tray while family members take items from the shelves. Those who do not read but understand symbols can help create a store "list" by placing labels from needed items into a bag or purse. Blind students who are nonreaders can do the same task by carrying object cards to remind them of what goods are needed at the store, for example, a card with a dried noodle or a card with the pouring section of a milk carton glued to it. Students who use speech can practice remembering needed items.
- Children with severe disabilities may not be able to provide physical assistance to others, but they can learn that they can be helpful in other ways, for example, by smiling, which makes others feel better, or by relaxing their bodies during dressing or extending their limbs to help others provide assistance more easily. They also need to be given positive support for cooperating in tasks that make the jobs of others easier.
- When a child with severe disabilities is involved in a community activity with other children, identify a small group of "special friends" who are interested in interacting with and assisting that child. For example, at religious services, two or three children can meet with the family of a child with severe disabilities to talk about how they can help get the child involved in activities. Neighborhood children can learn to understand the nonverbal communication of a child with severe disabilities and to recognize when the child enjoys an activity at the playground or when he or she wants to play something different. When teaching other children how to interact with nonverbal children, emphasize what the nonverbal children can do, rather than what they cannot do.

MAKING REALISTIC COMPARISONS AGAINST THE NORM: INITIATIVE

Many employers expect employees to begin their work each day without requiring specific directions about what needs to be done. For some employees, this expectation is limited to preparing supplies or work spaces for the day's activities, whereas for others, it extends to much more of the job. Employees who are self-starters and take the initiative on a job are valued because they contribute to the smooth operation of the business and require less supervision.

Without careful planning by adults, circumstances may not arise in which children with visual impairments have the opportunity to observe and practice performing tasks on their own initiative. Many visually impaired children find life unpredictable because they literally cannot see a cause and its accompanying effect, and they often find it safer and easier to wait until they are given directions before acting. Teachers and family members may sometimes unknowingly reinforce passivity by overprompting children with visual impairments instead of dealing appropriately with inaction that would not be tolerated in sighted children. In a sense, in these cases the adults are preempting the children's opportunities to develop self-direction and problem-solving skills.

Activities

- Although time with the teacher of visually impaired students is usually limited and should be spent wisely, it may be of value to establish routines in which the students are expected to work independently for a short period before they receive the teacher's full attention. Young children could be expected to get their materials ready—for example, to take the brailler off the shelf, the paper out of the box, and the textbook from the cubby—without having to be reminded and within a certain time. Other children can be made to understand that the first part of the time with the teacher is spent practicing handwriting or keyboarding and that they are expected to start to work on these tasks immediately. Older elementary school students can be instructed to check a special in-box at the beginning of each class for the assignment they are to complete without assistance before direct instruction by the teacher begins.

- At home, parents may want to establish routines at naturally occurring times of the day. For instance, children can be expected to hang their towels on the towel bars after they have used them each time or to feed the cat as soon as they arrive home from school.

Critical Points to Cover

- Having one's materials ready at the start of class is expected of all children.
- Getting down to work is a personal responsibility.
- Students can solve problems that interfere with their daily routines.
- Employers expect their employees to know how to start their day.
- Employees who are efficient and self-motivated are valued by their employers.

Helpful Hints

- Because successful participation in routine activities requires students to give up something that usually is highly motivating (for example, the attention they receive when an adult gives them directions), it may be necessary to use a reward system, at least at first and perhaps for some time afterward. Getting down to work is not intrinsically rewarding to most children.
- Help the students to understand that they are practicing initiative, independent functioning, and timeliness. At some point, make rewards contingent on independent work that is completed in a reasonable time. For example, when students have completed work without being prompted by their teachers, they need to be praised and allowed to choose a favorite activity as their reward. Remind the students that employers do not retain employees who do not get the job done promptly.
- Focus on praising the children for functioning independently in a timely manner. The quality of work is a related issue that needs to be addressed separately. During the introduction of and early practice in demonstrating initiative, reinforce the desired behavior with approval for the children's attention to tasks without direct adult intervention.
- Prepare (or have the children prepare) a checklist of materials that the children need to have on their desks at the start of each

school day. Tape the lists (in braille or print) to the children's desks or tape reminders on the desks to have the children check the lists they have placed in their notebooks or in their desks.

- Occasionally include a first activity that the students consider fun to do, such as preparing a snack for other students or sharing a story.
- Well-established routines provide natural opportunities for infusing problem solving into the school day. Routines can be interrupted in a variety of ways (someone else's towel can be hung on the rack or the paper box can be left empty), and the students can be encouraged to determine appropriate solutions to these roadblocks.
- Encourage the children to check their in-boxes or predetermined lists of chores or activities at home when they seem to be waiting for directions from adults, and reward them for doing so.

Evaluation Tips

- Ask other teachers whether the students immediately prepare to work after they arrive in class.
- Ask families whether their children perform necessary chores or tasks without having to be reminded.

For Students Who Need Additional Modifications

- Students with disabilities need to be involved in deciding what roles they can play in classroom activities in which they cannot fully participate. For example, if the class is completing a printed worksheet and a blind student with a physical disability cannot carry out this task, provide several options that will allow the student to do a similar activity with other children in the class. The student can sort cards with words or pictures, listen to a tape-recorded copy of the sheet and record a response, or complete the worksheet with a partner to reach the same goals.
- Students with disabilities need clear information about what they can do and what is difficult for them to do. Families and teachers can talk with students about what they can do if they work hard, and what is not possible because of physical differences. Adults with disabilities and medical personnel may be

helpful in discussing realistic and unrealistic expectations. It is not helpful or constructive for classmates and adults to use euphemisms or pretend that students can do things that are not possible, for example, pretending that a student with severe physical disabilities is "on" the football team, when he merely wears a uniform and sits in his wheelchair on the sidelines. Select activities that are based on what the students are really capable of doing.

ASSUMING RESPONSIBILITY

Chores are tasks that people know how to do and are responsible for completing and that others rely on them to do. When the assignment of chores is explained appropriately, youngsters who are required to perform them regularly can come to feel that they are making valuable contributions to their family or class. The performance of chores also gives children opportunities to practice already-mastered skills, to develop new skills, and to learn firsthand to be responsible for completing tasks.

Many youngsters with visual impairments are not assigned chores for a variety of reasons. Some teachers and families mistakenly believe that the children are incapable of performing chores. However, usually the reasons well-meaning people give for not assigning chores are that it takes the children too long to finish them or that it would be unfair to burden the children with chores when they have so many other things to learn. Neither reason is helpful in the long run because no one increases his or her speed at a task without practice, and the assignment of a chore is a chance to practice a skill and improve one's rate of completing it. Insisting that children contribute to family responsibilities by performing chores is a way of expressing confidence in the children's abilities.

Some adults believe that chores are performed by each member of the group for the good of the group and that no financial remuneration (that is, an allowance) or other type of reward is appropriate. Others believe that linking the performance of chores to a monetary or other reward is an excellent opportunity to help youngsters appreciate the direct relationship between work and spendable income. Therefore, depending on their viewpoints, family members and teachers need to decide whether they want to reward children for performing chores.

Activities

- With the students, create lists of tasks in which the students have demonstrated competence and that need to be accomplished for the classroom or home to run smoothly.
- Determine in advance the consequences of the children's performing or not performing assigned chores. One technique is to rely on natural consequences that have an impact on the entire group. For example, a child who is expected to put silverware at each place setting before dinner will feel pride when the other family members express their delight at not having to wait to eat. For many chores, however, such as cleaning a sink, the effect on the group is not as easy to determine, and it may be necessary to tie the timely and adequate performance of the chore to a predetermined reward. Rewards need to be selected carefully. Young children often need to have tangible rewards that are provided frequently, whereas older children can accumulate points or stickers over time. Behaviorists argue convincingly that rewards are more effective than punishments, that is, that it is better to have youngsters work for rewards than to take away scheduled activities when the children do not do their chores. They also recommend involving children in the selection of their rewards.
- Explain to the children that they contribute to the running of the class or home when performing chores. Also note that all children are expected to perform chores, although the chores performed by one child may be different from those performed by another.
- Have the youngsters select a chore or chores from a list of tasks and a desired reward from a list of acceptable consequences.
- Work with the children to determine the appropriate times of day to perform the chores.
- With the children's help, develop a system of keeping track of the performance of assigned chores. Examples of such systems include index cards in braille or large print that list common chores and that can be filed in boxes labeled *To Do* and *Done,* a chart on the refrigerator that lists chores in braille or large print and magnetic *Xs* or *Checks* that can be moved from the *To Do*

column to the *Done* column, and large-print or brailled lists of *To Do* chores that, when completed, print users can cross off with a pen or pencil and braille users can erase by flattening the dots.

- Provide appropriate feedback to the youngsters immediately after they perform the chores. Use these opportunities to recognize each child's initiation of the task, to shape further a particular skill, or to acknowledge once again the child's valuable contribution to the group.

Critical Points to Cover

- Many activities are necessary for the smooth running of a classroom or home.
- Each member of a group depends on the contributions of the other members.
- The work one contributes to a group is valuable and is recognized as such by the other group members.
- Work has to be done even if one does not feel like doing it.
- Many people working together as a team on a project will make performing the task easier than if one person works alone on the project.

Helpful Hints

- Remember that children learn from genuine praise and positive reinforcement.
- Noncompliance in regard to performing chores is often an indication that children are not convinced of the value of their contributions, that the reward system is ineffective, or that the negative attention the children receive for not performing the chores actually reinforces that noncompliance.
- Select chores that can be performed at predictable times of the day, such as refilling the braille paper in a tray before class begins or emptying the wastebaskets at home immediately after dinner. This kind of predictability helps youngsters remember to perform the tasks and helps adults organize their days to allow time for the children to do so.

- The chores assigned to young children should take a short amount of time (as little as 3 to 5 minutes). In general, the complexity and number of chores assigned during a day or week needs to increase as the children get older.
- Students can be assigned chores even when they have mastered only part of an activity. For example, youngsters who have learned to empty the silverware container can be assigned that part of the job when the dishwasher is being emptied. Similarly, children who have not yet learned to place plates in a cupboard may take them from the bottom rack of the dishwasher and stack them on the counter.
- Think carefully about defining personal hygiene and dressing tasks as chores, particularly for children who perform these skills routinely. Although these tasks contribute to the smooth running of the household by freeing the time and energy of others, they commonly are expected of all children and are thus considered expected behavior for children.
- Chores that are generally easy for young children are those that involve small spaces or well-defined activities, such as hanging up towels after a bath, cleaning a sink, filling a pet's bowl with food or water, emptying a dishwasher, setting the table for a meal, putting clothes into the hamper, emptying wastebaskets, wiping a small table or counter, and taking the kitchen trash to the outside garbage can. Tasks that are more difficult involve larger spaces, such as cleaning a bathtub, making a bed, vacuuming, erasing large chalkboards, and sweeping, as well as those tasks that are not well defined, such as cleaning one's room or straightening the closets.
- Children of elementary school age may be more inclined to participate in chores that can be accomplished at the same time and in the same area where other members of the class or family are working. For example, a child can clean a bathroom sink while an adult is cleaning the tub, thereby "sharing" the work or at least performing it in a social milieu.
- The regular rotation of chores among classmates or siblings can reduce boredom and increase the development of skills in a variety of areas.

Evaluation Tips

- Ask family members if their children are demonstrating increasing independence in chores performed at home.
- Ask the students to describe their contributions to their classrooms and families. Note when their voices and words indicate pride in their contributions.
- Ask the students to make periodic lists of the home and classroom tasks that they have mastered. Then ask them to explain what they have learned and what they think their contributions have been as a result.

For Students Who Need Additional Modifications

- Complete daily routines at the same time every day. Schedule a favorite activity right after a routine that the students dislike, so they will be encouraged to participate in and complete the routine.
- For routines in which the children require assistance, give them a choice about who will assist them on different days to add variety.
- Children who use adaptive equipment need to be involved in the storage and maintenance of the equipment at home. Establish a routine of returning the equipment to the same place after it is used, for instance, putting the hearing aid back on the tray on the dresser or placing the eyeglasses in their case on the bedstead.

PROMOTING KITCHEN SKILLS

Sighted children seem to develop a natural desire to do for themselves in the kitchen as they observe their parents, older siblings, and other children managing simple food-preparation tasks. By the time they enter elementary school, many sighted children can prepare simple uncooked breakfasts, pack their own lunches, and prepare simple snacks and meals in a microwave oven.

The development of kitchen skills may be delayed in children with visual impairments for a variety of reasons. Without appropriate interventions, many parents wait until their visually impaired children show the same kind of interest and initiative in the kitchen that sighted children demonstrate. Other parents are fearful that their children may be hurt physically when engaging in kitchen activities and protect them from these perceived dangers. Still other adults, unaware of the kinds of adaptations (such as wearing elbow-length flame-retardant gloves to place items in an oven) that people with visual impairments use, do not know how to start teaching what seem to be complex activities for young visually impaired children.

Children with visual impairments need to be taught to perform activities that sighted children learn incidentally, including those involving kitchen skills. Youngsters who participate in kitchen activities have more numerous opportunities to observe and practice organizational skills and are more aware of the "big picture" of how events surrounding them affect, and are affected by, their lives. For example, sighted children who watch parents prepare a salad or garlic bread have learned what ingredients are required for these foods, where the ingredients are stored, how they are prepared, and which kitchen tools were used to accomplish the task. In addition, children who are expected to contribute to their own care have a greater sense of autonomy and higher self-esteem than those who are not.

Children who always help prepare meals at homes gradually take over tasks for which they are developmentally ready, as families and early interventionists work together to provide them with appropriate opportunities for growth. For children who have not had these opportunities, teachers of visually impaired children in elementary schools may need to find creative ways to teach them how to perform kitchen skills.

Activities

- In cooperation with students and their families, select a mutually agreeable meal for the students to learn to prepare, such as cold cereal for breakfast or a simple sandwich for lunch. Assess the students' level of skill and determine the components of the skill that have not been mastered. Using a task analysis—that is, the process of breaking down a task into the smallest elements in the proper sequence to determine instruction of specific elements in the sequence—decide on the steps required to prepare the meal and use them to teach the task.
- As the students master part of the entire meal, their families can encourage them to perform that task during subsequent meal

preparation times. For example, if the students have learned to remove luncheon meat from its package, count two slices, and place them on a piece of plain bread, they can perform this task every time their lunch is being packed. Family members and children can work cooperatively to prepare lunch until the children have mastered the entire activity.

- Children who have mastered an entire activity should be expected to manage for themselves on a regular basis. Teachers and families can use this milestone to begin to teach them to prepare more complex meals or perform more difficult kitchen tasks, such as following a recipe, making desserts, or determining what ingredients need to be purchased to make a favorite meal or dessert.

Critical Points to Cover

- One's breakfast, lunch, and dinner do not automatically appear ready every day.
- Most children are expected to prepare their own breakfasts and lunches as they mature.
- When people prepare their own meals, they generally have more say as to what is included in the meals.

Helpful Hints

- Some of the tasks involved in making breakfast include getting the cereal from the cupboard, getting the milk from the refrigerator, carrying the milk to the table, pouring the cereal and milk, putting dirty dishes in the dishwasher or sink, and wiping the table. Other simple breakfast activities include making Pop-tarts, toast, frozen waffles, washing or peeling fruits, and making oatmeal or other hot cereals.
- Some of the tasks involved in packing a simple lunch include washing a piece of fruit, getting a drink package or chips from the cupboard, slicing cheese, opening packages of luncheon meat, wrapping cookies, spreading condiments, and opening and closing a bag of bread.
- Teachers may need to remind parents or other family members that most children make a mess when learning new kitchen

skills. An important part of each lesson is to learn to return the kitchen to its previous condition of tidiness.

- Teachers will want to remind themselves of the need to provide numerous teaching and practice opportunities for visually impaired students who are learning unfamiliar tasks. Children with vision seem to learn unfamiliar tasks more quickly because they have been able to acquire techniques through hundreds of prior observations of the task being completed by others.

- Families benefit when instruction by the teacher of visually impaired students occurs in their homes because they observe specialized techniques, hear the language of reinforcement and shaping of behaviors, and watch as their children perform tasks that once were difficult for them.

- Older children who prepare their own meals can begin to explore information about nutrition and the importance of a balanced diet.

Evaluation Tips

- Occasionally ask the children to list all the kitchen activities that they have mastered.

- Ask the students what they would like to be able to prepare in the kitchen and use this input to plan future lessons.

- Ask family members how much time is required for their children to prepare their meals, the amount of assistance their children request, their children's attitudes toward doing various tasks, and the quality of the clean-up their children perform.

- Relate other school or home activities to tasks learned in the kitchen (for example, "You need to sprinkle the cleansing powder in the sink in the same way that you shake salt or pepper on your food," or "Pour the liquid into the test tube slowly and carefully—as though you were pouring juice from a full container into a small glass"). Be sure students understand that the actions (shaking and pouring) are similar but that the substances are different (food versus cleaning products or chemicals).

For Students Who Need Additional Modifications

- For students with multiple disabilities to participate actively in the development of kitchen skills, it may be necessary to consider some environmental modifications, such as lowering countertops, cooking surfaces, and kitchen appliances so students in wheelchairs can reach them.

- Families and teachers need to be aware of and introduce modified kitchen tools like rocking knives, spiked platters to hold food in place, and nonslip mats to keep dishes from sliding on smooth surfaces.

- Students with multiple disabilities who are unable to read braille or print can often use recorded or pictorial recipes. Pictorial recipes, consisting of a pictured representation of each step, can help remind a student of ingredients needed and the sequence of actions to be followed.

ORDERING AND OBTAINING MATERIALS

A severe visual impairment often has a profound impact on an individual's ability to participate in the events of life through observation. Many youngsters with visual impairments cannot easily observe what the adults and other children in their world are doing and thus have difficulty becoming aware of an activity, learning how to perform the activity, and judging their own performance against a standard. To remedy this situation, it is frequently necessary to introduce an activity before it is age appropriate for the children's peers. With the carefully planned, sequential introduction of the components of a task, youngsters with visual impairments often are able to perform the entire task at the same time as their sighted classmates.

An example of a task in which sighted youngsters participate peripherally when they are young but are expected to perform independently later is the acquisition of school supplies. Teachers distribute a list of needed supplies on the first day of school, and parents or other family members, usually with their children, go to a local store to purchase the items on the list. Children may be asked which folders or notebook covers they prefer but otherwise are not directly involved in selecting the supplies. Still, they observe where school supplies can be purchased, the variety of options from which one can choose, and how the transaction is handled.

Some youngsters with visual impairments, particularly those who are totally blind, miss these learning opportunities because many of their school supplies are not sold at local stores. For instance, bold- or raised-line and braille paper, slates, braillers, large-print dictionaries, and canes generally must be ordered from distant locations. It is the job of the teacher of visually impaired students to make certain that these materials are available for the students. Furthermore, it is important for students to be aware of and participate in this process because they will be expected to order their own materials as adults. Elementary school age is the appropriate time to begin learning this process and responsibility.

Activities

- Teachers need to evaluate their own processes for ordering materials for students and determine how they can involve the students in the activity. At first, it may be enough to tell the students that certain merchandise is being ordered for them. Before long, however, it will be appropriate to have students participate directly in obtaining their supplies. Teachers can reproduce the order form (or parts of it) in the students' preferred reading media and review the directions for ordering by reading them to younger children or by having older students read and interpret them aloud. The students can then help decide what information to write on the form and where to find needed information (such as catalog numbers). Teachers also will want to be certain that the student understands (and participates in, if appropriate) the final steps in the ordering process—faxing, mailing, telephoning, or performing a computer entry.

- Another way in which students in elementary school can participate in acquiring their specialized materials is by helping school personnel with production efforts. For example, students with low vision who use materials that have been enlarged on a copy machine can be taught to make their own enlargements and then be expected to add this chore to their daily routine. Similarly, students who are blind can help produce braille on an electronic embosser by being taught the translation process, by making sure that paper in the embosser is aligned, and by removing paper from the printer. In some schools, visually impaired students fax materials they need brailled to the central office to help their classroom teachers.

Critical Points to Cover

- Books and materials do not just magically appear; they must be ordered.
- Ordering materials is a complex process involving many steps that must be carefully and accurately performed.
- Eventually students will need to assume responsibility for ordering their own materials.
- Children can be involved in the ordering process and can be responsible for the print accommodations that they need.

Helpful Hints

- Students can be exposed to and participate in the ordering of materials from a variety of sources, including the American Printing House for the Blind, Recording for the Blind and Dyslexic, and the National Library Service for the Blind and Physically Handicapped (see the Resources section). Have students begin to keep a file of the addresses and telephone numbers of the vendors from whom products are ordered so they can have this information on hand when they need to order supplies in the future.
- Have the children overhear a telephone call checking on the status of the order and then perform this task themselves.
- At home, family members can inform their children when orders are being placed from catalogs and similarly involve them in these purchases.
- Use this kind of lesson as an opportunity for the children to practice scanning and searching skills, and try to reinforce these skills through further practice with other print, on-line, or recorded catalogs that feature products often purchased by individuals with visual impairments. Students will also benefit from practicing organizational skills and becoming aware of the materials that can be purchased without leaving home.

Evaluation Tips

- When ordering materials, ask the students if they can tell you what the next step in the process should be.

- Ask families if their children are interested in and involved in ordering from catalogs that are mailed to the house.
- Have the students complete simulated order forms, using print, on-line, and recorded catalogs.

For Students Who Need Additional Modifications

- Students with multiple disabilities need to assume as much responsibility as possible for obtaining necessary materials. They may need assistance initially (or for an ongoing period) to telephone and order special tools or devices that they require. However, if they are able to use the telephone, they can call and place an order for books or materials they need for school.
- Students who are unable to hold a telephone receiver may be able to use a speakerphone or hands-free headset. If students are unable to use the phone independently, they can actively participate with the teacher by pointing to what they want or need in a catalog or by telling the teacher or aide and then by listening as the staff person places the order.

9

Encouraging Socialization

The ability to form working relationships with other people is of great importance in one's life work or career. This chapter focuses on social skills because socialization is an essential part of achieving success in one's work life. Individuals who can get along with their employers and coworkers are far more likely to be able to maintain employment and advance in their careers than are those who cannot.

Some of the social cues that people pick up on and respond to are visual—a smile, a shake of the head, a shrug of the shoulders, a frown, a teardrop, a defiant posture, or a depressed posture, among others. Because children with visual impairments often miss or misinterpret these visual cues, they need to learn how to interact successfully with others without relying on these cues. Communication skill-building activities, such as learning to use a telephone effectively and learning to start conversations, are included in this chapter, as are suggestions for opportunities for cooperative play during recess. In addition, activities related to self-awareness, such as understanding one's family history, to self-advocacy, such as learning to share information about one's functional needs, and to self-improvement, such as developing musical or artistic abilities, are described and incorporated into the discussion because they are important social competencies for visually impaired elementary school students to develop.

FOSTERING COMMUNICATION SKILLS

One component on which social communication is based is knowledge of one's peers. If a person knows that a fellow student or coworker has a particular interest or hobby, then he or she can start a casual conversation based on this information. Conversations built on shared interests often are the first steps toward friendship.

Children who are sighted pick up clues about their peers' interests from artifacts the peers choose to display. For example, students indicate their interest in a particular sport or sports team by wearing T-shirts decorated with the team's logo. An interest in a certain rock group or music style can be determined by the cassettes seen in an open bookbag. Favorite movies can be identified by pictures on lunch boxes or binders. Adults also display clues about their lifestyles and interests, such as family pictures on desks, a bike rack on the back of a car, or a gym bag left near one's workstation.

Some children with severe visual impairments are seen by teachers, parents, and other significant people in their lives as being self-centered in their conversation, that is, that they tend to talk exclusively about themselves. It may be that this egocentrism is related to having limited information about the interests and activities of their conversational partners.

Activities

- Have each child in the class make an "All About Me" book. Included in this book could be individual pages devoted to "People in My Family," "My Pets," "Sports I Play," "Favorite Movies," "Sports Heroes," "Best Bedtime Stories," and "My Classmates and Teachers." These books could be decorated with photographs, magazine cutouts, or children's artwork and stored in the classroom's book corner, where all the students, including children with visual impairments, could look at them. Each book should be transcribed and the pictures or artwork should be described for braille readers in the class. Another alternative would be to have each child read his or her book on cassette tape, providing the child who is blind with an auditory reminder of the sound of the other children's voices.

- Older students can be designated "reporters" by their teachers. Armed with a set of interview questions that they have created as a group, these students can interview members of the class about their personal interests and activities. These interviews could be used as the basis for writing human-interest stories to include in a class newspaper.

FROM A FAMILY PERSPECTIVE

Encouraging Socialization

One thing families can keep in mind when teaching social skills is just how central each member of the family is to the child's success. The youngest and oldest members of families can be powerful teachers. Allow children time to reflect and process what they have learned, perhaps during mealtime or when they are getting ready for bed. Talking with them about daily events and interactions helps reinforce any learning experiences.

Kevin O'Connor

Critical Points to Cover

- Everyone is different, but some students may have hobbies and interests that are similar to those of the visually impaired students.
- Knowing something about the person to whom the visually impaired student is talking helps him or her think of things to say.
- People like to talk about themselves, too, not just hear what one person has to say about himself or herself.

Helpful Hints

- Although it may not be evident, youngsters with visual impairments may not know the identity of their fellow classmates. Therefore, during interactions, such as a group activity during class, visually impaired children may participate but may not be able to name the other students involved in the activity. Teachers need to be alert to this situation and teach students with visual impairments strategies for finding out who else is participating. Strategies may include the following: Ask all the students at the beginning of group activities to announce who is in the group and to indicate their roles; ask the students to identify themselves when they speak, for example, "This is Tom, I'd like to suggest . . ." in group activities; teach children with visual impairments how to ask politely for clarification about who is who, for example, "Excuse me, please tell me your name again. Thanks."
- Teachers may also want to consider assigning partners for group activities to help visually impaired students identify participants;

for example, one person can observe and one person can record observations. A visually impaired student could ask his or her partner to identify other participants as the activity unfolds.

- To help identify students who are seated at the lunch table, a visually impaired student may want to walk to lunch with a friend who can then tell him or her who else is sitting at the table. Or, the student with a visual impairment may need to start a conversation at the table by saying, for example, "Hi, I'm Nancy, what's your name? Who's sitting next to you?"
- Even if visually impaired students have information about their peers, their conversation skills may not be well developed; in this case, role-playing with the teacher of visually impaired students may be helpful. Some students also benefit from developing a repertoire of phrases that can be used as conversation starters and conversation continuers. Some examples of phrases that can facilitate new conversations include asking about pets, siblings, favorite movies, popular singers, or hardest school subjects. Continuing conversations requires listening to what conversation partners have said previously and encouraging them to keep talking by asking specific questions (for example, "What kind of dog do you have?"); describing a connection ("Oh, I have a dog, too, but it's a cocker spaniel"); or using open-ended requests or questions ("So how do you and your dog play?").
- The teacher of visually impaired students can use the "All About Me" books to encourage students' use of handheld magnifiers.
- Reporters working on their stories have the opportunity to practice notetaking, listening, keyboarding, spelling, and writing skills.

Evaluation Tips

- Ask the students to tell what they know about other students in the class.
- Ask families if their children can provide more specific information about their classmates.
- Watch the students to see if they engage in conversations that are focused on the known likes and dislikes of their peers.
- Consider whether the quality of students' role-playing improves as they learn more about their peers and the ways to engage them.

For Students Who Need Additional Modifications

- Students need to be encouraged to develop an understanding of the feelings of like and dislike and, in the case of nonverbal students, to develop a gesture or sign to express these feelings. They can associate the concepts of like and dislike with other students during such social activities as games, mealtimes, and discussions about an outfit that they like and whether it is the same as or different from those their classmates like. The ability to express preference is an important step in making choices and communicating with others. When preferences are reinforced by others, a student is more likely to continue to communicate and to initiate communication.

- For nonverbal students, signs or touch symbols can be associated with other people to reinforce their distinctive identities. When the students have associated a touch symbol or sign with a person's presence, then it can be used to refer to the person when he or she is not present.

- When a student has difficulty taking turns during a conversation (for example, he or she talks too much or does not understand the reciprocal nature of communication), an object, such as a decorated "talking stick" or a toy microphone, can be held by the speaking member and handed to someone else when it is that person's turn to speak. This practice reinforces the idea that only one person speaks at once and that the other person has a role as the listener.

ENCOURAGING COOPERATIVE PLAY: RECESS

Recess at most schools can be a difficult time for children with visual impairments. Designed for students to work off their excess energy, most playgrounds offer unlimited opportunities to engage in activities such as running and playing ball, which can be difficult for some visually impaired students. In addition, children with visual impairments, even those who have mastered the intricacies of typical playground climbing equipment, may sometimes find the additional hustle and noise of several hundred students too distracting for enjoyable, safe play because the increased sound interferes with their efforts to orient themselves.

Teachers can help these students and others who are overwhelmed by too much activity by making slight changes or additions to the recess environment that facilitate interactions and cooperative activities among students. These can include providing manipulative toys in an enclosed area or having a designated space for games that involve more limited physical movement.

Activities

- Set up a games table for students at each recess, where board and card games are available for use by pairs or small groups of students.
- Invite parents and other family members and volunteers from the community to use the recess time to give students mini-lessons in a foreign language—a verbal activity that generally draws on the strengths of many youngsters with visual impairments.
- Establish a student garden area in some part of the schoolyard, even in raised planters. Interested students can plant seeds or seedlings and water, weed, and cultivate the garden.
- Ask a family member or volunteer to lead interested students in singing or folk dancing.
- Designate a reading room or area where students can sit quietly and read during recess. An extension of this activity could be a "book club," in which students agree to read a particular book and then discuss it among themselves.
- Set up a writing table for students who enjoy creative writing, where paper and writing implements are available. Adults could facilitate creative writing activities by providing interesting writing prompts or story starters, such as "On a cold, windy morning . . . ," or "A wolf was howling in the darkness . . . ," and older students could read their writings and critique one another's work.
- Ask a parent, volunteer, or older student to lead a group of interested students in aerobic exercises performed to music.
- Make simple weight–lifting equipment available for checkout or form a jogging club in which the participants are expected to run the track or other designated course with partners.
- Set up hobby tables for students who collect and trade sports cards, stamps, or coins. Other hobby tables could be established for students who are learning to tie knots, sew patches for quilts, or knit.

Critical Points to Cover

- There are many ways to spend one's free time.
- It is easier to talk with people who are engaging in a particular shared activity.
- Sharing an activity with a person allows one to get to know the person better.
- Sometimes, students are surprised to find that they can enjoy an activity that is new to them, especially as they gain familiarity and competence with the activity.
- Through self-evaluation of preferences (for certain people or activities), students learn more about themselves.

Helpful Hints

- Students may need to be taught, in advance, many of the visual activities just presented. For example, knowing that a games table is available to the students, teachers of visually impaired students need to be sure their students have played these games successfully. Also, it may be necessary to provide special instructions and practice for activities, such as folk dancing, gardening, and aerobics, privately at first.
- If a wide variety of activities is available, students may need to be encouraged to rotate through the various options to determine which activities they enjoy and which they do not.
- Students should not be assigned to these areas, but should be informed of their availability as an alternative to typical recess activities.
- Students, particularly those who are young, who do not naturally gravitate toward these recess alternatives and who are not otherwise occupied, may be asked to choose one before each recess and then be required to spend all or part of the recess engaged in it.
- Teachers may want to explore in depth the reasons behind a student's continued choice not to participate in any recess activities.
- Teachers should place tables, activities, and equipment in the same general area each day. Also, it is best to have the same activities offered every day or on a regularly scheduled day (or days) each week, so the youngsters do not spend the entire recess period trying to figure out what activities are available.

- Although at first it may be necessary for teachers of visually impaired students to be available for support during recess, their assistance should be gradually decreased.
- Work with the students to provide appropriate guidance for volunteers, parents or other family members, and older students who may be in charge of or presenting activities and who are unfamiliar or uncomfortable working with children with visual impairments.
- Use these opportunities to teach children with visual impairments self-advocacy skills, such as appropriate ways to express their needs related to their visual impairment or necessary adaptations and modifications.

Evaluation Tips

- Observe whether students report being more engaged at recess and enjoying the time more than previously.
- Ask the teachers if they have seen the students more engaged (with people or activities) during recess.
- Ask families about their children's descriptions of recess play.
- Observe whether the students report preferences, which is a good sign of individualization in their play at recess.
- Determine if the families or students report the students' engagement in similar activities during other leisure-time periods.

For Students Who Need Additional Modifications

- If the students enjoy listening to recordings as a leisure-time activity, they can work with a technology specialist to find a way to learn to turn on and turn off the recording. A switch can be used, so the recording will stop at regular intervals and the students will have to turn it on again, a step that reinforces the fact that the students can choose whether to continue listening. This process is better than letting the students listen for long periods without monitoring whether they are still interested in doing so. When possible, involve another student in a listening activity so that there is discussion and interaction between the two, rather than passive listening.
- Encourage learners to find the best position to assume to share materials and interact with children with physical disabilities.

For example, students with low vision who can bring their hands to their midline may want to have classmates sit directly in front of them. Students who are blind and have better use of one hand than another may want to have classmates sit to one side to make playing easier.

- When students with disabilities need regular assistance from classmates, it is preferable for them to receive assistance from different classmates, rather than always from the same ones, so they can get to know a variety of students. On some occasions, allow the students to choose their assistants.

- When students with disabilities are receiving related educational services (such as physical therapy), pair them with other students to make therapeutic activities cooperative interactions, in which both the classmate and learner can participate.

COMMUNICATING BY TELEPHONE

Learning to use a telephone effectively involves more than just knowing how to dial a friend's number and how to talk about the day's activities. Telephones are useful tools for such tasks as acquiring information, making appointments, and ordering products. As with all skills, a certain degree of teaching and practice of telephone skills is required before proficiency is achieved. Practicing communication skills on the telephone gives young children who are visually impaired additional opportunities to organize their thinking and materials, take notes, write, and learn about the world.

Activities

- Assess the students' current level of knowledge about the telephone. Depending on the students' previous experiences, instruction and practice in using the telephone may need to incorporate the following:
  1. memorizing the keypad
  2. dialing quickly
  3. knowing the parts of the telephone (including the jack)
  4. recognizing and understanding the significance of a dial tone, ringing, and busy signals

5. acquiring telephone numbers through directory assistance and use of the telephone book
6. understanding the organization of the white and yellow pages
7. dialing a telephone number that is written on paper
8. saving and organizing telephone numbers
9. learning telephone etiquette
10. taking messages

- Create opportunities for students to use the telephone. Students can call local businesses (such as a library, candy store, or movie theater) to get information about business hours, policies, or prices. They can order pizza or help teachers order office supplies. They can call recorded information lines, such as for the weather, the time, or sports scores. They can also make, break, or confirm appointments, such as with their orientation and mobility (O&M) instructors, guest speakers, readers, or other individuals with whom they have contact.

Critical Points to Cover

- There are many types of telephones, including pay phones (those for coin, credit-card, and prepaid calling cards), cellular phones, rotary dial and push-button, wall-mounted or desk phones, and portable phones.
- People use the telephone for many purposes, such as conducting business, socializing, and obtaining information.
- There are rules of etiquette that apply when using the telephone as a business or information-gathering tool.
- One can store telephone numbers in an organized way, such as in programmed storage, hard copy, or an electronic system, so they can be located easily again.
- To get a telephone number requires some knowledge of the organization of the telephone book and of the business with which one wishes to talk. Teach how to use directory assistance for local and long distance calling and for toll-free numbers.

Helpful Hints

- Try to incorporate the practice and refinement of telephone skills as one of the steps required for completing other activities, so the youngsters appreciate the value of these skills within the context of conducting the business of living.

- Students may benefit from a trip to the store to learn about all the different shapes and styles of telephones.
- Consider students' preferences and interests when selecting which numbers to call when students begin work on telephone skills.
- Teachers and parents or other family members can save the calls they want to make and ask children with emerging skills to "help" them get the information they need (for example, "I need to go to the stationery store to get some supplies after school today. Would you mind helping me by calling the store to see how late it is open while I get the chalkboard ready for the next lesson?").
- When developing a telephone list on index cards, some braille readers prefer to store the cards from the back of a card box to the front, with the cards inserted upside down and facing the back. This arrangement allows them to place their fingertips in the box to read the braille in a more comfortable position, without pulling each card out to read it. Likewise, some braille readers who use a Rolodex system will braille the cards upside down and on the back side.
- Role-playing conversations and the types of questions to be asked or answered by students is one way to prepare students for successful calls.
- Review the calls with the students. Were the numbers dialed correctly? Were the students polite? Did the students get the information the teacher wanted? What could the students do differently next time? A telephone recording and monitoring device attached to the phone so the teacher can also hear the information exchange can help the teacher and students develop strategies for solving similar problems in future situations.

Evaluation Tips

- Ask the children to role-play, write about, or orally describe the steps one uses to make a particular type of phone call.
- Observe the children at home and school to determine if they are using these skills spontaneously in natural environments.

- See if the students can teach younger students how to perform a task related to the telephone.

For Students Who Need Additional Modifications

- Students who are deaf or who have other physical disabilities should be introduced to adaptive equipment for using telephones. For instance, braille and print output telecommunications devices for the deaf (TDDs), hands-free headsets, and other devices may enable students with multiple disabilities to use telephones independently.
- Nonverbal students can avail themselves of an emergency information card marked with pertinent telephone numbers (such as the numbers of whom to contact in case of an emergency and a doctor's telephone number) to help with emergency telephone usage. If they cannot learn to present the card when appropriate, put the card in a logical place for easy access, such as their wallets, purses, or bookbags, or affix it to their wheelchairs.

PROMOTING SELF-AWARENESS

For all people, effective socialization is based on knowing themselves well and recognizing that they are separate entities. Children who are sighted receive constant visual reminders of their uniqueness, as individuals with a definite present and a unique past and future. They learn early that the experiences of others may differ from their own.

Many children with visual impairments are focused in the here and now because their formation of concepts is often inhibited by a lack of visual information. Without incidental information about their and others' developmental experiences, which is typically gained from sight, these children may be unaware of their place in the scheme of life. Teachers may find that some students have incomplete knowledge of their personal histories and inaccurate perceptions of their futures. Some youngsters actually do not grasp their own life cycle—that they were once babies and that they will grow into adults. Furthermore, some children recount that when they grow up, they will be able to see (like most of the adults they know).

These kinds of misperceptions develop from the lack of specific information that sighted children usually acquire incidentally over time. Direct instructional activities will probably be necessary for many youngsters with visual impairments to enable them to acquire a strong sense of their unique place within the span of time they spend on earth. This information will help them understand the world and thereby contribute to their ability to participate in more meaningful conversations, develop their own perspectives on life, and engage in intimate relationships with others.

Activities

- Have the students interview their parents and other family members about the history of their families. It may be necessary to help them prepare lists of questions to be asked. The students can audiotape or use an appropriate means of writing (such as a pencil, an electronic notetaker, or a slate and stylus) to take notes of the responses they receive. Possible questions for students to ask will depend on their families' structure, but they may include the following:
    1. Where and when were each of my parents and siblings born?
    2. Where and when was I born?
    3. What happened when I was born? Did you have to rush to the hospital? What was the name of the hospital? Who was there? How did they feel?
    4. Where are all the places we've lived? What were those houses like?
    5. What are the names of the schools I've attended? Where were they? Who've been my teachers?
    6. Have I ever had to go to the hospital? Why? For how long? How old was I?
    7. When did I get my first pet? What was its name? What happened to it?
    8. When and where did I meet my best friends?
    9. Questions for a child who has divorced or separated parents include: When did Dad or Mom move out? How did I react?
    10. Children who live with their extended families may ask, Who lives with us? When did other relatives or friends move in?
    11. Can you tell me something special that has happened during each year that I've been alive?

- After the students have conducted the interviews, they can be helped to create timelines of their lives. Students with visual impairments may need to be introduced to the concept of timelines, and braille readers may need help creating them as graphs. Sighted students who are involved in this activity may use photographs to decorate their timelines, whereas the visually impaired students may want to bring tactile artifacts that remind them of the events being described and to display these artifacts as part of their timelines.
- The students may be asked to write narratives of their histories. Older students can write biographies of other family members or classmates after conducting the research by using variations on the questions just listed. The students can make these stories more interesting by predicting futures for one another.
- The students can compare their timelines or biographies with those created by their classmates.
- As part of a history assignment, the students can include significant historical events in their timelines.

Critical Points to Cover

- Everyone's history is similar to other people's in some ways and different in some ways.
- Most people have good things and bad things happen to them in their lives.
- One's past cannot change, and one's history becomes more complex over time.

Helpful Hints

- It may be helpful to have students read the autobiographies and biographies of their heroes or the narratives created by older students as models before creating their own histories.
- While working on their stories, student can practice notetaking, listening, keyboarding, spelling, and writing skills.

Evaluation Tips

- Have students complete a simple application to attend a camp. Do they know most of the information requested?

- Ask the parents if the timeline project elicits more questions about other family members and significant events in their families' histories.
- Have the students complete a timeline of the main character in a biography or autobiography they have read. Do they apply the principles learned in this exercise when developing their own timelines?

For Students Who Need Additional Modifications

- Encourage the students to recognize similarities and differences among families at a level appropriate to them. Use photographs or drawings of families, audiotape recordings of family members' voices, and objects to remind them of their family members and to help them distinguish their own family members from the family members of other classmates.
- Encourage the students to tell about incidents that occurred in their lives and to distinguish between real and pretend events. Because many students with visual and multiple impairments spend time listening to television or the radio, they may believe that characters or situations broadcast by the media are real. For some students, a visit to a radio station, theater, or television studio may help them understand that some entertainment is pretending. In addition, discussion of the broadcasted material can be helpful, with students selecting a part of the broadcast to retell and to describe as "real" or "pretend."

REINFORCING SELF-ADVOCACY SKILLS

Students with visual impairments need to learn self-advocacy early in their lives. Because they may find themselves in educational settings where the teachers have not specialized in the education of children with visual impairments, these youngsters may need to articulate reliable information about their abilities and needs. Often, however, adults forget to ask students to provide important information about themselves and instead conduct this business privately, on a professional-to-professional or professional-to-parent basis. Children need to hear this exchange of information modeled and to become increasingly responsible for its content. If they are given guidance in the gradual acquisition of methods of

FROM A MULTICULTURAL PERSPECTIVE

During the elementary school years, children with visual impairments can distinguish that they are part of a specific racial-ethnic, religious, or disability group. Because identity is particularly affected by social interaction, they need to be guided in the process of self-assessment. As they compare themselves to others, their identity and esteem will be strengthened by their ability to recognize their uniqueness and talents and the areas in which they need to improve. Teachers and other adults need to help visually impaired children maintain a balanced perspective about themselves that is fundamental to the development of the inner strength that they will need to overcome others' negative attitudes toward them. Those who can describe their visual impairments and functional vision are already taking the initial steps toward self-advocacy.

At age 5 or 6, children begin to explore the cultures and other differences of classmates and friends and can identify stereotypes and act on their biases. For example, they may exclude a child from an activity because "it's for girls (or for boys) only" and not want to play with a child who is different in some way or call the child names or otherwise insult him or her. At this age, visually impaired children may be subject to such treatment for the first time.

From ages 7 to 9, children understand the concepts of discrimination, exclusion, prejudice, racism, disrespect, unfair treatment, and bias for or against their cultural and disability groups. When children are in situations in which there are no classmates from the same cultural group, they may feel less comfortable about their cultural identity and may identify with another ethnic or socioeconomic group because that group is treated better or has greater privileges.

During these years, children with visual impairments need to have accurate information about discrimination and in speaking out when they believe they have been treated unfairly. They need to develop critical thinking skills and to discover how to advocate for themselves as incidents occur. In general, building high self-esteem by fostering children's development and use of alternative abilities (for example, exploring auditorily and tactilely, asking questions, being assertive, handling teasing and put-downs, and helping others) can counteract

self-advocacy, they can learn the necessary skills that will serve them well in higher education settings, during job interviews, and on the job.

Activities

- Teachers of students with visual impairments can invite their youngest students to be with them while they explain the students' abilities and needs to the classroom teacher, instructional assistants, and other specialists who are assigned to work with

societal practices that limit the children's opportunities to participate, acquire skills, and even achieve.

Teachers and others need to intervene immediately when visually impaired or culturally distinct children are targets of discrimination. Intervention may take the form of discussions with individual children who were involved in the observed situation to clarify how they can interact appropriately. For classroom teachers, it may also include teaching separate units on such differences as disability, ethnicity, and religion that incorporate storytelling; serving foods of various cultures; playing with dolls that represent differences, including disabilities; and showing films about various cultures.

By age 9, children are usually interested in discovering their ancestry, and history and geography generally have great appeal to them. Teachers can encourage learning about differences by asking students to write or give oral reports on the books they read or the films they watched that relate to their individual cultures. In addition, because children at this age can put themselves in the place of others, they can also become sensitive to the feelings and abilities of others, especially people who may have experienced hardships as a result of their being different. For example, reading *The Diary of Anne Frank* or watching a film about the Underground Railroad and slavery, students may empathize with those who have had to endure great hardships because of their differences. Consequently, they may be inspired to be proud of their own differences and more sensitive to those of others.

Information on cultural values and practices can be incorporated into the classroom by involving the children's families in activities. For example, family members may be invited to contribute to classroom discussions about various cultural traditions. In planning lessons, teachers may need to make routine adjustments on the basis of cultural holidays, eating habits, gender expectations, dress codes, or restrictions related to religious beliefs. Learning about the skills and talents of visually impaired role models, along with the contributions of people of all cultures to science, mathematics, literature, music, art, and sports can foster cultural learning and acceptance.

Lila Cabbil

the students. The primary goal for young students is to allow them to hear the kinds of information provided by the teacher of visually impaired students, the types of questions asked by classroom teachers and others, and the teacher's responses. In addition to hearing these exchanges, youngsters can be more directly involved in providing information about themselves by demonstrating any specialized equipment they will be using, by helping to locate a desk whose location provides optimum lighting, or by selecting a place to store their braille paper.

- During each successive year, the children can be more and more involved in planning for beginning-of-the-school year meetings, as well as in the meetings themselves. The teacher of visually impaired students can prepare them by listing what is important for the classroom teacher to know about their functioning and visual impairments. (The list will vary from child to child, but it may include such information as what, if any, vision the child retains, what special devices the child may use to complete assignments, and what modifications the teacher may need to make to the classroom environment.) From this list, the children can be encouraged to select the information they feel comfortable sharing and the information they prefer the teacher of visually impaired students to give. The teacher and students then can role-play various verbal approaches to take with the classroom teacher. In addition, during these preparation sessions, the teacher and the students can determine how many of the classroom teacher's questions the students should try to answer and how many the teacher will answer.
- Over time, the children can be asked to generate more and more of the items that need to be explained to the classroom teacher. Working closely with the students, the teacher of visually impaired students can use these sessions to gather important information about the students' changing self-image and perceived needs. For example, a young adolescent who has always found it important to sit in the front of the class may now want to sit in another location. The teacher can use these opportunities to help the student clarify his or her reasoning and deal with competing needs (for instance, the desire to sit with friends versus the need to sit in a location that promotes visual efficiency).

Critical Points to Cover

- It is each student's responsibility to explain to teachers his or her abilities and needs.
- Most adults will need an explanation to understand that students with visual impairments will manage the job of learning grade-level material differently, but that expectations for the students' performance on that material should remain high.

- It is best to be open with teachers about one's visual impairment and its effect on one's functioning and needs.
- Telling adults about one's visual impairment gets easier the more the skill is practiced.
- Verbal strategies (such as the use of "I" messages and negotiation skills) are usually successful in situations when accommodations need to be negotiated.

Helpful Hints

- At first, the sessions involving the teacher of visually impaired students, individual students, and the classroom teacher need to be relatively brief and tailored to the child's attention span. For young children, it is best if the focus of meetings is on the visual impairment, how it affects their functioning in class, and any adaptations that are needed. A more comprehensive meeting between teaching professionals, either before or after this session, is usually necessary. As students gain skills through maturity, familiarization, and practice, however, teachers of visually impaired students should give the students greater responsibility for explaining their needs and abilities.
- Audiotaped or videotaped recordings of sessions with general education teachers can be made and reviewed before the next year's meeting as a starting point for the premeeting discussion and planning.
- Teachers of visually impaired students can model for their students the type of language that adults use in self-advocacy situations, such as predicting the concerns of others ("You're probably wondering how I'll take my spelling test"), using "I" statements ("What I will need is . . ."), and negotiation ("Which of these two test adaptations would you prefer?").
- Teachers can reinforce these skills throughout the year by having students share similar information about their visual impairments and associated adaptations in student-led presentations made to classes in which younger students with visual impairments are enrolled or to the students' own classes.
- Teachers working with students with more advanced skills in this area may want to plan ahead with the classroom teacher to

create situations that stretch the students' ability to think quickly, respond to unreasonable requests, and negotiate solutions
that are satisfactory to both parties. For example, the classroom
teacher may be prompted to ask questions for which students
have not specifically been prepared ("How will you know
when it's your turn to erase the chalkboard since this information changes daily and isn't discussed in class?"). Also, teachers
can be prompted to insist that students be helped when assistance is unnecessary ("Even though you say you can get to the
bathroom by yourself, I'll always be sure to send another student with you"). These kinds of situations will provide students
with opportunities to practice self-advocacy skills within con-
trolled circumstances.

Evaluation Tips

- Ask family members and other teachers whether they overhear
  the students acting as self-advocates with adults or other children.
- When role-playing these activities, observe whether the students appear to be gaining confidence in their capacity to
  describe their needs and abilities to others.
- Ask the students to explain how it feels to tell others about their
  visual impairments and to try to analyze why they feel the way
  they do.

For Students Who Need Additional Modifications

- Teach all the classmates the basics of the communication systems
  of students with disabilities, such as sign language, use of an adaptive device, or braille. Encourage nondisabled students to use
  these systems to communicate, even when the disabled students
  are not present, for instance, using a braillewriter during recess.
- For students who do not have a language system, respond to
  behaviors as if they are intentional communication. For example, if children turn their heads or put their heads down when
  an adult turns on the computer, respond as if they have said, "I
  don't want to do this today." In some cases the students do not
  have a choice, but the refusal should be acknowledged.

PROMOTING SELF-IMPROVEMENT

Participation in self-improvement classes is a shared experience of many children in elementary school. Among the types of classes in which young children partake are music, dance, self-defense, gymnastics, sports, and art lessons. Youngsters benefit from these classes in many ways, such as by refining their gross and fine motor skills; developing musical or artistic abilities and an appreciation of music and art; and experiencing social cooperation, teamwork, and competition. Students generally enjoy these activities and often use them to discover interests and talents through which they may define their competence. Likewise, involvement in Scouting or other groups may help students develop their talents and interests.

Youngsters with visual impairments need to engage in the same kinds of activities to help them develop their own identities as competent individuals. All children benefit from mastering the challenges of new tasks, performing for parents or caregivers and peers, and participating with other children in shared activities. Each of these experiences, though seemingly transitory, helps to form the foundation for future success in employment.

However, some families of students with visual impairments may be reluctant to enroll their children in self-improvement classes. Sometimes money and time are factors, but sometimes the reluctance is based on the possibility that the children will get hurt, be teased, or will experience failure. These concerns may often be unfounded or overly heightened, especially when schools and families work together to ensure that instructors are well informed about appropriate adaptations and supported in their efforts to experiment and learn how to share their skills and talents with visually impaired children.

Efforts to support students' success in appropriate group activities reap numerous benefits. Because all the participants are focused on mastering a particular task, they are more likely to converse and socialize around shared events and to form friendships that are based on common interests. Sighted children get the chance to know the visually impaired children as individuals in their own right, not just as children who have visual impairments. As the children with visual impairments experience success in achieving tasks that they perceive to be difficult for everyone, including their sighted peers, their self-esteem increases. In addition, as parents and other adults see the visually impaired youngsters achieving difficult tasks, they, too, will have higher expectations.

Activities

- Explore with the students and their families the types of lessons that seem most appropriate and desirable for the students. Some of the issues to consider during this discussion are the activities in which siblings or family members are involved; the activities in which the parents or other family members might have enrolled the children had there been no visual impairment; the activities the students have tried, would like to try, or have heard other children describe; and any special talents that the children may have displayed. If the parents or other family members cannot afford to pay for lessons, they may work with teachers to be creative in finding alternative options. One alternative is to involve other instructors who are employed by the school district. Carefully written IEP goals (and sensitive networking) may result in art or music teachers' providing private instructional support to facilitate students' successful participation in group lessons. Similarly, collaboration with an adapted physical education teacher may lead to a focus on the development of lifelong, community recreational skills, such as roller skating, bowling, or swimming. Another alternative for financial assistance with lessons is to approach a community service group and ask the members to sponsor the children's participation in lessons.
- After determining appropriate and desirable activities, the teacher of visually impaired students may need to work with the class instructors or coaches to help them understand the impact of congenital visual impairment on learning and to discover if the students need any adaptations. Students, especially older students, should be directly involved in this process. Although the techniques one uses to teach visually impaired children may differ, standards of acceptable performance do not. It is important to maintain high expectations.
- At first, teachers of visually impaired students or families will want to monitor the children's participation in lessons to ensure that any issues related to the visual impairment that arise are

immediately resolved. However, over time, it is important for the adults to encourage the children to solve any problems that occur. Observations during monitoring can also be used to inform parents and teachers about other areas that may need to be addressed on future IEPs, such as the development of social skills or particular fine- or gross motor activities.

- The adults may want to capitalize on emerging friendships that appear to be forming among the students. Students with visual impairments can be encouraged to invite class or team members who have made overtures of friendship for an after-class snack or to practice their newly learned skills during an off-lesson time (for example, a visually impaired student may ask, "Would you like to go bowling with me on Saturday morning?").

Critical Points to Cover

- People with visual impairments can learn difficult tasks, but they occasionally need specialized teaching techniques.
- Participating as a member of a group or team can be rewarding.
- It feels good to master a difficult task.
- Mastery of a difficult task takes practice, time, and energy.
- When one participates as a member of a group, one can socialize somewhat more easily because of the common focus of all the group members.
- Not everyone is good at (or enjoys) every task he or she tries.
- One can measure success in a difficult activity not only by the final outcome, but by the amount of effort expended or satisfaction gained.

Helpful Hints

- Teachers, parents, and other family members need to keep an open mind during discussions of possible activities and try not to eliminate any activities purely on the basis of visual demands. Many teachers and families have found that the most important factor in selecting an activity is the degree of teamwork required in it. Many students with visual impairments generally perform better in sports or athletic activities that demand an individual effort that contributes discretely to the whole, such as participation on wrestling, tai kwan do, swimming, skating, or gymnastics teams. Activities that require coordination with large groups of people (especially ball games) may tend to be more difficult for most children with significant visual impairments to perform.

- For some activities, children may need a period of individual instruction before they participate as members of a group or team. For example, a child could enroll in a quarter-hour private ballet lesson before participating in a group lesson. During the private time, the instructor can use coactive modeling to demonstrate the movements that will be introduced during the group lesson. The student, already familiar with the steps and hand movements, could then participate fully in the group lesson without requiring undue attention from the instructor and unwanted attention from the other students.

- Many youngsters with visual impairments benefit from a quick reminder of the names of the other students who are taking a lesson. Not being able easily to recognize faces from one lesson to the next can affect children's ability to socialize informally.

- It is natural for children to try a particular activity for a while, then move on to something else that interests them. Children with visual impairments should be encouraged to experiment with a variety of activities to determine where their true interests and talents lie. Because visually impaired youngsters cannot easily judge in advance whether an activity will be suitable for them, adults may need to be patient while the students explore their options.

Evaluation Tips

- Ask the parents about their children's comments or their involvement in the selected activities.
- Have the students demonstrate their newly acquired skills. Praise them for making genuine attempts and for their success and provide them with sensitive, realistic feedback.
- Have the students explain how they feel when they accomplish a difficult task.

For Students Who Need Additional Modifications

- Participation in self-improvement classes is an important experience for elementary students and needs to be encouraged with students who need additional modifications when they physically, emotionally, and cognitively are able to do so meaningfully. Often, the critical factor for meaningful participation is communication. For students who do not have symbolic language, encourage friends and family members to use a few basic object symbols or signs to reflect when the students are happy, angry, or sad. For example, when students begin to cry, place their hands on their cheeks and pat the tears to suggest a sign for sadness or for crying. Later, students will begin to understand that others have feelings too. The sign that each child has learned to express his or her own feelings can be generalized to others. In addition, by acquiring communicative intent (understanding and using object symbols or signs to relay basic feelings), students who do not have extensive language skills can improve their ability to integrate into classes or group activities.

- Make sure the students have and can use a signal or gesture to thank others for their assistance. The American Sign Language sign for "thank you" is a hand moved away from the mouth and down with the palm facing the signer. This is easy to teach and is widely understood. However, if a student does not have symbolic language, a handshake, smile, or pat on the hand of another person will work. Teach others in the school and work environment what the signal is so they will be able to understand the students' expressions of appreciation.

10

Developing Compensatory Skills

Compensatory skills are the skills or alternative techniques that students who are visually impaired need to learn to perform tasks that sighted students perform visually. For example, the ability to read and write with braille is a compensatory skill. Because career education promotes the use of academic skills in real-life, nonacademic situations, students with visual impairments need to have mastered the all-important compensatory skills of reading, writing, calculating, and traveling during their elementary school years.

This chapter addresses the necessary compensatory skills that elementary school students with visual impairments should be proficient in to move successfully into middle school. Each of the activities included—planning trips, writing letters, reading newspapers, measuring, using basic office tools, and researching and writing reports—leads to the development of alternative techniques that visually impaired students can use to participate in school and work.

PLANNING ACTIVITIES

Because students with visual impairments, like all students, learn through experiences and need repeated opportunities with similar experiences to make generalizations and draw conclusions about the world, they need to go on carefully planned and meaningful personal field trips to learn certain lessons. For example, visits to local businesses can be invaluable to students' ultimate understanding of, and participation in, the community.

Personal field trips can be made more meaningful if the skills that students are learning in school are infused into them and reinforced before, during, and after the trips. The activities outlined in this section list the steps in planning any short outing to a local community establishment. As much as possible, teachers should encourage their students to become increasingly involved and responsible for completing each step in the plan. The steps incorporate, in a meaningful, direct way, the self-help, vocational, and precareer skills that children at this age need to develop.

Activities

- Have the students call before the trip to see if the business is open and to get directions. Places to visit may include fast-food restaurants, post offices, dry cleaners, libraries, Laundromats, bakeries, shoe repair shops, bus stations, clothing stores, and grocery stores.
- Ask the students to plan the route and transportation alternatives.
- Have the students estimate the amount of time required to make the entire trip.
- Have the students write a confirmation letter if special considerations are needed.
- With the students, visit community establishments, and, if possible, use the services provided there.
- Ask the students to take notes of what they saw, what was discussed, and what happened, and to give their impressions of the trip.
- Have the students write thank-you notes if employees spent additional time with them (for example, describing their jobs, providing job-shadowing opportunities [chances to follow employees while they perform jobs], or demonstrating equipment).

Critical Points to Cover

- People rely on many specialty businesses in today's society.
- Frequently, many businesses perform the same function in one community.
- People choose to patronize a business on the basis of many factors, including location and service.
- Often the same item can be purchased at many types of stores.

FROM AN URBAN PERSPECTIVE

Elementary school students with visual impairments who live in urban areas are likely to receive disability-specific services in their local schools. However, these services may often be less tailored to their unique family and cultural needs than are those in rural areas where they may be the only children receiving these services. The advantages to attending schools in urban areas are that students in general have access to a wider array of medical, educational, and therapeutic professionals; adapted materials; specialized equipment; and transportation options for attending extracurricular and community events. They are also exposed to more diverse racial-ethnic and religious school populations and communities and more people with a variety of disabilities. Among the disadvantages are that considerably more students vie for specialists' attention and other available resources, and there may be greater or more concentrated evidence of some of the social ills of inner-city life (for example, gang activity, health problems, drug and alcohol abuse, violence, and poverty, as well as a feeling of anonymity).

Family members and professionals who work with visually impaired students will need to be diligent in advocating for individualized attention for these students so the children do not get lost in the large school systems they attend. They also need to provide as safe an environment as possible. In addition, they need to teach the children safety and other techniques to cope with crime and other dangers to which children with visual impairments may be particularly vulnerable because they cannot see visual cues of danger.

Furthermore, children in urban areas may have greater opportunities than those in rural areas to visit cultural institutions, such as museums and concert halls, and sports arenas, where they can attend various professional sports events. There are also more likely to be disability-specific support groups or recreational clubs that visually impaired children can attend with their families or friends. Activities such as these provide urban children with greater opportunities to build an awareness of themselves, the world around them, and the kinds of work people do than may be available in rural areas.

Victoria Tripodi

Helpful Hints

- It often is necessary to visit the same business or a similar business many times. For example, children with visual impairments may not be aware that the shoe repair store in the shopping mall smells the same as the shoe repair store in town and that the same kind of work is done at both places.
- Teachers need to instruct students in the various component tasks of these activities using the techniques that are appropriate

for each student. Many students need to listen to or observe the teacher performing a task, then gradually perform the task with increasing independence. For example, at first, the teacher may look up the establishment's telephone number in the white or yellow pages, dial the number, and record the information that the students repeat, whereas the students' only job may be to ask for the information and repeat it aloud. Later, each of these steps can be performed by the students as they gain confidence and competence in carrying out the task.

- Field trips are more valuable if the children can be involved in specific activities at the destination, such as mailing a letter, doing laundry, or buying cookies. Many repair-related activities are especially useful because they require two trips to the same location—one to drop an item off and one to pick it up.
- Each field trip to a business can be viewed as an opportunity to learn more about the employees. Help the students to prepare a list of questions to ask the employees, then have them compare the information given to them.
- These planned field-trip activities are important for reinforcing academic, communication, advocacy, orientation and mobility, daily living, problem-solving, and precareer skills.
- Students can begin to keep and organize telephone lists, route information, and business addresses, so these skills can be reinforced through practical application.

Evaluation Tips

- Ask the students to think about whether a job they have observed is one they would like to have in the future.
- Ask family members if their children seem to be more aware of the stores and businesses that they encounter in the course of their daily routines.
- Listen to the conversations and play of students to determine whether they refer to or incorporate their field-trip experiences in their interactions with their classmates.
- Observe whether the students are generalizing the skills learned in these activities as they approach new problems or activities. For instance, do students suggest that clothes that have been soiled need to go to the dry cleaner or do they independently

dial information and complete a telephone list entry when asked to get the number of a local pizza delivery establishment?

For Students Who Need Additional Modifications

- When the students visit adult workers, encourage them to ask how these people go to and from their jobs. Make sure that the students meet adults who have physical disabilities and talk with them about what kinds of transportation are available.
- Find opportunities for students to meet and observe workers who assist in transportation. Bus and taxi drivers and personal attendants may be willing to describe their jobs to the class and to talk about how they assist people who have special transportation needs.
- Before the students travel a familiar route, ask them to tell what landmarks exist along that route. For students who do not use language, provide objects or picture symbols to represent each landmark. For example, a place mat or spoon can represent the place where meals are served. A picture of a fire hydrant can remind a particular student of the corner where he turns on his way to the park. After each landmark is reached, the students can place the symbol for it in a purse, pocket, or backpack, and the next symbol can be presented.
- Give the students with severe physical disabilities choices about how they are moved. For example, if a student's wheelchair is moved by others, provide a symbol or teach a gesture for "fast" and "slow," so the student can request a change in speed. Make the left and right arms of the wheelchair distinctive (for example, use different colors or fabrics) and touch the student's arm on that side before a turn is made. When the student has mastered that concept, he or she can tap the right or left arm to request a right or left turn.
- Encourage the students to participate in planning field trips or visits to work sites. Work with the class to determine which questions to ask to ensure that all the classmates can enter a building or workplace.
- Involve the students in planning for special assistance on field trips or site visits, for example, by asking them, "How many adults will we need? Should each blind student have one sighted guide? Who can we ask to join us on our trip?"

FROM A FAMILY PERSPECTIVE

Developing Compensatory Skills

Children who are visually impaired need and appreciate help from their families as they develop compensatory skills, such as reading and writing in braille or using low vision devices; using a long cane, trailing techniques, or sighted guide assistance to get around in various environments; and accessing information from computers equipped with speech or braille output or screen enlargement programs. By learning about these adaptive techniques or compensatory skills, parents and other family members can effectively support their visually impaired child. The Hadley School for the Blind (see the Resources section) offers free correspondence courses for family members who are interested in learning braille (by sight or touch). The American Foundation for the Blind, American Printing House for the Blind, National Library Service, and other national organizations offer numerous publications and tools for teaching children how to perform alternative techniques for daily living, orientation and mobility, and accessing information (see Resources).

In instructing visually impaired children, some teachers help a class write a letter or persuasive essay and then post it in a public place for a week or two. It becomes an example of a communal project and a way for students to model future personal assignments. Families can perform similar activities in large print or braille. Celebrate your work together. When you write, build, compute, or discover, present the work publicly for the family to see (for example, by posting it on the refrigerator). Doing so will deepen the learning experience for everyone. One of the secrets of success for any family activity is simply to enjoy one another. Try not to let perfectionism, stress, wishes, rules, or expectations make the simple enjoyment of doing a task take a backseat. It is the feeling of enjoyment that is derived from performing a task that children will probably remember long after they have finished the task.

Kevin O'Connor

WRITING ACTIVITIES: LETTER WRITING

The ability to write letters is a skill used by most adults in their personal and business roles. Adults write letters to request information, explain a position, order materials, and thank another person for a kindness, among other reasons.

The inclusion of frequent letter writing in a program for elementary school students with visual impairments helps the students not only to prepare for future activities at home and at work, but also to develop clarity of thought and skills related to the use of writing tools, writing mechanics, and letter formatting. Although letter writing is taught to all children in school, most students with visual impairments will benefit from additional opportunities to practice the skill. In addition, some of these youngsters may need supplementary instruction in parts of the task that are not taught directly to sighted students, such as placement of the stamp or licking the envelope.

Activities

- For younger children or those who have not been exposed to the use of letters, it may be necessary to start instruction by giving them opportunities to learn the concept of mail, which includes letters from friends and relatives, information from businesses, and bills. This awareness may begin by having the children help carry the mail, place it in mailboxes, and open letters; by explaining what information is contained in the letters; and by letting them know when letters are being written. For instance, as she goes through the mail, mom might say, "Well here's a letter asking me if I want a credit card, this is an announcement of a picnic to be held at the church, this paper tells me I owe $40.23 to a department store, and here's a letter from Grandma."

- Students who are not yet writing can still begin to appreciate their role as letter writers. For example, immediately after holidays and birthdays, when writing thank-you notes is appropriate, ask the children to help compose a letter. Tell the children what is being included ("First, I'm writing the date") and then ask them what they want to convey ("What do you want to tell your Aunt Vicki about the toy she gave you?"). Use the children's wording as much as possible, though suggestions for changes can be made as the children become familiar with the process. Encourage the children to create their own "letters" at the same time by scribbling with a pen, pencil, crayon, slate and stylus, or brailler. Read the final product to the children, who then can help to fold the paper, insert it in an envelope, place a stamp in the corner, and lick the seal.

- As their penmanship, brailling, or word-processing skills improve, the students can be expected to create their own letters. A good way for them to start is to write to companies that send free products or coupons upon request. Some students have had good luck writing to movie or sports stars and asking for autographed pictures. Thank-you letters to volunteer braillists or others who provide services to the students are also appropriate. Teachers of more advanced students may want to encourage them to describe their school program in letters to legislators. The teachers need to teach the correct format of a business letter and still may be required to assist the students with appropriate wording. The students should sign their names to their letters, using a signature guide, if necessary. There are many types of signature guides, but most incorporate an opening in a piece of plastic, cardboard, or metal that provides a space in which the signature can be written.

- Preparation of the body of the letter is only part of the process. Many students need to be taught how to prepare an envelope so the writing is legible. They may also need continued practice folding letters, inserting them into envelopes, placing stamps in the correct place on envelopes, and licking and sealing envelopes. To reinforce organizational skills, students can also be taught to make copies of their letters on a copy machine; label the copies in braille, if necessary; and then file the copies for future reference. As letters and their replies accumulate, more complex filing systems (alphabetical, numeric, or alphanumeric) may be explored. They may want to consider filing correspondence by date, subject, receiver's last name, or some other variation of their own making (such as a color-coding system for students with low vision). This activity also gives students the opportunity to develop personal address lists and maintain them in an organized way, such as in a tabbed file or in an index card box, or, for more advanced students, by using computer or electronic notetaker programs.

Critical Points to Cover

- People use mail for many purposes.
- There are different formats for business and personal letters.
- There is a specific format to be followed when addressing and preparing an envelope.
- Many people enjoy receiving mail.
- One can store addresses in an organized way so they can easily be located again.

- One can store correspondence in an organized way so it can be located easily again.
- Stamps, which can be purchased at many locations, are used to pay the post office to deliver letters.
- The amount of postage required on an envelope is dependent on the weight of the materials in the envelope.
- Some materials can be sent as Free Matter for the Blind and Other Handicapped Persons.
- One can mail an envelope at a post office, from a mailbox at one's home, from a mail drop at school or in an apartment building or hotel, or from a different kind of mailbox on the street.

Helpful Hints

- Try to incorporate practice and refinement of letter-writing skills as a step required for other activities, such as after a field trip, part of an exercise exploring the availability and cost of braillewriters, or preparing for a party. Through these activities, youngsters can appreciate the value of letter-writing skills within the context of conducting the business of living.
- This activity can be enhanced by exploratory trips to the post office, where students can mail their letters; buy stamps; and learn about the people, materials, and other things associated with the post office.
- Discuss with the students the mailing privilege known as Free Matter for the Blind and Other Handicapped Persons. It is essential for the students to understand that to use "Free Matter" the sender or receiver must be blind or be print handicapped (the U.S. Postal Service defines those who are print handicapped as people who cannot read or use conventionally printed material) to mail material free of charge. The person sending materials "Free Matter" must be certified as eligible for this service by a competent authority (such as a family physician, ophthalmologist, or optometrist). Materials posted "Free Matter" must be in alternative formats, that is, braille, audiotape, large print (at least 14-point type), or other recorded formats. If a blind person sends letters or other materials in regular print, he or she will need to purchase the applicable postage. Special eligibility standards are specified in the *U.S. Post Office Manual,* section E040.2.1 (1996).

- As was mentioned previously, when developing an address box, some braille readers prefer to store the cards from the back of the box to the front, with the cards inserted upside down and facing the back. This arrangement allows them to place their fingertips into the box to read the braille in a more comfortable position without having to pull each card out to read.
- Stamps can be purchased at many locations. Try to expose the students to opportunities to buy stamps at supermarkets, chain drugstores, through the mail, or from vending machines.

Evaluation Tips

- Observe the students to determine their level of familiarity with the writing process. Are they performing the component tasks with greater independence?
- Ask the students, "What is the next step after I fold the letter?"
- Determine whether the students are maintaining address files in an order that makes sense to them.
- Ask family members whether their children have commented on letter writing and mailing practices at home and what they have said. Are the children becoming more involved in these activities?

For Students Who Need Additional Modifications

- Students who do not read and write can send messages to other people using other methods. Some examples include audiotaping messages, taking photographs that can be shown to others or used as pictures on communication boards, dictating letters to others, creating original drawings, or using adaptive technology to produce printed materials from a computer.

READING SKILLS: NEWSPAPER HELP-WANTED ADS

Youngsters with visual impairments need to have the opportunity to practice sophisticated as well as basic reading skills. One way to do so is to read newspaper help-wanted ads, a section of newspapers about which many sighted children may be aware, but that some youngsters with visual impairments may not have explored. For children who are blind, the information in the help-wanted ads can be typed or scanned into an accessible computer or retrieved through an on-line or telephone newspaper service.

Activities

- Explain to the students that many employers recruit new employees by listing job openings in a special part of the newspaper called the "help-wanted" section or "classified ads." To save money and space, employers write these ads using abbreviations that form a code that readers need to "break." Help the students use their reasoning skills to break the code to read newspaper help-wanted ads by analyzing ads with students.
- Once the students are familiar with the format of most help-wanted ads, they can categorize a group of ads by pay, education required, job cluster, or other classifications. Help the students draw conclusions from this exercise regarding the availability of jobs in certain fields, the relationship between pay and education or experience, and hiring trends. For example, students may note that there are more postings in the classified ads for jobs as a cashier than for jobs as a buyer. The teacher can use this observation to discuss similarities (for instance, that both jobs are listed under the heading *Retail*) and differences (such as that the position of cashier in general requires less education and experience than does one for a buyer, that a cashier may be in greater demand than a buyer because more cashiers are needed in a store than buyers, and that cashiers in general are paid less than buyers).
- Discuss other methods that employers use to let the public know that jobs are available, including placing signs in windows, telling their friends, contacting employment agencies, and using job listing services on the Internet.
- Introduce the students to the code used in ads to sell automobiles and houses or to rent apartments and help them break the code. This variation on the activity presents the opportunity to discuss the relative costs of these items with the students.

Critical Points to Cover

- One way that employers announce that they have jobs available is through help-wanted ads in local newspapers.

- Not all jobs are advertised in newspapers.
- All newspapers do not carry the same help-wanted ads.
- The information contained in newspapers is accessible to visually impaired students through the use of sighted readers, reading machines, or some on-line services.
- Some jobs pay better than others.
- Some jobs require more education than others.
- Some jobs offer more benefits than others.
- Some jobs are in greater demand than others.

Helpful Hints

- Reading help-wanted ads is an excellent way for students with low vision to practice the use of their low vision devices or other reading devices.
- Much of the vocabulary that is presented in this activity will be new to students (for example, *temporary, guaranteed, salary, staff development, qualified,* among other words) and they should be encouraged to use these new words in their discussions about jobs, employment-seeking strategies, and explorations of newspapers.
- Explain to students that many of the jobs listed may be unfamiliar to them. Make note of the jobs that seem to be foreign to students and use this list as a guide for future field trips or reports.
- Encourage the students to find a means to gain access to this information independently, so they do not have to rely on their teachers, families, or assistants to read directly to them. The use of on-line or telephone newspaper reading services, closed-circuit televisions, magnifiers, and scanning devices are methods by which visually impaired people can access help-wanted ads by themselves. The independent acquisition of this type of information will be critical to them when they are adults.
- Give the students help-wanted ads from newspapers in various locations and encourage them to identify the types of jobs that are available in large and small population areas.

Evaluation Tips

- Ask the parents if their children demonstrate greater interest in how relatives and workers acquired their jobs.

- Assess whether the students' rate of reading and interpreting help-wanted ads is increasing with practice by giving them examples (in accessible media) to interpret.
- Have the students write help-wanted ads for their "dream jobs" or for jobs that they have studied.

For Students Who Need Additional Modifications

- For students who do not read or write, encourage listening to help-wanted ads that are read aloud. Ask them to decide whether this is a good job for them, and practice making telephone calls to inquire about jobs that are available.

CALCULATING SKILLS: MEASURING

Although all youngsters spend some time in school learning how to measure, instruction often is based on the premise that students are familiar with the tools used for measurement and that they have observed adults taking or making measurements for a variety of purposes. The teacher may demonstrate the measuring activity in class, provide an opportunity for guided practice, and then assign workbook pages for the students to practice the task independently. However, many students with visual impairments may not have the prerequisite knowledge that is assumed necessary for the complete understanding and mastery of this task. Unless students have had frequent and direct experiences with measurement tools and activities, they may have difficulty developing the concept of measuring and facility with the use of measurement tools. They will therefore benefit from repeated opportunities to practice and apply these skills.

Activities

- As part of a special science experiment, have the older students take several measurements of a group of children in a first- or second-grade class, such as their height, weight, arm length, and palm width. The adventuresome ones may also measure the amount of water each subject can drink from a glass in one gulp. The students can then take the same measurements six months later as a follow-up.

- Have the students carefully record all findings using a technique that they have developed in consultation with the teacher of visually impaired students.
- Have the students reorganize the data, so that information about the group of students can be compared. For instance, height and weight information may be listed separately for boys and girls or by which part of the alphabet (first half or second half) students' last names fall. Remember that not all the potential ways to organize data will make sense to the grown-ups involved.
- Help the students to analyze the data.
- Teach the students to graph the data.

Critical Points to Cover

- People measure objects for a reason, not just because the activity is assigned to them.
- One uses different tools and strategies for measurement, depending on the object to be measured.
- Scientists must be consistent when taking measurements and must record the results carefully.
- Scientists use charts and graphs to organize and analyze findings.

Helpful Hints

- Some students have been observed to know how to measure using a ruler only when the object being measured is less than 12 inches long. Teach them how to align the ruler and flip or move it over to add to its length.
- Be sure that the students have been introduced to and can use a tape measure.
- Encourage the students to problem solve throughout the activity. Is there a better way to record the data? Is there a more efficient way to organize one's findings? What does this information tell the students?
- The students may need to be taught and encouraged to use appropriate strategies for working with and giving directions to younger children.
- Explain (and encourage the parents to explain) to the children when they are using measurement skills, what type of tool is

being used, and the purpose of the measurement. Involve the children in the task, if possible.

- Use the recording of personal data to reinforce the concept that people are different in many ways.
- This activity provides an opportunity for students with visual impairments to view themselves and be viewed by others as competent because they are performing tasks that are beyond the abilities of children being measured.
- This activity may be even more fun with sighted partners. Teachers need to make certain, however, that both partners have the opportunity to become proficient in all aspects of the activity.

Evaluation Tips

- Ask the students to measure unfamiliar objects of various sizes and to compare each other's results. Are the measurements by different students similar? What accounts for the differences?
- Ask the parents if the students are more interested in and desirous of helping when measuring tasks are being performed. Do the children demonstrate measuring skills at home?
- Ask the classroom teacher whether the children's ability to read charts and graphs has improved.
- Determine whether the students can teach younger children how to measure weight, length, or temperature.

For Students Who Need Additional Modifications

- Teach computational skills in the context of real activities and find opportunities for the students to compare "numbers" with "amounts" and "sizes." For example, adding the total number of students riding two school buses or subtracting the number of students absent from the total number of students in the class will provide applied practice. Children who are blind may have more difficulty making this distinction because they cannot compare large items with their hands; this difficulty may be greater if the students have a physical disability as well, since they cannot enclose sets or manipulate items.
- Use auditory approaches to emphasize the concepts of numeration and size or volume. For example, ask the students to com-

pare the difference between eight taps on the drum and one loud tap.

- In most cases, teach the use of a talking calculator only after the students have mastered basic operations. Encourage those students with mental retardation who cannot master mental calculation to memorize basic operations and to use a talking calculator to manage their own money.
- Encourage the students to notice real experiences that demonstrate the characteristics of sets by saying, for example, "There are usually 27 children in our room, but 2 are absent today, so how many people are in the class?"
- Students who have physical disabilities may want to use wire counting frames that can be created with large spools or beads. These frames may consist of a heavy wire in an arc shape on which counted beads can be moved to one side of the arc and uncounted items remain on the opposite side. With these frames, the students can separate counted from uncounted items without having the items roll away.

USE OF BASIC OFFICE TOOLS

The ability of most sighted children to use basic desk tools is, in all likelihood, learned primarily through incidental observations of their casual use by others. As with many other simple, everyday tasks, adults often wait until children express an interest in using a particular tool, for example, a stapler, and then informally demonstrate how the tool is used. Little direct instruction is necessary for sighted children to master the use of paper clips, binder clips, hole punches, clamps, three-ring binders, staplers, staple removers, rubber bands, adhesive tape, and scissors. Having observed the use of these items hundreds of times, most sighted children seem to know automatically how and when to use them appropriately.

Many children with visual impairments need deliberate direct instruction to learn to use these items. For most of these youngsters, the actual teaching time required to use each tool will be minimal. However, it is important for teachers and parents to require the children to use these tools regularly for functional purposes.

Activities

- Assess the students' recognition of and ability to use a variety of desk tools. Develop a plan to introduce items that the students are not using regularly within the functional context of the classroom or home. For example, ask students at home to place large-print or braille labels that have been prepared on index cards around canned or boxed goods and attach the labels with rubber bands. At school, students can assist the teacher by collating and stapling sets of papers. In addition, teach the students where the items are stored and how to retrieve them when needed. Encourage the students to use the tools by requiring them to turn in work that has been stapled, paper clipped, or organized in a three-ring binder.
- Encourage the parents to involve their children in the organization of bills, papers, and documents at home. For example, when the need to use a stapler, paper clip, tape, or other tool arises, they can ask the children to perform the task.
- Involve the students in school or community-association bulk-mailing efforts, such as preparing newsletters. This kind of activity requires repeated practice stapling, folding, punching, and collating.

Critical Points to Cover

- People use a variety of desk tools to assist them in organizing their documents and papers.
- Not all people use the same type of organizational device for the same activity.
- Staples are a fairly permanent method of keeping a set of papers together. Paper clips are used when papers may need to be separated again in the future. Tape and hole punches make permanent changes to documents, a sometimes undesirable result.

Helpful Hints

- Have the students explore the work spaces of a variety of workers who have desks (such as secretaries, managers, physicians, architects, and computer programmers) to discover for themselves the types of tools that these workers use and how they are organized.

- Rather than ask the students to buy prepunched paper, have them punch the holes in the pages that they use.
- Encourage the students to use rubber bands to attach labels to canned and frozen foods that are stored in the kitchen.
- Take the students on a field trip to an office supply store to explore the variety of tools (and their variations) that are sold.
- Encourage everyone who is involved with the students, including the parents and other family members, classroom teachers, classmates, to tell the students with visual impairments when and for what purpose different desk tools are being used.

Evaluation Tips

- Observe (and note, if appropriate) the students' spontaneous use of desk tools.
- Occasionally ask the students to explain why they have selected to use one tool rather than another.
- Ask families if they observe their children spontaneously using desk tools at home.

For Students Who Need Additional Modifications

- Review catalogs with students that include pictures and descriptions of office tools that are used by the general public and by people with special needs (for instance, one-handed keyboards) and bring examples into class, if possible.
- Consider ways to stabilize tools for students with physical disabilities (for example, the use of double-sided tape, jigs—devices that are used to guide a tool or hold work as it is fed into a tool-template—and so forth).
- Practice identifying categories of tools (such as types of staplers or paper clips) and ask students to describe how items in each category are similar or different.

RESEARCH AND REPORT-WRITING SKILLS

Because they may lack sufficient background and incidental learning experiences, many children with visual impairments often need to practice repeatedly the activities to which they are introduced in school before they can understand and incorporate them into their repertoire of skills that they can perform independently. Writing reports based on their own research is one skill that many students may not ordinarily practice enough to become truly proficient in.

Having little knowledge of the types of jobs that adults hold may also be a problem for many students with visual impairments. Although it is impossible to visit a large number of work sites, it is possible for students to discover information about a variety of jobs by reading numerous sources. Conducting research and then writing a report involve the use of many of the compensatory skills that students with visual impairments need to be successful workers, including reading, searching, scanning, using reference materials, taking notes, organizing information and thoughts, writing, editing, and using adaptive technologies.

Activities

- Have each student choose a job or career to study or use a random selection process, such as having each student draw a job title from a hat or place a finger on a selection from a page of the *Dictionary of Occupational Titles* (U. S. Department of Labor, 1991). The students then can practice using on-line, electronic, or print reference materials to discover information about their assigned jobs. After they have collected and organized their data, the students can write, edit, and rewrite papers of a predetermined length that they can include in files or binders that can be used as the basis for other activities related to career education.
- As a group project, have the students prepare oral presentations that describe the information they have collected about their assigned jobs.
- Use the reports of several students as the basis for other lessons in which the students compare jobs within and among occupational categories.

Critical Points to Cover

- Reading, searching, scanning, and gathering information get easier as one practices these skills.
- Drafting, writing, and editing represent a process of continual refinement and improvement of material.

- Punctuation, capitalization, and word choices matter when writing.
- There are many different ways to gather information, and each way has its own advantages and disadvantages.
- Information can be categorized and presented in a logical order.

Helpful Hints

- This task can be adapted for younger children by reading a story about a worker to the children (while they follow along in their own books) and then asking the children questions about that worker. The teacher of visually impaired students can write the children's responses in their preferred reading media, and the children can illustrate, with tactile objects or pictures, some of the content of the story. These reading times can be made much more meaningful by a field trip to a work site, such as that described in the story.
- At first, the teacher of visually impaired students can provide outlines or templates for students to use as they gather information and prepare their written reports. Older students who have completed this assignment before can be encouraged to add additional information, including their thoughts on the suitability of the particular job to them personally and on the kinds of adaptations that may be required for them to accomplish the job.
- Encourage the older elementary school students to use more than one source for their research. Also, expect them to conduct the research and prepare their reports more independently, using fewer templates or outlines and more complex technological tools, such as the Internet. For instance, although early reports may have been completed in the students' preferred writing medium, later reports need to be prepared in the medium preferred by the intended audience—the teacher.
- Introduce the students to and have them practice the use of live readers as they search for information about a particular occupational topic in the library or career resource center.

Evaluation Tips

- Check whether the students' reading speeds are increasing.

- Determine if students are making fewer errors in their writing for the teacher of visually impaired students.
- Ask other teachers whether the students' written assignments in other classes are improving.
- Ask families if their children are demonstrating a familiarity with and can discuss the roles of a large number of workers.
- In listening to the conversations and play of students, determine if they are projecting themselves more frequently into future job roles.
- Observe whether the students are more independent in their work at school.

For Students Who Need Additional Modifications

- Students who are unable to read and write may need to audio-tape their reports or to present them orally.
- Nonverbal students may need help developing pictorial journals of the places they have visited and the people they have met instead of using a report-type format. Videotaped observations can supplement the journals for students with adequate vision to review them.
- Deaf-blind students without functional vision or hearing may collect tactile objects as representational artifacts from observations to help them remember materials that other students may capture in reports. For example, samples of herbs and a package of seeds may be reminders of a visit to a farm. A paper cup and a new container of dental floss may represent a student's visit to the dentist.

References

U. S. Department of Labor. (1991). *Dictionary of occupational titles.* Washington, DC: U. S. Government Printing Office.

CHAPTER

Promoting Opportunities to Work

hile children are in elementary school, they need to have work opportunities, such as chores, available to them in school and at home. At the same time, they need to investigate the types of jobs that are available in their communities while they are still dreaming about what they want to be when they grow up. Consequently, students with visual impairments need to have contact with adults who are visually impaired to help them understand what jobs these people are engaged in and how they chose their particular fields.

Volunteer experiences can be important learning opportunities for elementary school students that help them explore career paths. Informational interviews and job-site explorations also can help young people with visual impairments discover what jobs are available to them. The activities in this chapter facilitate students' ability to handle responsibility and begin to investigate careers.

CAREER INVESTIGATION AT SCHOOL

Many individuals other than teachers are employed at a school. Sighted students learn about these employees (for example, coaches, administrators, secretaries, cafeteria workers, and janitors) and their general roles through frequent, casual encounters and informal observations. Even if sighted students never interact directly with these employees, the employees' existence and job tasks in support of the school are evident to these students.

The same information may not be readily available to many visually impaired students. These students are often not aware of the many support staff who are not directly involved in their classrooms but who are nonetheless involved in the school. They need to be taught who the employees at school are, what their roles are, and why they work. As with all instruction for students with visual impairments, these lessons are most effectively learned through direct interaction with the employees and direct involvement in the tasks they perform.

Activities

- Ask students to carry notes or messages to various school workers identifying tasks that need to be completed, and prompt the employees ahead of time to comment on the requests. (This activity can also be used as part of an orientation and mobility lesson or school orientation exercise.) For example, ask a student to carry a message to the janitor requesting that wastebaskets in a specific room be emptied. The janitor could respond by saying that the trash will be emptied after he or she has finished cleaning the sinks in the bathroom.
- Give the students opportunities to job shadow, or follow, school workers as they go about their duties. Even spending an occasional hour with employees who are willing to explain (and demonstrate) what they are doing as they perform their jobs can provide important insights into the nature of the jobs and work in general. Employees who encourage students to try parts of a job, such as answering a telephone or shelving books, are particularly good candidates for students who are job shadowing.
- Assign students to work with staff members whose jobs entail tasks that incorporate emerging skills that the students need to practice. For instance, assign a younger child who is developing the concept of one-to-one correspondence to work with the cafeteria staff, placing one carton of milk on each tray or at each place setting in front of each chair. Have an older child who needs practice aligning papers and using a stapler assist the school secretary in preparing materials that students need to take home.

- Help students to develop lists of interview questions and assign them various school workers to interview. Depending on their age level, the students might ask what time the employees arrive at work and go home, how much time is available for lunch, whether the employees bring their lunches or go to a restaurant to eat, the type of clothes they wear to work, what level of schooling is required for the job, the general salary range, and their level of job satisfaction, among other questions.

Critical Points to Cover

- It takes many people who perform various jobs and work together to run a school.
- Every job is important.
- People work for money and job satisfaction.
- Jobs often incorporate many different activities and require different skills.
- People select their jobs on the basis of their abilities, interests, values, and needs.

Helpful Hints

- Advise the students about their role and the behaviors expected of them when interacting with school employees.
- Brief the school employees about their role in these interactions.
- As often as possible, leave the students with the impression that the jobs being discussed can be accomplished by individuals who are visually impaired, as well as by those who are sighted. With older students, discuss how particular tasks may be adapted for employees with visual impairments.
- Use the errands, job experiences, interviews, or job shadowing as a springboard for discussing employees and their work. Relate the students' experiences with the school employees to other employees they have encountered in community outings, such as the secretary at the dentist's office or the janitor at the local mall. Is it the same person as the employee at the school? How are these jobs similar or different?
- Discuss with the students how they feel about these jobs. Are these the jobs they may want to do someday? Was there only a part of the jobs they enjoyed?

Evaluation Tips

- Observe whether the students incorporate, in conversations and play with other children, information they have learned about the employees at the school.
- Ask the parents what their children remember and tell them about the employees who have been interviewed or shadowed.
- Ask the students to describe or write about the employees they have interviewed or shadowed.
- Determine whether the students can act out (or role-play) the jobs they have studied.
- Ask the students who have had similar experiences to play a Twenty Questions-type game, by saying, for example, "I'm thinking of a worker who . . ."
- Ask employees whom the students have job shadowed about the students' performance. If they are comfortable doing so, ask them to provide feedback to the students.

For Students Who Need Additional Modifications

- Encourage the students to find out what parts of jobs people like and do not like. Nonverbal students may visit employees in the school and learn to use a sign or gesture for "like" or "dislike" and "happy" or "sad." For example, if the janitor is moving slowly as she mops the floors and is frowning, indicate, "She does not like to mop." If she is smiling as she finishes emptying the bucket of water, indicate, "She likes being finished." Students need to know that adults sometimes have to do things they do not enjoy. If they can understand the concept of money, they also need to know that employees are paid for performing their jobs.

CAREER INVESTIGATION THROUGH CONTACT WITH VISUALLY IMPAIRED ADULTS

Frequently, youngsters with visual impairments and the adults who work with them are unaware of the many jobs that can be performed by adults who are visually impaired. It is sometimes easier to think about why a person could not perform a particular job than to think about how that job may be performed with limited or no vision. The

best technique for overcoming a perception such as this is to introduce
students with visual impairments and the significant adults in their lives
to visually impaired adults who work.

The value of role models cannot be overestimated. By learning
about, reading about, or meeting role models, students can begin to
step outside their current experiences and imagine possibilities for
their future. People who can describe feelings similar to theirs and who
have a variety of experiences can help students lay out a road map
toward a future that seems plausible and attainable.

At the elementary school level, role models can be used to prevent, or at least minimize, the development of negative stereotypes and
attitudes. Elementary school students who regularly encounter and
interact with visually impaired adults learn that having jobs and families and being involved in the community are viable goals for the
future. They discover firsthand the kinds of adaptations that these individuals use to accomplish daily home, travel, and community tasks.
Equally important, they are given the opportunity to incorporate a
positive value about visual impairment into their sense of self.

Activities

- Invite visually impaired adults to visit the class to talk about
  themselves and what they do for a living. Teachers can meet
  visually impaired adults through contacts with local chapters of
  the National Federation of the Blind or the American Council
  of the Blind (see Resources), private agencies that provide services to people with visual impairments, or through friends and
  acquaintances of former students.
- Arrange (or have the students help arrange) meetings with visually
  impaired adults in the community. Prepare a list of questions for the
  adults related to their particular jobs, travel, school experiences, feelings about visual impairment, and home activities and determine in
  advance which technique (such as audiotaping or writing notes)
  the students will use to remember the adults' answers. Have the students conduct the interviews, being sure to leave some unstructured time for impromptu discussions on topics of shared interest.
- With the parents' permission, arrange for the students to spend
  a weekend day socializing with a known and trusted visually
  impaired adult.

- If they are unaware of consumer groups like the American Council of the Blind, the National Federation of the Blind, and the National Association for Parents of the Visually Impaired (see the Resources section), inform the students and their parents about the groups' existence and activities.

Critical Points to Cover

- Children who are visually impaired grow up to be adults who are visually impaired.
- Adults with visual impairments are members of families and have friends.
- Adults with visual impairments have many different types of jobs.
- Adults with visual impairments participate in a variety of community functions.
- Adults with visual impairments use numerous forms of transportation and travel techniques.
- Adults with visual impairments use many types of adaptations in their daily lives.

Helpful Hints

- Tell students that the adults with whom they are interacting are visually impaired.
- Participating adults should be known to, or interviewed in advance by, the teacher. If an adult with a visual impairment suggests illegal or questionable behavior (for example, "Oh, I drive even though I don't have a license"), then it is the teacher's responsibility to discuss laws, responsibility, and personal choice with the student.
- Former students who have established adult lives in the community can also be a source of role models for students.

Evaluation Tips

- Ask the parents to watch for and report instances when their children spontaneously discuss being employees or adults with visual impairments. What kinds of attitudes do these discussions reflect?
- Ask the students to describe what they plan to do as employees, family members, and citizens when they are adults.

- Ask the students to report orally, write about, or act out some of the experiences they have had when visiting visually impaired adults.

For Students Who Need Additional Modifications

- Find adults who have disabilities that are similar to the students' and arrange for visits. Talk about whether the adults do their jobs differently from others; for example, are their desks at a different height because of their wheelchairs? Do they use sign language interpreters when they go to meetings? What kinds of questions do they ask to find out what is printed on an overhead display or handout? How do they ask for assistance if needed when getting materials, finding information, or scheduling readers and interpreters?

CAREER INVESTIGATION THROUGH VOLUNTEER EXPERIENCES

Many adults engage in some work that is voluntary. Recognizing the two notions that everyone has needs that can be alleviated to some degree through the actions of another and that everyone has talents that can be used to alleviate the needs of another are important lessons in the moral and career development of all children. These lessons are as valuable for students with visual impairments as they are for sighted children. Since visually impaired youngsters are frequent recipients of volunteer services, it is especially important for them to realize that they, too, have much to offer people who are less fortunate than them.

Students need to be helped to understand that volunteer work is distinguished from "helping" others (usually a spontaneous action) in that it involves a greater commitment of one's time and energies toward a cause or need that one identifies with and helps to alleviate over a sustained period.

Activities

- Teachers can make several suggestions for volunteer projects, either for a single student or for a group. Although younger students may need help in selecting a preferred activity, older stu-

---

FROM A FAMILY PERSPECTIVE

Promoting Opportunities to Work

Performing work for pay is an important concept to teach children with visual impairments, especially to help them understand how important paid work will be for them when they are older. Historically speaking, visually impaired people in general have had a high rate of unemployment. Society, the government, and even many people who were blind assumed that blindness was a dead-end disability preventing work and full participation in life. We have known since before Helen Keller's time that this need not be so. Children who are visually impaired, like all children, need to develop a positive attitude toward work early in life and assume that they can do anything they set out to do. In your family, try to place few if any restrictions on what your child thinks he or she can accomplish.

Encourage your child to speak with a school guidance counselor about career resources. Talk to your child about volunteer activities in the community and take him or her to visit these sites, as well as potential job sites and professionals in various fields. In the same way that parents or other family members take juniors and seniors in high school on college visits, they can take younger children to places where they and friends work.

Kevin O'Connor

---

dents may be presented with these options and asked to choose a project. Some ideas for projects are as follows:

1. Hold a car wash and give the proceeds to a worthy cause (to be identified by the students).
2. Sell slice-and-bake cookies (prepared by the students) at the sports activities of peers (such as soccer, baseball, and basketball games) and give the proceeds to a worthy cause (to be identified by the students).
3. Recycle newspapers or empty aluminum cans collected from family members and friends.
4. Sing to groups at hospitals, nursing homes, or senior citizens' centers.
5. Grow flowers and donate flower arrangements to hospitals, nursing homes, or senior citizens' centers.
6. Read to residents at nursing homes or residential care facilities or take them on walks in the facilities.
7. Pick up litter at a local playground or park.

8. Help at a local charity's office (for example, answer phones, collate materials, and stuff envelopes).
9. Make solicitation calls for a school fund drive.
10. Collect magazines to donate to fire stations, senior citizens' centers, or shelters for homeless people.
11. Shop for groceries for people who are housebound.

- Depending on the ages and abilities of the students, help them learn any new skills that are necessary for the project's activities, help them make arrangements for their volunteer efforts, and supervise their work. As much as possible, the new required skills that are unfamiliar should be minimal, with the emphasis of instruction placed on the value of the volunteer efforts to others in the community or to the welfare of the community itself (such as recycling or picking up of litter).

Helpful Hints

- Students participating in community volunteer activities should truly be helping, not causing more work for already overworked staff or other volunteers. Therefore, teachers of visually impaired students may need to act as "job coaches" while the students learn the routines and skills necessary to perform the tasks expected of them.
- A delicate balance needs to be taken into consideration: Students need to commit to a project *and* learn about the various kinds of volunteer opportunities that exist in a community. Therefore, it is preferable to select only one new project each semester.
- If the students donate money to a worthy cause, they need to understand that cause through on-site visits, discussion, and readings. Similarly, students may need to be informed of how their time and efforts are helping others.
- Interviews and informal interactions with adult volunteers can help youngsters realize that these kinds of activities can continue to provide satisfaction throughout one's life.
- Be aware of and teach the students about safety concerns; for example, students who pick up litter on the playground or at a local park may need to wear protective gloves.

Critical Points to Cover

- People in a community have various talents and needs.
- Each person has the ability to help others in some way.
- Volunteering to help a person or a cause makes the volunteer feel good.
- Even people who are busy volunteer.

Evaluation Tips

- Ask the parents how their children have described their volunteer experiences.
- Ask the students to write about or describe the feelings they have when they are volunteering.
- Listen and watch for instances when students demonstrate an awareness of the value of giving to others or to the community at large.

For Students Who Need Additional Modifications

- Locate opportunities for the students to visit with others outside the home, preferably one on one with a neighbor or another child, for example, visiting an elderly neighbor to watch a favorite television show or having lunch at a classmate's house. If appropriate, let the classmates or neighbors know what jobs the students do at home and ask them to tell or show the students how the jobs are done in their houses. Although the visits are informal, they can be the foundation of students' understanding that they can do things for others who are not family members.

CAREER EXPLORATION THROUGH EXPERIENTIAL LEARNING

Many children experience their first paid work during the late elementary school years when their desire to purchase goods and services expands beyond the money they earn as allowances or that is given to them as birthday and other gifts. These first paid work experiences are usually arranged in the local neighborhood and involve temporary services, such as raking leaves, shoveling snow, washing cars, working as a mother's helper, walking pets, baby-sitting, ironing, and other chores that people are willing to pay others to do for them.

Activities

- Introduce the children to various types of work done in and around the home and gradually shape their ability to perform the work well and in a timely way.
- When the children express the need to have more spending money, introduce the concept of selling one's services to family members and neighbors—that there are some tasks that adults occasionally are willing to pay children to perform for them. Help the children determine their skills and evaluate the potential marketability of the skills.
- Ask the parents or other family members to set up jobs for their children with friendly neighbors in advance and have the students "sell" their services. It may be helpful for the students to role-play their marketing pitch at school and at home, thereby refining their approach.
- Have children whose work has been commendable ask their employers for letters of reference for use when searching for additional work.

Critical Points to Cover

- People usually need to work to earn money to pay for the goods and services they want.
- Working for money has both advantages and disadvantages.
- Employers have certain expectations of their employees, including punctuality, diligence, limited interruptions during work, and the delivery of acceptable products or services.
- An individual with a specific skill and a marketing plan can convince others to purchase his or her labors.
- Hard work is usually rewarded; unacceptable work also has its consequences.

- Some jobs may appear at first to be worth the effort but are unsatisfying (even when one is paid for the work).

Helpful Hints

- Students need to be reminded that one never goes into the home of a stranger without permission from one's parents or other adult caregivers. Provisions for going to the bathroom, getting a snack, or dealing with emergencies need to be arranged before students start their jobs.
- Keep in mind that children at this stage of their career development are experimenting with new roles and that most are only minimally motivated to continue such activities for long. Although students should be strongly encouraged to finish the jobs they have started, they should be allowed to change their minds about long-term commitments. However, if they change their minds, they will benefit the most if they are required to inform their neighborhood employers in person of their change in plans and their unavailability for this kind of work in the future.
- Children who have contracted to perform neighborhood jobs should be expected to show up for work on time, work diligently, complete all the tasks they have agreed to do, and perform them to a quality judged acceptable by their employers. Adults should expect that the children will make mistakes in these areas at one time or another and will experience the natural consequences of making those mistakes (for example, no pay or reduced pay and few, if any, calls back or referrals).
- Be creative. Help the students determine what their skills are and then help them try to market them. Neighbors may be willing to pay youngsters to push empty garbage cans from the street to near their houses on collection day or let cooped-up pets out for a five-minute run after school. Or the students can collect newspapers for recycling by loading them into a wagon and pulling it from house to house on the street where they live.
- Neighborhood work is often most successful when children and their parents or other family members have already established relationships with other families in the neighborhood. In such cases, the need to explain the children's abilities as people with visual impairments is frequently diminished.

- Try to avoid work that requires the additional labor of others, such as driving from one location to another. The most meaningful job is one that children do without relying on others because these jobs teach the children about their value as independent agents.
- The most likely candidates for neighborhood work are children who want to buy goods and services that they are not ordinarily able to. The frustrated desire to purchase or obtain something is often a strong motivating force for work.

Evaluation Tips

- Ask the students to describe how it feels to have jobs and to make their own money.
- Listen for the students' references to work in their conversations and play with their classmates. Do the students represent their roles positively?
- Ask the parents to report when their children ask to work for money at home.
- Have the students write creative stories about their work experiences.

For Students Who Need Additional Modifications

- Career exploration for students with multiple disabilities may require structured experiences that are set up for them by family members and instructional staff. For example, a family member who may have assumed responsibility for helping a neighbor with pet care during the neighbor's vacation can take along a child who is unable to negotiate such an experience independently to assist in feeding and caring for the animal. Instructional personnel may need to advocate for students with multiple disabilities to participate in work-related activities at school, for example, collecting tickets at an athletic or theatrical event. Some type of tangible reward for work well done will be an important requirement to help the students learn the work-for-pay concept.

CAREER EXPLORATION VIA INFORMATIONAL INTERVIEWING

Because many students with visual impairments have limited opportunities to derive common information about their environment through observation, sometimes simple details need to be brought to their attention through direct instruction. Children with visual impairments can understand the world of work better by obtaining information related to how people learn about and acquire the jobs they hold. Sighted youngsters receive this information as they interact with people and places in their environment. They see Help Wanted signs in stores, discuss the issue with their classmates, and observe actors in movies and on television portraying people who are involved in job-seeking activities. Visually impaired children need to have appropriate opportunities to absorb similar information.

As with all learning, information is more easily retained and better understood if students are encouraged to use active discovery methods. Instructional activities can be used to further develop students' abilities to conduct research, to solve problems, and to engage in interactions with others.

Activities

- Have the students (or teams of students) speculate about how adults and teenagers learn about the jobs they hold. Then, ask the students to question the workers whom they encounter during a specified period about the ways they found their jobs, write down (using print or a slate and stylus) or record the responses, along with information about the general ages and genders of the workers and the types of jobs they have. After the students have interviewed a large number (from 10 to 20) of people, help them to categorize the responses and discover any patterns. Do people in particular positions learn about their jobs from sources that are different from people in other fields? Does the age or gender of the individual make a difference?

Helpful Hints

- Be sure that the students remember to ask the same questions of all the people they interview. Depending on the information desired, one question may be, "What was your first job?" or "How did you learn about your first job?" or "How did you first learn about this job?" or "How did you get this job?"

- It may be interesting to have students collect this information from individuals who are working at particular locations, such as a medical office building, university, mall, construction site, or school, and compare the responses of employees at these sites with those from other sites. Are there patterns of responses?
- Another group of individuals from whom it may be interesting to gather data are people with disabilities. Are there patterns of responses?
- A variation on this activity may be to examine the *Occupational Outlook Handbook* (U. S. Department of Labor, 1998) to determine the general salaries of the jobs held by the individuals whom the students interviewed. Does there seem to be a connection between salary and how a person learns about a job?
- If the students are working on this project in groups, be certain that each group member has an opportunity to introduce the issue, ask the questions, and write responses. It may be necessary and helpful, at least at first, to teach the students with visual impairments how to scan, categorize, and review the data using adapted technology or sighted helpers before they work with a group of sighted classmates on these activities.

Critical Points to Cover

- People learn about the jobs they hold in a variety of ways.
- It is necessary to acquire and use a variety of job-seeking skills.
- Workers in certain categories use different means to learn about the jobs that they hold.
- A personal effort is involved in finding a job; that is, people with jobs have actively looked for employment (or paid others to look for them).

Evaluation Tips

- Have the students explain the meaning of, and spell, new words (such as *headhunter, networking, want ad,* or *recruiter*) they learned as a result of these interviews.
- Determine whether the students' predictions matched their findings. Ask them how people who use the scientific method feel when their predictions are confirmed or disproved.

- On trips in the community, ask the students to guess how particular workers may have acquired their jobs and then to explain the reasoning behind their suggestions. Are the students using appropriate reasoning techniques?

For Students Who Need Additional Modifications

- Students with multiple disabilities who are cognitively able may perform informational interviews in much the same way as their peers without multiple disabilities. However, make sure that interpreters are present for students who are deaf-blind.
- Students who are not cognitively able will have difficulty assimilating information gathered in interviews. They may learn more by doing actual on-site observations (if they have adequate vision) or performing in on-the-job training programs or job-shadowing activities to learn about jobs while performing them. Since generalization is often a problem for students with cognitive limitations, informational interviewing may be too far removed from the actual activities of the work sites. Learning about jobs on site is preferable for many students with multiple disabilities.
- For students with severe disabilities, mentoring relationships with employees at the school can be established or foster grandparents or volunteers can be paired with the students. Emphasize the establishment of rapport with these adults and a sense of familiarity, not teaching the students to do the jobs that adults do. Mentoring gives students the opportunity to practice interactive skills with adults who can give them individual attention and positive feedback about their communication.

CAREER EXPLORATION IN THE COMMUNITY

In their daily lives, sighted children observe the relationships between the household tasks they see their parents or caregivers doing and adult paid work activities. In images in books and magazines, on television, at the movies, and in real life, children see reflected the work that is done by parents, siblings, and other relatives in the home. For example, the work being done by an electrician depicted on a television show may seem similar to a parent's use of a screwdriver to tighten a screw in an electrical outlet. Similarly, children recognize a familiar activity when they catch a glimpse of a maid cleaning in a hotel room. Through incidental comments and experiences, sighted children learn that these people are paid for doing these seemingly common activities.

Many children with visual impairments cannot easily make the connections between the chores that they and their family members do and similar activities for which adults are paid. Therefore, teachers and families may need to plan carefully to assist children who are visually impaired to appreciate that most of the skills that they are being taught as youngsters are the same skills on which some paid employment is based.

Activities

- As children are taught how to perform household tasks, such as making beds, cooking, weeding the garden, preparing salads, ironing shirts, mopping floors, and washing cars, teachers can arrange for field trips to work sites where these tasks are expected of employees. The students can talk with the workers whom they meet about these jobs, shadow them while they work, and perhaps even try the tasks in the work situations. After the field trips, the adults need to use these visits as springboards for discussions about or further research on these jobs (such as the educational requirements, salaries, work hours, and job satisfaction) and the abilities of people with visual impairments to be employed in these positions. It is also beneficial for the teachers to help the students discover the characteristics of these jobs that make them personally desirable or undesirable.

Critical Points to Cover

- The activity that one considers a chore today may be a source of employment when one is older.
- Some jobs require little formal education, whereas others require advanced education.
- Some jobs are repetitive.
- Some jobs require a variety of skills.
- Some people find a particular job interesting and satisfying, while others would prefer not to have to do that type of work.
- Different jobs require various degrees of interaction with other people.

Helpful Hints

- Explain to the students that in some jobs, employees perform a variety of functions. For example, a maid in a hotel does not just make beds; she also cleans bathtubs, wipes counters, vacuums, and dusts. Similarly, most carpenters do not hammer nails all day, but are expected to carry lumber, read blueprints, and use electrical tools. However, a person who is employed at a Laundromat to iron or at a restaurant to wash dishes often performs only that task.
- Use these encounters with workers to discover which ones wear uniforms to work, bring lunch, or are generally satisfied with their jobs; what their salary levels are; and other information that will help the students understand the nature of the jobs they are exploring.
- Ask the parents and other family members to inform the students when workers they encounter are using skills that the students can perform.

Evaluation Tips

- Ask the students to describe the workers they have met and to explain the relationships between the chores they perform at home and the duties of these workers.
- Ask the students to consider whether there are particular jobs they would like to have and why they would like to have them.
- Have the students role-play or create a drama describing the jobs they have observed and any interactions the employees might have had with customers, superiors, and coworkers.

For Students Who Need Additional Modifications

- Provide opportunities for the students to notice the steps of a job. For example, when helping to do laundry at a Laundromat, they can learn not only that soap is put in, but that clothes are removed after the cycle and placed in the dryer and that they are folded and put away afterward. Children who are blind often notice only one step of a task. If they do not understand words, the only way they will know what happens next is to touch the materials and participate in the process.

- Encourage students with multiple disabilities to participate in community activities in which adults with multiple disabilities are present. For example, many communities have Independent Living Centers (ILCs) in which adults with disabilities, including those with multiple disabilities, are employed or visit with each other periodically. An outing at a local ILC to observe adults with disabilities at work or to socialize with them would give students with multiple disabilities opportunities to engage in conversations with adults who have similar disabilities in the community.

References

U. S. Department of Labor. (1998). *Occupational outlook handbook*. Washington, DC: U. S. Government Printing Office.

12

Providing Realistic Feedback

Realistic feedback is important to children who are visually impaired because they need to understand how their performances compare with those of others, including those who are sighted. Children who have not received realistic feedback may be unprepared to learn that they are not feasible candidates for certain jobs because their performance leaves something to be desired.

Issues related to both the quality and quantity of work are addressed in the activities presented in this chapter. Learning to manage time and set goals are also encouraged because they are skills that future teachers and employers will expect the students to have mastered. Included in the discussion are self-advocacy through participation in the Individualized Education Program (IEP) process, journal writing as a means of chronicling students' feelings and impressions, and learning to discriminate between wants and needs. By implementing these activities, adults can open up countless opportunities for providing students with realistic feedback.

INCREASING THE SPEED OF PERFORMANCE

People use their vision throughout the day to inform themselves of the quality of their work and to compare their performance with that of others. With one glance and without an explanation, they generally can determine how their product compares to another's with regard to neatness, accuracy, quantity, and speed of completion. Through this process, competitive sighted students can establish personal goals to improve in one or all these areas.

Students with visual impairments often rely on feedback from others, usually adults, to advise them of the quality of their performance. However, a sometimes omitted area of feedback is the speed with which tasks are completed. Because many people believe that students with visual impairments require a longer time to complete every kind of assigned work, these students are often not trained to develop the important work skill of promptly finishing tasks. But most employers generally value speed and timelines and are unlikely to hire anyone, sighted or visually impaired, who cannot perform desired tasks in the allotted time. Consequently, it may be necessary to teach visually impaired students to complete tasks quickly so they will be desired, effective workers.

Activities

- Select an activity that the students have mastered, such as collating and stapling papers, alphabetizing student work, or erasing the chalkboards. Have the students use a stopwatch to measure the amount of time required to complete the activity one time and then record this finding. To establish a baseline, have the students repeat these steps several times, until there is general agreement that the task usually requires a specific number of minutes to complete. Next, work with them to establish a goal for personal improvement. Ideally, the goal should be one that is achievable within a relatively short time. Encourage the students to practice the activity without being timed and then to complete a timed trial every day, recording, graphing, and analyzing the results.
- After the students are familiar with this process and have experienced positive results using the procedure, compare their performances with the performance of sighted students on the same tasks. Help the students to identify areas where continued improvement is necessary. Discuss with them the importance of working quickly, or at a pace that approximates the speed at which others perform the same tasks, and identify (using the process that was described at the beginning of this section) strategies for increasing their working rates.

Critical Points to Cover

- Practice improves speed on almost any task.
- Goal setting works best when the overall goal is broken down into smaller, more easily achieved, objectives.
- Setting and achieving personal goals positively affects the way one feels about oneself.
- One's performance can depend on many factors, including fatigue, illness, and anxiety. Occasional dips in the speed of performance are a natural part of life.

Helpful Hints

- It is essential to work on the speed of completing tasks only after the students have mastered the tasks. Students who are learning the components of an activity need to put their energies into thinking and learning, not into building speed.
- A balancing act is required of teachers who use the performance of sighted students as a standard of comparison and who want to preserve the self-esteem of their visually impaired students. Help the students realize that they have the power to change their performance with practice and work over time. The standards set by sighted students are only long-term goals that can be achieved with effort. Once the long-term goal is established, the focus should always be on the children's achievement of short-term objectives, which are increasingly closer to that goal.
- Help the students to discover that there is a wide range of performance speeds among members of the class that sometimes depends on the task being measured. It may be necessary to have students time the work rate of several sighted students on a variety of tasks to recognize the variability of performance speed.
- The activity of timing the completion of tasks is appropriate for academic subjects, such as mathematical problems and reading, as well as daily living skills (for example, the time required to dress, make the bed, and clear the table), mobility (the time it takes to walk from one class to another, to the library, or to the office), and prevocational activities (the time it takes to assemble tasks, collate papers, or distribute crayons).

- The speed with which tasks are completed is often related to the occasions to practice the task. This activity provides opportunities to practice within the context of a self-improvement "game" in which students work to "beat" their previous scores.
- If the students' speed in completing tasks does not increase and is still unrealistic when compared to that of other students in the class, then help them determine why their performance is not improving. Is there a better, easier, or faster way to accomplish the tasks? Which part of a task is taking the most time? Was the goal set too high? Is more practice needed?
- In many cases, the reward of charting progress and achieving the goal is all that is necessary. For young students who are not motivated to improve and for tasks that are difficult, a more tangible reward may be necessary. It is usually best to establish the reward for performance at the same time that the goal is set and to provide the reward immediately after the goal is achieved. Remember that rewards are very child-specific and should be determined on an individual basis.

Evaluation Tips

- Ask family members if their children seem to be working on tasks at home at a faster rate.
- Ask the classroom teachers if the visually impaired students in their classes have improved their speed in completing tasks.
- Ask the students to describe, act out, or illustrate how they feel when they get their work done at the same time as the other classmates or when they achieve a goal that has been set.

For Students Who Need Additional Modifications

- For students with multiple disabilities, learning to improve performance speed is a critical work skill. Use whatever means are available to communicate to the students that they have to do "more" of a task they have mastered (for example, use a manual sign, simple verbal cue, pictorial or tactile representation, or another symbol for "more").
- With discrete items, consider the use of pictures or tactile representations of the number of things the students need to pro-

duce, if feasible, for the students to compare their performance against. Use a counter, ticker, or abacus to count the number of objects produced and keep a simple graph or chart showing the students' improvement over time.

- When building speed, use a timing device (such as a kitchen timer, bell, stopwatch, or digital clock) to measure speed and encourage the students to set the device or note the start and finish times, as appropriate, at the beginning and end of each work session. Give positive, social reinforcement when the students' speed improves.

TIME MANAGEMENT SKILLS

Learning to manage one's time is a skill that generally is not expected of youngsters at the elementary school level, but it is one that they are learning nonetheless. Sighted children observe their parents, teachers, and other adults using wall and personal calendars to organize their days and to schedule appointments, and they use these early impressions later to establish and refine their own style of time management.

Many youngsters with visual impairments may have difficulty developing efficient time management skills because they have limited incidental visual access to calendars and clocks and few, if any, opportunities to observe easily the steps adults take when planning their time. Although most students with visual impairments are taught basic calendar concepts, they rarely are required to practice these skills within functional activities and contexts to make up for the loss of incidental exposure to them.

Activities

- Provide daily practice for students with visual impairments to use increasingly more complex calendar skills. Each student needs to have a personal calendar that is kept in a predictable location (see Helpful Hints for suggestions for making calendars). Young children have to practice the mechanics of using their calendars to provide information such as, "On what day of the month does the 16th fall?" or "How many days until Sunday?" Older elementary school students can record significant future information, such as the birthdays of relatives and friends, school holidays, and the dates on which planned events (such as field trips, spelling tests, or visits to the dentist) fall. These students require daily practice to discover how they can use calendars to make short- and long-term plans. Teachers need to vary the time management demands placed on their students. For example, a lesson may include planning when to send a birthday card to a pen pal or to a relative living in another part of the country so it arrives on time.

Critical Points to Cover

- People frequently refer to calendars at work, for school, and at home.
- People use many different types of calendar systems, and some people use more than one system.
- Calendars are used for more reasons than telling people what day of the month it is.
- Calendars help people organize and plan their time, for the present day as well as for the future.
- Planning one's time ultimately is a personal responsibility.

Helpful Hints

- Calendars for students who are visually impaired do not have to look like the seven-day by four-week grid pattern on a single page that is typically used by sighted people. Some students are more successful when their calendars are in three-ring binders with one page per day and weeks separated by tabbed pages. Others prefer to keep their calendars in file card boxes. An advantage of either system is that the pages can be removed, written on with a boldline pen, or inserted into a brailler or slate for notation of important events.
- The students may need to be introduced to a variety of braille and large-print calendars, as well as computer-based calendar systems.
- Brightly colored or textured stickers may be used in coding systems that some students prefer (for example, a fuzzy dot means that a test is scheduled).
- Once the students have mastered basic calendar skills, a valuable lesson may be to go to an office supply store to explore the wide

variety of calendar systems that are available for purchase. Encourage the students to try different systems, including those on computer disk and electronic notetakers, to determine for themselves which technique works best for them.

- Encourage the students to keep weekly assignment calendars (by subject area) and homework calendars.
- For young students, point out the presence of calendars in the environment, for example, on the secretary's desk, on the wall in the kitchen, or at the doctor's office.
- Have the adults with whom the students interact tell the students when they are using their calendars to determine whether they are available on a particular day, to organize their days, or to make business and medical appointments and dates with friends and relatives.
- Encourage the students to ask adults about the calendar systems they use or have used in the past. They can ask this question of adults whom they are interviewing about their jobs or whose jobs they are shadowing.

Evaluation Tips

- Use formal mathematics tests, for example, the *KeyMath* or *Kaufman Test of Educational Achievement (K-TEA)*, to determine the students' understanding and use of calendars.
- Ask the parents to report when students refer to calendars at home or remind them to write something on a calendar.
- Observe the students using their calendar skills at school: Can they find requested information more efficiently?
- Observe whether the students spontaneously use their calendars to write down when homework assignments are due.

For Students Who Need Additional Modifications

- Reinforce the concept of year for students who have the memory span. At first, emphasize experiences that take place during the year, rather than the names of months. For example, summer can be called the "no school time." Begin preparing the students for the end of the school year by showing this symbol several weeks before, and when they return to school, refer to the same symbol along with pictures or objects that represent summer activities. Include references to people they met who were doing jobs, such as a lifeguard at a beach, a waitress at a restaurant, or a camp counselor.

- Students with multiple disabilities may benefit from using modified calendars. For example, those who are blind can use laminated sheets of paper for each day's activities with sections for each time and activity. Affix Velcro to the sections, so the students can attach items backed with Velcro that represent different activities (such as a plastic spoon for lunch or a penny for time spent identifying and counting money) to mark upcoming, current, and completed stages in the day. Students with low vision can have similar calendars but can use pictures of activities, rather than tactile symbols. Once the students have mastered daily schedules, they can use similar calendars to represent a week's activities, a month's, and so forth.

- In weekly planning, provide some opportunities for students' choices. Use a variety of methods to communicate choices to students who do not use speech, including photographs or pictures of options, object symbols, tactile symbols, pictures drawn by the students, or an augmentative speech device.

PERSONAL IMPROVEMENT: SETTING GOALS

Like other youngsters, students with visual impairments can be taught an effective strategy for self-improvement at an early age. Activities in this area include setting goals, recording activities, monitoring their progress, and evaluating themselves. When young students successfully apply these steps to achieve their goals, they are laying the foundation for healthy change and for self-improvement as adults.

Activities

- Work with the youngsters to identify some area in which change is desired. Ideally, the activity should be one that the children choose and one in which the time spent on the activity needs to be increased or the activity needs to be done more often (for example, reading, shooting basketballs, preparing their lunch, or making kind comments to other children to initiate conversations).

FROM A FAMILY PERSPECTIVE

Providing Realistic Feedback

For all of us, especially for those family members with a disability, the family environment may be one of the few places where we are loved and accepted for who we are. Parents and other family members need to resist the temptation to have their children prove themselves. If there is anywhere in the world where we deserve total, unconditional acceptance just because we exist, it is within our family. However, to help your visually impaired children learn about the world around them and to enable them to compete with others in their future careers, we as parents and family members need to offer honest feedback about their performances. Family members need to observe their children in different environments and provide them with insight into how their performances compare to those of the other children in their lives. Honest, open feedback concerning what you observe will help your child understand what is and what is not working for him or her academically, socially, and ultimately, vocationally. Telling your child that his or her performance is exemplary when it may not be so sets the child up for disappointment and failure. By providing opportunities for constructive feedback, we help our children understand how they are performing in comparison with others and bolster their work on self-improvement goals. And all the time we are providing children with realistic feedback, we need always to encourage independence. The more our children—all of them—can do for themselves, the better they feel about their abilities. Learning to be independent becomes the root of sound self-esteem.

Kevin O'Connor

- Help students to determine the baseline level of the activity (the current rate of performance or the frequency of the activity), to establish realistic short- and long-term goals, and to determine appropriate rewards. The long-term goal represents the level of activity at which the youngsters would define the change as "fully achieved." Short-term goals are markers at which the students can identify and celebrate their progress toward the full achievement of the goal.

- Establish a realistic timeline at the time the goals are set and encourage the students to record and graph their work toward their goal each day.

- At the end of an established period (such as a week or a month), adults working with the children can help them evaluate their progress in achieving the goal and their feelings about that level of achievement.

Critical Points to Cover

- Careful setting of short- and long-term goals can lead to self-improvement.
- One feels a certain satisfaction in setting and achieving personal goals.
- Mutual support among people who are working toward goals is valuable.
- By achieving short-term objectives, one might find it less difficult to attain one's long-term goals.

Helpful Hints

- The purpose of this activity is to help the students understand the power of setting personal goals, measuring progress toward established goals, and evaluating themselves. Teachers, parents, and other family members need to avoid confusing their goals for the students with the students' own goals. The initial conversation about this kind of activity may begin with the question, "If you wanted to do something better, what would be some of the things you would like to try to do better?" or "Think about the things that people nag you about. Which of those things would it please you to do without having to be nagged?"
- Help the students define their goals precisely. If the goal is to be on time for class, has it been achieved if the student comes through the door when the bell rings? What constitutes the first on-time arrival? Specificity in describing the behavior and defining the acceptable frequency or rate are essential.
- If the students reach a plateau before they achieve their long-term goals, they may feel discouraged. It may be worthwhile at this time to encourage them to reevaluate the importance of their long-term goals and the appropriateness of their short-term objectives or to reconsider their timelines.
- Teachers and family members may want to set goals for themselves to model concurrently this self-improvement strategy for the students, thereby demonstrating the value of mutual support.
- Help the youngsters to select goals that are achievable by controlling their own actions and are not dependent on the cooperation or behavior of others. The goal of improving one's tetherball skills is realistic only if practice with a tetherball is available at school each day.

- Help the students to select goals that are easy to measure. For example, the number of compliments one gives one's classmates is measurable, whereas "being nice" to the classmates is not.
- Remember that it usually is much harder to reduce the frequency of a behavior than to increase it. If students want to reduce eye-poking behaviors, it might be effective to set "increase doodling" as a goal, because the activities are incompatible. (It is difficult to measure the number of times one does not poke one's eyes.) Students who choose reducing behavior as goals will want to define short-term objectives as smaller steps (for example, "Instead of rocking for a total of 15 minutes per day, I will rock for only 14 minutes") and reward themselves more frequently for making progress.
- For students who are blind, use Wikki Stix on special graph paper to measure their progress in reaching their goals. (Wikki Stix are 8-inch flexible cords made in assorted colors that stick to paper and can be used graphically to show shapes and letters. They can be used on embossed sheets of graph paper, with tactile lines and braille grids, that can be purchased from the American Printing House for the Blind [see Resources].)

Evaluation Tips

- Ask the students to keep a journal describing their results and their feelings when they reach a goal, get "stuck" at a plateau, or backslide.
- Ask families to report on changes in their children's attitudes about being able to accomplish difficult tasks.
- Describe scenarios in which the main character, visually impaired or sighted, adult or child, faces a problem. Ask the students what advice they would give that character. Does the advice incorporate the principles of self-improvement that the students have been learning? Use characters from popular culture (such as movies, television programs, or video games) in the scenarios.

For Students Who Need Additional Modifications

- The students should understand what represents the completion of a task. This concept can be conveyed in a variety of ways, for example, by using a model of a finished product or a picture list of all the elements or by presenting a timekeeping device and explaining, "When the bell goes off, we will finish." To the greatest degree possible, students need to understand how long they will work and what "finished" means for a particular activity, especially if it is an undesirable task. Students with short attention spans may work better if they have a checklist, a picture list, or a "finished" box to mark when each step of the task is completed.

STUDENTS' PARTICIPATION IN DEVELOPING THEIR IEPS

An increasingly common practice among special educators is to involve students in developing their own IEPs. This activity presents the opportunity for the students to learn of and describe their evolving strengths and needs, to evaluate and explain their progress through school, and to have some input into the direction that the progress will take. As the students take on an expanded role in directing their IEP meetings, not only do they learn to identify goals, but they also develop important leadership skills.

Activities

- Prepare young students to participate meaningfully in their own IEP meetings by explaining that in these meetings parents or other family members, teachers, and related services personnel plan what to teach for the next school year and that the process involves evaluating the students' performance and abilities and setting goals.
- Assist younger students in making a list of their strengths, collecting supporting documents, and identifying at least one area in which they would like to improve during the forthcoming year.
- Have the students read or orally present this information to the members of the IEP team at the start of the discussion of their current level of performance. Depending on the students' attention span and the expected complexity of the IEP discussion, the students may be thanked for their input and asked to leave or may be invited to stay for as long as they find the meeting interesting.
- Be sure to have the students sign the final documents as participants.

- With each passing year, students should be expected to participate to a greater degree in their own IEP meetings, including the discussions of their current levels of performance, which needs are priorities, the identification of goals, and placement. In addition, older students can be encouraged to open the meetings, welcome the participants, and state the meetings' purposes.

Critical Points to Cover

- Considerable planning goes into the education of students.
- The planning of students' education is a cooperative process among the students' parents, teachers, and other service providers.
- The students' opinions are important to all other members of the IEP team during the planning of educational programs.
- Meetings can run smoothly when they are organized in advance.

Helpful Hints

- Role-playing with the students before the meetings may help them to be more comfortable during the actual events. While role-playing, the students need to act in various roles, including those of a team leader, teacher, parent or other caregiver, and themselves, and to practice projecting the emotions of others.
- Ensure that the students understand that other special education students also have IEPs.
- The development of lists of strengths and areas that require improvement could be an assignment for all members of the general education class in which the students are enrolled. Encourage the students to date and save their lists and use them to evaluate their progress in academic areas over time.
- Older students can help the general education teacher and the special education teacher to collect and organize the data that will be presented at the IEP meetings in support of statements related to their current levels of performance.

Evaluation Tips

- Ask the students to tell what occurred during the IEP meetings. Older students may keep IEP journals in which they write descriptions of their IEP experiences and review these entries before each annual meeting.

- Ask the students if the meeting went as expected and what, if anything, they would change about the meeting if it could be held again.
- Ask the students to describe their feelings about participating in the meeting.
- Ask the students' parents about their feelings regarding the involvement of their children in this important educational planning process.

For Students Who Need Additional Modifications

- Students with multiple disabilities need to be included and encouraged to participate actively in the development of IEPs to the greatest possible extent. When feasible, teachers, parents, and other family members may develop some simple questions to ask the students about their educational programming (for example, do they like music class better than art class). Most important, give the students a list of activities from which to choose. Initially, the choices may be limited to two or three options; gradually, when possible, additional choices can be included. Encourage the students to choose from the alternatives posed either verbally or by some communication system (such as writing or using pictures, tactile representations, or communication boards, which provide pictures or words that students use to indicate ideas).

JOURNAL WRITING

Developing the ability to identify feelings and to know appropriate ways to react to the situations that create those feelings is often difficult for children who do not have the opportunity to observe other individuals visually. Many youngsters with visual impairments, who may not have close friends among their classmates and who may not identify closely with sighted children, may not be aware of ways to express and deal with the events in their lives that create strong emotions. Asking students to maintain journals that focus on their feelings may give both them and their teachers and other adults some insight into their emotional lives. The value of the journals can be increased when nonjudgmental adults respond privately to the expressed feelings and events, thereby affirming the students' sense of worth and increasing social competence.

Activities

- Ask the students to write in their "feelings journals" on a regular basis. In these journals, the students can note events that have stimulated strong emotional responses and that have occurred since their last entries. At a minimum, they can describe the events, their feelings at the time of the occurrence, and what they wish had happened instead. Older students can add their comments about what they may do if such situations recur and their guesses about the feelings of the other individuals involved. Teachers may give students who are new to this activity writing cues, such as "I felt important when . . ." or "I felt especially hurt when . . ." or "The thing that made me the happiest [saddest, scaredest, or maddest] was . . ."
- In the same writing medium used by the students, write responses to the students' entries that focus on helping the students to identify feelings more accurately, suggest how other participants might have felt, empathize with the students, and recommend other courses of action. As with other types of journals that teachers read, it is important to protect the students' confidentiality; ignore grammar, spelling, and writing errors; and be nonjudgmental about feelings that are shared.

Critical Points to Cover

- All people have feelings.
- People react differently to the same situation; a similar situation may result in a different emotional reaction at a different time.
- Although people may not be able to control their feelings, they do have control over their actions and their reactions to events.
- One's reactions to an event can influence the reactions, feelings, and opinions of others.
- Feelings are often transitory; the passage of time and other events can change the way a person feels.

Helpful Hints

- Nonwriters can audiotape their entries or dictate them to the teacher to write down. (If the students audiotape their journals, the teachers need to audiotape their responses.)
- Without referring to the students' journals, teachers can use both positive and negative situations that occur regularly as a starting point for activities that are designed to increase social awareness and improve social skills. For example, if a child has written about a teasing episode, the teacher can plan several lessons on how to handle teasing without having to mention that the idea for these lessons originated in the journal entry.
- Youngsters with less confidence and social maturity may benefit from more frequent opportunities to write in their feeling journals.
- This activity may be appropriate for all students in a general education class, especially if it is followed occasionally by an opportunity for the students to present their experiences and related feelings orally. Such oral presentations can help the students with visual impairments begin to realize that all children have similar feelings.

Evaluation Tips

- Have the students read previous journal entries and react to them. Ask them if they see changes in the way they handle difficult situations—if the events that made them feel a certain way when they were younger are the same events that influence their feelings today—and what elicits positive feelings, such as pride, joy, love, and respect.
- Ask family members and other teachers to determine if they have observed changes in the students' talk about themselves, attitudes, and behavior.
- Evaluate the students' entries for common themes and events and bring these commonalities to the students' attention by noting them in written responses to the entries.

For Students Who Need Additional Modifications

- Although some students with multiple disabilities may not have the written or spoken language skills to create a traditional journal, they may benefit from doing the activity with certain modifications. For example, they may choose to use pictures to represent their activities and special adventures, if they have sufficient vision to appreciate a pictorial journal. They may carry a notebook or envelope with them that can hold significant mementos, for example, leaves or pinecones from a park, shells from the seashore, tickets from a ball game or show, and so forth. An adult can assist students who do not have formal language skills in either recording or writing entries to accompany their pictures and mementos in a journal format.

DISCRIMINATING BETWEEN WANTS AND NEEDS

Learning to discriminate between what one wants and what one needs is an important factor in growing up. Most children have difficulty appreciating the differences between things that they want and things that they need. When someone is young and everything that he or she has is provided by another person, the differences between necessities and luxuries are particularly difficult to identify. Children are often overheard in toy or grocery stores proclaiming "But I want it! I need to have it!" However, sighted children, who have ready visual access to their homes and the homes of their friends and relatives, as well as those portrayed on television and in movies, have the chance to begin to differentiate subconsciously between what most people need to manage a home in today's society and items that they consider to be extras, or luxuries.

A lack of unconscious visual observations may inhibit the ability of many youngsters with visual impairments to make these same kinds of distinctions. Young blind children without opportunities to experience a number of residences may not even be aware that all homes have bathrooms, refrigerators, and beds. However, they can be helped by caring adults who allow them to explore, discover, and discuss similarities and differences in the environments in which they spend time. As the children mature, adults can use the children's "discoveries" to discuss why identified differences exist, how people define the concepts of luxuries and necessities uniquely, and how the amount of money that one earns and other circumstances (for example, health, number of family members, and culture) affect these definitions.

Receiving realistic feedback from those around them concerning what is considered to be a luxury and what is a necessity helps visually impaired youngsters comprehend what they may want to acquire through work. Feedback also helps students understand that with a visual impairment there are objects that they may consider to be necessities (a braillewriter or talking watch, for example) that sighted students may not. Likewise, there may be objects that their sighted classmates may believe are necessities that they may not (for example, a digital watch).

Activities

- For young or inexperienced children, it may be necessary to begin with planned, systematic explorations of the residences of a number of people. Help the children make lists of specific items (such as rooms, furniture, automobiles, services, appliances, electronics, types of food, toys, and clothes) for which to look. Work with them to develop an appropriate kind of system to record information. After the data have been collected, encourage the students to analyze the findings by searching for patterns. What kinds of items are common to the homes that have been explored? What kinds of items seem to be optional?
- Have students examine their own lives: What things do they define as necessities and luxuries at school and in their homes? Do all children have similar definitions? What explanations can be made about any differences? What would happen if each of the items on the students' lists were unavailable?
- Older students can interview their parents, teachers, and other adults regarding the luxuries and necessities in their lives. Again, using predetermined categories and a recording system devised by (or in conjunction with) the students, the students will need to review the collected data, analyze the information for patterns, and develop hypotheses to explain what they have found. Do all people define luxuries and necessities in the same way? What accounts for the differences?
- Teachers can help students appreciate the connections among the ability to purchase necessities, acquire luxuries, family and life circumstances, and earning power. Using hypothetical situations (perhaps as part of arithmetic assignments), students can manipulate these variables and discover their relationships.

Critical Points to Cover

- The things that people have in their home depend, to some degree, on the amount of money they earn.
- Most people purchase items that they consider to be necessities before they buy items that they judge to be luxuries.
- Not everyone defines the same things as necessities and luxuries.
- There are many family and life circumstances that affect one's definitions of a necessity.

Helpful Hints

- Blind children may choose to have a brailled list of the items for which they are searching and use fuzzy dots or some similar tactile items for marking.
- If possible, conduct the activities just described as a class and allow students to consolidate their data or compare and contrast their findings.
- Try to arrange for the students to explore the residences of people with visual impairments and ask these individuals their opinions on the luxuries and necessities in their lives. Help the students use this information to draw parallels between these needs and wants and their own needs and wants now and for the future. (Students will also learn that visually impaired people do or do not own cars, that they need to purchase adaptive equipment, or that most of what is in their homes is similar to what is in the homes of sighted individuals.)
- The students may enjoy reading books about children who come from families of different economic circumstances and discussing these stories in light of their increasing understanding of the concepts of necessity and luxury.
- Following field trips to historic homes, discuss how necessities and luxuries change or stay the same over time.

Evaluation Tips

- Ask parents or other family members about their young children's ability to make generalizations about the residences that they visit.
- Ask the students for their definitions of the terms *necessity* and *luxury.*

- As a concluding exercise, have the students identify the items (goods and services) they will need to purchase to live independently in apartments when they graduate from high school. Are the items on this list realistic, and do they truly reflect an understanding of necessities?

For Students Who Need Additional Modifications

- Students without formal language skills may find it difficult to make their needs known. Families or other caregivers and instructional personnel consciously need to note how the students with whom they work express their pleasure or dissatisfaction with things and activities. Once the adults who work with these students are clear about how the students express themselves most consistently, they can begin to work with the students on making choices. They can also begin to work on helping the students discriminate between what belongs to them and what belongs to others. Consistently labeling a student's personal belongings (such as a notebook, chair, coat, and toothbrush) with a tactile or visually interesting label can be helpful.

PART FOUR

The Middle School Years

Julie Lee Kay

Jane Erin

Activities for Students Who Need Additional Modifications

When children leave elementary school and enter middle school—usually defined as grades 6, 7, and 8—or junior high school—typically spanning grades 7, 8, and 9—they are usually also moving into adolescence. Adolescence is an emotionally tumultuous time in many young people's lives, and children and young people with visual impairments are no exception. Like their sighted peers, they may discover that their bodies are changing as their hormones take center stage, and they may experience frequent mood swings ranging from feelings of insecurity and confusion to fits of rebellion. This is the time that tries the patience of parents and teachers, but it is also a time for tremendous growth in such areas as independence and career development. It is therefore an opportune time to present young people with additional challenges from which they may learn and to encourage them to prepare for life beyond school.

In the chapters that follow, readers will find activities that enable teachers and families to do just that—challenge adolescents with visual impairments to prepare for the future. Although the same general areas that were covered in Parts Two and Three of this book are included here—activities that encourage students' high expectations of themselves, the fostering of social skills, the development of adaptive techniques and opportunities to work, and the attainment of realistic feedback—the materials presented demand a higher level of involvement and responsibility by students. By infusing these career education activities into the middle school years, teachers, parents, and other family members can help bolster the confidence of young people who are visually impaired and prepare them for the transition from middle school to high school and to the world of adult responsibilities and work.

CHAPTER

13

Conveying High Expectations

For young people with visual impairments to have others maintain high expectations of them, it is important that they continue to demonstrate comparable levels of competence with their sighted peers both at home and in school. The activities presented in this chapter encourage parents and teachers to assign chores to students to build the students' self-esteem and help them understand family responsibility. Students are supported in their efforts to join community-based groups, are instructed in organizational techniques, and are asked to implement the techniques that they believe are appropriate for their needs. By participating in these activities, students are setting the stage for performing and achieving at levels commensurate with those of their sighted peers. Moreover, because of their achievements, visually impaired students will be expected to perform at age level when they enter high school.

Visually impaired young people can acquire the career education skills that some of their same-aged peers are acquiring through incidental learning by mastering structured learning activities. If adults assume responsibilities for them, their classmates and teachers will tend to have diminished expectations of them. Therefore, it is essential that students are actively involved in the kinds of efforts that are presented in this chapter to maintain high expectations during and after their middle school experiences.

TAKING CARE OF ONESELF AND ONE'S POSSESSIONS

Young people who have visual impairments need to learn responsibility, just as their sighted peers do, by learning to take care of their pos-

279

sessions and themselves. Organizational skills need to be refined during the middle school years for youngsters to grow up to be as independent as possible. Many activities that occur at home and in school prepare adolescents with visual impairments for the world of work by requiring them to carry their share of the responsibilities necessary to make a home or workplace function efficiently. Requirements for visually impaired adolescents to take care of themselves and their belongings should be the same as those for sighted adolescents, with adaptations provided only as needed.

There are many ways adolescents with visual impairments can take responsibility for themselves. Grooming, doing the laundry, organizing space to accommodate personal belongings, cleaning one's bedroom and bathroom, and helping other family members to accomplish household tasks are ways in which the learning of responsibility can be reinforced. Learning to do laundry is one important way for middle school youngsters to gain independence. Other ways to foster independence and help students learn to take responsibility for their belongings include teaching them how to organize their desks, bookcases, and closets. When studying and storage areas are organized and neat, it is easier for visually impaired youngsters to find the materials they need, so they can save time searching for items and feel less frustrated in the process. And, as with so many of life's organizational demands, there are almost as many methods for organizing closets as there are people setting up the systems. Therefore, the students need to be made aware of as many systems as possible to choose what will work best for them. The following activities may help students learn to do laundry and to organize their desks, bookcases, and closets.

Activities

Tips for doing the laundry are as follows:

- Have two separate bags for dirty laundry—one for whites and one for darks. Mark the bag for dark laundry with puff paint or raised markings that can be felt, sewn-on buttons, or other tactile markings to signify the difference between the bags.
- Train the youngsters to check their clothes for items in pockets and to pin together matching socks (use brass safety pins) before placing them in the laundry bags.

FROM A FAMILY PERSPECTIVE

Organized People Are Made, Not Born!

Many of the tips and techniques in this chapter are based on this fundamental idea: Parents and family members need to teach their children with visual impairments things that their sighted classmates may pick up automatically.

When parents engage in such skill-building activities as assigning chores, visiting an office supply store to purchase organizational tools, and joining community organizations, at least two things happen simultaneously: Children learn a new and lifelong skill, and the parent-child bond strengthens, along with trust, reliance, and enjoyment.

Kevin O'Connor

- Mark the washing machine and dryer with puff paint, braille labels, or other raised markings to indicate where the dial should be set. Discuss with youngsters the different settings on the machines and explain the miscellaneous marks and the settings they represent (for instance, delicate, regular wash, heavy wash, and permanent press).
- Have the youngsters use a scoop that measures the soap accurately for most loads and ask them to keep the washing machine set on cold to reduce shrinking.
- Discuss the effect of washing fabrics in water that is too hot (shrinkage) or too cold (not as likely to come out clean if the material is a light color).
- Explain the importance of color separation (that dark-colored garments can bleed and ruin light-colored garments).
- Discuss the need to read care instructions on tags inside garments. Blind students can use a labeling system to help them sort clothes to avoid discoloration.
- Demonstrate how to use stain-removal products and discuss the importance of treating stains promptly. Also, discuss how to handle chewing gum and other difficult-to-remove substances on clothes.
- Explain how to add bleach to a load of white laundry.
- Teach the youngsters how to move wet clothes from the washer into the dryer and how to fold or hang the clothes promptly once they are dry.

- Discuss the importance of buying easy-care items, if one does not want to iron or dry-clean garments.

Tips for organizing desks and closets are as follows:

- Ask the students which items are important to keep near them to study effectively. Suggest that it is important to have a dictionary, calculator, paper, pencils, and pens or a slate and stylus on their desks.
- Discuss with the students where effective studying can take place, for example, at a desk or worktable, and have them select their preferred location.
- Visit an office furniture or supply store and have the students talk to the salespeople about the variety of desks and organizational supplies that are available and their particular features.
- Have the students become familiar with deep drawers for holding file folders; a pull-out extension or tray for holding keyboards; and compartmentalized drawers for storing paper clips, writing tools, staplers, and other office tools. Also have them investigate different types of file folders (such as tabbed, expandable, paper, plastic, manila, and colored), card filing systems (such as recipe-type boxes in wood or plastic, Rolodex systems, and two- and three-ring notebooks), and various office organizational tools.
- Have the students draw up organizational supply lists (of, for example, folders, stacking trays, letter bins, and disk and compact disc organizers) after the visit to the store. Ask them to compare the prices for these supplies to the budget they have available for purchasing supplies and to rank the supplies in order of priority.
- Once the desk and supplies are chosen, label folders or stacking devices (in the students' preferred medium—print, braille, or large print) to correspond to the items to be held. Have the students place items where they will be easily accessible, the most often used items in the most convenient locations.
- Revisit the study or work spaces after one week and help the students find ways to resolve any problems in organization that have arisen.
- Have students set up sections of books used in different classes, such as a section for books used in English class, a section for books used in science class, and a section for books used in history class to help organize their bookcases.

- Have the students label the spines of print books in their preferred medium, so the books can be easily identified. Braille readers can use braille labels, and print users can use large-print labels.
- Audiotape users may choose to store their cassette tapes in plastic storage containers by subject area and label the tape spines or to store them in cardboard boxes (such as shoe boxes) and label both the outside of the boxes and the tape spines in braille or large print.
- Explain the different ways of organizing clothing in closets—grouping like items (such as shirts, slacks, blouses, skirts, or dresses) in separate areas of the closet, putting similar colors together, or organizing clothing by fabric type or style (short sleeves versus long sleeves, for example)—and have the youngsters choose the way they prefer to do so.
- Teach the students the various ways of identifying clothing, for example, brailling index cards with information about the outfits, punching holes in the cards, and hanging the cards on their respective clothes hangers, or sewing braille labels or different-shaped buttons inside their clothes.

Critical Points to Cover

- Explain the effects of different water temperatures and washer settings (delicate, permanent press, or regular) on various fabrics.
- Discuss why some fabrics require dry cleaning.
- Provide some tips on how to remove stains.
- Explain how to ask for help when needed.
- Explain safety factors, such as removing lint from the dryer filter to prevent fires and not putting too many clothes in the washer to avoid overloading it.
- Emphasize to students that everyone organizes study and work spaces differently, so it is important for them to organize their own materials and space according to their needs. What may be the best organizational system for one person may not be the best for another.
- Explain that it is not necessary to purchase items to help organize a desk, bookcase, or closet. Boxes, thick cardboard, tins, and other household items can be recycled for use in organizing these spaces.

- Emphasize to students that they need to know where their things are kept and that they need to return them to the same place after items are used.

Helpful Hints

- Use puff paint (or other raised markings, such as Locator Dots and Hi-Marks) to help the students identify as many wash and dry settings as they may need.
- Develop a sequence for doing the laundry, such as adding soap first, then adding the clothes, and then turning on the machine.
- Designate a regular wash day to avoid having to nag students and to teach time management—note it on a calendar that is produced in an accessible medium (braille or large print).
- Keep items that are used the least in spaces (in the desk, bookcase, or closet) that are more difficult to access.
- Get to know a clerk at a favorite store. The clerk may be able to contact students when easily distinguishable clothes (due to buttons, cut, or other traits) are available in their size and preference.
- Have the students visit a store that sells supplies for organizing closets or the students' friends who keep their spaces organized. In order to learn useful tips in organizing the students' own closets, have the students ask their friends questions to determine why they have organized their spaces the way they have.

Evaluation Tips

- Encourage family members to comment on the students' efforts in doing their own laundry or organizing their belongings.
- When an article of clothing shrinks, have students compare the item to one that has not shrunk and give reasons why shrinking may have occurred.
- Assist the students with prompts when they are first learning the new organizational system for a desk, bookcase, or closet. Gradually reduce interactions with them in this activity so that only observation is necessary. Ask students what they believe they are doing well and what type of help they may need to improve the organizational system.

- Observe the students' performance over time and in different settings, such as in Laundromats while doing laundry or in school while organizing desks and lockers. Ask students to compare the similarities to and differences from these settings and the home environment. Have students problem solve how to adapt the organizational skills they have learned to the new settings.

For Students Who Need Additional Modifications

- Use a sequence of pictures to help the students remember the steps in doing laundry or other routines. These pictures can be placed on a bulletin board in the laundry room for easy reference or kept in a notebook or on individual cards with print or braille captions sequenced on a notebook ring. Students who cannot see pictures and do not read braille may benefit from having the sequence audiotaped.
- Use a front-loading washer and dryer for students whose physical disabilities make it difficult to load from the top.
- Select one or two steps that students with severe physical disabilities can carry out, such as placing items in a dryer, sorting items by color, or removing items from the hamper and carrying them to the laundry area.
- Encourage students with severe physical disabilities who cannot actively participate in loading or unloading the washer and dryer to listen for the machines to stop or for buzzers to go off. They may be able to alert others to the need to remove the clothes.
- Emphasize the concepts of clean and dirty and help the students place dirty clothes in a hamper or laundry chute at a consistent time. Establish how long each item should be worn; for example, underwear and socks go into the hamper each day before bedtime. Also have students practice identifying clothing that should be placed in a hamper even before it is worn an entire day, for example, when something is spilled on clothing or when an odor is evident.
- Practice with students to distinguish between "clean" spills and "dirty" spills. For example, water or soap suds splashed on a shirt do not require clothing to be changed, but ketchup or chocolate spills do.

- In all rooms of the house, place materials at a height where the students can use them. For example, tall wastebaskets are easier for students in wheelchairs to use, as are shelves located at elbow-to-shoulder height for storing the students' materials.

ASSUMING FAMILY RESPONSIBILITIES

Teaching adolescents with visual impairments to participate in household chores tends to be time consuming for most families. Because in many instances the parent or parents in a family usually work and have little time to spend on chores, teaching such family responsibilities can be a challenge. However, just as sighted adolescents are required to participate in household activities, adolescents with visual impairments also need to be expected to do their part. Learning that completing weekly chores is a family responsibility helps students understand the importance of contributing to the well-being of others and underscores the expectations of others that the young people can and will pitch in.

Activities

- Put together a "job jar," with jobs written on slips of paper (in the student's preferred reading medium and regular print). Be sure that the jobs listed are ones that all the students can do successfully and independently.
- Allow each youngster to select two or three jobs for the week at home or at school and place the slips in a jar or on a bulletin board with his or her name.
- Families or teachers may designate particular days of the week on which certain chores need to be completed; allow the youngsters to decide when other chores are done as long as they are completed in a specified period.
- Teach youngsters with visual impairments to use a "grid" pattern or a double-cross method when covering large areas during cleaning tasks. When working with the double-cross method to sweep or vacuum, students cover an area by sweeping across an open space vertically, use the opposite wall to square off, and then cross back to the wall from which they started. At the starting point, they move a full step to either the left or right and recross the space vertically, repeating that pat-

tern until they have covered the entire surface. When using a broom to sweep, the dirt is always swept toward the same wall. The students then cover the same area moving horizontally.

- As an alternative method, teach the students to sweep one path, deposit dirt at the end of the path, then return to the starting point, take a large step backward, and move toward the same wall again, repeating the process. The students can check their distance with an arm or the broom and continue until they finish sweeping the area. The final step is to sweep all the piles of dirt to a predetermined corner of the room.

Critical Points to Cover

- Emphasize to students that people are expected to be responsible for themselves and to contribute to the welfare of their family members.
- Explain that everyone in a family is expected to help out with day-to-day chores.
- Explain that when young people leave home to live in dormitories or other residential quarters, to set up their own homes or apartments, or to move in with others, they need to and are expected to know how to perform household chores.

Helpful Hints

- Be sure the youngsters have been taught how to do the chores before placing the slips of paper in the job jar.
- Keep cleaning materials in an assigned spot, so that adolescents with visual impairments can locate and identify them independently.
- Mark items, when necessary, in an appropriate reading medium (braille or large print).
- Include instructions on the safe use and disposal of all cleaning products. For example, explain to students that they need to throw away or recycle—but not reuse—bottles that contained cleaning products. They also need to know that it is dangerous to use bleach and abrasive cleansers together because the mixture will form a dangerous gas. They also need to understand the need for storing cleaning products in high or locked spaces so that young children will not accidentally ingest them.

- Start youngsters with small, well-defined areas first. For example, wiping a table would precede sweeping a small floor area, which would precede sweeping a larger floor area.
- Make chores as much fun as possible. If two or more youngsters are involved, offer a prize for the first who completes his or her chores in that week or who does the best job (unless the evaluation is unfair because of age, disability-specific, or other considerations).
- Praise the youngsters for work done well and let them hear their families or teachers compliment their work to other people. Such compliments give them a sense of self-respect and accomplishment and let other people know that the visually impaired youngsters are competent individuals.
- Let the young people with visual impairments and other family members generate the chores that need to be done. Doing so promotes decision making and working as members of a team.
- Jobs that are ongoing may warrant allowances if giving allowances is acceptable to the adolescents' families.
- Develop job charts that include descriptions of tangible rewards in appropriate media and post them in easily accessible locations.
- Initially, assign a day to do chores and give a reward when the work is completed.

Evaluation Tips

- Ask the youngsters to let their teachers or family members know when they have finished their chores. If the chores have been done satisfactorily, explain why the students did a good job. Be specific. "Good job" does not tell them a thing. "Thank you, the dishes are all in the right spot" is more explicit. Then return the job slip to the job jar.
- Redirect the students to get the job done correctly, if necessary. Help them solve any problem they may encounter in carrying out the job.
- Make rewards (perhaps including allowances) contingent upon completing the chores.

For Students Who Need Additional Modifications

- For students who do not read, place pictures of each task in the job jar or an object that relates to the task, such as a small laundry scoop for doing the laundry, a piece of dishrag for dish-washing, or a piece of sponge for cleaning floors.

- Create a calendar on which an object representing each day's job is placed. For students with limited memory spans, place an object that represents the day's job into a basket or box each day and teach them to begin the task by removing the object from the basket or box. These objects are concrete reminders of the jobs to be done.

- To help students remember the sequence of steps in a task, place the materials in a row from left to right in the order in which they will be used. Before the students begin the task, call their attention to each object and have them describe the steps if they use language.

- For students who cannot do a complete task, find one or two steps that they can do. Try to find several tasks that use the step to give them plenty of practice. For example, if the students can pour water, they can help rinse dishes, water plants, or empty a bucket after someone washes the floor.

- Provide opportunities for the students to understand the jobs that others are doing; for example, have them touch the ingredients before their parents or siblings prepare food, explore the textures of brooms and brushes to see how they push materials on the floor, or observe others emptying trash into a bin.

ENCOURAGING COMMUNITY INVOLVEMENT

If youngsters with visual impairments have positive experiences as members of school and community organizations, they will be more likely to learn or refine socially appropriate behaviors. Community experiences allow young people to increase their responsibilities, learn to organize their time, have opportunities to interact with their sight-ed peers, and, possibly, discover the variety of jobs that are available in their community.

Activities

- If the youngsters are not already involved in the community, encourage them to join a community-based group, such as Boy Scouts or Girl Scouts, Young Men's Christian Association (YMCA)

FROM A RURAL PERSPECTIVE

During the middle school years, visually impaired children who live in rural areas are frequently the only ones in their districts with sensory impairments. As with other students their age, they are struggling to belong to a peer group—to identify with others their own age and to break away from parental influences. To join their classmates in exploring social and vocational options in their rural communities, they need to be mobile and have a notion of what options are available to them. Consequently, one of the more pressing needs of these students is access to role models and the provision of community supports to encourage them to be actively involved in exploring careers.

Children in middle school are entering adolescence and hence are in the process of setting expectations for themselves that are often based on the possibilities they see in their own lives. In many rural communities, a lack of appropriate, vital services, such as public transportation, diminished opportunities to interact with other visually impaired children and adult role models, and a scarcity of work programs and job opportunities, can often lead visually impaired students to lower their expectations.

Families and teachers who live in rural communities can make a joint effort to have the communities offer support by identifying solutions to problems posed by the lack of needed services for children and adolescents with visual impairments. The key is to be creative in devising solutions. When public transportation is not available, the question becomes, How does a visually impaired student get from place to place in a timely manner? Solutions may vary and include arranging for car pools and tapping into other transportation sys-

or Young Women's Christian Association (YWCA) youth groups, and church or synagogue youth groups.

- Family members or teachers may want to research local youth groups and their leaders by asking questions such as the following:
  1. Does the group leader facilitate positive communication between peers?
  2. Has the group been formed in an environment that fosters friendships?
  3. Does the leader set realistic goals with members of the group and assist them, including youngsters with disabilities, in meeting those goals?
  4. Would the leader come to a parent or a vision teacher for help, if necessary?
- Involve the visually impaired youngsters in the research process to the maximum extent possible.

tems, such as medical transportation services or transportation provided by service organizations.

With regard to meeting the needs of visually impaired youngsters to interact with visually impaired role models, the question becomes, How can other visually impaired individuals be located in the rural environment? Contacting the state vocational rehabilitation agency that offers services to visually impaired people and consumer organizations for adults (such as the American Council of the Blind or the National Federation of the Blind; see Resources section) or consulting a teacher of visually impaired students could certainly be a part of the solution. And, at least for training purposes, students may need to leave their communities to obtain specialized training in the skills they need to succeed in school or at work. For example, during field trips to a state residential school for blind students, children can meet adult role models in a variety of work situations, as well as other students who are visually impaired. (Many states offer special summer transition job programs for older students through state residential schools or vocational rehabilitation programs, which younger students and their families can visit for help in future career planning.)

Visually impaired students in rural areas may also want or need to attend a residential school for advanced instruction in disability-specific skills, such as literary braille or the Nemeth Code (used in mathematics and science), orientation and mobility techniques, or vocational skills training with adapted equipment or tools. In addition, teachers may contact personnel offices within businesses outside these communities to expand young people's opportunities for interviews for jobs that are not commonly found in the communities in which they live.

Elaine Sveen

- Once such groups are located, suggest that the leaders promote interactions in small groups so the youngsters with visual impairments can have greater opportunities to get to know the other group members.

Critical Points to Cover

- Discuss with students that community involvement is important to young people because it is a way for them to make friends and participate in age-appropriate activities they enjoy.
- Explain to students that participation in group activities enables young people to refine skills that may be transferable to work environments. These skills may include solving problems, setting goals, keeping notes, working with others, writing reports, presenting ideas, and negotiating with group members and leaders.

- Emphasize that participation in group activities also provides opportunities to network with adults and other young people who may be able to provide job leads in the future.

Helpful Hints

- Encourage the youngsters to explain their visual impairments to the group leaders and other participants to facilitate positive behavior and realistic expectations.
- Be available to assist the group leaders in developing ways to make any necessary adaptations so the visually impaired youngsters may participate in most, if not all, the group activities. Some adaptations may include locating sources to produce braille or large-print training materials, labeling items with tactile markings or braille, providing sighted-guide assistance, arranging field trips that are accessible to visually impaired students, and lending adapted games or tools.
- Have visually impaired youngsters demonstrate their adaptive equipment to the entire group.
- Be sure to help the group leaders obtain or convert required reading materials, including the group manual, that are in the visually impaired youngsters' preferred reading medium.
- Allow the youngsters with visual impairments to make suggestions or solve problems when things are not going smoothly or when communication is difficult.
- Encourage the youngsters with visual impairments to invite other participants to their homes between meetings to advance developing friendships.
- Consider holding an awareness session for the group facilitated by family members, parents, teachers, or students in cooperation with the group leaders to explain visual impairments by using videos or by performing vision loss simulation activities. These activities may include using goggles that simulate different visual impairments, donning sleep shades to simulate total blindness while doing routine chores, or demonstrating how people with particular types of vision loss adapt various tasks for accomplishing them. An interesting activity is to have sighted students try to follow a simple recipe without using vision and then have them follow the same recipe after they been shown how to use marked measuring cups,

spoons, and a stove with the dials marked. Another useful activity is to have sighted students wear vision loss simulators or sleep shades and try to eat a meal or put together a simple puzzle.

- Rehearse with the students what they will say in the group.
- If the youngsters are not interested in the groups mentioned previously, suggest that they join after-school clubs like the Spanish club, debate team, or drama club; take classes to learn new skills, such as sculpting, swimming, gymnastics, wrestling, or photography; or participate in volunteer activities.

Evaluation Tips

- Monitor the youngsters' comments and actions after group meetings. Ask them with whom they interacted, what games or activities they did, how they were involved in those activities, and what they talked about in meetings.
- If there are difficulties, assist the youngsters with problem-solving strategies and role-play solution-oriented scenarios.

For Students Who Need Additional Modifications

- Find ways in which the students with severe disabilities can assist others and not just receive assistance. Assistance may be as basic as moving a wheelchair to a position where another person can use the individual's tray to hold objects, but the importance of the students' role should be acknowledged as that of a helper.
- Encourage members of the Scout troop, including the students with severe disabilities, to consider wheelchair access when they plan activities and to find ways to include the disabled students. If an activity is not possible for the students with severe disabilities (for example, hiking on rough terrain), encourage the group to plan alternative activities during the same period for other members who may also choose not to participate in the inaccessible activity, as well as for the students with severe disabilities.
- Save objects, slides, and photographs from Scouting trips and talk with the disabled students and the group about the experiences after they have taken place as a way to encourage the students to remember and refer to their experiences on the trip. Slides are especially useful for students with physical disabilities

because the students can operate an adaptive switch to show the slides to others.

- When participants are deaf, teach the Scout troop or social group the basics of sign language. Before each new activity, introduce one or two new signs that the members can use to refer to their experiences with the deaf participants; for example, if they are going camping, teach the signs for *tent, campfire,* and *marshmallows.*
- When activities are done in groups, make sure that the group members take turns working with each other. In this way, all the participants get to know the students with disabilities and can help to think of new ways for them to participate.
- When disabled participants do not use spoken or sign language, encourage each member of the group to find a special symbol that will represent him or her to them. For example, a Girl Scout who wears her hair in braids may place her friend's hand on her braid so the friend will know who she is.

ORGANIZING SCHOOL WORK

Many young people with visual impairments have been successfully integrated into mainstream public and private schools. Although classroom education teachers work with these students on an ongoing basis and teachers of visually impaired students are available to help support their efforts, it is sometimes possible that lower expectations are set for these young people, primarily because it may take them longer to complete certain tasks. Families and teachers can support youngsters with visual impairments by continuing to have high expectations for them while making many tasks more organized and therefore easier to complete. They need to take time to teach skills thoroughly, so young people feel good about mastering these skills; to model good behavior; and to give the youngsters praise when it is earned. For youngsters to have positive self-images, it is important for family members and those working with them to expect them to perform at levels comparable to sighted youngsters of the same age.

Activities

- Have the students organize a notebook or notebooks for school and personal purposes to promote independence. Middle school students have to change classes several times during a school day, which increases their need to be orderly.

- Have the youngsters each purchase a three-ring binder with two pocket folders and a notebook zipper bag. Ask them to label the folders in their preferred medium: One folder may be marked Homework or To Do, and the other may be marked Return to Teacher or Completed. In addition to completed homework assignments, the students can place notes from their families to the teacher (regarding absences or scheduled appointments, for example) in the return folder.

- The youngsters with low vision may keep pens, pencils, optical devices, and markers in the notebook zipper bag, whereas those who are blind may keep a slate and stylus, a couple of pens for signatures, and a signature guide in that section. All the students may benefit from having a single-sheet hole punch and a stapler in their bag. Although it may require additional expense to have duplicate items in each notebook, doing so prevents the visually impaired youngsters from having to shift items from classroom to classroom, allowing them more time to change classes with their sighted peers.

Critical Points to Cover

- Explain to students that to keep up with schoolwork, they need organizational systems.
- Explain that although people use different kinds of organizational systems, three-ring binders and file folders are common tools both in schools and offices.
- Emphasize that it is the visually impaired students' responsibility to keep up with their materials and tools.
- Learning to deal with decisions that one has made is just as important as having the right tools.

Helpful Hints

- Involve the youngsters as much as possible in setting up their organizational systems. After discussing the needs for each notebook (its size and contents), have the students select which notebooks they want to purchase, even if the parents or teacher may not agree with their selection.

- A classroom teacher may have specific requirements for a folder. The students should learn about these requirements and integrate them into their notebook systems.
- Encourage students to use other available resources, such as the *Transition Tote System: Navigating the Rapids of Life* (Wolffe & Johnson, 1997), available from the American Printing House for the Blind (see the Resources section).
- Emphasize literacy, reading speed, and use of technology as well as organizational skills, to maximize the visually impaired students' chances of keeping up with their sighted classmates.
- If the students have numerous braille or large-print books, ask the school administrators to assign them two or more lockers or a place in each classroom to store necessary materials. It is important that students with visual impairments have space for storage that they can gain access to independently.

Evaluation Tips

- Review with the students how their organizational folders are working for them. Are there any items that may need to be added or deleted? Are there any notebooks that could be combined or added?
- Suggest that the students speak with their sighted peers to gain any organizational tips that they may have. Revise the tips to meet the needs of individuals with visual impairments.
- Monitor the students' progress using the notebooks and folders. Help the students solve problems if they are confused or if the system fails to meet their needs.

For Students Who Need Additional Modifications

- For students who cannot turn pages in a notebook or handle paper, organize schedules and work activities by using different materials. These materials may include a picture or object calendar on an easily accessible bulletin board, an audiotape recorder to keep a schedule and to record deadlines, a set of picture or object cards on a notebook ring or in a waist pack, or a series of hooks on wallboard on which objects or pictures can be placed.

- Students who travel independently can carry pictures or objects to remind them of their destinations.
- Students who cannot communicate using spoken language should learn a way of communicating with others when assistance is needed. This method of communication should include a way of getting another's attention acceptably and, in some cases, using cards to request assistance or state their destinations.
- The students' way of carrying materials should be similar to that used by others in school. If others use backpacks, then a backpack should be adapted to attach to the students' wheelchairs. If girls carry purses, then the girls with disabilities should also have purses. Velcro can often be substituted for complex buckles or zippers on backpacks and purses to make them easier to use.
- If the students require more time to travel between classes than what is normally provided, arrange for one or two nondisabled classmates to travel with them at the same time. In this way, the disabled students will not miss out on the socialization aspects of changing classes.
- Encourage classmates without disabilities to participate in developing adapted materials for the disabled students. They can often find creative solutions to problems regarding materials, and making new materials can be a project for home economics, industrial arts, or art classes.
- Decorate special equipment or adaptive devices, such as braces, wheelchairs, or monoculars, according to the preferences of the disabled students. Bright colors, stickers, pictures of rock stars, and graphics can elicit comments from others and promote interaction among peers.

References

Wolffe, K., & Johnson, D. (1997). *The transition tote system: Navigating the rapids of life.* Louisville, KY: American Printing House for the Blind.

CHAPTER

14

Encouraging Socialization

Before students embark on their high school and postsecondary school journeys, they need to master the social skills that are critical to life success. This chapter presents activities that stimulate young people to identify their career goals, interests, and abilities and the personal attributes that are necessary to keep jobs, clarify values, learn assertiveness skills, connect with mentors, and take risks. By performing these activities, students can come to recognize their strengths and weaknesses and the strengths and weaknesses of those around them at school and in the community.

After students with visual impairments leave the public school system at age 18 or shortly thereafter (typically no later than age 22), they may leave their families' homes and begin lives that revolve, to a large degree, around others—roommates, employers, professors, readers, attendants, and friends. Or they may stay in their families' homes but become involved in activities that occur predominantly outside home, for example, in work (paid or volunteer), further studies (at a community college, university, or technical or vocational school), and relationships outside the family (with acquaintances or friends). To make mature choices and establish viable, long-term relationships outside their families, the students first need to master social skills. This chapter gives readers some of the means to make the development of these skills a reality.

THE CONCEPT OF SELF-AWARENESS

Like all young people, those with visual impairments need to know who they are and how they fit into the world around them. Self-awareness, or an awareness of one's individuality, is an essential ingredient in personality development and plays a significant role in interactions with others. Blind students may need to be taught greater self-awareness and social interaction skills because many of the social behaviors people manifest are displayed by visible body language, including eye contact. Being able to voice opinions, join in conversations, and be a good listener and respond appropriately are all examples of good communication and social skills. As students with visual impairments grow up, they will need to have adults explain the effects of their interactions with others because many responses to how a person acts are typically noted through visual cues. The more aware visually impaired students are of such social interaction issues, the more socially comfortable and successful they may be.

It is important for adults to help youngsters identify their interests, abilities, values, strengths, and weaknesses. By knowing about these things and thinking about them as they grow, youngsters are better able to make connections not only to other people but also to work environments that they would enjoy and in which they will be able to perform. If young people do not have ideas about the kind of work they would like to do, others may select work for them. And given that society often tends to stereotype people with disabilities as having limited interests and abilities and, therefore, limited occupational choices as adults, youngsters with visual impairments need to be given opportunities to explore a wide range of hobbies and activities. Doing so will give them not only a strong foundation of information on which to make life decisions, but social opportunities to belong within the community.

Activities

- Encourage young people to consult career-investigation reference books that can take young people through a series of questions about their values, interests, hobbies, and skills. These books, many of which may be found in junior high or high school libraries, are informative for students and for adults who work with them. The students are usually excited about evaluating themselves in guided learning experiences.
- Ask the students to complete the exercises in the career-investigation books to help them identify whether they would prefer to work (and would work best) with people, data, or things.

FROM A FAMILY PERSPECTIVE

The Concept of Self-Awareness

Children's feelings of self-esteem and self-awareness are greatly influenced by family discussions, and a natural place to have these discussions is around the family dinner table. Make the family mealtime the definite calming social event of the day. (Make it a priority to eat together as a family at least once a week, if not once a day.) If you need to do disciplining, serious talking, and the like, then try to select another time for these actions. Make the family mealtime a guaranteed "together time." *Come to the Table* (Cannon & Cooney, 1997) is a guide to reviving the lively art of dinnertime conversation. It presents 52 easy-to-use exercises that are designed to get family members talking to each other.

Understanding the Effect of One's Behavior on Others

Family meetings are an essential way to encourage family members to understand the effect of their behavior on others. These meetings, which can be conducted weekly, are a simple, effective, and time-tested formula that allows the family members to share the ups and downs of daily life in a democratic forum. The book *Active Parenting: Teaching Courage, Cooperation, and Responsibility* (Popkin, 1987) and the pamphlet *The Family Council* (Rigney & Corsini, 1970) provide additional information on helping children understand the effects of their behavior on others.

Kevin O'Connor

Many of these guided learning experiences indicate which jobs match the interests, values, and skills that the students currently have. Just as important, the exercises may indicate that the students are considering fields in which they have little or no current interest or aptitude and hence may encourage them to think of different occupations.

- Have the students take interest inventories like the *Self-Directed Search* (Holland, 1985), to assist them in exploring their potential for particular jobs.
- Ask students to discuss with their teachers, family members, or counselors what aspects of an experience they liked and disliked while volunteering or working.
- Have students read books about people who have undergone life experiences—and have them explain what interests them about those experiences—and consider what they like best

about their involvement in school, community activities, and family life.

Critical Points to Cover

- Discuss the differences and similarities between people's interests, abilities, values, strengths, and weaknesses. Give examples of activities that may be of interest to one person but be considered a chore to another (for example, gardening, walking, or cooking).
- Talk about how interests, abilities, values, strengths, and weaknesses affect getting and keeping a job.
- Exchange views on which qualities (that is, work habits or behaviors) a person needs to demonstrate to be successful at work. These qualities may include initiative; good listening skills; the ability to ask questions, follow directions, and demonstrate an interest in what one is doing; and the willingness to learn new things and to work with other people.
- Examine ways that people can learn more about themselves to help them discover their abilities for certain jobs, for example, by taking interest inventories.
- Explain to students that one highly effective way to determine one's vocational abilities is to experience a wide variety of work experiences through job shadowing (that is, following an employee while he or she performs a job to better understand the employee's responsibilities) or volunteering or performing work for pay and then evaluating what one likes or dislikes.

Helpful Hints

- Have the students discuss what they see as each other's strengths.
- Perform activities with the students that help them identify the differences among values, interests, and abilities.
- Role-play situations that may occur at work and that help the youngsters identify their value systems. Audiotape these sessions for review and write down critical points for later discussion.
- Help the adolescents to build assertive communication skills by encouraging them to join speech, drama, or debate clubs; to

role-play communication techniques with adults or other students; to practice what to say in situations that involve conflict; and to play games and participate in sports activities. By providing guidance, helping students understand their extracurricular options, and supporting their choices, adults can foster active involvement and opportunities for building assertiveness skills.

- When students are researching jobs or job shadowing others who are working, discuss which hobbies, clubs, and other activities could help students learn critical concepts and skills to obtain specific positions.
- Ask the adolescents to interview adults whom they admire to determine the adults' values, interests, and abilities and ask how these values, interests, and abilities affected their choice of careers.
- Have the students gather information from others on what abilities they think they have that will affect their career choices and success.

Evaluation Tips

- Ask the students to tell what they have learned about their strengths and weaknesses.
- Ask the youngsters to set one goal that will help them further assess their values, interests, or abilities.
- As other activities are performed with students, whether in the classroom or in the home, have them assess what values are being applied as they make decisions. For example, when members of the students' families discuss what they want to do on their vacation, suggest that each person list three activities. Review these activities with students: What does each person's choice indicate about his or her values? Were the family members motivated by a desire for money, excitement, or a desire to be in a group, be alone, be active, or to be outdoors in making these choices? Likewise, when the students decide in class which activities they want to participate in, help them identify the values that influence the reasons for their choices: For example, are their choices based on issues related to security, adventure, health, creativity, or independence?

FROM A MULTICULTURAL PERSPECTIVE

During the preteenage and teenage years, young people refine a range of social skills to address many situations and people of diverse ages and backgrounds. Students who are outside the dominant culture, which is made up of people without disabilities, are bombarded with challenges, such as others' negativity toward or misunderstanding of their differences. In addition, some students with disabilities face discrimination and rejection because of their race, ethnicity, gender identity, or religious beliefs. As a consequence, they need to learn to stand up for themselves.

Like all young people, those who are visually impaired need to draw on their repertoire of life experiences to become assertive adults. They need to be able not only to express their feelings and desires, but also to give and receive feedback and respect. And they need to enlist the support of others by helping others and engaging in individual, group, and community activism. Assuming leadership responsibilities is another way for them to become more self-assured.

Establishing and maintaining relationships with people in the dominant culture help middle school youngsters with visual impairments minimize stereotyping and maximize their opportunities to learn about various differences among people and educate others about visual impairments. In addition, selecting appropriate strategies for establishing, managing, and maintaining relationships strengthens these young people's decision-making skills.

The onset of visual impairment during preadolescence or adolescence requires special consideration, especially when young people face racial or ethnic biases in addition to bias related to visual impairments. Thus, young people

For Students Who Need Additional Modifications

- After the students meet unfamiliar people, encourage them to describe ways in which they are similar to and different from the people they have met. These descriptions can begin with physical characteristics: Are the people male or female? Are they taller or shorter than the student? Older or younger?
- Use a symbol to mark possessions and spaces that belong specifically to the students. For students who do not read, this symbol can be a picture or a tactile object (such as a sticker with a smiling face or coarse Velcro stick-on tabs).
- Find adults who have disabling conditions similar to those of the students. If the students use language, encourage them to talk with the adults about what the adults experience. Arrange several visits so the students can see what activities these adults include in their day.

who become visually impaired at this time may need extra supports, such as counseling or support groups, through which they can explore their feelings about differences. Family members and friends may find that participating in such counseling or support groups is vital in helping the young people adjust to their visual impairments. Visually impaired youngsters feel validated when others fully understand that they can be contributing members of the community.

Most children and youths easily internalize spoken and unspoken messages (such as stereotypic and negative images on television or videotapes and in books, newspapers, magazines, advertisements, and cartoons) about who they are and how they are valued. Because many visually impaired children and youths rely on the interpretations of sighted persons, they often may be more profoundly influenced by the prejudices and stereotypes of others. Hence, teachers and family members need to be more conscious of expressions of prejudice so they can avoid behaviors that perpetuate misconceptions or stereotypes that are based on disability, race-ethnicity, gender, religion, and values that are different from those of the dominant culture. They also need to be aware that prejudice and even dehumanization may be reflected in such actions as avoidance, discrimination, devaluing, and disrespect. The primary goal of multicultural competence is to prevent harmful messages from being transmitted or to interrupt those that are attempted. As teachers and family members help visually impaired young people attain a high level of awareness, knowledge, and skill in cross-cultural communication, they foster the youngsters' ability to compete in a multicultural world and the global workforce.

Lila Cabbil

- Encourage the students to visit adults in the school and audio-tape descriptions of their occupations. Later, they can practice identifying the adults whose voices they recorded.
- Provide choices of leisure-time activities and vary these choices from day to day. Object or picture cues (see Chapter 3) can be used with students who do not have an established language system.
- Ask the students to interview parents and friends about their hobbies and leisure-time activities. Have them compare their likes and dislikes to those of the people they have interviewed and talk about whether they may want to try another person's hobby.

SOCIAL INTERACTION SKILLS

Cooperative social interactions frequently occur when children are members of organized groups that have a specified purpose, such as to perform a community service, play a sport, or refine competencies, such as playing a musical instrument or singing. In such groups, young people learn to follow directions from a leader, to develop self-confidence in a group setting, and to cope with success and failure as they discover how a group operates. Group activities are important to adolescents because they offer the participants opportunities to learn social skills that will carry over into adulthood. Students with visual impairments may miss out on a variety of cooperative social opportunities during the middle school years if they are not part of an organized social group. Thus, their families and teachers may need to encourage them to participate in school and extracurricular group activities. The students' participation in these activities can help them develop skills that will assist them in their chosen careers. Furthermore, they should be given numerous opportunities every day to make choices and decisions and to give feedback to others. As they master a skill, such as a sport, a hobby, or another interest, their confidence in their abilities grows, which encourages them to take on bigger challenges ultimately. It is important for teachers and families to have high expectations of students with visual impairments. By setting high expectations, adults subtly convey a message of confidence in the students' abilities. Students who frequently receive such messages rise to the challenge; perform to the best of their abilities; and, consequently, build their confidence levels.

Activities

- Encourage middle school students to pursue their interests (for example, hobbies, sports, or crafts projects).
- Support students in developing their interests further by encouraging them to join clubs, participate in hobby shows, and go on family vacations to places that expand their knowledge of these interests.
- Promote team and individual sports as important learning opportunities for students. Traditionally, swimming, wrestling, and track have been sports in which youngsters with visual impairments have participated successfully. In addition, many visually impaired people have gone beyond traditional sports and have played football, basketball, and soccer or participated in cheerleading and other extracurricular activities.

FROM AN URBAN PERSPECTIVE

During the middle school years, visually impaired students, like their sighted peers, may expand their involvement in sports, Scouting, youth groups, performing arts, language clubs, and other extracurricular activities. Not only are these opportunities more numerous and readily available in urban than in rural areas, but transportation is less likely to be a barrier to involvement in urban areas.

In addition, youths who are visually impaired may have a greater chance of meeting adults who are visually impaired in urban than in rural communities, which can help them determine the types of careers they can pursue as adults. They also have the opportunity to meet other young people with visual impairments, as well as those with other disabilities and those from various racial-ethnic, cultural, and religious backgrounds, all of whom can broaden their view of the world.

Furthermore, there are in general more work opportunities in large urban areas than in most rural areas. Consequently, there are likely to be more opportunities to learn about jobs through job shadowing or informational interviews and to receive internships or trial work experiences when students are ready to go to work.

Victoria Tripodi

Critical Points to Cover

- Discuss the importance of the students' active participation in group activities.
- Discuss how work environments are similar in many ways to organized groups.
- Discuss jobs that are related to the activity in which the students participate and encourage the students to take written notes (using braille, large print, or an electronic notetaker) about the comparisons.
- Discuss how accommodations can be made for students' participation and include strategies for meeting transportation needs. For example, ask the students where they need to go (for instance, to swimming practice or a play rehearsal) and talk about the travel options that are available. Can the students walk; ride a bicycle; ride in a car with a friend or family member; or take a bus, train, or taxi? If older students or friends drive and can give visually impaired students a lift, the students can reciprocate by giving them money for gas or snacks for practice

meets, by making phone calls to solicit help with transportation for future practice sessions, or by repaying the favor in some other way. Other options include carpooling and sharing the cost of taxi rides to "even out" transportation responsibilities. It is important to discuss with the students the concept of interdependence (people helping one another) and its significance in the lives of all people. Because many visually impaired students are unlikely to be able to drive automobiles independently, they need to understand the issue of interdependence (and its integral component, reciprocity) and apply it throughout their lives.

- Discuss how social skills are imperative for success in group activities, including work.

Helpful Hints

- Enlist the assistance and support of the activity leader before encouraging students to join a group.
- Encourage the students to read stories about athletes or other active people with visual impairments.
- Be available to discuss any difficulties that may arise from the students' participation in the group activity.
- Several sports have been adapted to allow for the full inclusion of people with visual impairments, including beep baseball, goal ball, bowling with gutter guards, and tandem biking, as have numerous board games, such as Monopoly, Scrabble, checkers, chess, dominos, and backgammon. Young people with visual impairments who learn sports and games are likely candidates for acceptance into groups or clubs by their sighted peers with similar interests.
- Find mentors for students who are active in areas of the students' interest.
- Encourage the students to develop hobbies that require skills that are transferable to group endeavors (such as ham radio, reading, musical skills, computer games, and crafts projects).

Evaluation Tips

- Ask the students for feedback on what they are learning from group participation that could be applicable to a work environment.
- Ask the students to evaluate their involvement in the group.

- Ask the group leader to evaluate the students' involvement.
- Ask family members and other concerned adults to observe whether the students actively participate in the group activity.

For Students Who Need Additional Modifications

- Encourage the students to visit different after-school activities and clubs before they choose their favorites. Talk with them about which activities would be easier for them to perform and which would be more difficult.
- Talk about activities that younger children can participate in and those that older children can. Have the students play a game in which the adult names (or shows a picture of) a game or activity and the students state whether it is usually done by people their own age or by younger or older people. Examples may include playing with dolls, driving race cars, or riding bicycles. This exercise may be particularly helpful for students who prefer leisure-time activities that are more appropriate for younger children than older children.
- Identify objects or materials that are associated with a particular sport, game, or activity. Invite speakers (such as a scuba diver or flower arranger) to class who have participated in that activity and ask them to demonstrate their equipment.
- Play a game in which an adult names an activity or hobby and the students state whether it is done individually, in a group, or both.
- Talk about whether students prefer to be with others or alone when they have free time.
- Find alternative ways for students who do not read or write to keep score during games. These alternatives can include dropping a poker chip into a container, punching a hole in a card, or ringing a bell (with someone else recording a point). Use the task of keeping score as a way of talking about the concepts of more and less.
- Have the students make a list of things they can do independently when others are busy. Even though these may not be challenging activities, they should be things that will keep the students' attention and keep them active. For example, writing letters, working on a craft, or keeping a journal may be meaningful activities that can be performed in a group setting.

ASSERTIVE COMMUNICATION SKILLS

Strong communication skills are an asset for anyone in today's world. Although the use of technology, particularly the use of electronic mail, has equalized communication for people with visual impairments in various ways, communicating face to face is a problem at times for some visually impaired individuals. Because of the public's stereotypical notions of blindness fueled by such factors as frequent portrayals on television and in films, books, and plays as needing help to voice their needs or as not being able to make eye contact or having other pronounced mannerisms, social interactions between visually impaired and sighted people have sometimes been negatively influenced. Therefore, young people with visual impairments benefit from learning assertive communication skills to address their needs and wants and make their wishes known, as well as to attend to the needs, wants, and wishes of others. By being able to communicate assertively, they can compensate for some people's tendencies toward overprotectiveness, which in turn can contribute to patterns of helplessness and lower self-esteem. In general, being assertive helps people have their needs met while respecting the needs of others.

Activities

- Assertiveness skills may be taught in group or individual settings, but a group setting may be preferable because of the increased likelihood of receiving structured feedback from peers and adults. The teacher may wish to coordinate either groups of students with visual impairments only or have a mix of children with and without visual impairments.
- Ask the students to discuss the differences among aggressive, passive, and assertive communication skills and to give examples of each. The following is an example of a scenario that may be used:

    A young man who is blind goes to a restaurant to have lunch. He discovers that the menu is inaccessible—it appears on a chalkboard and on a printed list. He cites the accessibility laws and says he will call his lawyer because the restaurant does not have a braille menu. The young man's response may be interpreted as aggressive communication by most people. Or the young man may react passively by ordering a hamburger, rather than what he really wants to eat, because he knows the restaurant serves hamburgers. An assertive communication by the young man might be for him to ask a waiter or another employee to read the menu aloud so he can make a selection.

- Separate the large group into subgroups and give them instructions to read a card with a scenario described on it. Have them discuss the scenario and ask the first subgroup to role-play the situation with a response that is passive, assertive, or aggressive. Let the other subgroups critique the first group's effort and say whether it was passive, assertive, or aggressive. The other groups can also be encouraged to give feedback on whether they felt positively or negatively about the first group's communication style. Examples of scenarios may include the following:
    1. The visually impaired student is in a restaurant, and the waiter asks the sighted person who is sitting with the student what the student wants to order. How does the student respond?
    2. The student is waiting for a street light to change. When it changes, someone grabs the student's arm and starts pulling him or her across the street. How would the student respond?
    3. The student who is blind is helping his or her mother to prepare a meal when a younger brother enters the kitchen and says he will take over because he can do the job faster. How would the student respond?
    4. The student has recently joined a new club. During break time, people are talking to one another, but the student has not been included. How would the student respond?
    5. The student is interviewing for a position in the marching band, and the supervising teacher tells the student that she does not see how a blind person can perform in the band. How would the student respond?
- Encourage the students to read stories or watch movies and television shows and discuss the characters, noting who demonstrated passive, assertive, or aggressive communication skills.
- Let the students research two leaders from the past or present (for example, Martin Luther King, Jr., Franklin D. Roosevelt, Mother Teresa, Colin Powell, and Margaret Thatcher). Ask them to compare these leaders' communication styles and leadership qualities.

Critical Points to Cover

- Discuss the differences among passive, assertive, and aggressive styles of communication and the consequences for oneself and others of using each style.
- Stress the importance of using an assertive approach in the workplace, at home, and in the community for personal satisfaction and self-esteem.
- Discuss the importance of analyzing the degree to which jobs require assertive communication skills.
- Discuss the appropriateness of an assertive communication style in the employment process.

Helpful Hints

- Invite a panel of people with visual impairments to come to the class to describe their life experiences, how they communicated as teens and as adults, and the outcome of their efforts.
- Structure the group to be a safe environment for all the students. Emphasize trust and honesty when working on communication skills.
- Infuse assertiveness skills training into orientation and mobility lessons, regular classroom interactions, and activities in the community.

Evaluation Tips

- After completing role-plays and discussion, encourage the students to talk about situations in which they could have been more assertive. Analyze how well they have understood the lesson by reviewing the nature of their responses.
- Use both audiotapes and videotapes of sessions to help the students evaluate their verbal and nonverbal behaviors.
- Ask the students to write down the feelings they experienced during the sessions in their preferred medium so they can refer to their responses later.
- Observe the students and note when they are using assertiveness skills. Point out the positive consequences of their efforts.
- Have the students define in their own words the terms *passive, assertive,* and *aggressive.*

For Students Who Need Additional Modifications

- Make sure the students are able to initiate appropriate greetings in public places and role-play appropriate greetings for different situations, such as meeting a friend at a grocery store, passing a neighbor on the street, or being introduced to a new person. For students with physical disabilities, find the most appropriate ways of adapting a handshake or substituting a gesture; for example, have the students extend their hands for another to shake, smile, turn their heads, or wave.

- Find the best way for students to request assistance from strangers and try activities that allow them to use that skill, for example, by having them hand picture cards to salesclerks at a store if the students are nonverbal.

- Role-play conversations with others and talk about how to recognize when someone is ready to end the conversation. Some visually impaired individuals with other disabilities enjoy talking with others and do not realize when someone else is ready to discontinue the conversation. Signals such as shortening sentences, turning away from the speaker, and mentioning another commitment should be recognized as signs that an individual is ready to finish a conversation.

- The students can visit people on their jobs and ask for permission to audiotape the employees' conversations while they are working. Afterward, the students can listen to the recordings and talk about what the speakers' conversations meant: Did they want someone to do something? Were they trying to find out something? Did they sound happy, nervous, or bored?

- Work with students who use a different system of communication (for example, sign language) to teach their classmates to use the system. Emphasize words that are interesting to middle school students.

- Encourage the students with physical disabilities to consider how they like to communicate with others; for example, if they use wheelchairs, do they feel more comfortable when others sit next to them, rather than stand over them? If they have hearing impairments, does it help if others do not play the radio while speaking to them? Role-play interactions in which the students tell others what would help them during communication.

UNDERSTANDING THE EFFECT OF ONE'S BEHAVIORS ON OTHERS

Society conveys many subtle social messages to children as they grow up, primarily through nonverbal communication. Because children with visual impairments often miss these nonverbal messages, they are frequently unaware of the effect of their behaviors on other people. Although the majority of youngsters who are visually impaired are mainstreamed, or placed in regular classes, they often are not included in social activities with their sighted peers. Appropriate social behaviors typically cannot be learned incidentally by children and youths with visual impairments; they need to be taught. It is critical for families and teachers to help youngsters with visual impairments interpret and analyze how their behaviors affect others and how others feel when they behave in certain ways, to help the youngsters correct inappropriate social behaviors and to explain nonverbal cues or behaviors to them.

Activities

- If possible, arrange for the students with visual impairments and some sighted peers (from school, church or synagogue, or other organizations) to enroll in a challenge or ropes course. These courses are designed to help young people with team building and facilitate communication skills, self-advocacy skills, and leadership skills through a range of activities that involve both physical challenges and mental problem-solving skills. The instructors are usually social workers or counselors who promote realistic feedback among the participants. When told about the students' behavioral goals, they will address any negative behaviors the students exhibit. A weekend outing or repeated sessions will provide the students with a great deal of feedback on their social interactions and the effect of their behaviors on others.

Critical Points to Cover

- Explain that although people have different personal values, there are fixed mores—habits, values, moral codes, and ethics—in each social milieu that all people are expected to observe and demonstrate through their behaviors.

- Discuss that people see each other differently from the way they see themselves, and that these differences may be important. It is by soliciting and attending to others' feedback (when it is valid) that people resolve problems with social interaction skills. Students with visual impairments need to understand that feedback or constructive criticisms are tools for self-improvement. They also need to understand that people sometimes misinterpret behaviors and give feedback that is hurtful or inappropriate. When behaviors are misinterpreted, it is important to understand what in the behaviors misled the other people and how to behave in ways to ensure that people perceive what one really intended.
- Discuss the importance of understanding the effects of one's behaviors on others in the work environment.

Helpful Hints

- Encourage the students with visual impairments who are enrolled in a challenge or ropes course to go to the activity center before their sighted peers, so they can gather information firsthand that their sighted peers will observe, that is, how the course is laid out, what kinds of obstacles are present, and so forth. Work with an orientation and mobility (O&M) instructor to ensure that safety techniques are taught to the students and that information-gathering tips are shared.
- Encourage students to read stories about adolescents who have experienced social difficulties and have resolved them productively. Ask a librarian to help you identify appropriate books for the students to read.
- Be sure to praise the students when you observe positive social behaviors.
- Encourage the students to work with older students and adult mentors.
- Encourage the students to keep journals of their social interactions and analyze why some situations go well and others do not. Discuss their journals with them privately and brainstorm suggestions for future social exchanges.
- Encourage students to attend group meetings at school that are often led by social workers or counselors to address issues of

concern to the students, such as dating, weight control, and social etiquette.

- Ask the classroom teachers and other professionals who work with the students to meet with students privately when they observe positive or negative behaviors that the students have demonstrated and to discuss how to improve or maintain their efforts when similar situations arise in the future.
- Role-play a variety of social situations with the students to give them additional ideas regarding social interactions. Have the students role-play all the different roles inherent in such situations to help them understand the situations from other people's perspectives.

Evaluation Tips

- Ask the students to describe their experiences in the challenge or ropes course. Ask them questions such as these: What behaviors of their peers did the students find acceptable or unacceptable? What feedback did the students receive from others, both positive and negative?
- Discuss with the challenge- or ropes-course instructors the behaviors that they noted were accepted or not accepted by the group.
- Ask the instructors for suggestions about other activities that would help the students learn more about themselves and others.

For Students Who Need Additional Modifications

- Discuss with the students how others may react to adaptive equipment associated with their disabilities, such as a wheelchair, hearing aid, or orthopedic devices. Role-play the ways in which the students may respond when others mention the equipment and discuss the approaches that may make others feel comfortable or alienate them (for example, using humor or anger, ignoring questions, or providing information).
- Have the students watch videos or listen to stories in which teenagers have conflicts with others. Talk about ways of solving conflicts before the students listen to the part of the story in which a solution is presented.

- Have the students practice identifying an individual's feelings from voice (for blind students) or from facial expressions (for students with low vision). Role-play individuals who are showing a variety of emotions and encourage the students to react to the way people are feeling.

References

Cannon, N., & Cooney, N. (1997). *Come to the table.* New York: Sheed & Ward.

Holland, J. L. (1985). *The self-directed search manual.* Odessa, FL: Psychological Assessment Resources.

Popkin, M. (1987). *Active parenting: teaching courage, cooperation, and responsibility.* New York: HarperCollins.

Rigney, K., & Corsini, R. (1970). *The family council.* (Available from Adler School of Psychology, 65 East Wacker Place, Suite 2100, Chicago, IL 60601; phone 312-201-5900).

CHAPTER

Developing Compensatory Skills

This chapter discusses the ways in which families and teachers can encourage adolescents with visual impairments to develop work-related vocabularies; conduct informational interviews with visually impaired and sighted adults who are employed; develop and write out their own career plans; participate in job-shadowing activities; practice job-seeking skills, such as filling out applications and writing cover letters; develop a budget; learn to use adaptive devices and computer technology; and learn the provisions of the Americans with Disabilities Act of 1990. All the students' functional academic and independent living skills are taught in the context of their next environment: work and adult responsibilities.

Although middle school students still have the high school years to refine their work-related skills and obtain paid work experience, the more active that young people who are visually impaired are, the more likely they will make a successful transition from middle school to high school and beyond. Most students learn by engaging in meaningful activities in which they can apply what they are learning to real-life situations. Compensatory skills can make the difference between full and partial inclusion for young people with visual impairments. By being able to read, write, perform calculations, travel independently, and solve life problems without assistance from sighted persons, they will be in a position to obtain training opportunities and jobs and to establish and maintain relationships after high school. This chapter presents vehicles for refining compensatory skills in meaningful real-life activities that set young people on the path to greater life satisfaction.

CONCEPT DEVELOPMENT

When young sighted people leave high school, they are generally expected to have plans to enter the workforce either immediately or following vocational training or graduation from college. However, this is not the case for many young people with visual impairments. School curricula often do not include students with visual impairments in their vocational programs or, if the students are in the academic track, encourage the students to maintain strong scholastic records and help them apply to college. Transition planning needs to begin at an early age to ensure that visually impaired students develop realistic concepts of the world of work. Informational interviews, job-shadowing experiences, talks given by work-related speakers, work-training efforts, and volunteer or paid work experiences are all methods of exploring possible career interests for youngsters with visual impairments.

An important information resource for people who are visually impaired is the Careers and Technology Information Bank (CTIB), maintained by the American Foundation for the Blind (AFB). Through the CTIB, adults who are blind or have low vision act as mentors to discuss work-related issues, such as using adaptive technology, obtaining training for a job, and using transportation effectively. (For information on the CTIB, write to AFB, 11 Penn Plaza, Suite 300, New York, NY 10001; or CTIB can be accessed by telephone at 212-502-7642 or E-mail at techctr@afb.net.)

Activities

- The world of work has a vocabulary all its own. Key concepts that students in the middle school years should be able to differentiate are job and career. The concept of job may mean a person's position in a workplace, whereas the concept of career may mean a person's lifework or profession. Discuss the differences between the two concepts with the students and ask them which *jobs* they would like to have while in high school and after high school which *careers* they would like to pursue. Have them each make a list of five jobs they would like to have as potential careers. Ask them to call CTIB for the names, address-es, and telephone numbers of people who are currently employed in these jobs or career areas. Have students generate questions to ask these employees, including the following:

1. What is your current job title?
2. What do you do in a typical day?
3. What jobs have you held in your working life?
4. What is your career goal?
5. How did the variety of jobs that you have held assist you in achieving your career goals?
6. How did you discover what your current career choice would be?
7. Have you changed your career? If so, why?
8. What training (for example, a college degree) was required to obtain your job?
9. How do you handle your transportation needs?
10. What equipment do you use on the job? Is it adapted to meet your needs?
11. What do you wear to work?

- Allow the students a week to contact one or more of the CTIB mentors. Ask them to discuss their results in a group or with the teacher individually and to consider any trends or patterns they may see among the mentors' suggestions. These discussions will reveal the complex nature of career decision making, including the fact that all jobs are beneficial because they are learning experiences.

Critical Points to Cover

- Discuss the benefits of pursuing a career versus a series of jobs.
- Discuss the benefits of having jobs that are not specifically relat-ed to a career.
- Discuss the reasons why a person with a visual impairment may need more time and energy than a sighted person to research a possible career path.

Helpful Hints

- In addition to the CTIB contacts, the students can contact peo-ple who are working locally in their areas of interest. Ask the students to compare the answers of the sighted and visually impaired people with whom they have spoken. They should find similarities as well as differences.

- Ask the students to develop a career plan with a timeline based on their current interests.
- Have the students rotate among several jobs during their job-shadowing experiences and discuss which parts of the jobs they shadowed seem of interest to them.
- Discuss the adaptations, materials, or equipment that may be required to be successful in each job with the students.
- Assist the students in generating additional questions (general to their situations) if they are unfamiliar with information seeking.
- Audiotape role-playing sessions to practice and review appropriate telephone manners.
- Discuss work-related concepts, such as part-time work, full-time work, temporary work, and a probationary period, because these terms may come up in conversations with the public and with CTIB members.
- Allow students who have difficulty with verbal communication to contact the first person on their list by mail and then have them speak to the person in a follow-up phone call. Doing so may allay their fears of speaking with people with whom they are unacquainted.

Evaluation Tips

- Listen to and observe the students while they are making telephone calls. With the other persons' permission, audiotape the phone calls for later discussion.
- Review and critique any written communication the students produce.
- Listen to and observe the students during group sessions. Later, set aside individual time to discuss the results of their conversations with the mentors.
- Ask the students to write papers outlining the difference between a job and a career and the results of what they discovered about themselves while they were speaking with the mentors.

For Students Who Need Additional Modifications

- Have the students distinguish between paid jobs and leisure-time activities. When in the community, describe people that the students pass (for example, a woman running by in a jogging suit, a man digging a hole in the sidewalk, and two people drinking coffee at a café while looking at some papers) and ask the students, "Do you think the person is working or having fun?"
- Invite persons with disabilities to speak to the students or arrange for students to visit them on their jobs. Encourage the students to ask how these people do their jobs differently from others, for example, are their desks at a different height because of their wheelchairs? How do those who are deaf talk to people at work who do not know sign language?
- Have the students visit people who do not work for pay but serve as volunteers, work in their own homes, or attend activity centers. Emphasize that people can do valuable work that does not necessarily involve paid employment.
- Have the students identify tools and materials that are used in different types of jobs. Talk about which tools they can use already, which tools they could learn to use easily, and which tools would be more difficult to learn to use.
- Discuss the concept of working cooperatively and find jobs in which the students can partially participate. Make sure the students know which steps other people are doing and the signs that indicate that the jobs are finished; for example, when planting seedlings, the students can scoop dirt into the pots but other workers may place the seedlings into the dirt and water the plants.

READING AND WRITING SKILLS

Literacy is a focus of concern in this country because despite society's goal of a fully literate citizenry, large numbers of Americans are thought to be functionally illiterate, that is, they are unable to read or to understand the written language of everyday life. Since people who have strong reading and writing skills usually are more marketable than are those who do not, people with visual impairments who communicate well in writing and read proficiently will have an advantage over some sighted people with limited abilities in these areas. By being able to write résumés and cover letters, fill out applications, and read help-wanted ads and job descriptions (in braille or large print), visually impaired students can be productive in their job search. The ability to follow written instructions, complete forms, write memos and reports, and perform other work tasks is essential for keeping most jobs. Given the ongoing importance of information services, people with visual impairments need to become as literate as possible. They also need to develop competence in using technology to give them access to the written word.

Activities

- An excellent way for middle school students to become familiar with the literacy demands of the world of work is to fill out job applications, which usually require a summary of the applicant's education, skills, and work experiences. After they complete these applications, students are often more aware of the need to complete their education, volunteer, or gain paid work experiences.
- Ask the students to obtain applications at work sites where they would like to work when they are able to get jobs. In small groups, have them choose one application and fill it out together. (Students who are unable to read print will need to ask for assistance and to use personal data sheets to help whomever assists them. Personal data sheets include all the pertinent information that an applicant would include on a job application.) After the group has filled out an application, ask the members to discuss the following:
  1. what they filled in for each question
  2. which items gave them difficulty
  3. which items they were unable to fill out because of their lack of experience, education, skills, or knowledge
- Complete an application with the entire class and emphasize the importance of completing the application neatly, telling the truth, having a list of references handy and being brief when answering some questions. For homework, have each student complete an application.

Critical Points to Cover

- Explain the importance of memorizing your social security number or carrying it with you.

- Discuss the kinds of identification a prospective employee must have available to show to a person who is hiring for a position.
- Discuss who should be listed as references and the need to contact potential references for permission before using their names.
- Explain how an applicant can cover such points as volunteer experiences, which are not asked for on an application.
- Clarify how a person who is blind and a person with low vision fill out an application.
- Discuss which laws protect a person with a disability from discrimination in the hiring process.
- Explain what a functional vision statement is and how to present one. (A functional vision statement reports the measurement of a person's vision by the functions the person can perform, rather than by a person's acuity, or sharpness of vision.)

Helpful Hints

- Give students who read braille a brailled version of an application for reference, but caution them that braille applications are not usually available at workplaces, so they will need to obtain assistance from sighted people to complete standard applications unless they are filling out applications on-line.
- Review when to fill in "NA" or "not applicable" and how to write dates on applications; give other hints on filling out applications.
- Take a field trip with the students to a motor vehicle bureau to obtain picture identification cards.
- Assign the students who have had some work experience as the leaders in discussions. (Peers can be excellent teachers.)
- Build language skills with concepts like nondiscrimination, résumé, cover letter, thank-you letter, and references.

Evaluation Tips

- As a group, let the students critique each completed application for feedback from peers.
- Ask each student to complete a different application and then have the class compare and contrast the applications.
- Invite an employer to come to the class and give feedback on the students' applications.

- Ask the students to research the laws that relate to employment practices.
- Teach the students to write a cover letter that points out additional information that may enhance the application, such as volunteer work activities, leadership positions in extra-curricular activities, hobbies, and so forth.
- Ask the students to obtain permission from three sources who would be willing to act as references for them.
- Research which companies require résumés in addition to or instead of applications and which companies accept only applications.
- Discuss with a human resources person the pros and cons of résumés and applications.

For Students Who Need Additional Modifications

- Teach verbal students who do not read how to use a sighted reader. Explain that it is their responsibility to give instructions to the reader and to let that person know what material is to be read.
- For students who do not read, discuss other ways of getting information. Have them practice using a library reference service or telephone information services.
- Have the students visit and observe people who use a variety of tools (like a speech-activated computer, low vision devices, and braille) to help them read and write. Talk about what makes different tools right for certain people.
- Have the students observe friends or family members for a day and tell when these people used reading and writing. Talk about ways of doing the same jobs (for example, looking up a number in the telephone book or making a shopping list) when reading and writing are not possible.
- Associate pictures or objects that represent jobs with the words that stand for the jobs. After the students have learned to associate a word with an object or picture, present the word and object or picture separately and encourage them to match the pairs.
- Look for signs in the community (such as Help Wanted or Men Working) that relate to jobs that people do. Have the students practice reading signs and discussing what kind of work people may be doing nearby.

FROM A FAMILY PERSPECTIVE

Developing Compensatory Skills

It is critical for parents and family members to help visually impaired children develop compensatory skills because these skills are directly related to children's ability to advocate and stand up for themselves in the real world.

To help children master these skills, it may be helpful to learn firsthand the challenges they face. Parents who attempt to learn braille will have a deeper appreciation of their children's struggle and will be in a better position to help the children learn as well. When sighted adults begin to struggle with reading and writing skills as if they were visually impaired, they see just what kinds of skills, attitudes, and knowledge children need to become independent. When they role-play with children as interviewers or interviewees, employers or employees, workers or coworkers, then they have the opportunity to help the children learn the real-world skills they will use daily.

Encourage middle school youngsters to get involved in reading, writing, and calculating with their hobbies as well as with their homework. For example, suggest that they write letters to extended family members, compile vacation logs, or keep personal or family journals. These writing activities can also serve as incentives for improving students' keyboarding skills.

Kevin O'Connor

- Ask the students to dictate a letter to another person to volunteer for work or apply for a job.

COMPUTATIONAL SKILLS

Incidental learning is a term that professionals often use when they discuss information that people pick up by chance or through casual observations. Sighted children learn numerous concepts without being taught them directly. Examples of these concepts are that a traffic signal has three colors to inform drivers about what to do (stop on red, yield on yellow, and go on green), that facial expressions indicate whether a person is receptive to being spoken with at a particular moment, and that a shrug of the shoulders often means, "I don't know." A significant area in which students with visual impairments may miss key concepts because they are unable to pick up information through incidental learning is computation. Although the ability to calculate is a skill that is taught in school, it is an area in which incidental learning also takes place. For instance, sighted youngsters often note how much items cost when they accompany a person who is shopping and are usually given the opportunity to start purchasing items at an earlier age than are children with visual impairments. These shopping experiences at an early age prepare them to become informed consumers as adults. Therefore, it is necessary to give children with visual impairments the same opportunities in this area as sighted children have and to teach them these informal computational skills. The real-life activities presented next will help students make computational skills a useful part of their lives.

Activities

- Give the students a reasonable budget for a meal and ask them to choose a meal that either they or an adult will prepare. Have the students complete a grocery list for the items needed to prepare the meal. Then take them to a grocery store to price the items, making use of a customer service representative, if necessary, to find the items on the list. Discuss the differences in prices and how quality may be affected by prices in some cases. Have the students calculate the amounts of all the items and total the bill. Ask them if the budget will cover the cost of the groceries. If not, ask them what changes they need to make in the menu or whether they could purchase less expensive ingredients.
- Once they have mastered these skills, give the students the task of computing the budget needed for groceries. For example, the students may figure the menu and budget for one day, then for a weekend, and then for a week.
- Have the students explore ways to cut the cost of groceries by comparison shopping, comparing meat dishes with vegetarian dishes, buying in bulk, and using leftovers for another meal.
- Take the students to shop at a bulk food store to compare prices with regular grocery stores.
- Teach the students about unit pricing.

Critical Points to Cover

- Explain that employees of grocery stores perform many different roles. For example, a cashier handles money, a stocker places grocery items on the shelves, and a manager oversees personnel and all the processes that involve the grocery store.

- Discuss the ways to request assistance when shopping alone, for example, by asking a customer service representative, a personal shopper, or another customer.
- Emphasize that the cost of a prepared meal purchased in a store is higher than that of a meal prepared at home.
- Discuss how grocery coupons can help lower the costs of food. People with visual impairments can use coupons by obtaining assistance from sighted individuals to read advertisements and circulars and to remove coupons for them. Then they can use a slate and stylus to note the products and amounts of the coupons or can make braille or large-print labels and paper clip them to each coupon.

Helpful Hints

- Together with an O&M instructor, take the students on a tour of a grocery store with a store employee to discuss the layout of the store.
- During the budgeting exercise, review terms such as *bulk, promotional sales* and *generic* or *store* labels, so the students are familiar with them while shopping and can make more meaningful comparisons.
- Tour a variety of grocery stores, from small ones to large supermarkets. Many students with visual impairments do not realize that different stores offer different services and products.
- Ensure that the students know the basics of using calculators or abacuses before they start these shopping activities.
- Some banks establish "free" checking accounts for visually impaired students to use in lessons, so the students can practice writing checks under supervision.
- Discuss debit and credit cards and explore options for making purchases without cash. Explain that debit cards are shaped like credit cards but that with debit cards, the purchasers' money is deducted immediately from their checking accounts rather than tallied and billed on a monthly basis as with credit cards.
- If shopping via computer is available in the community, teach the students how to use an on-line grocery service, which

enables a person to E-mail a grocery list to a store and have the groceries delivered to the person's house. This service is available to the general public and makes the task of grocery shopping easier for people with visual impairments or physical disabilities.

- Have the students practice asking for assistance in stores. Suggest that they frequent the same stores to develop relationships with the store personnel and to become familiar with the items in stock, so they can purchase items without the help of friends and family members.
- Help the students draw up a budget that includes housing, utilities, food, transportation, taxes, clothing, recreation, retirement, savings, and miscellaneous costs. Help them determine the monthly salary they would need to cover these costs. Will the careers the students are interested in pursuing pay enough to cover these costs? If not, what alternative lifestyles or career goals would the students need to investigate?

Evaluation Tips

- Have the students estimate the budget needed for a mock meal. Ask them to list ways of lowering the cost of the meal.
- In follow-up activities that involve purchases, ask students to do comparison shopping.
- Give a budget to a group of students and ask them to purchase and prepare a meal on their own, reminding them to include the cost of their transportation to and from the store. Ask them to compare how working on a team was different from working individually.

For Students Who Need Additional Modifications

- Consider the most appropriate method for students with physical disabilities to handle and store money. If the students cannot use a standard wallet, a coin pouch with a Velcro closing may be more manageable. A bank that sorts coins by denomination may simplify access to coins at home.
- Compare the costs and time involved in alternative ways of grocery shopping, for example, paying for the delivery of groceries versus paying an individual to shop or waiting for assistance

from store personnel. When possible, prepare amounts of money in advance for known costs, such as change for bus fare, soft drinks, or movies, so students with physical disabilities can locate the entire amounts quickly when needed.

- Have the students interview workers in a store and consider which tasks could be done from a wheelchair, which could be done without speaking with others, and which could be done without the need to read and write.
- Acquire several types of calculators to give the students the opportunity to compare adaptations (for example, large visible buttons or large buttons that are easy to press and have speech output) that allow them to calculate quickly.
- Compare the weights of foods sold in different-size boxes.
- Purchase examples of foods that are packaged in large boxes and contain lighter weights to help students understand that large boxes are not always less expensive.
- Consider alternative ways for students with physical disabilities who cannot carry large quantities of groceries to transport their purchases. Point out the advantages and disadvantages of buying smaller, lighter containers for physical convenience.
- Make an appointment to talk with a bank representative about the ways of making services accessible to people with disabilities (for example, paying bills by telephone, using checks printed in braille, and having braille and private audio output at automatic teller machines).
- If the students are involved in paid work activities, encourage them to establish a plan for saving money and for determining a budget and choosing the ways they want to spend their money. However, emphasize the students' responsibility in keeping to a budget; for example, if students do not have enough money at the end of the month to go to a movie or pursue other activities, help them plan how they can make different choices the next month so they can save enough money to engage in these activities.
- Encourage students who cannot tell dollar bills from other denominations to request change in one dollar bills, so they can check for the correct change.

USE OF ADAPTIVE DEVICES

People with visual impairments may need to make minor adjustments to complete many chores done at home, at school, and in volunteer or work settings. Technology is helpful in many situations, but everyday materials that are available to the general public can usually be more easily and less expensively obtained. Using common sense and applying good problem-solving skills are often the best "tools" that students with visual impairments can have. For example, some variety stores, department stores, and kitchen stores sell small pieces of rubberized material to help people grip lids to open jars—such an implement may help a student with limited hand strength open doors.

Activities

- Schools, churches or synagogues, and other facilities with offices are some examples of settings in which visually impaired people can make simple adaptations or use adaptive devices to participate. Collating mail, answering telephones, delivering mail, and filing are among the tasks that are routinely performed in these settings. Ask an office manager to allow a group of students to observe the work duties of employees for one hour while the manager explains the job duties required in the entire office, not just for one job. Then ask a group of students to come up with adaptive devices or tasks that could be done by people who are blind or have low vision. Give them one hour to make a list with detailed descriptions of the adaptations. Some of their suggestions may include the following:
  1. Brailling files or labeling them in large print.
  2. Using an audiotape recorder to record and retrieve telephone messages and then writing the messages down on a brailler or notepad.
  3. Having a sighted person separate the mail and then put it into brailled or large-print folders for mail delivery.
  4. Setting up a jig that enables a blind person to fold mail correctly. A jig is a device used to accomplish a task. For example, a jig for folding paper may be a flat board with two raised borders connected at a corner to form an "L" shape. If a student fits a piece of paper onto this board and rests the

bottom and left edge of the paper against the two raised borders, the paper is held in place. There are typically two grooves or raised-line marks on the right side of the jig to indicate thirds of a standard 8½-inch x 11-inch sheet. The student can fold the top edge of the paper toward himself or herself at the first mark and fold the sheet again to meet the bottom border. This procedure results in an evenly folded piece of paper that will fit into a standard business-size envelope. The student can fold the paper in half by bringing the top edge of the sheet to the bottom border of the jig.

5. Doing the task without a jig.
6. Making a list of telephone extensions in braille or large print so calls can be forwarded.
7. Using magnifiers, closed-circuit televisions, or other low vision devices to read mail or notes.

Critical Points to Cover

- Discuss what jobs tend to be more easily adapted than others.
- Explain when technology is more efficient to use than adaptive material.
- Summarize which adaptations visually impaired employees would need to explain to their supervisors or coworkers and why. These adaptations may include marking the door of the appropriate rest room with a braille or large-print label; putting memos in braille or large print or on disk, if print memos are distributed to other employees; and providing verbal and written warnings and notices when there are obstacles in the workplace or when office equipment has been removed. Adaptive equipment that an employer may need to provide (if it meets the "reasonable accommodation" definition of the ADA) may include enlarged text, speech output, refreshable braille displays, or other adaptations to a computer. (The Job Accommodation Network [JAN], a database sponsored by the President's Committee on Employment of People with Disabilities, provides technical support and assistance to people with disabilities and to businesses on how to make job-site accommodations [http://janweb.icdi.wvu.edu/kinder/jan.htm].) An example of adapted equipment that may need to be explained when being

used is speech output from a computer, because it initially may disrupt other workers or draw their attention away from their own work.

- Discuss when employers are responsible for paying for "reasonable accommodations" and when employees with visual impairments need to purchase their own adaptive equipment. Information about such guidelines can be obtained from JAN.

Helpful Hints

- Apply the same principles for adapting a chore at home or at another work site.
- Interview other people with visual impairments and ask them, "What tools have you adapted to assist you in your job, at home, or at play?"
- Have a group of students with and without visual impairments read about the ADA. Ask the group to teach others in their classes about the ADA in the form of a skit, a game, or a panel presentation.
- Ask the students to gather information about the ADA themselves, rather than give them the information. Then they will know where to get the information if they need it as adults.
- Give examples of adaptive devices before the students begin their experiences in a workplace. Inviting a panel of people with visual impairments or mentors through the CTIB to talk with the students about their work experiences and methods for adaptation would be helpful in gathering information.
- Assist the students in solving problems and coming up with ideas on their own, rather than give the students the answers.
- Encourage students to share their experiences with methods for adaptation with other visually impaired workers to help the students think about adaptations for work and living spaces.
- Teach students who are blind to print numbers and the alphabet so they can write down telephone numbers and messages for sighted family members without having to use a typewriter or computer and printer.

Evaluation Tips

- Ask the students to list five or more items or tasks that were easily adapted at the work site they visited.

- Have the students demonstrate to their parents or other students what adaptations were made.

For Students Who Need Additional Modifications

- Take the students on field trips to centers where adaptive materials and devices for people with disabilities are sold or distributed. After the trips, discuss the concepts related to these materials and devices with the students. For example, ask the students, "Why would people operate a computer with their voice instead of a keyboard?" "Why would it be helpful to have a control on a wheelchair?"
- Have the students identify tools that are used by their parents or other familiar people. Emphasize the difference between tools that must be used to do a job and those that just make a job easier.
- Give the students choices about the adaptive tools they use and encourage them to try doing a job with and without the tool, for example, by asking them, "Did you like having a bookboard to hold your books?" "Was it easier or harder to do this task without the tray on the wheelchair?"
- Explain to students that those who use technological devices need to have the devices available to them when necessary. Teach them a signal, sign, or word to request each device.
- Reinforce safety issues related to the use of devices; for example, explain to the students that they should not touch outlets or pull on plugs. When teaching students who may model adult behaviors, plug in devices before they come to the work area.
- When devices are purchased, introduce the students to the vendor who has sold the devices. Encourage the students to ask questions. Students who have low vision can keep a photograph of the vendor and the vendor's name and telephone number close to the device. Blind students can audiotape the person giving his or her name and contact information, and students who read braille can braille a card and place it in an index card file.
- Ask the students to demonstrate technological devices to their classmates and supervise classmates who are trying out the devices. Make sure that the classmates clearly understand the use of these devices and the rules for using them. For disabled students who cannot monitor the use of their own equipment,

assign each classmate to serve as "caretaker," who can make sure that the devices are kept clean, used appropriately, and stored in designated places.

- Encourage the students to interview others, including people with physical disabilities, about the tools or devices they use to accomplish tasks. Have the students identify the purposes of each device; for example, does the device allow a person to work more quickly, provide access to print, or stabilize or position materials needed to perform a task?

- Identify tasks that are in the school environment (such as emptying the trash and picking up mail) and have the students identify adaptations that may enable them to accomplish these tasks.

- Identify devices that may give students more control over how they receive assistance; for example, students who do not use speech or sign language can use a bell, buzzer, or augmentative communication device to signal the need for assistance. Encourage the staff members to require students to request assistance before they offer help.

SOLVING PROBLEMS INDEPENDENTLY

Problems arise almost daily in a person's life. How well people deal with problems in part reflects the training in solving problems independently that they received at home and at school. Being able to solve problems successfully is an essential skill that students need, but youngsters with visual impairments may not have as many opportunities to solve problems while they are growing up as do sighted youngsters because many people work with and for them to enhance their learning. Since some learning about how to be independent may be sacrificed because the challenges the students experience are resolved for them by others, adolescents with visual impairments need to be taught problem-solving skills.

Activities

- Describe a disability-related problem to an individual or a group of adolescents with visual impairments. For instance, a person with a visual impairment goes to work one day and finds that his or her speech-access computer is not functioning properly and the company's technical support person is on vacation for a week. Ask the individual or group to answer the following questions:

1. What is the problem?
2. Whose problem is it?
3. What is the preferred outcome?
4. What are some alternative solutions to the problem?
5. Which solution would the student or group pick and why?
6. What is the next best solution in case the first solution does not work?

- Discuss each individual's or the group's answers. Do individuals agree or disagree? How is each person different in his or her approach to solving problems?

Critical Points to Cover

- Discuss the differences and similarities between a problem and a challenge.
- Explain how one evaluates whether a possible solution is the best one.
- Discuss how leadership affects solving problems in groups.
- Examine the typical problems that may occur in the workplace.

Helpful Hints

- Encourage the students to participate as much as possible in group activities.
- Help build the language and communication skills necessary to foster strong communication among group members by facilitating and role-modeling the skills during group activities.
- Introduce students to stories about people, including those with disabilities, who overcome difficulties by using good problem-solving skills. Determine whether the heroes followed the model given in this activity.
- Suggest to the students that they join a club that deals with social problems, such as Students Against Drunk Driving, or an environmental club, such as the Sierra Club. A club can provide an opportunity to practice group problem-solving skills.
- Whenever a problem arises at home or in the classroom, involve the student or the group in identifying the problem, the

expected outcome, the possible solutions, and in suggesting a plan of action.

Evaluation Tips

- Ask the students to write down (using their preferred reading medium) a problem, the desired outcome, and five alternative solutions and to list their choice of first and second alternatives and why they selected these alternatives.
- Ask the students to list their own strengths and weaknesses in solving problems and how this activity may have helped them become better at solving problems.
- Discuss a problem in school or at home. Examine possible solutions with the student or group of students to determine if they can help solve the problem.

For Students Who Need Additional Modifications

- When a problem arises, represent several solutions in a medium that the students can understand. For example, if the students use some sign language and have low vision, draw or sign several possible ways of solving the problem.
- Find ways to help the students understand that they have influenced events. For example, if they burned cookies they were baking or forgot to put their favorite shirt in the wash, ask them to role-play or demonstrate how they would do the task differently in the future. For students who cannot use and understand speech or sign language, use a picture or symbol of them to label things they have made or tasks they have completed.
- When tools and equipment need to be fixed, involve the students in calling the appropriate repair persons and making the arrangements for the repair. For students who are verbal, encourage them to describe or write the problem down clearly so the service person will be able to assist them.

USE OF TECHNOLOGY

Technology continues to open up opportunities for children and adults with visual impairments. Scanners have made available the world of print to many people with visual impairments. Textbooks are beginning to be accessible in electronic formats (for example, on disk or CD-ROM), which benefit a wide range of people including those with visual impairments. The use of technology breaks down the boundaries of race, age, disability, and sex. According to Hatlen (1996, p. 30), "Technology can be a great equalizer . . . it enhances communication and learning and expands the world of blind and visually impaired persons in many significant ways."

Students with visual impairments who have good computer skills may find it easier to keep up with their schoolwork than those who do not. In the world of work, technology has enabled people with visual impairments to enter many fields that were previously closed to them. Computer-related jobs are increasing, allowing visually impaired people to have access to more work opportunities. Even most entry-level jobs require the use of technology. Therefore, it is critical for adolescents with visual impairments to become familiar with and competent in using technology and keeping their skills up to date.

Activities

- Ask the students to list three jobs or careers in which they are interested and then help them contact three people who have those jobs. Ask the students to make appointments to meet with these employees, informing them that the meeting is designed to discuss job responsibilities and the use of technology for each major job duty. During their interviews with these employees the students can ask the following questions in addition to their own:
  1. What types of technology do you use at the work site?
  2. Is technology essential to completing your job duties?
  3. Are there other pieces of technology that you could use on the job but do not yet have?
  4. What are the pros and cons of using technology?

  After the students have gathered this information, schedule an in-person or telephone meeting with a member of the technology staff of a vocational center or rehabilitation agency that serves people with visual impairments. During this meeting the students can share the information they gathered at the three work sites and ask the staff person to discuss which pieces of technology that the employees use may be adapted for use by people who have low vision or are blind.

Critical Points to Cover

- Determine what types of technology the students use. Then ask students the following questions: Will that technology be used in the workplace? If it will not be used, when will the students begin using technology that is compatible with the workplace?
- Discuss where training is available for the students to learn to use appropriate technology.

Helpful Hints

- Discuss the pros and cons of relying on technology.
- Before the activity begins, teach the students the basic types of technology that are available, including electronic notetaking devices, computers with speech or braille output or screen-enlargement programs, reading machines, braille embossers, and everyday tools with speech or available tone output (such as calculators, watches and clocks, scales, and liquid-level indicators).
- Work with the school to encourage the use of technology for the students whenever possible.
- Set up demonstrations by technology vendors at the school.
- Visit technology exhibits at conferences and gather print, audiotape, braille, or electronic materials about assistive technology.
- Tour an adaptive technology center with students to discover what types of technology are available and how they are adapted for use by people who are visually impaired.
- Research training centers and trainers to determine where students can learn to use adapted technology.
- Teach the students about the ADA and its implications for reasonable accommodations for people with disabilities in the workplace.
- Have the students phone the CTIB to speak with mentors about their use of technology.
- Encourage the students to use the Internet for homework and for the development of interests.
- Continue to emphasize the impact of technology on a wide variety of jobs. Point out how technology is being used during trips in the community with the students.

Evaluation Tips

- Ask the students to outline the types of technology with which they are already familiar and the kinds of training they would need to do their three jobs of interest.
- Obtain information from the school and from the teacher of visually impaired students about possible technology training that will be available in the future. Ask the students to share their ideas of what their training needs will be in the future.

For Students Who Need Additional Modifications

- Find ways that technology can be used to enhance communication with people in the community, for example, using a loop-system tape (repeating tape) recorder or a small speech device to greet others.
- Make a list of the physical skills that the students use most frequently and consider the jobs that incorporate these skills. Find people who do similar jobs by using technological adaptations and encourage the students to meet them.
- Explore ways of acquiring technology for adults who will not be competitively employed. Maintain a resource list of sources and agencies that can help individuals continue to use technological equipment after they graduate from school.
- Consider ways in which household appliances and electronic devices can be activated with switches by individuals with physical disabilities to provide more independence at home.

O&M

The ability to travel independently is an important factor in obtaining and retaining employment. More important, it affects how people with visual impairments feel about themselves. People with visual impairments may experience difficulty maintaining social or vocational relationships if they are not able to travel independently. Therefore, it is essential for students to be as competent as possible in their use of O&M skills.

As with most learning experiences, both visually impaired and sighted students learn best when they have meaningful learning opportunities, including the chance to build on their previous experiences to reinforce the skills they have learned. If students engage in activities that are particularly meaningful to them because of the social and intellectual stimuli the activities provide, they are far more likely to remember and use skills that they have learned previously. For example, if students learn to walk with long canes but are not allowed to walk beyond the parameters of their school or home yards, it is possible that the O&M skills they acquired may not be sufficiently reinforced to transfer into a new environment. However, if they enjoy visiting local stores and are encouraged to walk to the stores using their canes, the O&M skills they have learned will be reinforced in a meaningful and enjoyable activity and thus are more likely to be retained.

Activities

- Incorporate O&M skills into career education by planning scavenger hunts for students in the immediate community. A scavenger hunt is a game in which players generally try to acquire specified objects within a time limit. However, for the purposes of this activity, students can try to obtain information about various jobs. Teachers or families can provide students with a list of specific jobs and then ask students to try to locate, within a certain time frame, the workers who perform the jobs. For example, in planning a scavenger hunt in a shopping mall, decide how many areas should be included in the hunt on the basis of input from the O&M instructor who works with the students. If the students know only one area of the mall, write questions for the students to locate shops only in that area. If the students are more experienced travelers, they may use the entire mall as their "hunting" area. After informing the people who have agreed to participate in the scavenger hunt of the time frame when the activity will occur, write questions or clues in the appropriate medium with the students to help them think of the job skills that are necessary for each job being hunted. For instance, a stocker in a store may be described as follows: "This person puts items to sell out on shelves for customers to examine." The students will take the list of questions, decide who meets the clue's descriptions, find the person at his or her workstation, obtain a signature (or tactile object representing that person's workstation), and return the completed form or group of objects to the teacher. Rewards for completing the hunt can be given. Have the students review the experience as a group to facilitate discussion about the different jobs. Consider using tactile maps or raised-line drawings to help the students during the scavenger hunt.

- Have the students participate in orienteering. In orienteering activities, students are given directions or a map (printed, brailled, or audiotaped) to different locations in an unfamiliar area and must find their way to various points. For example, the students may be given a map of a local park with specific landmarks numbered from 1 to 10 and asked to locate each landmark in the sequence and end up at the appropriate spot to finish the activity. Often, orienteering activities are incorporated into individual or team competitions.

- Ask the students to plan and implement a road rally. In this activity, visually impaired students are paired with sighted drivers. The students with visual impairments have the written directions in their preferred reading medium and act as navigators while their partners drive to the unfamiliar destination.

Critical Points to Cover

- Discuss the types of jobs the workers in the various mall stores perform.
- Explain the layout of the mall.
- Review the logic of the numbering system that is used for the stores.
- Discuss the jobs in a school system that may interest students.
- Explain where else in the community similar jobs are performed.
- Compare how staff members communicate with each other.
- Explain why it is helpful to work as a team for an orienteering activity.
- Discuss the importance of details when giving or receiving directions.

Helpful Hints

- Divide the group of students into teams and ensure that totally blind students are given as much responsibility for the activity as those adolescents with some vision.
- Clarify any unfamiliar words or map concepts with students that may cause them difficulty in doing these activities.
- Have the completion of the hunt, rather than a time limit for the hunt, be the goal to allow the students who are blind to have the same opportunities as their sighted peers.
- Encourage the use of low vision devices to facilitate locating stores or other points of interest.
- Encourage students to ask for assistance; this is a critical travel skill.
- Ensure that the staff members are at their jobs during the scavenger hunt, so the participants will not be disappointed.

Evaluation Tips

- Discuss the variety of jobs available in a mall.
- Ask the students to design a scavenger hunt, orienteering, or road rally for their neighborhood.
- Ask the students for their opinions about the easiest and hardest travel situations in these exercises. How did they learn the easier routes? How could they improve their mastery of the difficult routes? What worked or did not work in the orienteering and road rally exercises?
- Ask the students to discuss and present what they believe to be the most time-efficient route if the scavenger hunt was timed.

For Students Who Need Additional Modifications

- Have the students carry photographs or object symbols to remind them of a destination that they can check en route while they are traveling without assistance.
- Encourage the students to consider options for traveling to and from class, including whether they would like classmates to accompany them and what route they would like to travel.

- Have the students compare the time needed to reach a destination by timing their trips using each route; they can then choose the fastest route.
- Have the classmates of students who use wheelchairs do an accessibility inventory in the school and in various locations in the community. Have them list the places that cannot be reached by wheelchair and advocate with the administrators or business owners to make these sites accessible.
- For students who do not have symbolic communication, choose an object or picture symbol to represent travel. Involve the students' classmates to make sure that the students always wear or carry that symbol so it can be associated with travel. The object can be a real one, such as a cane, cap, or purse that tells the students that they will be going somewhere whenever they wear or use it.
- Students with multiple disabilities can explore transportation options in their community by telephoning the public transit system to ask what arrangements are available for people who use wheelchairs or by talking with others who use alternative transportation. They also need to practice consistent routines for entering and exiting vehicles and requesting assistance. Students who are nonverbal may be able to learn a signal to indicate that they are ready to be moved in or out of a van or automobile.
- Ride with the students on public transportation to or from their work-experience sites, so the students learn what adaptations, if any, are available. For example, wheelchair accessible buses and preferred seating are provided by many bus companies. If appropriate, bring a speaker from the public transit system who can discuss options for transportation with the students.
- Encourage the students to role-play requesting appropriate sighted guide assistance or assistance with a wheelchair. For example, a student who is requesting sighted guide assistance might ask, "May I hold your arm while we cross this street?" rather than using general terms that do not describe the type of assistance needed. After they have role-played, try the same role-playing activity in the community to see whether the students will ask strangers for help.

- Work with deaf-blind students who have language skills to prepare a card to request assistance from others. Prepare several
types of cards based on the types of assistance needed. These
cards might display common requests: "Please tap my arm
when Bus No, 25 is here"; "Please let me take your arm to cross
the street."

References

Hatlen, P. (1996). The core curriculum for blind and visually impaired students,
including those with additional modifications. *RE:view*, 28, 25–32.

CHAPTER

16

Promoting Opportunities to Work

This chapter presents specific ideas for activities that help young people with visual impairments to work in paid or unpaid jobs. Students are encouraged to participate in helpful efforts in their immediate neighborhoods, schools, and communities and engage in fund-raising events. Summer jobs are promoted and the activities to prepare for them are presented. There are also activities to help students keep up with job leads, attend job fairs, apply for jobs, interview with prospective employers, and participate in volunteer experiences. All the activities in this chapter focus on moving students into work-related experiences and jobs.

Work and volunteer experiences are integral to career education. The goal of each person's education is his or her participation in the labor market, which ultimately leads to self-sufficiency and, it is hoped, to life satisfaction. Students who participate in work activities while in school are in general more likely to move from middle school to high school and to graduate from high school with more realistic ideas of what they can do to support themselves than are those who have never worked. Consequently, it is essential for teachers and families to address work-related experiences as early as possible in children's lives to help them flourish in the years ahead. Any work-related experience that is given to middle school students needs to be assigned with a full understanding of the child labor laws. The U.S. Department of Labor has guidelines on child labor in the Fair Labor Standards Act, a copy of which can be obtained by contacting the U.S. Government Printing Office in Washington, D.C.

HELPING AT HOME AND IN THE NEIGHBORHOOD

It is important for all young people to gain a sense of belonging in their homes and neighborhoods. Frequently, many youngsters with visual impairments are not expected to be responsible members of their families and contributing neighbors and are not included in activities that promote such roles. As a result, they do not have many opportunities to enhance their positive self-esteem and self-identity. Therefore, it is critical for them to engage in activities that reinforce the fact that they can contribute to their families and communities while they are learning critical life skills.

Activities

- Have middle school students perform a wide variety of jobs both at home and for neighbors. These jobs may include baby-sitting, watering plants and yards, cleaning houses, and taking care of pets. Any of these jobs can enhance the students' concept of self and help them to learn skills they will need in adult life. Steps similar to the ones in the following sequence that describes watering plants can be applied to any of the other jobs just listed.
- Teach each student where all the plants that need to be watered are located. Have a pitcher available that restricts spills. Devise a sequence in which plants are watered and how much water each plant requires.
- Have the students do the task repeatedly as part of their chores.
- When the students are able to do the chore independently, they can notify their neighbors that they are available to take care of plants when the neighbors are away from home.
- When the neighbors are ready for the students' services, go with the students to their first "jobs" not only to assure the neighbors but to bolster the students' confidence in resolving any difficulties that may arise.
- Role-play with the students how to ask for instructions on caring for the plants. Make recommendations at first and then assist the students in brainstorming ways to make the chore easier. For

instance, the students may request that the neighbors group their plants in one or two areas for easy access.

- Shadow the youngsters while they complete the actual work, but let them know that the shadowing is similar to the role a supervisor on a job would play.

Critical Points to Cover

- Discuss with students that it is important for them to contribute to their home and community environments to help them develop and enhance their sense of self.
- Explain the importance of organizing work tasks and work flow.
- Encourage the students to read about plant care, so they are knowledgeable about their work.

Helpful Hints

- Visually impaired middle school students need to be actively involved in the entire process of performing a job from beginning to end, if possible. Doing part of a job does not give the students the full sense of satisfaction that completing the entire job can.
- Be available to assist the first few times that the students do jobs for neighbors. Then, gradually decrease the amount of assistance until the students can perform independently. Allow extra time for the students to learn the process, if necessary.
- Before the youngsters notify neighbors of their skills and availability, encourage them to use computers and printers to create flyers that advertise their services.
- Spend time orienting the youngsters to their neighbors' residences so they may complete the jobs independently.
- Work with the youngsters on organizing their work space and work flow. For example, if they are cleaning a house, have them put all cleaning supplies in a bucket. Have them clean bathrooms first, then have them dust, vacuum, and then mop.
- If possible, enroll the youngsters in community or school classes that teach the skills needed to complete the jobs. Many communities have baby-sitting classes for teenagers. Garden clubs hold classes on a wide range of plant care activities. Science

classes offer opportunities to learn about plants. (An additional benefit is the networking aspect of attending these classes.)

- Similar experiences can be offered at school. The students may collect attendance cards, answer telephones or take messages, and water plants for the teachers.

Evaluation Tips

- Discuss the outcome of each day's work with the students. What went well? What did not go well?
- Have the students request feedback from the neighbors who used their services. Since neighbors may not wish to criticize the students directly, follow up with them to see how the students did and then address their concerns with the students.

For Students Who Need Additional Modifications

- All young people should have regular tasks to carry out at home. Devise a way of ensuring that these tasks are done at a consistent time. If the youngsters use a visual or tactile calendar or calendar box system (see Chapter 3), include a symbol or picture for the task in the calendar system. If they cannot remember sequences for weeks or days, give them an object representing the task just before it is to be done, for example, a watering pitcher for plants to hold on the tray of their wheelchairs as they move toward the sink to fill the pitcher.
- For tasks that are unpleasant or undesirable, plan a pleasant activity for the students immediately afterward. For the students whose memory span does not allow them to remember the pleasant task to come, create a positive effect while doing the unpleasant task (for example, play the students' favorite music while they are putting dishes away).
- For students with physical disabilities, consider how the position or location of a task can be changed so they can do it more easily; for instance, they can sort silverware while lying prone on the floor.

JOB SHADOWING AND WORK EXPLORATION

It has already been mentioned that because students with visual impairments are not able to take in all the information about people

FROM A FAMILY PERSPECTIVE

Helping at Home and in the Community

The best time to give responsibility is when children are almost ready for it. Help the children to prepare for responsibility; do not pamper them, and always allow some aspect to be a challenge. Come to the children's rescue only when you have to, such as when their safety is imperiled.

Family members can help prepare children for the world of work in at least two ways. First, the children can run part of the house in a businesslike way. They can monitor the family members' performance of various tasks, such as emptying the garbage, doing various house-cleaning chores, recycling newspapers, and sharing computer time, using charts, lists, and time-management techniques. Consequently, the house will be run more efficiently, and the children will learn valuable skills at the same time. Second, they can get family members involved in an activity beyond themselves and the home, such as helping at a soup kitchen, shelter for homeless people, church or synagogue, hospital, or nursing home. Participating in one of these activities as a family gives parents the opportunity to observe their visually impaired children first-hand in a worklike situation.

Finding Summer Jobs

Let your child's obtaining a job be as educational as the job itself and, as much as possible, let him or her have the satisfaction of finding the job, applying for it, and getting it himself or herself.

Middle school students might experience some difficulty in finding jobs because many employers use the age of 16 as the minimum age for hiring purposes. However, there are few restrictions for churches or synagogues, schools, and family-owned businesses, or for services done at home through the computer, for lawn and garden work, or for direct sales clubs aimed at children as the sales agents. Olympia Sales Club (located in Enfield, Connecticut) and Sales Leadership Club (located in Springfield, Massachusetts) are two businesses that distribute their seasonal products year-round through a sales force of middle school students. Students receive commissions, have to take care of accounts payable and receivable, and get a start-up kit to canvas the neighborhood.

If you decide to employ your child at home or at your office, resist the temptation to become his or her direct supervisor. Ask someone else to take that job and make sure that person has the freedom and your support to supervise the student as he or she would any employee. In addition, discuss expectations, rules, and roles with the student early on in the job-training experience.

Kevin O'Connor

working around them that their sighted peers can, it is necessary for families and teachers to create experiences to expand their knowledge of the world of work. After a number of these experiences, visually impaired students will be able to identify what aspects of different jobs they like and dislike. As a result of their early exploration activities, they will be better able to choose a satisfying career path.

Job shadowing is an activity that allows the students to spend time with people who are working in a field in which the students have expressed interest but may know little or nothing about. Job-shadowing experiences enable students to learn more about jobs in an experiential manner (see Chapter 15).

Activities

- Have the students list three jobs about which they would like to gather information.
- Discuss why the students like these jobs.
- Ask the students to pick one of the jobs to explore.
- With the students, brainstorm 10 or more questions they would like to ask to learn more about the particular job. Questions may include such topics as salary, training, benefits, skills needed, educational level required, and necessary personality traits for the job.
- Have the students write the questions in their preferred reading medium.
- Help the students each contact a person who does the job in the community and set up a one-hour to a half-day session with the worker. Suggest that the person choose a day for the visit during which he or she will be doing a variety of job duties. Ask if the student can complete one or more tasks at the job site that would not have an impact on the effective performance of the job. Activities may include tearing up lettuce, stuffing envelopes, or delivering messages.
- Accompany the students to their job-shadowing sites. Have them ask the questions they drafted earlier and then ask the employees to describe their work sites and the work exploration activities. Have the students "shadow" or follow the employees through their regular work activities.

Critical Points to Cover

- Discuss appropriate behavior for the students while shadowing the employees, including shaking hands while introducing themselves and not interrupting while the employees are talking.
- Review terminology that may be used at the workplace.
- Explain to the employees the need to describe the job tasks when completing work that the students may not be able to see.

Helpful Hints

- Encourage the students to have similar job-shadowing experiences with family members or friends in occupations that the students have not indicated an interest. These experiences will broaden the students' knowledge of the world of work and how what others do for a living affects them indirectly.
- If employees in the students' home communities are not available to take part in actual job-shadowing experiences, phone calls to adults who can talk to the students about job experiences are the next best option.
- Help the students telephone the Careers and Technology Information Bank (CTIB) of the American Foundation for the Blind (at 212-502-7642) to arrange for informational telephone interviews with visually impaired people who are working in a wide range of occupations.
- The more often the students perform these job-shadowing activities, the more sophisticated their questions become.
- When possible, contact employees who are visually impaired. Staff at rehabilitation agencies may be able to contact these employees, or consumer organizations, such as the American Council of the Blind or the National Federation of the Blind (see Resources), may be able to do so on the teacher's behalf.

Evaluation Tips

- Following the activity, review the information gathered with the students. What did they learn? Clarify items or topics that the students may not have understood.

- Set up similar experiences with the students to explore other related occupations. When the students have completed these other job-shadowing experiences, compare with the students the information they gathered. For example, which position paid a higher salary? Which job required more education?
- Observe the students during their job-shadowing experiences.
- Ask the employees who are being job shadowed to share the steps they took toward selecting their careers, and to describe the pros and cons of their chosen career.
- Ask the employees who worked with students about how the students performed during the job-shadowing experience. Also ask the workers whether students asked questions or took notes.

For Students Who Need Additional Modifications

- Expand the activity to include "walking in an adult's shoes." Have the students shadow people who have daytime occupations that do not include competitive employment, such as homemakers, volunteers, and participants at senior citizens' centers and day activities centers.
- Arrange for the students to spend time in different work environments, for example, restaurants, libraries, and manufacturing sites. Ask them to remember as many different types of workers as possible and describe the jobs.
- Have the students distinguish between work they like and work they do not like. The students can do so by sorting pictures, photographs, or printed or brailled cards or by responding verbally with "yes" or "no" when they are asked, "Do you like to____?" Once they have identified work they like, arrange for them to visit employees whose jobs include tasks the students like to perform.
- When visiting work sites, call attention to ways that help employees be on time for work. Checking a clock or watch and noticing when others begin working are ways of monitoring promptness. Ask the employees how they know that it is time to start and stop work. Punching time cards, listening for signal bells, or counting the number of items completed are ways that people know when work has been finished. These methods can be used to monitor classroom routines, so the students know

that they are similar to the ways in which days are organized in the workplace.

- Use titles during classroom activities that are similar to those used in the workplace, for example, "supervisor," "team member," or "secretary" can be applied to students during classroom activities.

SUMMER JOB EXPERIENCES

Most people learn by doing. Although child labor laws prohibit middle school students from participating in most forms of paid work during the school year, there are several summer job opportunities in which visually impaired students may choose to participate. These job possibilities include baby-sitting, summer work programs through school or rehabilitation agencies, community-based work programs through Interfaith or Private Industry Council subcontractors, and assisting neighbors. (Remember that child labor laws need to be checked first.) Some parents may choose to "hire" their children for the summer to perform duties that are beyond what the children need to do to receive their allowances. These experiences help young people with visual impairments learn good work habits and strong work skills.

Sometimes the hardest part about finding jobs is identifying positions that match people's interests and strengths. With assistance, the students can determine their strengths, by asking themselves questions such as these: Do I like to talk on the phone? Do I know the entire neighborhood? Do I like children? After the students list their strengths, discuss with them the job opportunities that may match those strengths.

Activities

- Either individually or in small groups, discuss how people find jobs. Explain that the majority of people find jobs through networking.
- Ask the students to list at least 10 people who know them and consider them to be responsible, able workers. Have the students contact at least three people to ask about summer job opportunities.
- Have the students gather other ideas for summer jobs by going to the school counselor for suggestions, and help them gain

access to help-wanted ads in newspapers and obtain applications from three or more businesses that have Help-Wanted signs.
- Ask the students to review all the possibilities and rank the job options that seem best in order of priority.
- Have the students apply for available positions.

Critical Points to Cover

- Emphasize to students that clear communication is important in finding and maintaining a job.
- Explain to students that it is necessary for them to explain to prospective employers the job accommodations they will make so they can perform the jobs successfully.

Helpful Hints

- If students are too young or are otherwise unable to work in paid positions, they may search for either volunteer work or short-term jobs like feeding or walking a neighbor's pet or watering a neighbor's flowers or garden while the neighbors are away on vacation.
- Encourage the students to complete most of the activity independently, including making telephone calls, writing lists, and performing other tasks, to promote self-esteem.
- Help the students develop filing systems for organizing the job search and keeping up with activities.
- Develop and role-play how to contact potential employers.
- Engage the students in the following:
    1. calling prospective employers to ask about job openings
    2. filling out applications
    3. practicing interviews
    4. developing references
    5. writing résumés or personal data sheets
    6. writing thank-you notes

Evaluation Tips

- After each contact, review with the students what went well and what did not go well and why.
- Listen to the students make their contacts. Discuss how well they communicated their goals and ideas.

- If the students do not get summer jobs, discuss other options for learning work skills and developing possible work contacts for the next summer (for example, volunteering, camping, helping around the house, or assisting relatives or friends).

For Students Who Need Additional Modifications

- Arrange for the students to visit the job sites of their older brothers and sisters or other family members during the summer. Assist them in describing the tasks that are performed on these jobs by using pictures, signs, words, or demonstrations.
- Arrange for the students (or those with them every day) to keep journals of how the students do particular jobs throughout the summer. These jobs can be chores around the house, such as emptying trash or watering plants, volunteer work, or paid jobs. The journal entries need to show how the students did the jobs differently at the beginning and end, how they kept on schedule, what adaptations they used, whether they liked doing the jobs, and how the journal writer could tell when the student liked or disliked the work.

VOLUNTEERING IN THE COMMUNITY

Students with visual impairments should be involved in as many activities in their communities as possible when they are young, so when they grow up, they will have a network of people whom they can contact for possible jobs. While gaining volunteer experience, students learn to work cooperatively with others as part of a team, have opportunities to be leaders, and learn about the various paid jobs that are related to volunteer work. Participating in a wide range of volunteer experiences will help the students identify their interests and aptitudes, as well as develop actual work skills.

Activities

- Have the students each identify a volunteer opportunity by asking the adults in their lives about the charities or volunteer agencies to which they have contributed or volunteered. Have the students bring their list of options to class and "market" their choices. Then have the class vote on two options. Phone the organizations and ask whether there are any requirements for volunteering in them. The students can determine if they meet these requirements and decide which organization to volunteer at on that basis. The next step is for the students to develop a participants' plan (for example, staffing booths at health fairs). The plan needs to cover the students' roles, the dates and timelines of the planning process and actual participation, and the contact person at the organization. (The students can either keep notes or help the teacher document the process. Students who do not write can use pictures of activities for their documentation.)

- Have the students implement the plan, continuing to document their participation in an appropriate medium.
- After the final activity, have the students rate their participation in the process by asking the following questions:
  1. How did I participate in planning this activity?
  2. In which ways did I participate in the actual activity?
  3. How well did I work with my peers?
  4. How could I improve my participation?
  5. Do I consider the project to have been a success?
- Discuss the students' self-evaluations and ask them how they would complete the activity if they did it again. What would they change, and what would they keep the same?
- If possible, have the students do the same or a similar volunteer experience again, so they can apply their analysis and implement their recommended changes.

Critical Points to Cover

- Discuss the concept of teamwork: that by working as a team, people with different strengths can create a better product or idea or accomplish a goal because of their cooperation.
- Explain the benefits of performing volunteer work.
- Review the kinds of paid jobs that are related to volunteer experience. For example, helping in a church nursery may later turn into a paid day care position or weeding yards for friends or neighbors may lead to a landscaping job.
- Explain the concept of marketing, or the skill of persuading others to believe in an idea or product.

Helpful Hints

- Encourage the students to complete as much of the work as possible.
- Allow students to make mistakes and learn from those mistakes.
- Encourage the students to read materials that are related to the volunteer experience.
- Teach the students terms, such as *fund-raiser, health fair,* and *in-kind,* that will be used in the volunteer experience.
- Encourage the students to support each other through the learning process.

Evaluation Tips

- Observe the students in volunteer experiences.
- Ask the students' supervisors to evaluate their performance.
- Ask the students to evaluate their performance.
- Have the students watch two commercials on television or listen to two commercials that are broadcast on the radio to critique the ads in terms of marketing techniques.

For Students Who Need Additional Modifications

- Find community volunteer activities that the students can participate in (for example, helping shopkeepers clean the sidewalks, planting wildflowers in empty lots, or helping in the community's recycling program). Encourage the students to tell others what they can do so they can participate. Work with the students before the events to practice an element of the task that they can accomplish. After the activity, ask the students to talk about how they feel: Did they like volunteering? What did they like? What did they dislike?
- Discuss the concepts of volunteering and working, and explain how they are different. Encourage the parents who are involved in volunteer work to come and talk with the students about why they participate in volunteer activities.
- In school, find places where volunteers are used. Find out what their jobs are. Discover other projects that volunteers could perform in the school and encourage the students to volunteer for these tasks.

- Find ways to recognize the students who volunteer. Students who have limited language and cognitive skills may be given tangible recognition, such as a framed photograph of the student at work or an audiotape of people in the community saying thank you in unique ways.

SPECIAL EVENTS

Many job-related events that occur in the community are tailored for the general population as well as for people with disabilities. Career fairs are often held at local high schools or city coliseums. In many large cities, job fairs are held for people who are interested in particular career areas, such as the food industry or health care industry. Rehabilitation and other agencies may hold special sessions to enlist the community's participation in providing work opportunities for people with disabilities. Any of these events can help students with visual impairments understand better the availability of a wide variety of careers.

Career fairs are often held in high schools to expose the students to the many job opportunities in their community or state. Despite the frequent lack of information in accessible media at these fairs, students with visual impairments may still find it helpful to attend them because they provide an opportunity to talk to people in a wide range of positions and careers.

Activities

- To help students prepare to attend a job fair, get a list of the employers who will be at the fair and, if possible, the booth-arrangement map. Review the employers and their companies with the students and ask the students which employers interest them. Then, locate those employers' booths on the map, so the students have an idea of the layout and the location of the employers at the fair.
- Assist the students in making a list of questions for each employer or business. Role-play introducing oneself and asking for business cards and information about the business.
- Attend the fair with the students and, referring to the map, orient the students to the layout. Help the students, when necessary, locate the employers' booths. Have the students initiate

conversations and prompt them, when necessary, to ensure that they ask the questions they generated earlier.

Critical Points to Cover

- Explain how to speak to a stranger (like a prospective employer or a recruiter) in a formal setting. Include in the discussion such points as how to make an introduction, how to listen, how to shake hands, how to ask socially acceptable questions, and how to end a conversation.
- Review how to locate prospective employers to reinforce mobility skills. If a map is not available ahead of time, get to the job fair before employers arrive, locate the booths where employers of interest will be, and practice walking to that area. A sighted guide may be necessary for those students who do not have the O&M skills needed to complete this task independently.
- Strengthen the students' work concepts by using and discussing terms, such as *informational interviewing, first impressions,* and *networking.*

Helpful Hints

- The students may want to use portable technology, such as a an electronic notetaker, audiotape recorder, or portable talking word processor, to take notes at the job fair. If they use a small audiotape recorder to record conversations, remind the students to make sure that they first get permission from the employers to record their comments. A slate and stylus or notepad may be used if portable technology is unavailable or if it would interfere with dialogue.
- Encourage the students to project themselves with confidence by shaking the hands of the people they meet, making eye contact, using appropriate body language and facial expressions, and carrying on conversations.
- Related activities may include attending transition forums, school-to-work weekends, volunteer fairs, and community job fairs.
- Students may use tactile maps or raised-line drawings with representations of the booths to locate booths of interest on their own.

Evaluation Tips

- Review with the students the conversations that took place. Analyze which companies appealed to them and why.
- If particular companies had great appeal to the students, ask them to set up informational interviews with representatives of these companies to determine the training, education, and work skills that are needed to be employed by these companies and to learn about the various jobs available.
- Attend another job fair with the students and observe the students' participation. After the event, discuss the situations that students found easier to deal with the second time and ask them what information they believe they need to have to be even more successful at the next job fair.

For Students Who Need Additional Modifications

- Arrange for students to attend a technology conference for people with disabilities and encourage them to ask the exhibitors what jobs have been done using the technology they sell.
- Assist the students in developing a greeting routine and using it when meeting strangers at special events. If they do not use words, help each student create a card that can be handed to someone that contains a greeting, the student's name, and information about how to communicate with the student.
- Hold an "occupation day" at the school, inviting adults who have a variety of life roles, including people who attend day-activities centers and the individuals who work with them.
- Encourage the classmates of the students to consider career options in working with people who have disabilities.

WORK-STUDY PROGRAMS

One important way for young people with visual impairments to learn what they like and dislike about jobs is to work. This work may be paid or volunteer work, but regardless of the pay structure (or lack thereof), it is essential for the students to be exposed to a wide variety of work experiences. While the students are in middle school, job-shadowing experiences, working for neighbors, and volunteering in the community are significant ways to get realistic information about the world of work. As they grow older, they should gradually focus on learning actual job skills. Through each of these experiences, the students may increase their knowledge and refine their skills, as well as receive feedback from coworkers, supervisors, and parents on their accomplishment of job duties and on personal relations. Each experience then becomes a learning tool, helping to shape and define the students as future workers and contributors to their own prosperity and that of the companies for whom they work.

Many rehabilitation and education programs sponsor summer work programs. Similarly, many schools provide career or vocational education programs, although these programs are usually available only during the high school years. Volunteer centers coordinate volunteers who come from a variety of backgrounds. Many of these places can help middle school students with visual impairments find volunteer or paid work. Middle school students who are 14 to 16 years old may be employed in certain occupations if the work is after school and meets the Fair Labor Standards Act regarding the number of hours worked per day and week. There are also restrictions on the time of day these children can work. Fourteen year olds are allowed to work in retail, food service, and gasoline service establishments, at such jobs as cashier, clerical worker, packager, bagger, and delivery worker (on foot or using bicycles or public transportation). (Employers need to consult the Fair Labor Standards Act's child labor laws.)

Activities

- Have the students approach a volunteer center to help them obtain volunteer or paid work experience. If they are unable to establish such a connection, ask them to approach churches, neighbors, and friends for work ideas.
- Once the students have held a job or gone through a short-term experience, help them to assess what they have learned by asking themselves the following questions:
  1. What were my strengths in the workplace?
  2. What were my weaknesses?
  3. Was I always dressed appropriately?
  4. Did I always arrive on time to work?
  5. How well did I get along with my coworkers and boss?

   6. Did I initiate work, or did I frequently need direction?

   7. Did I complete my work on time?

   8. Did I spend my time on the job constructively?

   9. Was I able to work independently?

  10. Was I energetic?

- After the students have completed their self-assessments, ask them to obtain realistic feedback on the same questions from their employers. Compare the two sets of answers with the students. Have the students suggest ways in which they can improve in their next jobs.
- Ask the students to research employment practices and the retention of workers. What skills or traits are most valued by employers?
- Invite a panel of employers to the classroom to discuss their experiences in hiring and firing employees.
- Have a group of students go through the steps they believe are necessary in setting up a small business. Rotate each student in the "boss" position over a certain period. Then have the group members discuss what they have learned.

Critical Points to Cover

- Discuss what aspects of the job may affect employees' efficiency (for example, training, support services, transportation, low salaries, or problems at home).
- Itemize the traits or qualities that supervisors tend to value most in workers. These characteristics may include punctuality, initiative, honesty, good social skills, and a willingness to learn new tasks.
- Explain that some jobs are oriented more toward people, others are oriented more toward tasks, and still others are oriented more toward data. Just as people differ, so do the jobs that people perform.
- Discuss how people cope with jobs that are viewed as unpopular. For example, some people consider maintenance work to be a menial job. Point out all the skills needed to complete the job, discuss what would happen if the job were not completed by anyone, and discuss the positive aspects of the job. A positive feature may include having flexible hours that allow the person to stay at home with children during the day while a spouse

works, therefore reducing the need for child-care costs. A maintenance worker in a school may enjoy working around children, having autonomy over job tasks, or the variety of tasks to be completed each day.

Helpful Hints

- Encourage the students to minimize their negative comments about the jobs and emphasize the positive, since the idea behind this activity is to help the students recognize their strengths and identify what types of workplaces would suit them.
- Share personal experiences, so the students understand that all employees have strengths and weaknesses.
- Have the students read stories about various kinds of workers and describe these workers' strengths and weaknesses so students can more clearly identify these concepts.
- Try to place the students in job experiences that fit their interests, at least in the first placement.

Evaluation Tips

- Review the students' self-assessments and the employers' assessments and analyze with students the similarities and differences among them.
- Ask the students to describe how they felt about the self-assessment exercise and about being assessed by others. Who gave the most valuable information? (Remember that students are often harder on themselves than others are.)
- Compare assessments from the students' current work experiences with their previous work assessments, if applicable.
- Take the students to observe employees in another setting. Ask them to critique the employees using the same questions listed earlier. How would they rate the employees if they were doing evaluations?

For Students Who Need Additional Modifications

- In a work-study setting, pair the students with disabilities with classmates without disabilities who have the same or similar interests. Teach the students without disabilities to work with the disabled students in completing work tasks; for example, the students without disabilities may prepare a mailing and the disabled students may stuff the envelopes, or the students without disabilities may copy a flyer on the photocopy machine and the disabled students may place the flyers in mail slots.

- Hold in-service sessions or brown-bag lunch sessions in a workplace to teach the employees about the needs of the students with disabilities. These sessions may include once-a-week meetings at lunchtime to teach them sign language or to show videos about disabled people in the workplace. Involve the students with disabilities in planning and preparing for these sessions.

Providing Realistic Feedback

As youngsters approach their teenage years, it is important for teachers and family members to give them responsibilities, encourage them to take risks, and foster their performance of activities independently while providing support and care.

In this chapter, activities are presented that teach students with visual impairments how to make appointments with doctors, arrange travel, set goals, and encourage them to critique their classmates' work behaviors, as well as their own, and obtain feedback from others. The chapter also includes strategies for meeting visually impaired adults or older students who can share ideas and dreams with them.

PLANNING AHEAD

Families and teachers often forget that youngsters with visual impairments may not learn incidentally that adults spend a lot of their time planning for scheduled events. To keep one's life running smoothly, one needs to master the art of scheduling. It is especially important for visually impaired people to learn how to schedule their time to arrange for such important aspects of life as transportation and for sighted assistance, to help read their mail, pay bills, and to help with shopping trips, among other tasks. One way to accustom students with visual impairments gradually to the concept of planning is to let them assume responsibility for scheduling various appointments.

Activities

- Brainstorm with students in a group or individually about what appointments they routinely have to make, such as those with doctors, dentists, or eye care specialists.
- Have students find out when their last appointment took place and when the next one should occur and locate the names, telephone numbers, and addresses of their doctors.
- Ask the students to make their own appointments (or confirm scheduled appointments) once they have the information about their next appointments, and ask them to keep them in a calendar in their computer system or develop a tickler calendar system. (Using a tickler calendar, a student writes the details of an appointment—the time, the place, and with whom the appointment is scheduled—on a notecard or index card and files the cards chronologically. Once the appointment has been kept, the student throws out the corresponding card or files it in a "finished" file.)
- Check with the students every two weeks to review their calendars.
- Ask students to confirm their appointment, if they have one scheduled within the next two weeks.
- Have them determine how to get to the appointment, arrange transportation (even if they only have to ask a family member or staff member to drive them), make a list of questions to ask at the appointment, and be prepared to pay for the visit. An adult's assistance may be needed for the first few appointments, but gradually the students will be able to complete the steps independently.

Critical Points to Cover

- Teach the students how to use tickler files in their preferred reading medium, how the files work, and how to use a desk or notebook-style calendar for planning.
- Review proper telephone etiquette for making and confirming appointments.
- Discuss with students the variety of payment options and insurance available for different circumstances. Students may ask their families what types of insurance they have chosen and why they selected those particular plans.

Helpful Hints

- Students may need individualized instruction because of their unique needs and the sensitive nature of various appointments. Also, the students may not want the teacher to know which doctors they visit, so do not push them to schedule all appointments.
- Rewards are always appreciated. If the students do much of the work in scheduling appointments, teachers or families can offer them a choice of rewards for completing the task.
- Related activities include scheduling travel plans, planning transportation to after-school activities, arranging appointments for other family members, preparing clothes for the next day's activities, assisting the teacher in planning a field trip, and planning and giving a birthday party.

Evaluation Tips

- While monitoring the students' progress in scheduling, help the students evaluate what they have done well or in what areas they need improvement before they can complete the entire appointment process independently. After the appointments, ask students to report on how the appointments were managed, what worked well, and what needs to be changed for making future appointments.
- Questions to ask the students include these:
  1. Were you on time?
  2. Were the directions adequate for you to find your way?
  3. Was the method of transportation you used the most effective and efficient way of getting there?
  4. Did you check in appropriately at the office? (For example, did you notify the receptionist of your arrival?)
  5. Were you prepared to ask or answer questions?
  6. Did you pay for the visit?
  7. Did you arrange for your next appointment?
- Continue to monitor the students' progress to facilitate further learning.

For Students Who Need Additional Modifications

- Use a consistent scheduling system and make sure that it uses a meaningful medium (such as a calendar box with objects that represent an appointment [a toothbrush for a dentist's appointment or eyeglasses for an ophthalmologist's appointment], a wall calendar with picture or tactile symbols, or an audiotaped schedule that the students can play at the beginning of each day) and is concrete enough for the students to understand.

- When possible, encourage the students to monitor changes in their routines. The use of an appropriate and consistent signal, such as a bell (for a blind student), a flashing light (for a deaf student), or a tap on the hand (for a deaf-blind student), should provide the information that it is time for a change in the routine. For students who have difficulty changing, a second signal can be provided a few minutes later. If they still do not respond, help them put away materials and remind them of the next activity.

- When a special event is planned, draw attention to it each day when the calendar or morning activities are presented. The students should consider what needs to be done on that day to prepare for the upcoming activity.

- When planning for an activity in an unfamiliar area of the community, the students need to consider whether the sites in the area are wheelchair accessible. A team or an individual can be appointed to make telephone calls or visits to determine the accessibility of the sites.

- Have the students with special transportation needs practice scheduling transportation. Will an adapted van be needed? How far in advance must it be ordered? How long does the actual trip take?

SETTING GOALS

It is essential to help middle school students with visual impairments learn to set goals. They need to understand the difference between short-, intermediate-, and long-term goals. For example, to pass a test at the end of the week is a short-term goal; to graduate from eighth grade is an intermediate-term goal, and to graduate from high school is a long-term goal. Students also need to recognize that their career goals are long-term goals and that most people change their life and career goals over time—as they mature. In addition, students need to understand that goals can usually be broken down into small steps or objectives that can help them achieve the goal.

Students in middle school need to begin setting short-term goals that will help them to define what skills they need to obtain and retain jobs. The particular jobs they choose for themselves later they may recognize as intermediate goals—jobs they may actively pursue either in the late middle school years or during the high school years. Once the students have set these short- and intermediate-term goals, they may want to define the long-term career goals that will relate to the jobs and skills they have mastered earlier.

Activities

- Ask the students to list three adults whom they would like to interview to find out about their life goals. Have the students interview at least two of the adults and ask the following questions:
  1. What are three of your long-term goals, including one work goal?
  2. How did you come up with your goals?
  3. What short-term goals or objectives have you set to reach your long-term goals?
  4. Have your goals changed much in the past 5 to 10 years? In what ways?
  5. If you knew 10 years ago what you know now, what would you do differently?
- Then ask the students to compare the adults' answers. You may ask them to list the answers in categories of long-term goals, short-term goals or objectives, and changes.

Critical Points to Cover

- Explain to students that setting too many goals often results in lower motivation, which may affect goal setting in the future.
- Discuss with students that to avoid distraction, they need to set only a reachable number of goals.
- Emphasize to students that they need to set realistic time limits.
- Encourage students to be flexible, since goals change as young people mature.

Helpful Hints

- Have the students with visual impairments determine their own goals, as simple or as complex as they want them to be. If the students reach the goals easily, then discuss how the goals could have been made more complex or challenging or help them expand the goals into new goals. If the goals were not met, discuss how the students could have changed the outcomes.
- Relate the students' goals to the goals the adults mentioned in the interviews. This exercise gives the students a feeling of maturity and belonging.
- Encourage the students to ask questions.
- As the students get older, relate setting goals more to career interests and training options.
- The following are some related activities:
  1. Suggest that the students join a summer reading program at the local library. In these programs, young people usually receive rewards for reaching their goals of reading a certain number of books.
  2. There are many activities in a wide variety of lessons that encourage goal setting. Ask academic teachers to incorporate these activities in their lessons as often as possible. Also look at the goals and objectives on the students' IEPs.
  3. Encourage the students to earn and save money to purchase desired items, using the terms *long-range* and *short-range* goals.

Evaluation Tips

- Have students list one goal that they each want to accomplish in a month and the weekly short-range goals it would take for them to reach the goal. Ask them at the end of the month if setting short-range goals helped them achieve their long-range goal.
- Discuss whether the goal was reachable. If it was not, did they lose their motivation to achieve it? How could they revise or update the goal to achieve what they want, need, or desire?

For Students Who Need Additional Modifications

- Through the use of calendars and daily activity discussions, encourage the students to set daily or weekly goals. Each goal can

FROM A FAMILY PERSPECTIVE

Job Maintenance Skills

Parents' occasional, short reflections about their first jobs can be helpful. Try not to teach with these reminiscences; just tell the stories, since stories are powerful teaching tools in themselves.

Discussing newspaper and magazine articles, television programs, and local events can also be good starting points for talking about how people succeed or fail and what can be learned from their experiences. As part of these conversations, ask your children to imagine that they are employers in a business they might want to own or are employees doing work that might interest them. Talking about what makes a business successful and an employee effective can help children begin to learn about how to retain a desirable job.

Kevin O' Connor

be placed on a card or a bulletin board, and the students can be responsible for documenting when they have reached their goals by placing the card in a "finished" box, punching a hole in it with a paper punch, checking it off on a To Do list, or using any other method they wish to indicate that they achieved the goal.

- Before a task begins, help the students understand what will indicate that the task has been completed. Showing the students an example of a finished product, indicating that the box of materials will be empty when the task is completed, or incorporating any other tangible indicator of completion will help them keep the goal in mind.

JOB MAINTENANCE SKILLS

Many youngsters may believe that getting a job is the hardest part of the job search, but maintaining a job may actually be the most challenging part of the career development process. Many of the behaviors necessary to keep a job are observed or unspoken behaviors, such as good grooming, getting to work on time, helping coworkers, and showing enthusiasm for one's work. Other expected work behaviors are usually explained or outlined when people begin jobs, such as following the employer's policies and procedures, being at work on time, and calling in when ill. People in the workplace may feel uncomfortable telling visually impaired people if they display inappropriate work behaviors that may result in the termination of their jobs or in limited social acceptance at the workplace. Therefore, it is necessary to teach acceptable behaviors to the students with visual impairments by considering both the home and the school as the training grounds for the anticipated behaviors in the workplace.

A job-maintenance skill that is often not formally addressed is assisting coworkers when one's own work is done. Mutual reliance on each other, or teamwork, is a primary ingredient of today's workplace and needs to be emphasized to all students. Helping others with their work is an area of which young people with visual impairments may not be especially aware because people tend to help them. One effective way to teach this skill is by involving the youngsters in class, community, or family projects.

Activities

- Ask students to participate in class and community projects that involve teamwork and helping others. These projects may include selecting a senior citizen center or nursing home, where the students could assist in special activities (such as performing a play, singing songs, and reading to residents) every month; painting a mural on a wall of the school; keeping the school yard clean; and raising money through bake or craft sales to purchase books for the school library.
- Have the students become involved in one family undertaking, such as cleaning up the yard. This project entails cutting the grass, trimming the hedges, sweeping the walk, and raking the leaves. Throughout the year, the students can learn one task at one time. (To accomplish the most complicated task, namely, learning how to mow the grass, set up one stake in one corner and another stake in the opposite corner of the yard and attach a rope to them. Have the youngsters mow with the rope at waist height. Once a row is mowed, the youngsters can move the stakes over approximately two feet and then mow the next row.)
- After all the tasks are learned, have the students complete a task that involves the least amount of time. When the students are done with their chore, redirect them to assist another person. If

others finish before the student completes the chore, then assist the student by modeling the behavior.

- Select different work behaviors that relate to important activities of daily life, for instance, getting ready for school, being there promptly, and turning in homework that is accurate, neat, and on time. One important work behavior is getting along with other workers. Encourage the students to be helpful, respectful, and friendly in social situations.

Critical Points to Cover

- Explain to students what are acceptable behaviors at work.
- Discuss the unacceptable behaviors at work.
- Explain the issues that may influence which behaviors are considered to be acceptable or unacceptable in a job, including social rules that are exhibited by others. For instance, it may be all right for a person to come to work late if he or she made prior arrangements with the employer.
- Review the benefits of exhibiting good work behaviors, such as social acceptance, job maintenance, and career advancement.

Helpful Hints

- Emphasize the importance of infusing these work behaviors into all aspects of the students' lives so they become part of the students' normal patterns of living.
- Encourage the students to ask questions.
- Discuss how it felt to help others and when others helped them.
- Ask the students to critique the work of other people. For example, at a restaurant, did the waiters or waitresses provide exceptional or inferior service? Ask the students to compare the work behaviors to those they exhibited when their work was not effective. Discuss the benefits of being a good worker.
- Ensure that the students are honestly evaluated.

Evaluation Tips

- Ask students to list the work habits they exhibited while doing yard work or participating in a community service project.

- Ask the other family members how they felt when they received assistance.
- Observe students' current work behaviors. Discuss with the students any weak areas and whether these are areas in which the students want to improve. If not, ask students about what kinds of workplaces they think may allow these behaviors?
- When other activities have been completed, have the students compare the experiences.

For Students Who Need Additional Modifications

- Make sure that each student has a signal or gesture to indicate that assistance is needed. For students with severe physical disabilities, this signal can be the use of a switch to activate a message saying, "I need help, please" or the activation of a light or bell to gain the attention of others.
- Provide feedback to students about their physical appearance, so they will know what facial expressions are pleasing, what posture is attractive, and what clothing is appropriate for the workplace.
- For verbal students, practice role-playing different types of language to be used in different settings. Point out that slang can be used with friends but may not be the correct way to speak to adults in the workplace.
- Reinforce the students for working hard at difficult tasks. Encourage them to work a little longer by saying, "It does look hard, but you are a hard worker, and I'll bet you can go a little longer," rather than allow them to stop working as soon as they are fatigued.

MENTORSHIPS

Because visual impairment is a low-incidence disability, many visually impaired children and their families may not know any visually impaired adults who are in the workforce. Therefore, it is helpful when both families and children can observe visually impaired adults functioning as productive members of society. Since the mass media frequently continue to portray people who are blind as helpless members of society, it is essential to provide mentors for visually impaired students and their families to overcome such stereotypes and expand their knowledge of the abilities of people with similar impairments.

Activities

- Ask students to set up a mentorship directory and contact the mentors who have agreed to work with the students. A mentorship directory is a list of people who are visually impaired and who could act as role models. The entries on the list need to reflect the following:
  1. a variety of jobs
  2. positive traits (that is, they have high self-esteem, are as independent as possible, and have good social skills)
  3. various degrees of vision loss
  4. the ability to use a wide variety of modes of transportation
  5. the skills to use a wide range of technology for work and independent living
  6. the ability to interact well with teenagers

  Setting up such a directory takes a considerable amount of time, but the resource is invaluable. If the students reside in an urban area, they may find enough adults living in the immediate area to contact; if they live in a rural area, their search may extend over several counties or even across the state. People who may be willing to participate as mentors can be found by contacting the Careers and Technology Information Bank (CTIB) of the American Foundation for the Blind or the National Federation of the Blind (see the Resources section). Once the mentors are contacted and have agreed to be included in the directory as mentors, produce the listing on disk and in print and braille and distribute it to the visually impaired students who want it. Teach the students how to phone or write the mentors and to ask such questions as how they chose their line of work, the training they received, how they get to work, and how and when they socialize with their coworkers.

Critical Points to Cover

- Have students list some of the traditional jobs that visually impaired persons have held.

- Ask the students how technology has affected the jobs that visually impaired people now hold.
- Ask the students whether they would like the types of jobs they have discussed with the mentors and ask the students to explain their reasons for liking them or disliking them.
- Ask the students to name the jobs that are not held by persons with visual impairments. Will technology and training change the trend, or is vision an integral part of those jobs? If people with visual impairments are interested in these fields, what are the related jobs that they can do?

Helpful Hints

- Encourage the students with visual impairments to locate as many of the mentors in the directory as possible.
- Have the students set up the directory for distribution.
- The students may need help in their first phone calls to the mentors.
- Ask the mentors whether they will participate in other activities so they can have more contact with and develop relationships with the students.
- Encourage the students to contact people who do jobs that they may not be interested in but who have dog guides, use trains for transportation, or use particular types of technology or tools to broaden the students' information base.
- Help the students compare and contrast the jobs that the mentors hold.
- Set up a "buddy" system by which the mentors and students meet periodically.
- Find mentors with visual impairments who hold a variety of jobs.

Evaluation Tips

- Contact both the mentors and students to assess whether their interactions are benefiting the students.
- Ask the students to write a report about one of the mentors with whom they have been in contact.
- Ask the students' teachers and families whether the students' contact with the mentors has been meaningful.

- Ask a group of students who have used the directory for a few months to revise it.
- Ask the students to research particular jobs in more depth if they indicate interest in these jobs after they have spoken with the mentors. Observe the students' efforts.

For Students Who Need Additional Modifications

- Include successful adults with disabilities in addition to those with visual impairments in the directory. Include people who are successful in roles as family and community members, whether or not they are competitively employed.
- Encourage the students to develop a list of questions to ask their mentors when they contact them. Get them to think about subjects that may be problems for them at school.

PART FIVE

The Career Caravan

Anna Lee Braunstein

As demonstrated by the activities included in the previous sections of *Skills for Success,* there are many ways in which to teach children and adolescents work behaviors and career skills and expand their awareness of the meaning of work and possible career options. Depending on students' ages and innate abilities, various efforts can be effective. With younger children, families and teachers need to take the primary role in guiding children's learning experiences and providing appropriate exploratory activities, such as field trips and structured storytelling, arts and crafts projects, and creative dramatics activities. As children mature, however, they can take on increasing responsibility for their own learning efforts and experiences, such as trips to businesses or organizations of particular interest to them. In general, activities for older students tend to be more student directed and those for younger students more adult directed. In the following section of this book, a program for students in middle school and beyond is described, in which student-directed and adult-directed activities are combined.

The Career Caravan program is a career exploration process designed to be implemented by teachers during school summer sessions. Ideally, career education activities such as those described in the Career Caravan are often introduced to students while they are in middle school or junior high school. However, the Career Caravan program can also be relevant for high school students to deepen understanding of certain available career options and the work behaviors expected of all employees. (Students, especially those who have completed the Career Caravan or a similar career exploration program during middle school or junior high school, can also make use of *The Transition Tote System,* a set of materials designed to reinforce organizational and job-seeking skills and support their career-related activities [Wolffe & Johnson, 1997; see the Resources section].)

The description that follows gives readers an overview of the Career Caravan program, specifically how to set up a five-week summer experience for visually impaired students. In addition, suggestions are provided for incorporating Career Caravan content into the schedule of the regular school year. Examples of the form letters and flyers that can be used in the program are also presented. Although some readers may prefer to use these form letters and forms that can be duplicated easily, others may want to develop more detailed forms and letters for specific programs they plan to initiate. Finally, some lesson examples from the Career Caravan program are presented as an appendix, which, when used with the activities from Parts Three and Four (the elementary school and middle school years) of this book, can help teachers and families provide a well-designed and rewarding career education program that can facilitate the transition of visually impaired students from school to the workplace.

The Career Caravan

To obtain employment, job seekers need to know what jobs are available and how to get them. The Career Caravan is a five-week experiential program for visually impaired students in middle school (usually grades 6, 7, and 8) or junior high school (typically grades 7, 8, and 9) that is designed to expose students to various jobs and how they are performed. The program is typically offered in the summer because of the extensive academic requirements of the school year. As with many summer school programs, it is organized around a school day that is approximately four hours long. Schools in some parts of the country have accepted the program as credit for their career exploration requirement for graduation.

The Career Caravan program encourages students to go into their communities and visit a wide variety of job sites. The students visit businesses and organizations three times per week to gain an understanding of the many job possibilities available in particular career areas and to meet workers who perform these jobs. These trips are scheduled as part of a weekly theme; for example, careers in food service, health care, business, or communication may each be the focus of a week's job-site visits.

In addition to the job-site visits, the students have the opportunity to develop specific skills that are necessary for both work and school. These skills range from the academic—using a calculator, for example—to the social—such as learning the skills necessary to eat in a restaurant. Also included are skills for obtaining a job, such as completing applications and interviewing techniques. Lessons are taught daily and often require repetition. All activities included in the cur-

Note: The Career Caravan is an abridged version of the complete Career Caravan Program. Additional information about the comprehensive program can be obtained from the author, Anna Lee Braunstein, 6608 Chiquita Way, Carmichael, CA 95608.

riculum have a job-related focus. Although the description of the program provided here details a model used in California to show readers how the program can work, the program can be modified to suit individual circumstances.

PREPARATION

In the spring, a flyer (see Example 1) and welcome letter (see Example 2) inform students and parents of the purpose of the Career Caravan program. The welcome letter explains the types of activities planned, including both classroom and community-based activities. It also explains the teacher's expectations regarding dress and behavior. Because the program is a career exploration experience, each student's appearance and conduct are important, and work clothes are required for most visits. All students and adults need to dress appropriately for

---

CATCH THE CARAVAN!

The CAREER CARAVAN is heading out in June for its travels about the county. Planned stops include 15 businesses, 4 restaurants, and a special finale. Passengers will

- participate in an intense career-exploration program

- meet a variety of workers and learn how they do their jobs

- learn how to complete job applications, how to handle interviews, and how to write résumés

- develop skills for writing business letters, taking telephone messages, and scheduling transportation

- demonstrate work habits (attendance, punctuality, working cooperatively, and following instructions)

- try new places to eat

Admission price: your attendance

Make your reservations now!

Call your teacher to get a ticket to a work-filled future!

EXAMPLE 1. Career Caravan Flyer

CAREER CARAVAN ANNOUNCEMENT

(Date)

Dear Students and Families:

This announcement is to inform you of Career Caravan, a work-exploration program developed specifically for junior and senior high students who are visually impaired. The purpose of the program is to give students opportunities to learn about the variety of jobs and careers that are available in the local community. In addition, such job-obtaining skills as completing applications, developing résumés, writing business letters, being interviewed, and developing work ethics are taught. To further the social aspect of work, opportunities to share business lunches are included. Upon the successful completion of this program, a student should have several informed ideas for possible careers and the skills necessary to take the first step toward employment.

Each week's visits are based on a specific theme. If you have an area that you would like to explore, please request it with your application, which is enclosed, and we will try to accommodate you. The more meaningful the visits are to you, the more you will benefit from the experiences.

When we visit a job site, we practice the appearance and behavior of a job applicant. Students are to wear clothes that are suitable for each visit. These clothes will vary from neat jeans and shirts to slacks or skirts and dress shirts or blouses. For some visits, shorts will be acceptable. The students will know a week in advance what the theme of the visit will be and what attire will be appropriate. At no time are torn or dirty clothes to be worn. Short shorts, tank tops, halter tops, and printed T-shirts are also inappropriate business attire.

If you have any questions about this program, please call me. I look forward to your joining us.

Yours truly,

Career Caravan Coordinator

EXAMPLE 2. Career Caravan Welcome Letter

the location to be visited. Depending on the destination, clothing may range from dresses and slacks to shorts. In terms of expectations for socially appropriate behavior, promptness, reliability, and courtesy are areas of emphasis in all daily work. A permission form is also included in the mailing (see Example 3). In addition, each participant is required to complete an application to attend the program (see Example 4).

PERMISSION LETTER

Dear Parent or Other Family Member:

Students in CAREER CARAVAN will travel each week to job sites and to lunch. We will use public transportation or private cars driven by teachers or instructional assistants. We need your permission to transport your child for this career-exploration program.

I give permission for _____ to travel with the Career Caravan program.

Signature _____

Relationship _____

Date _____

Yours truly,

Career Caravan Director

EXAMPLE 3. Permission Form

STUDENTS AND STAFF

The students invited to participate in the Career Caravan are usually middle school or junior high school students with visual impairments. However, high school students without set career goals or with a limited understanding of the labor market are occasionally included as well. In addition to their visual impairments, the students may have mild learning disabilities or moderate physical impairments.

The Career Caravan staff is headed by a teacher of students with visual impairments who can teach students how to use adapted computer equipment, complete tasks like signing their names, and use appropriate social skills. This teacher also provides the program's classroom instruction. Having an orientation and mobility (O&M) instructor as a team teacher or contract provider is ideal for teaching travel skills, reinforcing social skills, and providing valuable insights into mobility issues on the jobs observed. In addition, one or two instruc-

---

CAREER CARAVAN APPLICATION

Name: _____

Address: _____

City: _____ State: _____ Zip code: _____

Telephone number: _____

School: _____ Grade: _____

Teacher of visually impaired students:

What would you like to do
for your first job while in school?

What career would you like to pursue
after you graduate from high school or college?

EXAMPLE 4. Application Form

tional assistants are needed. The ratio of staff to students needs to be no greater than one to four because of the probable need for students to be driven to the job visits. All staff members participate in group discussions, sharing their own job experiences but not overshadowing the students' contributions. Both the teachers and the instructional assistants help the students during their individual work periods. The equipment and supplies that are useful to have when conducting the Career Caravan program are listed in Example 5.

DAILY ROUTINE

On the first day of the Career Caravan program, the students need to get acquainted with each other and the entire staff. The instructional staff—teachers and assistants—need to emphasize the adventure inherent in visiting community businesses and organizations to investigate jobs and participating in the special activities planned, such as eating out with classmates and staff once a week. The daily Career Caravan schedule is from 8:00 A.M. to 12:00 P.M. Students start each day in the classroom with the instructional staff. On Mondays, Tuesdays, and Thursdays, the class begins with individual or group classroom activi-

SUGGESTED EQUIPMENT AND MATERIALS FOR SETTING UP CAREER CARAVAN PROGRAMS

Furnishings:
computers (one for every two
 students)
  program for writing envelopes or an
 electric typewriter
  printers
  word-processing programs
large white board
sufficient power outlets
surge protectors
tables with separate chairs
working telephone

Basic Office supplies:
8½ x 11-inch paper
binder with dividers for each student
binder paper
computer disks
envelopes
erasers
felt-tip pens
message pads (enlarged or in braille)
name badges
paper clips
paper punch
paste
pencils
pens
poster paper
scissors
stamps
stapler and staples
tape

telephone book
tissues
white board pens and eraser

Specialized equipment:
braille notetaker
braillewriters and paper
calculators (talking and large-print
 display)
closed-circuit television
electronic dictionary (such as the
 Franklin Talking Dictionary, which is
 a handheld fully speaking electronic
 dictionary, thesaurus, spelling
 corrector, and grammar guide)
handheld telescopes
large-print dictionary
magnifiers
speech access for computers
audiotape recorders and
 audiocassettes

Career Caravan materials:
applications
articles on jobs
classified advertisements
clothing catalogs
brochures about the Careers and
 Technology Information Bank
 (CTIB) (available from the
 American Foundation for the Blind;
 see Resources)
menus

Reference materials and magazines:
Attmore, M. (1990). *Career perspectives: Interviews with blind and visually
 impaired professionals.* New York: American Foundation for the Blind. A book
 that includes interviews with 20 blind or visually impaired professionals.
Bissonnette-Lemendells, D. (1987). *Pathways: A job search curriculum
 instructor's guide.* Northridge, CA: Milt Wright and Associates. A guide that

EXAMPLE 5. Suggested Equipment and Materials List

contains worksheets for discussion on applications, interviews, résumés, and work ethics.

CAREERS & The disABLED. Equal Opportunity Publications, Inc., 1160 East Jericho Turnpike, Suite 2000, Huntington, NY 11743. A quarterly magazine that covers employment opportunities for people with disabilities.

Dialogue. Blindskills, Inc., P.O. Box 5181, Salem, OR 97304. A general-interest magazine, published quarterly, for adolescents and adults.

Hosler, M. M. (1995). *20,000+ words.* New York: Glencoe/McGraw-Hill. Louisville, KY: American Printing House for the Blind. (Large-print ed.) A quick reference speller in which words are divided into syllables.

Kendrick, D. (1993). *Jobs to be proud of: Profiles of workers who are blind or visually impaired.* New York: AFB Press. A book that is available in large print, braille, or cassette and profiles 12 jobholders who are blind or visually impaired and the work they perform without an advanced academic education or extensive technological adaptations.

Kendrick, D. (1998). *Teachers who are blind or visually impaired.* Jobs That Matter series. New York: AFB Press. A book that is available in large print, braille, or cassette and includes the life stories of 18 individuals who have fulfilled their dreams to be teachers.

National Library Service for the Blind and Physically Handicapped. (1993). *Assistive devices for reading.* Compiled by Carol Strauss [Reference circular]. Washington, DC: Author. (Available from the National Library Service for the Blind and Physically Handicapped, 1291 Taylor Street, N.W., Washington, DC 20542; 800-252-9205). A circular that lists devices designed to assist people with low vision to access print materials with magnification devices and screen enlargement programs. It also includes addresses and telephone numbers of manufacturers and vendors and journal articles that evaluate specific devices.

National Library Service for the Blind and Physically Handicapped. (1998). *Assistive devices for use with personal computers.* Compiled by Carol Strauss [Reference circular]. Washington, DC: Author. (Available from the National Library Service for the Blind and Physically Handicapped, 1291 Taylor Street, N.W., Washington, DC 20542; 800-252-9205). A circular that lists devices designed for people who are blind to access print materials using auditory output or braille output. It includes a list of producers and vendors (and addresses and telephone numbers), as well as books and journal articles in which specific devices have been evaluated.

Pamperin, M. (Ed.). (1995). *Access to resources for students with visual impairments.* Los Angeles: California Transcribers and Educators of the Visually Handicapped. A comprehensive reference for students in transition from high school to independence that contains information on 150 resources for materials, equipment, and services.

Rabby, R., & Croft, D. (1989). *Take charge: A strategic guide for blind job seekers.* Boston: National Braille Press. A firsthand account of how to seek employment.

DAILY JOURNAL

☐ Check here if this is a place or job you liked.

Date:

Name of company:

What does this company do?

Name of the person who led the tour:

  His or her job:

Most of the work was

      a. inside

      b. outside

The employees worked

      a. by themselves

      b. together

They wore

      a. uniforms

      b. dressy clothes

      c. casual clothes

List the types of jobs seen:

What seemed to be the best job?

What training would you need to work here?

What type of supervision do the employees have?

What job or jobs there would you like to perform?

What job or jobs would you not like to perform?

EXAMPLE 6. Student's Journal

ties that last for approximately one hour. Following the classroom activities, the students and staff visit the job sites. These visits usually take 2½ hours, including travel time. Finally, everyone returns to the classroom and spends the last half hour of the day discussing the day's visit, and the students chronicle their adventures in special journals (see Example 6). The entire four hours are spent in the classroom on

Wednesdays engaged in job-readiness classes and planning activities, as detailed in the following sections. On Fridays, students begin their day in the classroom engaged in group or individual work. They leave the class at approximately 10:30 A.M. to go to a local restaurant for a business luncheon, returning to school in time to catch the bus home. A typical week's schedule is included as Example 7. The following sections detail the main components of the Career Caravan program.

CLASSROOM ACTIVITIES

When students arrive each morning, they complete time cards and pick up personalized work schedules for the day. The use of time cards reinforces the work behaviors of promptness and dependability and demonstrates the necessity of monitoring one's own work hours as required on a job. Each student is responsible for keeping track of the time and changing activities as directed by the daily schedule. The schedule for each student's activities can be kept on a computer disk for the student to print out each morning. The students can update the disk file at the end of the day and add the next day's schedule. Alternatively, they can maintain work files in three-ring notebooks containing assignments, worksheets, and their entries in their journals.

Classroom activities consist of lessons related to developing or improving general work skills and appropriate work behaviors. These skills generally fall into the areas of writing, mathematics, oral skills, social skills, and transportation skills. Some of the specific work-related skills and behaviors in each area may include the following:

Writing

- cursive writing of a legal signature, as required by law in most states for signing checks or legal documents (a signature should fit on a three-inch-long line)
- printing on forms (such as applications, W-2 and W-4 forms, proof-of-citizenship and legal-alien-status forms)
- creating résumés
- printing one's name, address, city, state, zip code, telephone number, birth date, birthplace, name of school, social security number, and parents' complete names, with everything spelled correctly, on an information sheet

THEME: COMMUNICATION

Time	Monday	Tuesday	Wednesday	Thursday	Friday
8:00 A.M.	Individual work: Spelling Cursive signature	Individual work: Continue journal	Group lesson on applications Complete sample application together	Individual work: Finalize menu choices Compute cost with tip and tax	Spelling bee Check homework Complete journal for the week
8:30 A.M.	Group work: Discuss theme, jobs, questions	Group discussion: Sample scenarios related to honesty Anticipate jobs and refine questions for site visit to television station	Individual spelling tests, including information for application	Group discussion: References Discuss upcoming visit, anticipating jobs	Write thank-you letters Group discussion: Salary, benefits
9:00 A.M.	Leave for radio station: On-site visit	Leave for television station: On-site visit	Group work: Announce restaurant choice Individually read menus	Leave for telephone company: On-site visit	

Time				
9:30 A.M.			Group lesson on message taking Role-playing Individual practice on real phone with instructional assistants	Compute hourly, weekly, monthly, yearly wages Discuss taxes, FICA deductions
10:00 A.M.			Review dress codes for various work sites	Review etiquette for restaurant
10:30 A.M.			Make collage of casual, sporty, and dressy work clothes	Leave for Chinese restaurant
11:00 A.M.		Return to class Individual work: Continue journal Thank-you letters Signature Group discussion: Company visits	Return to class Continue journal Continue message practice Practice eating marshmallows with chopsticks	
11:30 A.M.	Return to class Journal writing	Job charades	Homework: One reference— Name, address, phone, job	Return to class Complete account of meal expenses
12:00 P.M.	Dismissal	Dismissal	Dismissal	Dismissal

EXAMPLE 7. Sample Schedule for One Week

- printing one's height, weight, eye and hair color, vision condition, clothing sizes, and other identifying characteristics
- writing two or more references—from teachers, family, friends, or neighbors (students first need to ask permission of the persons to list them as references)
- writing entries in a daily journal of businesses visited, the job titles of persons interviewed, and opinions of jobs observed
- writing checks, including the recipient's name, date, and amounts spelled out and in figures
- typing thank-you notes and business letters

Mathematics

- managing a checking account: determining deposits, withdrawals, and bank balance
- calculating sales and income taxes
- using a calculator: calculating percentages and tallying bank accounts and purchases
- managing money: making change, determining typical monthly payments, calculating tips, and budgeting
- managing time: determining how many hours worked per pay period, what time to return from a break or lunch, and hours in a typical workday
- calculating payments—wages per hour and pay period, raises and deductions (FICA, state and federal taxes, union dues, and insurance)
- using an adding machine (if possible, borrow machines from local businesses for practice)

Oral Skills

- using telephone skills: ordering materials or meals, making appointments and reservations, answering a business telephone, getting information, and taking and leaving messages
- taking orders (using templates for cash registers of fast-food outlets to take practice orders)
- discussing jobs and developing questions to ask regarding job descriptions, employees' titles, tools and equipment used, hours worked, type of training and experience required, promotion, and benefits

- comparing various jobs visited
- interviewing, including answering questions about oneself
- talking to employers
- talking to coworkers

Social Skills

- shaking hands properly and smiling when first meeting some-one
- ordering from a menu in a restaurant
- eating properly: using a napkin and the proper utensils
- dressing: using catalogs and advertisements; creating a small portfolio of suitable attire for casual and business establishments; and visiting a clothing store to learn about affordable and appropriate wardrobes for various types of interviews, skilled labor positions, and office or professional work
- demonstrating a strong work ethic (showing up on time, coming to work or class every day, cooperating with authority figures and peers, following instructions, and so forth)

Transportation Skills

- reading a map
- reading a bus or train schedule
- telephoning a bus or train company to ask for information
- planning a route for the class to a restaurant or job site
- writing directions to one's home from the nearest major intersection (or directing a driver if sharing a ride to work)

Sample lessons for each of these content areas are included as an appendix to this part.

Classroom activities for students are individualized according to their needs. For instance, an older student may need assistance developing a résumé, while a younger student may need to learn how to write a simple thank-you note. Assessments completed during the school year and reflected on the students' Individualized Education Programs (IEPs) can be used to determine the students' academic skill levels. Specific skills assessments can be conducted during the first week of the summer program to determine the students' knowledge of work and their work-related abilities, such as signature writing, practical math, and keyboarding. Group or individual instruction is provided according to the students' current level of performance. If various workstations can be set up in the classroom that is used, many activities can be conducted at the same time, much like at a regular work site.

Classroom activities will be more meaningful if the skills are applied or used on visits to actual job sites or during business lunch activities. For instance, students can complete job applications for particular organizations or businesses they will be visiting and submit them to the personnel directors or the business managers for evaluation. The comments of people who do the actual hiring add weight to those of the teacher. Holding private practice interviews conducted by personnel representatives that require applications to be submitted and proper dress and conduct gives the students nonthreatening experience with interviewing. In addition, mock practice interviews can be performed that are evaluated anonymously by class members. An adult observer can summarize these evaluations and discuss privately with each student the positive features of their interviews and the areas that need to be improved.

JOB-SITE VISITS

Selecting Themes and Job Sites

Using a theme for each week's job-site visits enables students to gain an understanding of the breadth of jobs available in different occupational categories. The idea of a theme, such as investigating jobs in restaurants, cafeterias, and fast-food places during a unit on food service, helps students categorize career options. Because the students visit a different location each day for three days, several different work sites that fit the theme for the week are needed. These work sites can be selected from the teacher's knowledge of the community or from newspaper classified ads or the local telephone book yellow pages. Themes may be established in advance by the instructional staff in concert with the students, and the most meaningful themes may come from the students themselves. Staff can ask students what jobs they would like to have or are interested in learning about and can then include those job sites as part of a week's theme. In this way, students learn not only about their identified interests, but about other jobs in related fields.

The following are some suggested themes and specific job sites that may be appropriate to include in the Career Caravan. Each community has its own particular pool of job categories. For example, some communities have numerous job examples in the agriculture field, whereas others may have few in that area but many in communication. Some potential sites to visit include the following:

- food service: fast-food establishments, small restaurants, large restaurants, grocery stores, bakeries, restaurant-supply firms, and Business Enterprise Program operations (federal and state vending stand or food-service endeavors that are provided for and managed by people with visual impairments)
- communications: radio stations, including radio reading services for the blind; commercial and public television stations; telephone companies; and newspaper or magazine companies
- medical services: physicians', dentists', and chiropractors' offices; pharmacies; emergency care units of hospitals; ambulance services; convalescent homes; and medical and dental laboratories
- law and law enforcement: fire stations, police or sheriffs' offices, state police offices, courts, law offices, highway patrol offices, and law enforcement academies
- retail establishments: gas stations, department stores, specialty stores, catalog sales and customer service offices, discount stores, grocery stores, and office and computer supply stores
- business: construction, banking, manufacturing, insurance, financial investment, agriculture, and service industry (convention centers, resorts, hotels, and motels)
- education: public and private schools, district offices, colleges and universities, technical or vocational schools, and day care facilities
- government: federal, state, county, and civic sites (choices will vary with each community)
- transportation: private and public bus companies, taxicab companies, train or subway stations, regional transit centers, airports, and airline companies
- recreation: parks, golf courses, bowling alleys, YMCA/YWCA, stables, sporting goods stores, sports complexes or arenas, zoos, fairgrounds, neighborhood recreation centers, movie and live-performance theaters, and art galleries

Use of the *Dictionary of Occupational Titles (DOT)* (U.S. Department of Labor, 1991) offers another way to develop themes. The *DOT* provides succinct descriptions of more than 12,000 jobs represented in the U.S. labor market. The *Occupational Outlook Handbook (OOH)* (U.S. Department of Labor, 1998–99), published every other year, provides more detailed information about the 250 most common jobs available at the time of its publication. Occupational categories and representative jobs presented in both books include these:

- professional, technical, and managerial occupations, such as architect, teacher, computer systems analyst, dentist, lawyer, clergy, writer, and commercial artist
- clerical and sales occupations, such as secretary, bookkeeper, cashier, stock clerk, ticket agent, and sales clerk
- service occupations, such as domestic cook, housekeeper, innkeeper, hairdresser, and amusement or recreation worker
- agricultural, fishery, forestry, and related occupations, such as farmer, horticulturist, conservation worker, logger, and hunter
- processing occupations, such as metal caster, mold maker, foundry supervisor, threshing machine operator, winery worker, cotton puller, fish smoker, and coffee roaster
- machine trades occupations, such as toolmaker, cabinetmaker, stonecutter, bookbinder, and printer
- benchwork occupations, such as jeweler, assembler, sander, furrier, piano tuner, shoemaker, and tailor
- structural work occupations, such as riveter, steelworker, engine assembler, boilermaker, cable television installer-repairer, and electrician
- miscellaneous occupations, such as driver, station agent, dispatcher, packer, film editor, and model

Preparing for the Visit

Once the themes are selected, preparation is vital to the success of the job-site visits. During the initial contact with an owner or manager of a business, in person or by telephone (see Example 8), the teacher needs to explain the program, request a possible visit, and make an appointment for a preliminary visit to see the site and learn about the various types of workers and equipment in order to prepare the stu-

**TEACHER'S CHECKLIST FOR CONTACTING
A BUSINESS MANAGER OR OWNER**

1. Explain purpose of visit

    a. To see range of jobs

    b. To learn standards of hiring and employment

2. State needs of students

    a. To have direct contact with work materials and equipment

    b. To have personal opportunity to meet workers and hear what they have
    to say about their jobs

3. List sample questions by students

    a. How did you get your job?

    b. What kind of training do you need?

    c. Do you like your job?

    d. What are the benefits of working here?

4. Emphasize positive aspects for students and workers

    a. Personal experience for students in learning about jobs

    b. Opportunity for workers to share job information with an eager
    audience

    c. Pleasurable contact between two groups

    d. Favorable exposure of the business to school staff and students'
    families

5. Send confirmation letter with specific information

    a. Date and time of tour

    b. Number of people to expect in tour group

    c. Teacher's name and daytime telephone number

    d. Statement of appreciation for time and support

EXAMPLE 8. Teacher's Contact Checklist

dents for what they will encounter. The preliminary visit is also the
time to acquaint the manager with the needs of the visiting students.
The manager needs to know that the students can learn the purpose
of equipment and tools more accurately when then can safely handle

---

School Name/Address

(Date)

Contact person (with business title)

Business address

Dear Mr./Ms. _____ :

The purpose of this letter is to confirm the visit of my class on (date) at (time) to your company. We appreciate your making the time available to us for this tour. There will be (number) students with visual impairments and (number) adults accompanying them. We want to be as unobtrusive as possible, so please feel free to contact me if you think we are too large a group or if you have any other concerns. You may reach me by telephone (phone number) at (name of school) between the hours of (time available), or, if it is more convenient for you, I can also be reached at my home (phone number) between the hours of (time available).

For your information, I have enclosed a one-page sheet that covers the guidelines for this visit, which we talked about in our initial conversation. Again, many thanks for having us—we are looking forward to our visit.

Sincerely,

Career Caravan Instructor

enclosure

EXAMPLE 9. Confirmation Letter to Business Contact

items, that the students will harm neither themselves nor the equipment, and that there will be enough adults along to supervise the students closely. The students will need time to ask questions of the various workers whom they meet. It is important for it to be explained that although the interviewing will take time from the workers' jobs, the benefit to the visually impaired students is invaluable, and the cooperation of everyone at the site is a service on behalf of the students that is genuinely appreciated.

A week before the visit to a job site, the teacher needs to send a letter confirming the date and time the students and staff will visit and containing the teacher's work and home telephone numbers in case the manager needs to contact the teacher for any reason (see Example 9).

The teacher also needs to include a printed insert restating what has already been explained to the manager regarding staff supervision of students and the students' handling of materials and equipment (see Example 10) with the confirmation letter.

Once a job-site visit is arranged, transportation for the students to the site needs to be planned, preferably in consultation with the O&M instructor. If possible, public transportation should be used. Preparatory sessions can incorporate lessons in reading maps and bus schedules and telephoning to make travel inquiries. Small groups of students working together can develop a travel itinerary for the visit and can divide the responsibility to give each student an opportunity to plan various aspects of travel during the session. For example, one student may call the bus station to find out whether the business in question is located on a bus route. Another may read a city map to determine whether the business is within walking distance (walking to a location is an important opportunity for mobility and exercise). Another student can call the business to ask what the suggested travel route is. If the group determines that neither public transportation nor walking is viable, the students, together with the instructional assistants, can arrange for vans or cars driven by district-approved personnel to take the students to the site.

The Visit and Follow-Up

The students will need guidance before going on their first job-site visit. The teacher should develop preliminary, general questions to direct the students in their observations of individual workers, such as these:

- What job tasks do you perform?
- What qualifications did you have to have to get this job?
- Where can a person get the training necessary to perform this job?
- What equipment or tools do you use to do this job?
- Where else can one apply the skills used in this job?

During the first job-site visit, students' questions tend to be general and basic. Questioning will become more sophisticated as the students gain more knowledge of work. After each visit, a discussion of what has been seen and learned will reinforce the trip and clarify any misconceptions.

Before they leave for the visit, the students need to discuss what they know about the weekly occupational theme and the specific job

A VISIT BY THE CAREER CARAVAN

Guidelines for the Business Manager or Owner

The students who will visit your business are learning about many jobs that are available in the community. They are interested in how your particular business operates and the types of jobs that you offer. By being able to visit businesses like yours, they will be able to make wise choices about the jobs they will want to do as adults.

These students have visual impairments. This means that their vision ranges from low vision (that is, to see their work they have to get close to it or to use special magnifiers) to blind (they have to use braille for reading and writing). Since visually impaired students learn best by handling items rather than by demonstration, each of these students would benefit from being able to examine equipment tactilely under the guidance of your employees.

Because of the lessons we teach before they enter a business, you can expect questions from the students. Please make your answers as complete as possible. The students therefore will be able to gain accurate knowledge about the jobs you perform. They will be able to decide if these jobs, with special training and equipment, are possible for them. When they return to the classroom, the students will need to explain accurately the information they have learned from you.

Some possible questions that you and your employees may expect to be asked are the following:

How did you get your job?

What kind of training did you need?

What types of equipment do you use?

What other jobs do you do?

Where else can this job be performed?

In addition, we would like the students to become aware of the expectations of supervisors. Your explanation of how you expect an employee to behave while at work can help make the students more sensitive to their future responsibilities. They can also profit from learning about what you seek in applicants when hiring new employees. This information may include appearance, speech, and behavior, as well as knowledge of the job. Our classroom discussions become more meaningful when students hear what employers want from their employees.

Although the purpose of this program is the students' preparation for future employment, we are having a good time learning about the world of work and we hope you and your staff enjoy our visit. Please encourage your staff to relax and feel comfortable with these students. Words such as *look* and *see* are a part of the students' vocabulary and appropriate to use.

We look forward to visiting your company!

EXAMPLE 10. Guidelines for the Business Manager or Owner

location. The teacher's familiarity with the work site can enable him or her to guide the discussion. Using information that the students already know and their own curiosity, the students can prepare more specific questions to ask the manager and workers whom they meet.

Two factors largely determine the size of a group at a particular location: the age range and the number of students in the program. If the ages of the students vary widely, different approaches to the visit may be warranted. The class can be divided into groups of those who are acquiring preliminary job information (younger students) and those who are closer to actual job experiences (older students), with each group participating in a separate tour. In this way, the students will ask age-appropriate questions and gain answers they can understand and use. Also, if the work site is small, the class should be divided into groups of four to six to prevent the students' visit from having a negative impact on the ability of the workers to conduct business. Each small group should visit a comparable site, sharing observations of differences and similarities during the follow-up session at the end of the day.

Visiting work sites where visually impaired people are employed can enhance the learning experience for students as well. Vocational rehabilitation counselors can help identify locations where visually impaired workers are employed, but if the teacher does not have a working relationship with a local vocational rehabilitation counselor, a call to the state rehabilitation services agency can provide information on which employers to contact. Governmental agencies continue to be primary employers of people with visual impairments. Watching and talking to an employee with a visual impairment at a work site provides concrete evidence to the students that employment can be a reality for them. In addition, the students are usually interested in the equipment being used by visually impaired workers and the means of transportation the workers use to get to the job site. Under ideal circumstances, each session of the Career Caravan will include opportunities to meet visually impaired workers.

After the visit, the students need to review what they have observed. They need to check to see if their questions were answered and to compare observations to share the facts they learned. In addition, they need to determine individually their own attitudes toward the jobs and the work site. After several visits, the students will be able to generalize about the jobs they have visited. Keeping a journal of facts to remember and opinions about their visits helps the students formulate their own ideas about particular jobs.

To determine possible jobs to seek or careers to enter, the students need to consider which jobs they find appealing, as well as those they do not think are desirable. If the students begin to show interest in a particular field, follow-up visits and further exploration can be included during the regular school year.

Within a day of the visits, each business should receive two thank-you notes—one from the teacher on school stationery and the other from a representative of the students (the students should take turns writing an appropriate letter using a business letter format). The letter from the student representative should be written on a typewriter or a computer and be signed "Career Caravan Representative" to lend authority to the student and the letter. Writing letters such as these helps students develop good business practices and demonstrate proper social skills.

THE BUSINESS MEAL

Because working people often eat breakfast or lunch with their fellow employees, prospective clients, or acquaintances, the development of proper eating skills and restaurant manners fits well in the Career Caravan approach. One day of the week can be set aside for a business meal. Although students are usually already skilled in eating bag lunches or at fast-food outlets, the business meal provides the more adult dimension of eating at a restaurant. Preparing for business meals is a highly motivating activity that encourages the development of both eating etiquette and social skills. Having a reason to demonstrate correct social skills greatly influences the probability of successful learning, and the opportunity to eat out is just such a motivation.

This meal is the only part of the Career Caravan program that requires a fiscal expenditure by the students. In cases in which students are unable to pay $5 to $10 per week, school staff can attempt to find sponsors from the school or charitable organizations in the community.

Before the first business meal, each student should be assessed for the correct use of napkins and utensils and given tips on how to place an order and pay the waiter or cashier. Practice lessons may be necessary for some students as part of the course work. If an Asian restaurant is a destination, the students may want to practice using chopsticks (marshmallows are a good food for a first try). If a Mexican restaurant is a destination, the students may need to be instructed on how to shuck a tamale. In general, the students also need to be reminded of the appropriate dress for the particular restaurant.

Another necessary classroom activity before each business meal is for the students to read the restaurant menu for that day; decide what to order; and compute what the meal will cost, including the tax and tip. Doing so will prevent embarrassment or delays at the restaurant, and the students will be able to place their orders and pay their bills independently.

Choosing different types of restaurants, including ethnic restaurants (Mexican, Chinese, Italian, French), pasta or salad restaurants, or vegetarian or general-menu restaurants, will make this activity more interesting. One student can make the reservation during the week to ensure that there is enough seating for the class. It may also be wise to tell the restaurant staff of any time constraints, such as bus schedules, that could affect the serving of the meal. It may also be helpful to tell the waiter or waitress beforehand that the students will be requesting separate checks.

A practical application of the business meal activity is teaching budgeting skills. A reasonable budget for the program may be $7 per week. Because the restaurants chosen are ones that use menus and have waiters or waitresses, part of the cost of the food will be a 10–15 percent tip. Students need to learn to limit themselves to their discretionary funds. Generally, allowing 20 percent of the cost of the meal to cover a tip and local taxes is a good guideline. If they start the program with $35, they can spend up to $7 per week or $5 one week and $9 the following week. It is essential for the teachers and students to determine the amount allowable for each student at the beginning of the program and for the students to understand that they must budget their money to last the full five weeks of the program. To stay within their budgets may mean drinking water instead of milk or soda if the food alone costs the amount allocated for the entire meal. To help the students learn about living on a budget, the staff can instruct parents not to allow them to bring extra money.

As part of a related activity, the students need to keep weekly expense records and tally their balances. Using a calculator to keep their records accurately and to compute upcoming expenses provides students with practical experience. This effort needs to be a part of each student's daily activity.

The weekly meal can also provide a forum for work-related discussions. The students may want to use the business meal as an opportunity to invite an occupational role model to visit and speak informally with them about work in a particular field. The role model may be someone who works in an organization the students have already visited or someone who works in an area in which a student has expressed interest. Guidelines for speakers who meet with students are included in Example 11.

Another food-related experience that occurs both at work and in social situations is the potluck lunch, in which people share a meal that they have helped to prepare. If students choose to organize a potluck lunch rather than go out to eat, they need to plan for an appropriate range of food. The expenses still should fall within the $5 to $10 per person limit, and some students may have to share expenses. No food should be brought from home, since bringing food would violate the budget constraints. After a shopping trip to the local grocery, the students can use the school's cooking classroom to prepare the food. Each student needs to be responsible for preparing a portion of the meal, depending on his or her cooking ability, with supervision from the teacher. Knowing how to serve oneself appropriately at a potluck meal is a social skill that many teenagers benefit from learning.

FINAL ACTIVITY

At the end of the Career Caravan journey, the students can enjoy a final activity, such as a trip to a major spot of interest like an amusement park, a picnic, or a swimming party. This activity represents the company picnic or trip. The students can plan and budget for this culminating event, using the money remaining in their respective budgets for such expenses as transportation, admission fees, and food. Planning for this activity becomes an opportunity to work on a committee and share responsibilities. The activity itself can be described and organized as the culmination of all the program's experiences and should be an exciting finale to work well done.

VARIATIONS

Although the Career Caravan has traditionally been a summer program, the lessons and visits can be addressed during the school year. In a resource program for students who are visually impaired, the curriculum can be devoted to the Career Caravan classroom lessons one day a

---

GUIDELINES FOR PRESENTERS AT CAREER SEMINARS

The purpose of this workshop is to help visually impaired students become aware of the requirements for employment in organizations such as yours. Some suggestions for points to include in your presentation are as follows:

1. Explain the range of jobs available in your organization.

2. Provide specific information and examples about your standards for job applicants, including

   a. Appearance of an applicant

   b. Neatness and content of an application

   c. Conduct during an interview

   d. Sample questions and responses for an interview

   e. Content of a résumé

3. Describe the dress code for various jobs at your site.

4. Explain the work standards in the following areas for a variety of jobs:

   a. Deadlines

   b. Attendance

   c. Attitude

   d. Appearance

5. Describe a "good" employee.

6. Give examples of employees who have received positive attention (such as awards, bonuses, or promotions) and those who have received negative attention (such as being demoted, reprimanded, or fired).

If you have materials that you would like to share with the audience, please send them to us so we can transcribe them into braille or large print for our students. Please be comfortable using words like *see* or *look.* Our students use them appropriately. Although the subject of this workshop is serious, we hope you and your audience will relax and enjoy sharing and learning.

EXAMPLE 11. Guidelines for Speakers

week. The job-site visits can be field trips during the school year or on nonstudent instruction days such as teachers' conference days. These lessons and trips can involve fewer students or perhaps just one student at a time. Because of time constraints, they may focus directly on a student's interests and less on general community awareness as indicated by the student's level of familiarity. Adjustments in the lessons involving discussion would be driven by the needs of the participating students.

Many high schools now require a career exploration course for graduation. Working with the regular classroom teacher, the teacher of students with visual impairments can adapt and supplement lessons specifically needed by students with visual impairments. With some team teaching, the class can include Career Caravan trips and lessons. By spreading the lessons out over the school year, students can have more time to refine their skills.

In a year-round school program, the Career Caravan can also fit into a one- or two-week intersession twice a year. This program would not have the advantage of giving students time to polish their skills throughout the year. However, the theme approach would still be appropriate, but specific lessons, such as learning about résumés, would be grouped together rather than taught in a five-week program.

For a program based on an itinerant model, where the students attend the schools closest to their homes, the lessons and trips need to be individualized. A successful team approach may involve the teacher's presenting the classroom lessons and the O&M instructor's orchestrating the visits. The advantage of this method is that the lessons and visits can proceed over a longer period, giving the students ample opportunities to develop their skills. Also, the lessons are personalized to the students' needs and interests.

Another plan for teaching career-related skills is to offer intensive career workshops on Saturdays. Students can spend several Saturdays— for example, every other Saturday or four Saturdays in a row—working on the lessons; the group discussions would be included; and the job-site visits would be limited to businesses open on Saturdays or be part of a group field trip during the school day.

For the modified Career Caravan programs, the business meal, with its social and mathematical lessons, can occur any time during the school year. Either the teacher or the O&M instructor can provide opportunities for several students to get together and eat in a restaurant for lunch or dinner.

CONCLUSION

Upon completion of the Career Caravan program, the students with visual impairments will have moved toward a basic understanding of how to go about obtaining their first jobs. They will have learned techniques for researching future jobs and careers. They will also have received instruction in how to apply for and interview for their first jobs while in high school or after graduation. Their knowledge of jobs and work sites in their communities will help them compete with other potential job applicants, and they will also have a better understanding of the social requirements and etiquette of being with coworkers. The Career Caravan helps students with the necessary skills to succeed in finding their first jobs and in making meaningful career choices and can be a vital part of students' transition to the world of work.

APPENDIX
Sample Career Caravan Lessons

WRITING LESSON

Accurate writing is a basic requirement for getting a job. From an application to a résumé, written information about job seekers is what an employer notices about applicants first. Inaccuracies on these forms will usually eliminate an applicant from receiving an interview. Students who are visually impaired have additional concerns in writing. If they have poor handwriting, should they type the application or have someone else complete it? Lessons, drills, and practice all pay off when an application is acceptable to a prospective employer.

Activities

- The students need to be able to write their legal name in script on a 3-inch line—about the amount of space provided on both applications and checks. For students who are blind, individualized lessons should be developed in the strokes needed to write their name.
- In the beginning of the program, the students can prepare a personal information sheet containing the following information: full name, address, city, state, zip code, telephone number, birth date, birthplace, name of current and former schools, and social security number. This is the basic information needed for completing job applications.
- The students should complete a variety of job applications collected from fast-food restaurants and governmental and general business sources. Practice in completing these accurately and neatly is essential. By the end of the program, each student should have three perfectly completed applications to use as models for the real thing.

- Students who use braille, rather than print, need to select a responsible person to write for them—a teacher, relative, or friend. The person chosen must have neat handwriting and accurate spelling skills. It is the applicant who directs what is entered in each space on the application, not the writer, and it is the applicant who will be held responsible for what is written.
- Ask an employment agency representative to talk with the students about the application process.
- Have the students make copies of an application to practice on and then complete one to be submitted.

Critical Points to Cover

- Accuracy in completing an application cannot be overemphasized. The information contained in an application is that by which an employer first judges a candidate. An incomplete, messy, or inaccurate application is unattractive to most employers and usually means no interview and no job for the applicant.

Helpful Hints

- Enlarge the applications for easier reading and writing, then reduce them for submission.
- Some students may wish to use a closed-circuit television to complete applications.
- Most applications have questions that some applicants cannot answer, for example, military service for school-aged youths. The students need to be instructed to write "N/A" for not applicable. Leaving the space empty could indicate the applicant did not read the question.
- Printing is better than cursive writing on applications because it is easier to read, and it is usually required.

Evaluation Tips

- Have students submit three completed applications for review by the staff.
- Request that an employer or human resources person critique each student's application.

MATH LESSON

Although most students realize that adults work for pay, they may not understand what a salary is in terms of real money. Students with visual impairments seldom have opportunities to examine a paycheck to see the effect of taxes and other deductions. Knowing the terminology and doing basic computations regarding gross and net salaries increase the students' understanding of a paycheck.

Activities

- By calling a state or federal government employment agency, the students can learn what the current minimum wage is. On the basis of that information, they can calculate the weekly, monthly, and yearly salaries of an entry-level employee. Then they can find out about the range of income tax rates and which rate applies to most entry-level employees to determine an annual after-tax income for an entry-level employee.
- Using newspaper ads or telephone inquiries, the students can next estimate the monthly costs of food, rent, transportation, entertainment, clothing, and any other necessary expenses. They can then compare these costs to projected income based on the minimum wage or advertised salaries for jobs of interest and establish a monthly or weekly budget based on a realistically anticipated salary.
- Have the students ask employees in jobs similar to those in which they are interested about the rate and frequency of raises. Then, have them calculate the actual value of projected raises in terms of net income.

Critical Points to Cover

- Gross income (salary before tax and benefit deductions) and net income (take-home salary or money remaining after deductions) are different, and the students need to understand the difference. They also need to understand that one's net salary minus fixed expenses like rent, transportation, and food makes up one's discretionary or "disposable" income.

- Living independently has associated costs, and each student needs to anticipate those costs on the basis of an understanding of the cost of living.
- The students also need to understand that their cost of living is contingent on decisions they will make about where they live, with whom they live, what form of transportation they use, and what amenities they choose (cable television, private telephone services, and so forth).

Helpful Hints

- Many school math and practical economics books have exercises in budgeting that the students can use for practice.
- Help the students understand that as entry-level employees, they will generally start at a lower rate of pay than individuals with more experience or credentials.
- These computations can be performed as approximates, not as precise mathematical problems.
- Both federal and state government agencies publish free employment guides to help determine these figures.

Evaluation Tips

- Have the students analyze fictitious paychecks, noting gross and net income.
- Have the students submit a viable budget that is based on a predetermined wage.

ORAL SKILLS LESSON

The conversation of adolescents generally is not appropriate for a business environment. Knowing how to talk to fellow workers and supervisors is a skill that can be learned. In today's climate, workers also need to know how to make casual remarks and what jokes are appropriate. Career Caravan is an important place to practice acceptable conversation.

Activities

- Discuss how and where workers talk to each other and their supervisors. Compare the way workers talk with one another and how they talk to supervisors or employers. What are possible conversation topics regarding both work and personal interests? Have the students identify potential topics for conversations at work. They can use their knowledge of the company where they are or would like to be working, school, news, sports, hobbies, community events, and so forth as conversational topics.
- Have the students share examples of conversations and advice from adult workers, such as parents.
- Have the students collect jokes that are acceptable in the workplace. Discuss what is inappropriate and why. Discuss when and where jokes can be shared judiciously. Have the students and staff share appropriate jokes.
- Using various scenarios, practice talking to an employer about a job, a problem, or a request for time off.
- Have the students talk to the school principal about a problem or request.

Critical Points to Cover

- Voice tone and volume are important characteristics of expression in speaking on the job. One must speak loudly enough to be heard but not so loudly as to be annoying. Courtesy and pleasantness are essential in the workplace, whereas sarcasm and complaining have no place on the job.

Helpful Hints

- The staff needs to model proper on-the-job conversations and tone of voice when working with students.

Evaluation Tips

- Ask the principal to give the students feedback if they approach him or her with a problem or request.

- The teacher and staff need to provide the students with feedback on their oral communication skills: what is working for them and what is not.

SOCIAL SKILLS LESSON

Although getting a job is the first task of a job seeker, keeping the job is what really matters. Employers state that they can teach job skills, but employees must have well-developed work behaviors, such as promptness, honesty, and responsibility, to retain their jobs. As future employees, students with visual impairments need to demonstrate comprehension of these work-related behaviors or social skills. These traits need to be promoted and rewarded so the students understand the importance of positive work behaviors.

Activities

- As a group or with the teacher, the students can discuss the traits that make someone a good worker. The discussion needs to include such behaviors as attendance, promptness, honesty, and reliability, as well as the behaviors that could result in a worker's being fired. Additional discussions can cover such issues as, What are good reasons for being absent or late? How does one report an absence?
- The students can develop problem-solving scenarios to determine if an employee's behavior is honest, for example, taking home pencils from work or using the office computer to write personal letters. These sessions let the students openly share their values and learn what is appropriate in a work situation.
- Have the students calculate what time they would need to return to work from a 15-minute break or a 30- to 60-minute lunch.

Critical Points to Cover

- Work behaviors, such as punctuality, dependability, honesty, cooperation, following directions, and getting along with others, are essential in getting and keeping a job.
- Work behaviors are often referred to in recommendations both by personal references and by previous employers.

- Inappropriate work behaviors may mean the loss of a job and failure to find another.

Helpful Hints

- Give the students frequent opportunities to demonstrate good work habits.
- Have the students observe each other's work habits and rate them.

Evaluation Tips

- Have the students maintain their own Career Caravan attendance sheet, including latenesses, for self-evaluation.
- Have the students complete a checklist rating themselves on such characteristics as being on time, having good attendance, being honest, being responsible, and working well with others. (Areas that need improvement can also be noted, and a plan to improve them can be developed.)

TRANSPORTATION ISSUES LESSON

Traveling to a job site is a way of demonstrating independence. Carpooling is a popular way to get to work and one that can be used successfully by people who are visually impaired. However, students with visual impairments are frequently passive passengers when riding in automobiles. They tend to depend on and trust others to know how to get to places. To prepare for going to work with other employees, students need to be able to provide instructions to a driver on how to find their homes.

Activities

- The student, working with a teacher, O&M instructor, or parent or other family member, learns the major intersections and landmarks to get home from school. Then the student can direct others to his or her home using the school as a starting point.
- The student can call public transportation to learn the best bus route to school or to a possible work site from his or her home.
- The student can learn alternate routes to get home from family members, friends, or teachers.

Critical Points to Cover

- It is essential to know one's house number and street name, including the proper pronunciation and spelling.
- It is also important to know where one's house is in relation to an identifiable (northeast, northwest, southeast, or southwest) corner, left or right (north, south, east, or west) side of the street, and distinctive features (color, single or multifamily dwelling, single or multistory, brick, clapboard, adobe, and so forth).
- It is helpful to know the closest major intersection.
- It is helpful to know what notable landmarks indicate that the driver is getting close to one's home or neighborhood.

Helpful Hints

- Obtain copies of local bus and train maps and schedules to confirm what students have learned about the locations of their homes and the job sites they will visit.

Evaluation Tips

- Can the teacher or O&M instructor drive the student home following the student's directions?

Afterword

Students who are visually impaired often leave the safe havens of home and school to take on their roles in the workplace and community before they are properly prepared to do so. Preparation for becoming independent, capable, and successful adults needs to begin early in students' lives, and it needs to be formally outlined as a plan in their Individualized Education Programs (IEPs).

At the beginning of my professional career as a teacher of children with visual impairments in the late 1970s, formal written curricula identifying age-appropriate activities that supported career education programs for children with visual impairments did not exist. Furthermore, little attention was given to teaching career education in general to children in the regular classroom. Today, however, with the availability of written curricula and books such as *Skills for Success: A Career Education Handbook for Children and Adolescents with Visual Impairments*, families and teachers can interweave career education and lifelong learning into the unique skill areas that visually impaired children need for their future success.

Skills for Success is aimed at teaching visually impaired children—from the preschool years through the middle school years and beyond—life and career skills to enable them to maximize their independence, employability, and participation in the community. Caring adults can integrate the activities that are presented in *Skills for Success* in meaningful ways throughout a visually impaired child's day—whether the child is at home, at school, or in the community. In addition, families, teachers, and members of the community can help youngsters apply what they learn daily to new situations as they grow up, so they can become independent and have a broad range of choices in their lives—including unlimited opportunities to pursue the career paths they have chosen.

I wish that *Skills for Success* had been available as a resource years ago to help me and other service providers teach in a practical way the concepts and skills our visually impaired students needed within the regular school curriculum. The comprehensive sets of activities that are addressed in this handbook are practical and versatile enough to be used by families as well as service providers. The children and adolescents who complete them will be better prepared to take on their roles as competent and successful citizens.

The community-based foundations that financially supported the development and publication of *Skills for Success* recognized the significance of families, teachers, and members of the community sharing the responsibility of helping visually impaired children at an early age develop skills for future personal and job-related success. These organizations also understood that by helping to provide young visually impaired people with practical knowledge early in their education, they could assist these youngsters in learning to contribute to the community as they became adults and thereby help the community as a whole prosper. We at the American Foundation for the Blind (AFB) are grateful to the Texas community foundations that grasped the full meaning and impact of working as partners with families and teachers in offering career education activities to visually impaired children at an early age and throughout the school curriculum to help them become productive citizens.

Skills for Success salutes the importance of lifelong learning and the collaboration among teachers, families, and communities in teaching career-related skills to visually impaired youngsters to enable these youngsters to flourish.

Mary Ann Siller
National Program Associate in Education
Co-chair, National Education Program
American Foundation for the Blind

Resources

This resource guide is an attempt to supply readers with a representative listing of materials and organizations that are supportive of career education efforts for children and adolescents who are visually impaired. The resources are listed in categories: books and pamphlets, journal articles, videotapes, agencies and organizations, camps, and on-line resources. For information on vendors of aids and adaptive devices, readers are encouraged to attend consumer and professional conferences and to review the many catalogs available on request from specific companies and organizations. Materials are not listed in age-specific groupings, although all ages covered in this handbook—preschool, elementary, and middle school—are represented. In addition, listings include representative titles for the supplementary areas identified in *Skills for Success*: sources of materials for students who need additional modifications, for students living in urban and rural areas, for students from a variety of cultural backgrounds, and for families.

Many organizations of and for people who have visual impairments are provided with contact information. Also included are organizations that are not specifically focused on issues concerning visual impairment but that may be of related interest. Many of the listings are annotated. For each organization and company listed, the most current address and telephone number available at the time of publication are included. A more thorough coverage of agencies and organizations serving people with visual impairments may be found in the *AFB Directory of Services for Blind and Visually Impaired Persons in the United States and Canada* (New York: AFB Press, 1997). Similar information about U.S. agencies and organizations that serve people with disabilities is published in the U.S. Department of Education's *Directory of National Information Sources on Disabilities* (Washington, DC: U. S. Office of Special Education and Rehabilitative Services,1994).

BOOKS AND PAMPHLETS

Anderson, S., Boigon, S., & Davis, K. (1991). *The Oregon Project for Visually Impaired and Blind Preschool Children* (5th ed., rev.). Medford, OR: Jackson County Educational District.

An inventory of skills in eight developmental areas (cognitive, language, social, vision, compensatory, self-help, fine motor, and gross motor), this curriculum for early intervention can be used to identify instructional goals for and record the acquisition of skills by young children with visual impairments.

Source: Jackson County Education Service District, 101 North Grape Street, Medford, OR 97501

Attmore, M. (1990). *Career perspectives: Interviews with blind and visually impaired professionals.* New York: American Foundation for the Blind.

Available in large print and braille and on audiocassette, this publication highlights the career choices of college-educated workers who are visually impaired. Although inspirational in tone, the book focuses on such practical issues as transportation, education, and social aspects of the 22 professionals who are profiled.

Source: AFB Press, 11 Penn Plaza, Suite 300, New York, NY 10001

Barraga, N. C., & Erin, J. N. (1992). *Visual handicaps and learning* (3rd ed.). Austin, TX: PRO-ED.

This book provides insights into the educational impact of visual impairment on children from birth through high school. Case histories help the reader follow a comprehensive discussion of curriculum adaptations and specialized materials for students with visual impairments.

Source: PRO-ED, 8700 Shoal Creek, Austin, TX 78757-6897

Bingham, M., & Stryker, S. (1996). *Career choices: A guide for teens and young adults: Who am I? What do I want? How do I get it?* Santa Barbara, CA: Academic Innovations.

A nontraditional approach to career planning, *Career Choices* focuses on high school students determining who they are and what they want from life. Sections of the book can be incorporated into English, mathematics, and social studies classes. Unique activities and self-directed learning make the book an exciting way for teenagers to discover who they are and to empower them to make wise career choices.

Source: Academic Innovations, 3463 State Street, Suite 219, Santa Barbara, CA 93105

Blind Childrens Center (1993). *First steps: A handbook for teaching young children who are visually impaired.* Los Angeles: Blind Childrens Center.
The manual covers early childhood development, professionals on the child's instructional team, the anatomy of the eye, working with the family, behavioral management, speech and language development, sensorimotor integration, motor development, self-help skills, developing IEPs and IFSPs (Individualized Family Service Plans), and materials and devices for young children with visual impairments.
Source: Blind Childrens Center, 4120 Marathon Street, Los Angeles, CA 90029

Bolles, R. N. (1998). *What color is your parachute?* Berkeley, CA: Ten Speed Press. Considered a classic among job hunters and career changers, Bolles's book assists readers with setting goals, looking for a job, and interviewing successfully and provides tips for people who want to be satisfied with their career choices. It includes an extensive list of career planning resources. Revised annually.
Source: Ten Speed Press, P.O. Box 7123, Berkeley, CA 94707

Bredekamp, S., & Copple, C. (Eds.). (1996). *Developmentally appropriate practice in early childhood programs* (rev. ed.). Washington, DC: National Association for the Education of Young Children.
A comprehensive guide to the principles that form the foundation of developmentally appropriate practice, this book includes guidelines for classroom decision making. It focuses on the natural developmental sequences for children without disabilities and can serve as an important reference for parents and teachers.
Source: National Association for the Education of Young Children, 1509 16th Street, N.W., Washington, DC 20036-1426

Brolin, D. E. (1992). *Life-centered career education: The complete curriculum and assessment package.* Reston, VA: Council for Exceptional Children.
This package includes more than 1,100 lesson plans in the areas of living skills, personal social skills, and occupational skills. Although designed for students with disabilities in general, most of the lesson plans can be easily adapted for visually impaired students. Sequential lesson plans reflect the career development process of awareness, exploration, and preparation in each of these areas. For each lesson, objectives; activities for community, school, and home; and evaluation methods are detailed. Lesson plans also identify the career role that is being considered, such as family member, employee, citizen, or hobbyist. The comprehensive package also includes a competency

rating scale, two equivalent forms of a knowledge battery, and two equivalent forms of a performance battery. Although the package is extensive in size (it is contained in eight three-ring binders), these carefully designed curricula can be invaluable for teachers in a program committed to facilitating the development of career education, especially for students who will be able to participate in the program over a period of several years.
Source: CEC Publications, P.O. Box 79026, Baltimore, MD 21279-0026

Chandler, P. (1992). *A place for me: Including children with special needs in early care and education settings.* Washington, DC: National Association for the Education of Young Children.
A Place for Me gives teachers and caregivers practical help for integrating children with disabilities into early childhood settings.
Source: National Association for the Education of Young Children, 1509 16th Street, N.W., Washington, DC 20036-1426

Chen, D., & Dote-Kwan, J. (1995). *Starting points: Instructional practices for young children whose multiple disabilities include visual impairment.* Los Angeles: Blind Childrens Center.
This manual provides a conceptual framework and specific strategies for developing a meaningful program for young children with visual impairments and other disabilities. Chapter topics include identifying the characteristics and learning needs of young children whose multiple disabilities include visual impairment, guiding principles for instruction and program development, steps for getting started, instructional strategies, developing communication, teaching daily living skills, positive behavioral support, orientation and mobility, occupational therapy, roles of itinerant teachers, and a family's perspective.
Source: Blind Childrens Center, 4120 Marathon Street, Los Angeles, CA 90029

The Childhood of Famous Americans series. Aladdin Paperbacks. New York: Simon & Schuster.
This collection of biographies of famous Americans is written for juvenile readers (ages 8–12) and is available from the publisher in 14-point type, double spaced. It is also available from the National Library Service in braille or on audiocassette. Biographies in the series include Susan B. Anthony, Crispus Attucks, Clara Barton, Daniel Boone, Buffalo Bill, Davy Crockett, Thomas A. Edison, Albert Einstein, Henry Ford, Benjamin Franklin, Lou Gehrig, Harry Houdini, Thomas Jefferson, Helen Keller, John F. Kennedy, Martin Luther King, Jr., Robert E. Lee, Abraham Lincoln, Annie Oakley, Molly Pitcher, Paul Revere, Knute Rockne, Eleanor Roosevelt, Teddy Roosevelt,

Betsy Ross, Babe Ruth, Sacagawea, Jim Thorpe, Mark Twain, George Washington, Martha Washington, and Wilbur and Orville Wright.
Source: Simon & Schuster, 1230 Avenue of the Americas, New York, NY 10020

Cooper, J. (1992). *For parents: How to develop your child's self esteem.* White Bear Lake, MN: J. Cooper Associates.
This book is filled with activities and ideas to help children feel good about themselves.
Source: J. Cooper Associates, 7230 101st Street North, White Bear Lake, MN 55110-1322

Cooper, J., & Harvatin, J. (1992). *Worry free parenting.* White Bear Lake, MN: J. Cooper Associates.
A publication that contains useful information about child development to help parents understand natural aspects of a child's emotional development, *Worry Free Parenting* includes a section on adolescence.
Source: J. Cooper Associates, 7230 101st Street North, White Bear Lake, MN 55110-1322

Corn, A., Cowan, C., & Moses, E. (1988). *You seem like a regular kid to me.* New York: American Foundation for the Blind.
This pamphlet is designed to build the public's understanding of children who are visually impaired.
Source: AFB Press, 11 Penn Plaza, Suite 300, New York, NY 10001

Crary, E. (1984). *Kids can cooperate: A practical guide to teaching problem solving.* Seattle, WA: Parenting Press.
This practical book by a parent educator focuses on teaching children how to solve problems and cooperate. Although it is written for parents, teachers and counselors will also welcome the straightforward approaches the author suggests.
Source: Parenting Press, P.O. Box 75267, Seattle, WA 98125

Crary, E. (1990). *Pick up your socks . . . and other skills growing children need! A practical guide to raising responsible children.* Seattle, WA: Parenting Press.
The author details techniques for parents and teachers to help young children learn to assume responsibility; it contains numerous practical exercises for home and school.
Source: Parenting Press, Inc., P.O. Box 75267, Seattle, WA 98125

Crystal, J., & Bolles, R. (1974). *Where do I go from here with my life?* Berkeley, CA: Ten Speed Press.

A classic, easy-to-read reference manual for people who are interested in self-directed career and life planning.
Source: Ten Speed Press, P.O. Box 7123, Berkeley, CA 94707

Derman-Sparks, L., & ABC Task Force. (1989). *Anti-bias curriculum tools for empowering young children.* Washington, DC: National Association for the Education of Young Children.
A readable book, full of suggestions to help staff and children learn to respect individual differences.
Source: National Association for the Education of Young Children, 1509 16th Street, N.W., Washington, DC 20036-1426

Dobson-Burk, B., & Hill, E. (1989). *An orientation and mobility primer for families and young children.* New York: American Foundation for the Blind.
This book provides information on the development of orientation and mobility skills, including sensory training, concept development, and motor development, and includes a glossary of key terms.
Source: AFB Press, 11 Penn Plaza, New York, NY 10001

Downing, J. E. (1996). *Including students with severe and multiple disabilities in typical classrooms: Practical strategies for teachers.* Baltimore: Paul H. Brookes.
The author has written a practical resource to help teachers who have students in their classrooms with one or more sensory impairments in addition to cognitive and physical disabilities. The text includes suggestions for modifying the general educational curriculum and adapting instructional techniques. It is appropriate for those working with students in preschool, elementary, or secondary settings.
Source: Paul H. Brookes, Box 10624, Baltimore, MD 21285-0624

Everson, J. (1995). *Supporting young adults who are deaf-blind in their communities: A transition planning guide for service providers, families, and friends.* Baltimore: Paul H. Brookes.
A guide for the future-planning process, with an emphasis on living and occupational options for individuals who are deaf-blind, this publication incorporates approaches that address the diversity of the deaf-blind population and provides information on medical and transition services, postsecondary education, housing and work options, and planning processes. A strong transdisciplinary team model is emphasized in planning with and for individuals who will require ongoing adaptations because of sensory impairments.
Source: Paul H. Brookes, Box 10624, Baltimore, MD 21285-0624

Farr, J. M., & Christophersen, S. (1991). *Your career: Thinking about jobs and careers.* Indianapolis: JIST Works.

This book and others published by JIST Works are geared toward teenagers' interests and reading levels. It is a useful resource for working with adolescents.
Source: JIST Works, 720 North Park Avenue, Indianapolis, IN 46202-3490

Ferrell, K. A. (1985). *Reach out and teach: Meeting the training needs of parents of visually and multiply handicapped young children.* New York: American Foundation for the Blind.
This two-volume set consists of a parents' handbook that gives families the background and step-by-step training techniques they need to facilitate motor and cognitive development and a workbook for recording the child's developmental progress.
Source: AFB Press, 11 Penn Plaza, New York, NY 10001

Frey, W. D., Jakwerth, P., Lynch, L., & Purcell, R. (1992). *Addressing unique educational needs of individuals with disabilities: An outcome based approach.* Lansing, MI: Disability Research Systems.
These unique materials are particularly valuable in that they present examples of educational expectations for students with visual impairments when exiting kindergarten and the 2nd, 5th, 8th, and 12th grades. Expected outcomes are identified in four domains: academics, mathematics and English-language effectiveness, personal management and daily living, and life-role orientation. One of the two outcomes included in this last domain is "Proceed toward the fulfillment of realistic career, independent living, and other life pursuits." Interrelationships among adult-role expectations, unique educational needs, and the 10 expected outcomes are clearly described. Teachers can use the lists of exiting grade-level competencies or "selected educational considerations" to identify areas in which instruction may be appropriate for students. Also included in this volume are observation-assessment instruments to rate students' functioning with regard to the selected outcomes. Different assessment protocols are included for students in grades 1–4, 5–7, 8–10, and 11–12.
Source: Disability Research Systems, 2500 Kerry Street, Suite 208, Lansing, MI 48912

Glenn, H. S., & Nelson, J. (1989). *Raising self-reliant children in a self-indulgent world: Seven building blocks for developing capable young people.* Rocklin, CA: Prima Publishing & Communications.
Written for parents and teachers, this book discusses seven building blocks, including the concepts of capabilities, interpersonal skills, systemic skills, and personal control.
Source: Prima Publishing, 3875 Atherson Road, Rocklin, CA 95765

Guelda, J. O., & Robinson, K. B. (1992). *Hands on: Functional activities for visually impaired preschoolers.* Louisville, KY: American Printing House for the Blind.

This publication provides activities for developing sorting and classification skills. *Source:* American Printing House for the Blind, P.O. Box 6085, Louisville, KY 40206-0085

Harris, J. M. (1989). *You and your child's self-esteem: Building for the future.* New York: Carroll & Graff.
This book offers advice to parents about the role that self-esteem plays in children's development and fostering the ability to take the initiative. It includes discussions of discipline, creativity, and self-esteem in children with disabilities. *Source:* Carroll & Graff Publishers, 260 Fifth Avenue, New York, NY 10001

Huebner, K. M., Prickett, J. G., Welch, T. R., & Joffee, E. (1995). *Hand in hand: Essentials of communication and orientation and mobility to your students who are deaf-blind.* New York: AFB Press.
This comprehensive manual contains essential information about the needs and capabilities of individuals who are deaf-blind, with emphases on communication and orientation and mobility (O&M). It provides key concepts, main instructional strategies, and learning activities for encouraging the development of communication and O&M skills in students who are deaf-blind, from toddlers to adolescents. The final module of the O&M unit addresses transition, with extensive discussion on the O&M skills needed for adult living. Topics addressed in this chapter include communicating with the public, making decisions about when assistance is needed, travel at the work site, and problem solving. *Source:* AFB Press, 11 Penn Plaza, New York, NY 10001

Johnson, D. W., & Johnson, F. P. (1994). *Joining together.* Needham Heights, MA: Allyn & Bacon.
This reference includes activities for building group interaction skills. *Source:* Allyn & Bacon, 160 Gould Street, Needham Heights, MA 02194

Kay, J. L., & Locke, L. (1997). *Career education teacher handbook.* Austin: Texas School for the Blind and Visually Impaired.
Guidelines for planning students' work experiences are presented in this handbook, which discusses vocational assessments, and outlines a community-based vocational education approach to employment for students with visual impairments. *Source:* Texas School for the Blind and Visually Impaired, 1100 West 45th Street, Austin, TX 78756

Kendrick, D. (1993). *Jobs to be proud of: Profiles of workers who are blind or visually impaired.* New York: AFB Press.

A companion to *Career perspectives: Interviews with blind and visually impaired professionals,* this book focuses on jobs that do not require a college degree. The many jobs discussed in the book are helpful to those who are unfamiliar with career options for people with visual impairments who are not interested in or able to attend college.
Source: AFB Press, 11 Penn Plaza, New York, NY 10001

Kendrick, D. (1998). *Teachers who are blind or visually impaired.* Jobs That Matter series. New York: AFB Press.
The author introduces readers to 18 individuals who have successfully fulfilled their dreams of teaching.
Sources: AFB Press, 11 Penn Plaza, New York, NY 10001

Lansky, Vicki. (1985). *Practical parenting tips for the school-age years.* New York: Bantam Books.
Although this book was not written specifically for parents of children with visual impairments, it is a sensible guide that helps parents let go of their children and assist them in developing self-esteem through getting out on their own, learning to play, and assuming responsibility for themselves and others. It includes lots of fun ideas and source information.
Source: Bantam Books, 1540 Broadway, New York, NY 10036

Levack, N., Hauser, S., Newton, L., & Stephenson, P. (1996). *Basic skills for community living: A curriculum for students with visual impairments and multiple disabilities.* Austin: Texas School for the Blind and Visually Impaired.
A description of the curriculum developed at Texas School for the Blind and Visually Impaired for students with multiple disabilities who also have visual impairments, this book addresses a wide variety of topics, many of which relate to transition issues, including community-based instruction, transition plans, domestic activities, social skills, and career education. The curriculum includes specific objectives and forms for assessment and instructional documentation.
Source: Texas School for the Blind and Visually Impaired, 1100 West 45th Street, Austin, TX 78756

Linder, T. W. (1993). *Transdisciplinary play-based intervention.* Baltimore: Paul H. Brookes.
The author provides a curricular framework for developing interventions that infuse discipline-specific learning objectives for preschoolers with disabilities into play situations.
Source: Paul H. Brookes, Box 10624, Baltimore, MD 21285-0624

Loumiet, R., & Levack, N. (1993). *Independent living: A curriculum with adaptations for students with visual impairments: Vol. 1. Social competence* (2nd ed.). Austin: Texas School for the Blind and Visually Impaired.

This curriculum is designed for use with students aged 5 to 21 who are visually impaired. It is divided into 11 goals that address the following aspects of independent living: interaction, self-concept, emotions, nonverbal communication, values clarification, personal and social aspects of sexuality, physical aspects of sexuality, courteous behavior, problem solving and decision making, scholastic success, and personal and civic responsibility. For each goal, a brief explanation of its importance is provided, general teaching considerations are described, and associated skills are identified. Skills are sequenced by age groups, on the basis of developmental norms of typical children. For each skill, examples of competence are described and adaptations of methods and materials are suggested.

This curriculum can be used as a source of critical skills for educational planning, ideas for activities, and suggestions for adapted instructional techniques. Included in the appendixes are sample lesson plans, a list of social skills curricula, a compilation of titles of books for students related to social competence (by age level), lists of appropriate audio and audiovisual materials, resource lists, and evaluation forms that can be used for assessment or to track students' acquisition of competence in the identified skill areas.
Source: Texas School for the Blind and Visually Impaired, 1100 West 45th Street, Austin, TX 78756

Loumiet, R., & Levack, N. (1993). *Independent living: A curriculum with adaptations for students with visual impairments: Vol. 2. Self-care and maintenance* (2nd ed.). Austin: Texas School for the Blind and Visually Impaired.

This curriculum is designed for use with students aged 5 to 21 who are visually impaired. It is divided into 14 goals that address the following aspects of self-care: dressing, clothing management, hygiene, toileting and feminine hygiene, eating, eating in different settings, food management, housekeeping, housing, telephone, time, money, health and safety, and self-advocacy. For each goal, a brief explanation of its importance is provided, general teaching considerations are described, and associated skills are identified. Skills are sequenced by age groups, on the basis of developmental norms of typical children. For each skill, examples of competence are described and adaptations of methods and materials suggested.

This curriculum can be used as a source of critical skills for educational planning, ideas of activities, and suggestions for adapted instructional techniques. Included in the appendixes are sample lesson plans, lists of appropriate audio and audiovisual materials, resource lists, and evaluation forms that

can be used for assessment or to track students' acquisition of competence in the identified skill areas.
Source: Texas School for the Blind and Visually Impaired, 1100 West 45th Street, Austin, TX 78756

Loumiet, R., & Levack, N. (1993). *Independent living: A curriculum with adaptations for students with visual impairments: Vol. 3. Play and leisure* (2nd ed.). Austin: Texas School for the Blind and Visually Impaired.
Designed for visually impaired students ages 5 to 21, this curriculum is geared toward helping those who can live independently or with minimal assistance when they become adults. The 9 content areas covered in the volume include the management of leisure time; solitary play; social play; physical games and sports; pets and nature; music and dance; arts and crafts; reading, writing, speaking, and drama; and science and technology.
Source: Texas School for the Blind and Visually Impaired, 1100 West 45th Street, Austin, TX 78756

Lynch, E. W., & Hanson, M. J. (1992). *Developing cross-cultural competence: A guide for working with young children and their families* (2nd ed.). Baltimore: Paul H. Brookes.
This publication provides information and advice for professionals who work with children and families from diverse cultural and linguistic backgrounds. It discusses the influence of culture on people's values, challenges inherent in adapting to a different culture, and strategies for developing effective relationships built on mutual respect. Specific cultural groups discussed include Anglo-European, Native American, African American, Latino, Asian, Filipino, Native Hawaiian and Samoan, and Middle Eastern.
Source: Paul H. Brookes, Box 10624, Baltimore, MD 21285-0624.

MacCuspie, P. A. (1996). *Promoting acceptance of children with disabilities: From tolerance to inclusion.* Halifax, NS: Atlantic Provinces Special Education Authority.
The social impact of academic integration on children with visual impairments is examined in this book. The author shares details from a qualitative research project that explored the social integration of 5 elementary students. Specific suggestions are recommended to enhance the social integration of visually impaired students.
Source: Atlantic Provinces Special Education Authority, 5940 South Street, Halifax, Nova Scotia, Canada B3H1S6

Manolson, A. (1984). *It takes two to talk.* Toronto, Ontario, Canada: Hanen Early Language Resource Centre.

This handbook presents strategies for supporting the early communication of children with disabilities through turn taking; instructional prompts; and creating conversations within a variety of music, play, and art activities.
Source: Hanen Early Language Resource Centre, 40 Roxborough Street West, Toronto, Ontario M5R 1T8, Canada.

McCallum, B. J., & Sacks, S. Z. (1993). *Social skills curriculum for children with visual impairments.* Santa Clara, CA: Santa Clara County Schools.
The authors of this curriculum provide teachers, parents, and others with a variety of strategies to facilitate the development of the social skills of students who are visually impaired. They present some introductory material on the theoretical basis for the development of social skills and include an assessment instrument, the Social Skills Assessment Tool for Children with Visual Impairments (SSAT-VI). This rating scale provides a framework for evaluating students' basic social behaviors, interpersonal relationships, and cognitive social behaviors. These same three areas form the categories for which the three age-appropriate curricula (preschool, elementary, and secondary) are presented. Each curriculum contains a series of objectives, written with specific measurable criteria, and suggested strategies for achieving skill acquisition with the particular age group of interest. The authors, teachers of visually impaired students from northern California, keep their teaching ideas relatively simple, assuming that innovative teachers will individualize instruction to meet their students' needs.
Source: B. J. McCallum, 1296 Mariposa Avenue, San Jose, CA 95126

McCallum, B. J., & Sacks, S. Z. (1994). *Personal management skills for children with visual impairments.* Santa Clara, CA: Santa Clara County Schools.
This curriculum provides teachers, parents, and others with a variety of strategies to facilitate the development of the personal management skills of students with visual impairments. The authors, teachers of students with visual impairments in northern California, explain that through this curriculum, teachers can implement a "fluid, flexible, and effective program of empowerment" for these students. A simple assessment instrument is included. This rating scale provides a framework for evaluating students' personal care, food, organizational, housekeeping, time and money management, and self-advocacy and decision-making skills. These six areas form the categories for which the three age-appropriate curricula (preschool, elementary, and secondary) are presented. Each curriculum contains a series of general objectives, written without measurable criteria, and suggested strategies for achieving skill acquisition with the particular age group of interest. The teaching ideas are fairly general; teachers will need to review this curriculum

frequently to make certain that their students are being given opportunities to master the many important skills.
Source: B. J. McCallum, 1296 Mariposa Avenue, San Jose, CA 95126

McLoughlin, C., Garner, J., & Callahan, M. (1987). *Getting employed, staying employed.* Baltimore: Paul H. Brookes.
The authors provide practical suggestions for locating jobs and describe appropriate supports in the workplace for people with severe disabilities. The manual emphasizes employment training in community settings.
Source: Paul H. Brookes, Box 10624, Baltimore, MD 21285-0624.

Morgan, E. (1994). *Resources for family centered interventions for infants, toddlers, and preschoolers who are visually impaired.* VIISA Project, Vols. 1 and 2. (2nd ed.). Logan, UT: HOPE, Inc.
These manuals provide strategies for collaborating with families of young children who are visually impaired in promoting their children's development. Topics include working with families and support services, implementing an early intervention program, facilitating transitioning and educational placement, and working with preschoolers with visual impairments in a center-based setting. Specific curriculum units include developing communication and language; learning about social-emotional skills, child care, self-care, gross motor skills, and orientation and mobility; learning through the senses (vision, hearing, and touch); getting ready for braille; and improving cognitive skills.
Source: HOPE, Inc., 809 North 800 East, Logan, UT 84321

O'Neil, M. (1972). *Hailstones and halibut bones.* New York: Doubleday.
This entertaining children's book of poetry about colors is particularly meaningful for students who are blind or severely visually impaired.
Source: Bantam Doubleday, 1540 Broadway, New York, NY 10036

Pogrund, R. L., Fazzi, D. L., & Lambert, J. S. (1992). *Early focus: Working with young blind and visually impaired children and their families.* New York: American Foundation for the Blind.
Chapters of this book address working with families; understanding the medical and functional implications of visual impairment; developing concepts and language; developing social, play and self-help skills; developing strategies for behavioral management, orientation and mobility, and service delivery models; professional roles; and advocacy.
Source: AFB Press, 11 Penn Plaza, New York, NY 10001

Sacks, S. Z., Kekelis. L. S., & Gaylord-Ross, R. J. (Eds.). (1992). *The development of social skills by blind and visually impaired students: Exploratory studies and strategies.* New York: American Foundation for the Blind.
This book is designed to help teachers increase the likelihood that children who are visually impaired will integrate successfully in social and emotional relationships with sighted children. Theories of social development, research results, and strategies for teachers are outlined and discussed in a practical manner.
Source: AFB Press, 11 Penn Plaza, New York, NY 10001

Sacks, S. Z., & Silberman, R. K. (Eds.). (1998). *Educating students who have visual impairments with other disabilities.* Baltimore: Paul H. Brookes.
This publication helps prepare teachers to work with visually impaired students with other disabilities, including deaf-blindness, learning disabilities, orthopedic disabilities or health impairments, neurological disabilities, and emotional and behavioral problems.
Source: Paul H. Brookes, Box 10624, Baltimore, MD 21285-0624

Secretary's Commission on Achieving Necessary Skills. (1992). *Learning a living: A blueprint for high performance.* Washington, DC: U.S. Department of Labor.
This publication provides information on the skills and competencies students need to learn while in school to become effective employees.
Source: Superintendent of Documents, P. O. Box 371954, Pittsburgh, PA 15250-7954

Secretary's Commission on Achieving Necessary Skills. (1991). *What work requires of schools: A SCANS report for America 2000.* Washington, DC: U.S. Department of Labor.
This document discusses the skills and competencies that students need to learn while in school to become successful workers.
Source: Superintendent of Documents, P.O. Box 371954, Pittsburgh, PA 15250-7954

SKI★HI Institute (1993). *A resource manual for understanding and interacting with infants, toddlers, and preschool age children with deaf-blindness.* Logan, UT: HOPE, Inc.
This manual provides practical information on a variety of intervention topics and learning activities. Specific areas include auditory training, the use of functional vision, communication, daily care, motor skills, orientation and mobility, and working with medically fragile children.
Source: HOPE, Inc., 809 North 800 East, Logan, UT 84321

Smith, M., & Levack, N. (1996). *Teaching students with visual and multiple impairments: A resource guide.* Austin: Texas School for the Blind and Visually Impaired.

The authors of this resource guide address topics that are important to teachers of visually impaired students who work on a transdisciplinary team serving students with multiple and visual impairments. They provide in-depth information on the assessment of students with severe disabilities, including a chapter on transition planning and resources that are important for adults with severe disabilities. Although many of the resources are specific to Texas, general information about vocational opportunities, living arrangements, and guardianship provide a starting point for families and professionals who are seeking appropriate adult services.
Source: Texas School for the Blind and Visually Impaired, 1100 West 45th Street, Austin, TX 78756

Steveley, J., Houghton, J., Goehl, K., & Bailey, B. (1996). *Planning today, creating tomorrow: Guide to transition.* Terre Haute: Indiana Deaf-Blind Services Project.
This publication furnishes information about the transition planning process for those who work with people who are deaf-blind, as well as terminology and resources.
Source: Indiana Deaf-Blind Services Project, Lumberg Center School of Education, Room 502, Indiana State University, Terre Haute, IN 47809

Swallow, R. M., & Huebner, K. M. (Eds.). (1987). *How to thrive, not just survive: A guide to developing independent life skills for blind and visually impaired children and youths.* New York: American Foundation for the Blind.
This is a short, simple-to-read, straightforward book that can be shared with parents, paraprofessionals, and general education teachers of students with visual impairments. It presents guidelines and strategies for teaching students to develop skills needed for independence, travel, and recreation. Its particular value is its concise presentation of the many instructional needs of students with visual impairments. Because it is concise, readers begin to appreciate the importance of beginning instruction in skills early, of integrating the use of skills in many environments, and of having high expectations for the performance of these students.
Source: AFB Press, 11 Penn Plaza, New York, NY 10001

Trujillo, T., Tavarez, T., Rubald, T., & Roach, W. (Eds.). (1966). *I'm moving on: This book will help me as I move on into my community.* Santa Fe: New Mexico Deaf/Blind Services.
This book is intended to provide a means of personal record keeping for individuals who are deaf-blind and are entering community life. It provides for documentation of communication forms, medical and health needs, and preferences for recreational activities and personal possessions. It can be used

as a means of informing caregivers about the needs and interests of people with severe disabilities.
Source: New Mexico Deaf/Blind Services, 1060 Cerillos Road, Santa Fe, NM 87503.

Tuttle, D. W., & Tuttle, N. R. (1996). *Self-esteem and adjusting to blindness: The process of responding to life's demands* (2nd ed.). Springfield, IL: Charles C Thomas. The authors provide readers with insights into the development of self-esteem in children, youths, and adults who are blind. They explore how blind individual's attitude toward blindness and the attitudes of others influence the individual's self-esteem and feelings about himself or herself. The book is liberally illustrated with statements from the writings of and about people who are blind.
Source: Charles C Thomas, Publishers, 2600 South First Street, Springfield, IL 62794-9265

Watkins, S. (Ed.). (1989). *The INSITE model: Home intervention for infant, toddler, and preschool aged multihandicapped sensory impaired children.* Logan, UT: HOPE, Inc.
These two volumes of a home-based curriculum discuss identifying the child with multiple disabilities or sensory impairments and identifying family needs; providing family support; and planning, delivering, and evaluating programs. Specific curriculum units include home-based lessons in communication, hearing, vision, cognition, and motor areas.
Source: HOPE, Inc., 809 North 800 East, Logan, UT 84321

Wehman, P. (1992). *Life beyond the classroom: Transition strategies for young people with disabilities.* Baltimore: Paul Brookes.
The author presents models for transition planning for individuals with various disabilities and follows the transition process from job development through placement. This book is intended for individuals who are part of the transition planning team.
Source: Paul H. Brookes, Box 10624, Baltimore, MD 21285-0624

Wolffe, K. E. (1997). *Career counseling for people with disabilities: A practical guide to finding employment.* Austin, TX: PRO-ED.
The author describes career counseling techniques for practitioners who work with youths and adults with disabilities. Specific content areas detailed include self-awareness, vocational selection, job-seeking skills, job-maintenance skills, and job-search skills. Techniques for counseling people of all ability levels are discussed.
Source: PRO-ED, 8700 Shoal Creek, Austin, TX 78757-6897

Wolffe, K., & Johnson, D. (1997). *The transition tote system: Navigating the rapids of life.* Louisville, KY: American Printing House for the Blind.

These unique materials include a tote (a briefcase and organizer with a padded center section for holding a laptop computer or four-track audiotape recorder, numerous pockets for other adaptive tools and folders, a clipboard, and a braille and large-print calendar) and two manuals—a students' manual (available in print or braille and on audiocassette), with self-directed career education activities for high school students and an informational supplement, and a facilitator's guide for directing students who are less able or motivated in those same career education activities.

Source: American Printing House for the Blind, P.O. Box 6085, Louisville, KY 40206-0085

Yolen, J. H. (1977). *The seeing stick.* New York: Thomas Y. Crowell Junior Books.

The Seeing Stick is a Chinese folk tale: The princess is sad because she is blind, until she learns to "see with her fingers."

Source: HarperCollins Publishers, 10 East 53rd Street, New York, NY 10022

JOURNAL ARTICLES

Bagley, M. (1985). Service providers' assessment of career development needs of blind and visually impaired students and rehabilitation clients and the resources available to meet those needs. *Journal of Visual Impairment & Blindness, 79*(10), 434–443.

Being blind and being a woman. (1983). [Special issue]. *Journal of Visual Impairment & Blindness, 77*(6).

Bush-LaFrance, B. A. C. (1988). Unseen expectations of blind youth: Educational and occupational ideas. *Journal of Visual Impairment & Blindness, 82*(4), 132–136.

Career development. (1985). [Special issue]. *Journal of Visual Impairment & Blindness, 79*(10).

Clayton, I. (1983). Career preparation and the visually handicapped student. *Education of the Visually Handicapped, 14*(4), 115–120.

Corn, A. L., & Bishop, V. E. (1985). Occupational interests of visually handicapped secondary students. *Journal of Visual Impairment & Blindness, 79*(10), 475–478.

Corn, A. L., Muscella, D. B., Cannon, G. B., & Shepler, R. C. (1985). Perceived barriers to employment for visually impaired women: A preliminary study. *Journal of Visual Impairment & Blindness, 79*(10), 458–461.

Corn, A. L., & Sacks, S. Z. (Eds.). (1997). Adolescence and early adulthood [Special issue]. *Journal of Visual Impairment & Blindness, 91*(3).

Craig, C. J. (1996). Family support of the emergent literacy of children with visual impairments. *Journal of Visual Impairment & Blindness, 90*(3), 194–200.

DeLaGarza, D. V., & Erin, J. N. (1993). Employment status and quality of life of graduates of a state residential school. *Journal of Visual Impairment & Blindness, 87*(6), 229–233.

DeMario, N. (1992). Skills needed for successful employment: A review of the literature, *RE:view, 24*(3), 115–125.

Dixon, J. M. (1983). Attitudinal barriers and strategies for overcoming them. *Journal of Visual Impairment & Blindness, 77*(6), 290–292.

Etheridge, E. G. (1978). An approach to career development for visually impaired students on the elementary level. *Education of the Visually Handicapped, 10*(3), 87–91.

Ferris, A. (1991). Easing a blind student's transition to employment. *RE:view, 23*(2), 85–90.

Fiorito, E. (1983). Choices and chances in the 80s. *Journal of Visual Impairment & Blindness, 9*(2), 286–287.

Forest, M., & Lusthaus, E. (1990). Everyone belongs with the MAPS Action Planning System. *Teaching Exceptional Children, 22*(2), 32–35.

Geruschat, D. R. (1993). Employment and residential status of graduates from a residential school. *Journal of Visual Impairment & Blindness, 87*(6), 234–237.

Gossett, L. P. (1983). Blind ambitions. *Education of the Visually Handicapped, 14*(4), 140–141.

Graves, W. H. (1983). Career development theory applied to the delivery of services to blind and visually impaired persons. *Yearbook of the Association for Education and Rehabilitation of the Blind,* 2–17.

Graves, W., & Lyon, S. (1985). Career development: Linking education and careers of blind and visually impaired ninth graders. *Journal of Visual Impairment & Blindness, 79*(10), 444–449.

Hagemoser, S. D. (1996). The relationship of personality traits to the employment status of persons who are blind. *Journal of Visual Impairment & Blindness, 90*(2), 134–144.

Hale, L. D., Smith, D. H., & Gandy, M. J. (1991). Vocational rehabilitation services for blind persons: The experience of sibling twins. *Journal of Visual Impairment & Blindness, 85*(8), 341–342.

Hatlen, P. (1996). The core curriculum for blind and visually impaired students, including those with additional disabilities. *RE:view, 28*(1), 25–32.

Holmes, D. L., Wanner, C. R., & Bishel, M. A. (1983). Career education in an educational program for visually impaired. *Education of the Visually Handicapped, 14*(4), 120–125.

Howze, Y. S. (1983). The use of social skills training to improve interview skills of visually impaired young adults: A pilot study. *Journal of Visual Impairment & Blindness, 81*(6), 251–255.

Huvelle, N. F., Budoff, M., & Arnholz, D. (1984). To tell or not to tell: Disability disclosure and the job interview. *Journal of Visual Impairment & Blindness, 78*(6), 241–244.

Jeppson, D. L., & Hammer, F. (1992). Summer employment for youth. *RE:view, 24*(1), 29–32.

Kirkman, R. E. (1983). Career awareness and the visually impaired student. *Education of the Visually Handicapped, 14*(4), 105–113.

Lamb, G. (1996). Beginning braille: A whole language–based strategy. *Journal of Visual Impairment & Blindness, 90*(3), 184–189.

Liebman, J. (1990). Supported employment: Does it really work? *RE:view, 22*(2), 84–89.

Mather, J. (1994). Computers, automation, and the employment of persons who are blind or visually impaired. *Journal of Visual Impairment & Blindness, 88*(6), 544–549.

Miller, G. (1991). The challenge of upward mobility. *Journal of Visual Impairment & Blindness, 85*(8), 332–335.

Miller, G. (1993). Expanding vocational options. *RE:view, 25*(1), 27–31.

Miller, G., & Rossi, P. (1988). Placement of visually impaired persons: A survey of current practices. *Journal of Visual Impairment & Blindness, 82*(8), 318–324.

Peterson, M. (1985). Vocation evaluation of blind and visually impaired persons for technical, professional, and managerial positions. *Journal of Visual Impairment & Blindness, 79*(10), 478–480.

Pfanstiehl, M. R. (1983). Role models for high-achieving visually impaired women. *Journal of Visual Impairment & Blindness, 77*(6), 259–261.

Roberts, A. H. (1992). Looking at vocational placement for the blind: A personal perspective. *RE:view, 23*(4), 177.

Sacks, S. Z., & Pruett, K. M. (1992). Summer transition training project for professionals who work with adolescents and young adults. *Journal of Visual Impairment & Blindness, 86*(4), 211–214.

Sacks, S. Z., & Wolffe, K. (1992). The importance of social skills in the transition process for students with visual impairments. *Journal of Vocational Rehabilitation, 2*(1), 46–55.

Spungin, S. J. (1983). Career development: The educational context. *Yearbook of the Association for Education and Rehabilitation of the Blind and Visually Impaired,* 18–29.

Stith, A. (1996). Résumés that get results. *CAREERS & the disABLED,* 38–41.

Stratton, J. M., & Wright, S. (1991). On the way to literacy: Early experiences for visually impaired children. *RE:view, 23*(2), 55–61.

Storey, K., Sacks, S. Z., & Olmstead, J. (1985). Community-referenced instruction in a technological work setting: A vocational education option for visually handicapped students. *Journal of Visual Impairment & Blindness, 79*(10), 481–486.

Temelini, D., & Fesko, S. (1997, January). Shared responsibility: Job search practices from the consumer and state vocational rehabilitation perspective. *Research Practice.* Boston: Institute for Community Inclusion, 1–2.

Whitman, D. (1990). Paid summer work experience for rural blind youth. *Journal of Visual Impairment & Blindness, 84*(2), 77–78.

Wolffe, K. (1985). Don't give those kids fish! Teach 'em how to fish! *Journal of Visual Impairment & Blindness, 79*(10), 470–472.

Wolffe, K. (1996). Career education for students with visual impairments. *RE:view, 28*(2), 89–93.

Wolffe, K. (1997). The key to successful school-to-work programs for blind or visually impaired students. *JVIB News Service, 91*(4), 5–7.

Wolffe, K. E., Roessler, R. T., & Schriner, K. F. (1992). Employment concerns of people with blindness or visual impairment. *Journal of Visual Impairment & Blindness, 86*(4), 185–187.

Young, C. E. (1995). A focus group on employment. *Journal of Visual Impairment & Blindness, JVIB News Service, 89*(1), 14–17.

Young, C. E. (1996). How successful vocational rehabilitation counselors place clients in jobs: Results of a focus group. *Journal of Visual Impairment & Blindness, JVIB News Service, 90*(2), 1–6.

VIDEOTAPES

Activity-based intervention, produced by Diane Bricker
This video demonstrates teaching strategies involving everyday activities as essential learning opportunities for infants and preschoolers with disabilities.
Source: Paul H. Brookes, Box 10624, Baltimore, MD 21285-0624

Anti-bias curriculum videotape, produced by Louise Derman-Sparks
A practical approach to helping young children achieve a nonbiased worldview for the classroom teacher, *Anti-Bias Curriculum* demonstrates through actual classroom incidents how teachers and children can address physical and cultural differences among people.
Source: Pacific Oaks College, 5 and 6 Westmoreland Place, Pasadena, CA 91103

Braille literacy at work, produced by Sally Mangold & Mary Ellen Pesavento
This video demonstrates the importance of braille literacy for workers who are blind or have low vision. People working at a variety of jobs discuss their reliance on braille for managing their workloads efficiently.
Source: Exceptional Teaching Aids, 20102 Woodbine Avenue, Castro Valley, CA 94546

Bringing out the best: Encouraging expressive communication in children with multiple handicaps and ***Getting in touch: Communicating with a child who is deaf-blind,*** produced by Elizabeth Cooley, Oregon Research Institute
These two videos demonstrate touch and object cues, interrupted routines, and other communication strategies used with children with multiple disabilities, including visual and hearing impairments.
Source: Research Press, 2612 North Mattis Avenue, Champaign, IL 61821

Can Do Series
Seeing things in a new way: What happens when you have a blind baby
Learning about the world: Concept development
Becoming a can do kid: Self help skills
Making friends: Social skills
Going places: O&M
In this series of five videos, infants, preschoolers, and children who are visually impaired are shown with their families in everyday situations. Highlights include specific instructional strategies and interviews with blind adults.
Source: Visually Impaired Preschool Services, 1215 South 3rd Street, Louisville, KY 40203

Coactive signs
Introduction to tactile communication for children who are deaf-blind
Using tactile signals and cues with children who are deaf-blind
A coactive sign system for children who are deaf-blind
This series of videos demonstrates the use of tactile signals and coactive signs for communicating with children who are deaf-blind.
Source: HOPE, Inc., 809 North 800 East, Logan, UT 84321

Communicating with preverbal infants and young children
This video shows strategies for developing turn taking and early conversations with infants and preschoolers with disabilities.
Source: Learned Managed Designs, Inc., P.O. Box 747, Lawrence, KS 66047

Functional vision: Learning to LOOK, produced by the Blumberg Center at Indiana State University, North Dakota Department of Public Instruction & South Dakota Department of Education and Cultural Affairs

In this video simulations of vision loss are presented along with an introduction to different visual skills and strategies for encouraging child's use of functional vision during everyday situations. It is available dubbed in Spanish.
Source: BVD Promo Services, P.O. Box 930182, Verona, WI 53593-0182

Functional vision: Learning to SEE, produced by the South Dakota Department of Education and Cultural Affairs and the Blumberg Center at Indiana State University
This video was developed to help parents and educators understand how children with visual impairments see and use their vision to learn. It demonstrates how to conduct a functional vision assessment and is available dubbed in Spanish.

Getting there: A look at early mobility skills of four young blind children
This video demonstrates instructional strategies for encouraging orientation and mobility skills of infants and preschoolers who are blind.
Source: Blind Babies Foundation, 1200 Gough Street, San Francisco, CA 94104

Hand in hand: It can be done!
A video and its accompanying discussion guide focus on key concepts and instructional strategies for working on communication and orientation and mobility skills with a wide age range of students, toddlers through adolescents, who are deaf-blind.
Source: AFB Press, 11 Penn Plaza, Suite 300, New York, NY 10001

Helping your child learn series
Vol. 1: When and where to teach, Teaching self control, Teaching playtime skills
Vol. 2: What to teach, Teaching choices, Teaching dressing skills
Vol. 3: How to teach, Teaching with adaptations, Teaching mealtime skills
This series of videos shows young children with multiple disabilities or visual and hearing impairments in a variety of home activities. They demonstrate instructional strategies for working on specific skills within the family routine.
Source: BVD Promo Services, P.O. Box 930182, Verona, WI 53593-0182

Navigating the rapids of life
The skills and experiences necessary for life success are described in this video. Children and youths are shown actively participating in social, academic, and vocational skill-building activities at home, in school, in their communities, and at work.
Source: American Printing House for the Blind, P.O. Box 6085, Louisville, KY 40206

AGENCIES AND ORGANIZATIONS THAT SERVE PEOPLE WHO ARE VISUALLY IMPAIRED

American Action Fund for Blind Children and Adults
18440 Oxnard Street
Tarzana, CA 91356
(818) 343-2022
Publishes children's books that combine print and braille on facing pages, so blind and sighted people can read together. Also has a lending service of Twin Vision Books, Twin Vision Lending Library, and other braille publications appropriate for preschool to high school reading levels. Provides free braille calendars to people who are visually impaired.

American Council of the Blind
1155 15th Street, N.W., Suite 720
Washington, DC 20005
(202) 467-5081 or (800) 424-8666
Fax: 202-467-5085
E-mail: ncrabb@access.digex.net
URL: http://www.acb.org
Seeks to improve the social, economic, and cultural participation of people who are blind in all aspects of society. Services include consulting with industry regarding the employment of individuals who are visually impaired; publication of *The Braille Forum,* which contains articles on employment; and a legislative hotline. Includes a parent support group, American Council of the Blind Parents.

American Foundation for the Blind
11 Penn Plaza, Suite 300
New York, NY 10001
(212) 502-7600 or (800) 232-5463
Fax: (212) 502-7777
E-mail: afbinfo@afb.net
URL: http://www.afb.org
Provides services to and acts as an information clearinghouse for people who are visually impaired and their families, professionals, organizations, schools, and corporations. Conducts research and mounts program initiatives to improve services to visually impaired persons, including the National Initiative on Literacy; advocates for services and legislation; maintains the M. C. Migel Library and Information Center, the Helen Keller Archives, and a toll-

free information line; provides information and referral services; produces videos and publishes books, pamphlets, the *Directory of Services for Blind and Visually Impaired Persons in the United States and Canada,* and the *Journal of Visual Impairment & Blindness.* Specific to career education is the Careers and Technology Information Bank (CTIB), which offers career and technology information, as well as peer support for visually impaired people who want to learn about or seek employment. Adults who are visually impaired have agreed to be mentors to discuss issues such as using technology, obtaining training for a job, and using transportation effectively. Individuals may request a brochure or contact CTIB directly by calling AFB's toll-free information line or via E-mail at techctr@afb.net.

American Printing House for the Blind
P.O. Box 6085
Louisville, KY 40206-0085
(502) 895-2405 or (800) 223-1839
Fax: (502) 899-2274
E-mail: info@aph.org
URL: http://www.aph.org
Products include a variety of books and learning materials in braille and large print and on audiocassettes, as well as equipment for students in grades kindergarten through 12 who are visually impaired, available at no cost through national quota funds. Products include the Sewell Raised-Line Drawing Kit, the Classroom Calendar Kit, the Individual Calendar Kit, Work-Play Trays, Colored Shape Cards, Plexiglas Block with the Light Box, the Transition Tote System, and the video *Navigating the Rapids of Life.*

Association for Education and Rehabilitation (AER) of the Blind and Visually Impaired
4600 Duke Street, Suite 430
Alexandria, VA 22304
(703) 823-9690
Fax: (703) 823-9695
E-mail: aernet@laser.net
Represents teachers, counselors, and orientation and mobility instructors whose area of expertise is the field of blindness and low vision. Sponsors regional and international conferences, as well as teleseminars of interest to professionals and parents on topics related to career education. Promotes all phases of education and work for people of all ages who are visually impaired, strives to expand their opportunities to take a contributory place in society, and disseminates information. Publishes *RE:view* and *AER Report.*

Blind Childrens Center
4120 Marathon Street
Los Angeles, CA 90029
(213) 664-2153 or in California (800) 222-3567
Fax: (213) 665-3828
Provides services to young children who are visually impaired. Produces a variety of publications and materials pertinent to families of children with visual impairments and service providers.

Descriptive Video Service/WGBH
125 Western Avenue
Boston, MA 02134
(800) 333-1203
URL: http://www.wgbh.org/dvs
Makes television broadcast programs and movies on video accessible to visually impaired people via narrated descriptions of a program's or movie's key visual elements.

DO-IT (Disabilities, Opportunities, Internetworking, and Technology)
University of Washington
4545 15th Avenue, N.E., Room 206
Seattle, WA 98105-4527
(206) 685-DOIT (685-3648) (Voice/TTY)
Fax: (206) 685-4045
E-mail: doit@u.washington.edu
URL: http://weber.u.washington.edu/~doit
Supports high school students with disabilities to prepare for academic study and careers in science, engineering, and mathematics through the loan of computers and adaptive technology, mentoring, and summer study programs. Provides information, publications, videos, and resources on related issues and financial aid for students with disabilities. Publishes *DO-IT News.*

Foundation Fighting Blindness
Executive Plaza, Suite 800
11350 McCormick Road
Hunt Valley, MD 21031-1014
(410) 785-1414 or (800) 683-5551
TTY/TDD: (410) 785-9687
Fax: (410) 771-7470
URL: http://www.blindness.org

Finds treatments and cures for retinal diseases, such as retinitis pigmentosa, macular degeneration, and Usher syndrome. Provides public education, information and referral, workshops, and research through its main office and 60 affiliates. Raises funds for research into the cause, prevention, and treatment of retinitis pigmentosa. Publishes *Fighting Blindness News.*

Hadley School for the Blind
700 Elm Street
Winnetka, IL 60093-0299
(847) 446-8111 or (800) 323-4238
Fax: (847) 446-9916
URL: http://www.hadley-school.org
Allows students to study at home with free correspondence course materials through its accredited distance education program. Courses are offered to parents of blind children, professionals working with people who are visually impaired, high school students preparing for college, and adults who have become blind. Hadley offers three courses in its *Transition to the American University* program: Preparation Starts Early, Personal and Social Adjustment to Campus Life, and Classroom Survival Strategies. The career and employment courses offered are Assessing Yourself and Your Options and Principles of Job Acquisition.

Helen Keller National Center for Deaf-Blind Youths and Adults
111 Middle Neck Road
Sands Point, NY 11050-1299
(516) 944-8900
TDD: (516) 944-8637
Fax: (516) 944-7302
Provides short-term rehabilitation services, job preparation and placement, and diagnostic services to people who are deaf-blind through its national center and 10 regional offices. Provides technical assistance and training to those who work with deaf-blind people. Publishes *Nat-Cent News.* Sponsors the National Family Association for Deaf-Blind ([800] 255-0411, ext. 275).

Howe Press
Perkins School for the Blind
175 North Beacon Street
Watertown, MA 02172-2790
(617) 924-3490
Fax: (617) 926-2027
Manufactures the Perkins Brailler; standard, large cell, or jumbo dot braille; braille paper; slates; styli; mathematical aids; and braille games.

Jewish Braille Institute of America
110 East 30th Street
New York, NY 10016
(212) 889-2525 or (800) 433-1531
Fax: (212) 689-3692
Supplies hard-to-find hand-copied braille books that students may need in their post-secondary academic careers.

Lions Clubs International
300 22nd Street
Oak Brook, IL 60521-8842
(630) 571-5466
Fax (630) 571-8890
Provides summer camping opportunities for blind or visually impaired students. Offers support for technology and training to young students with financial need.

Minnesota State Academy for the Blind
P.O. Box 298, Box 68
Faribault, MN 55021
(507) 332-3226
Fax: (507) 332-3631
Offers materials and consultative assistance to people nationwide who are interested in organizing a family transition weekend and is a residential school for students in Minnesota.

National Association for Parents of the Visually Impaired (NAPVI)
P.O. Box 317
Watertown, MA 02471-0317
(800) 562-6265
Fax: (617) 972-7444
Provides support to parents and families of children and youths with visual impairments. Publishes a newsletter, *Awareness.*

National Association for Visually Handicapped
22 West 21st Street, 6th floor
New York, NY 10010
(212) 889-3141
Fax: (212) 727-2951
E-mail: staff@navh.org
URL: http://www.navh.org
Provides information and services to people with low vision, their families, and professionals. Offers a catalog of low vision devices and large-print publications.

National Braille Association
3 Townline Circle
Rochester, NY 14623-2513
(716) 427-8260
Fax: (716) 427-0263
Provides transcription services and a duplication service for masters in its braille book collection. Produces catalogs of textbooks, music, and general-interest braille books. Supplies braille textbooks and other materials at below cost. Provides assistance and education to transcribers and professionals.

National Braille Press
88 St. Stephen Street
Boston, MA 02115
(617) 266-6160 or (800) 548-7323
Fax: (617) 437-0456
E-mail: orders@nbp.org
URL: http://www.nbp.org
Provides braille printing services and sponsors the Children's Braille Book-of-the-Month Club. Publishes regular-print picture books of the month with plastic brailled over each page.

National Eye Institute Information Center
National Institutes of Health
U.S. Department of Health and Human Services
Building 31, Room 6A03
9000 Rockville Pike
Bethesda, MD 20892
(301) 496-2234
Fax: (301) 402-1065
URL: http://www.nei.nih.gov
Conducts research on the eye and vision disorders.

National Family Association for Deaf-Blind
c/o Helen Keller National Center
111 Middle Neck Road
Sands Point, NY 11050-1299
(516) 944-8900 (voice/TTY/TDD) or (800) 255-0411, ext. 275
Fax: (516) 944-7302
Acts as a support network for families of children, youths, and adults who are deaf-blind. Encourages and supports parent leadership, intragency partnerships, training, advocacy, and representation in national and state projects serving individuals who are deaf-blind. Publishes *NFADB Newsletter.*

National Federation of the Blind
1800 Johnson Street
Baltimore, MD 21230
(410) 659-9314
Fax: (410) 685-5653
URL: http://www.nfb.org
The National Federation of the Blind is a membership organization whose intent is to integrate people who are visually impaired as equal members of society. Publishes *The Braille Monitor* and *Future Reflections*, a magazine for parents. Provides a parent support group. In cooperation with the U.S. Department of Labor, NFB developed Job Opportunities for the Blind (JOB), a program that helps skilled blind people find job openings. Also holds career planning seminars for blind people seeking employment.

National Industries for the Blind
1901 North Beauregard Street, Suite 200
Alexandria, VA 22311-1727
(703) 998-0770
Fax: (703) 820-7816
URL: http://www.nib.org
Enhances opportunities for economic and personal independence for individuals who are blind by creating, sustaining, and improving employment. Allocates, among qualified industries for blind persons, purchase orders of the federal government for approved goods and services. Coordinates the production of 106 industries and 36 states. Devises quality-control systems and provides management and engineering services to increase plant efficiency and broaden production opportunities for people who are blind. Publishes *Opportunity*.

National Information Center for Children and Youth with Disabilities
P.O. Box 1492
Washington, DC 20013-1492
Fax: (202) 884-8441
(202) 884-8200
TDD: (800) 695-0285
Fax: (202) 884-8441
Serves as a national clearinghouse for information about children and youths with disabilities. Publishes *Transition Summary*, an annual compilation of articles on transition.

**National Information Clearinghouse on Children
Who Are Deaf-Blind (DB-LINK)**
c/o Teaching Research
Western Oregon State College
345 North Monmouth Avenue
Monmouth, OR 97361
(800) 854-7013
TDD: (800) 848-9376
Fax: (503) 838-8150
Identifies, coordinates, and disseminates information concerning children and
young adults who are deaf-blind as a collaborative effort among Helen Keller
National Center, Perkins School for the Blind, and Teaching Research.

National Library Service for the Blind and Physically Handicapped
Library of Congress
1291 Taylor Street, N.W.
Washington, DC 20542
(202) 707-5100 or (800) 424-8567
Fax: (202) 707-0712
URL: http://LCweb.loc.gov/nls/nls.html
Conducts a national program that allows individuals who are visually impaired
or have physical disabilities to borrow books and magazines in braille, large
print, on flexible disk or audiocassette free of charge through a network of
regional libraries.

National Organization for Albinism and Hypopigmentation
1530 Locust Street, No. 29
Philadelphia, PA 19102-4415
(215) 545-2322 or (800) 473-2310
Provides information on albinism and hypopigmentation. Publishes a newsletter and provides peer support through a network of state chapters.

Oakmont Visual Aids Workshop
310 White Oak Drive
Santa Rosa, CA 95409-5942
Produces a series of tactile books that demonstrate basic concepts (for example, same and different, long and short, and above and below) and recognition of familiar objects (such as paper, buttons, fasteners, and floor coverings).
All pages have hand-lettered and braille labels.

Prevent Blindness America
500 East Remington Road
Schaumburg, IL 60173
(847) 843-2020 or (800) 221-3004
PBA Center for Sight (800) 331-2020
Fax: (847) 843-8458
Conducts, through a network of state affiliates, a program devoted to public education on the conservation of vision through vision screenings in schools and the sharing of industrial eye-safety strategies. Collects data on the nature and extent of causes of visual impairment.

Recording for the Blind and Dyslexic
20 Roszel Road
Princeton, NJ 08540
(609) 452-0606 or (800) 221-4792
Fax: (609) 987-8116
URL: http://www.rfbd.org
Lends recorded and computerized educational books to people who cannot read standard print because of visual, physical, or specific learning disabilities.

Seedlings: Braille Books for Children
P.O. Box 51924
Livonia, MI 48151-5924
(313) 427-8552 or (800) 777-5882
Fax: (313) 427-8552
E-mail: seedlink@aol.com
URL: http://www.22cent.com/seedlings/
Provides low-cost braille and combination print and braille books appropriate for children.

Texas School for the Blind and Visually Impaired
1100 West 45th Street
Austin, TX 78756
(512) 454-8631
Fax: (512) 454-3395
URL: http://www.tsbvi.edu
Serves as a residential school and educational center. Publishes curricular materials, including an annotated bibliography.

United States Association for Blind Athletes
33 North Institute Street
Colorado Springs, CO 80903

(719) 630-0422
Fax: (719) 630-0616
E-mail: usaba@usa.net
Provides athletic opportunities, including swimming, track, wrestling, goal
ball, and skiing, for people who are blind or have low vision.

SOURCES OF RELATED INFORMATION

Boy Scouts of America
Special Needs and Disabilities
1325 West Walnut Hill Lane
P.O. Box 152079
Irving, TX 75038-3039
(214) 580-2417

Council for Exceptional Children
1920 Association Drive
Reston, VA 22091-1589
(703) 620-3660 or (800) 328-0272

Girl Scouts of the U.S.A.
Services for Girls with Disabilities
420 5th Avenue
New York, NY 10018
(212) 852-8000

**Higher Education and the Handicapped (HEATH)
Resource Center**
One Dupont Circle, N.W., Suite 800
Washington, DC 20036-1193
(202) 939-9320 or (800) 544-3284
Fax: (202) 833-4760

National Parent Network on Disability
1727 King Street, Suite 305
Alexandria, VA 22314
(703) 684-6763

President's Committee on Employment of People with Disabilities
1331 F Street, N.W.
Washington, DC 20004-1107

(202) 376-6200
TDD: (202) 376-6205
Fax: (202) 376-6200

CAMPS

Participating in a well-run camp gives students who are visually impaired the opportunity to meet peers with visual impairments, to learn from the experiences of older individuals who are blind or visually impaired, and to develop and use new skills.

Camp Allen
56 Camp Allen Road
Bedford, NH 03110-6606
(603) 622-8471
Fax: (603) 626-4295
This private, nonprofit camp provides a summer residential program.

National Camps for Blind Children
4444 South 52nd Street
Lincoln, NE 68506
(402) 488-0981
Fax: (402) 488-7582
Sponsored by Christian Record Services, these camps are made available through financial gifts from private individuals. Week-long programs are scheduled at various campsites throughout the country that have been selected for their standards of excellence. The camps are operated by professional staff, with one counselor assigned to four campers. Camp programs are suitable for children aged 9 to 19, and activities vary by location.

Pennsylvania Lions Beacon Lodge Camp
114 SR 103 South
Mt. Union, PA 17066-9601
(814) 542-2511
Fax: (814) 542-7437
The lodge provides a summer residential camp for children and adults with disabilities, including people with visual impairments. Activities offered at the camp include fishing, hiking, swimming, archery, indoor and outdoor games, and talent shows.

Space Camp—West Virginia School for the Deaf and Blind
301 East Main Street
Romney, WV 26757

(304) 822-4883
Fax: (304) 822-3370
The staff at the West Virginia School for the Blind coordinates Space Camp
for Children with Visual Disabilities, held in the fall of the year for students
who are enrolled in Grade 4 or higher. Different programs are offered; some
provide experiences with sighted students, whereas others do not.

Vacation Camp for the Blind
817 Broadway, 11th floor (Office)
New York, NY 10003
(212) 625-1616, ext. 124
Located in Rockland County, New York, the camp offers summer vacations
and weekend retreats to people who are blind or visually impaired. Special
features of the camp include a 5-acre lake and a self-guided nature trail.

Summit Park Road (Camp)
111 Summit Park Road
Spring Valley, NY 10977
(914) 354-3003
This program offers a camp experience for individuals who are visually
impaired and their families.

ON-LINE RESOURCES

These listings include Internet addresses for sources of electronic information. E-mail addresses for agencies and organizations listed elsewhere in this section are included in the main organizational listing.
Because of the rapid changes in technology, the Internet addresses listed here are subject to frequent change.

able-job
Adaptations to the workplace and issues relating to finding employment are
considered in this forum.

America's Job Bank
http://www.ajb.dni.us/
A partnership between the U. S. Department of Labor and state-operated
Public Employment Service, America's Job Bank provides labor exchange
services to employers and job seekers through a network of 1,800 offices
throughout the United States.

BLINDFAM

listserv@sjuvm.stjohns.edu

The everyday life experiences of blind persons, family members, and friends are discussed.

BLINDJOB

listserv@maelstrom.stjohns.edu

Employment issues and opportunities for visually impaired people are discussed, including the accessibility of jobs, creative ways of making jobs accessible, difficulties that people face in obtaining jobs because of their visual impairment, and problems employers face in hiring visually impaired people.

Career Resources Center

http://www.careers.org

Links to Career Gems, a selection of 100 career Web sites; job postings; learning sites; and career services are provided by the center.

Federal Jobs Central

http://www.fedjobs.com/

A database for federal job openings, Federal Jobs Central is compiled by Federal Reserach Service, Inc., a company with more than 24 years of experience in the federal employment field.

Job Accommodation Network (JAN)

http://janweb.icdi.wvu.edu

Sponsored by the President's Committee on Employment of People with Disabilities, JAN provides information about job accommodations and the employability of people with disabilities. It also provides information regarding the Americans with Disabilities Act and puts employers who are considering the possibility of hiring a person with a disability in touch with employers who have already been through the process.

JOBTRAK

http://www.jobtrak.com/

College students and alumni can post résumés on-line and participate in career forums. A job search manual and a list of graduate schools can also be accessed.

The mission of the American Foundation for the Blind (AFB) is to enable persons who are blind or visually impaired to achieve equality of access and opportunity that will ensure freedom of choice in their lives.